THE ENCYCLOPEDIA OF AIRBRUSH TECHNIQUES

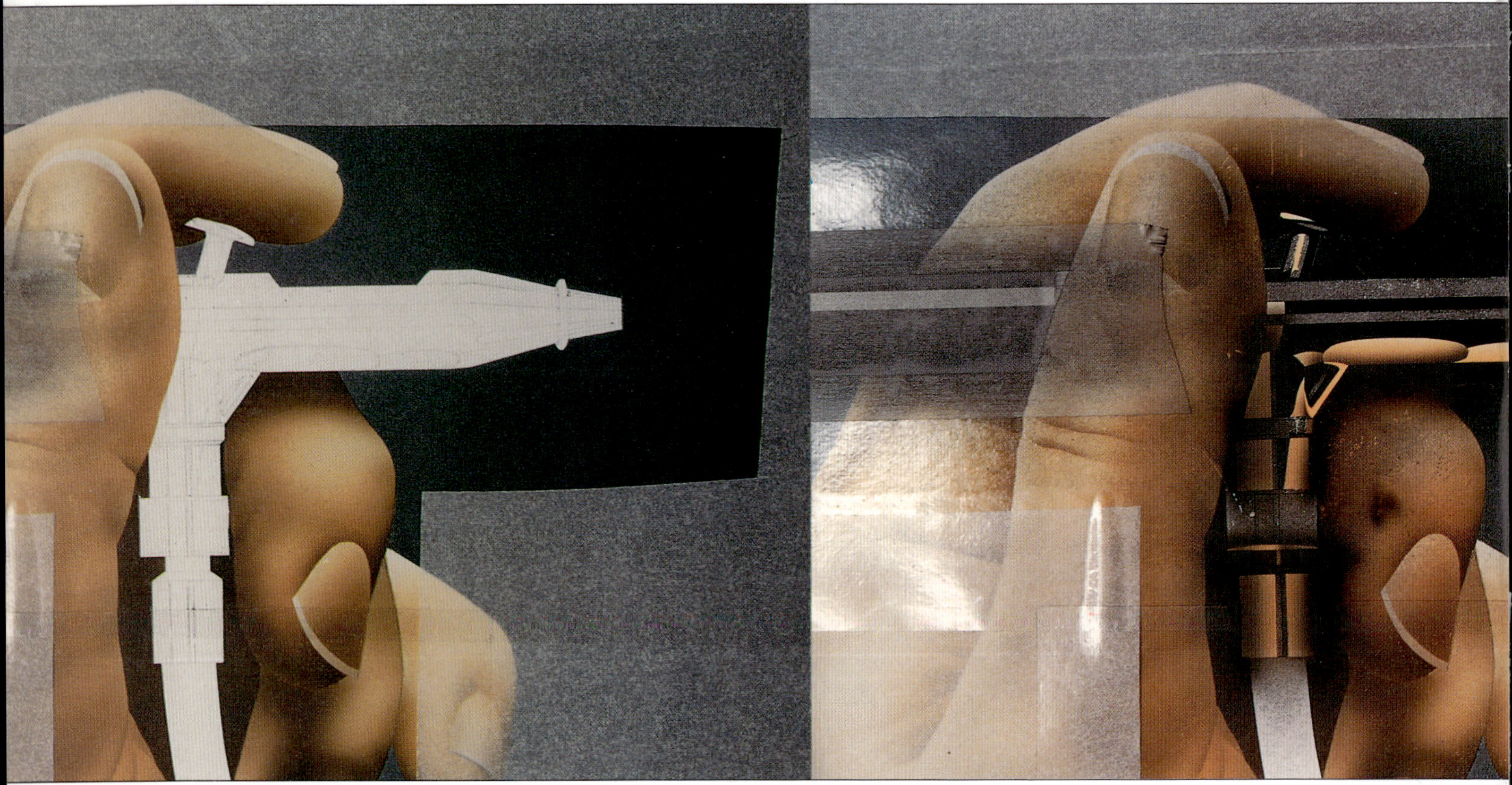

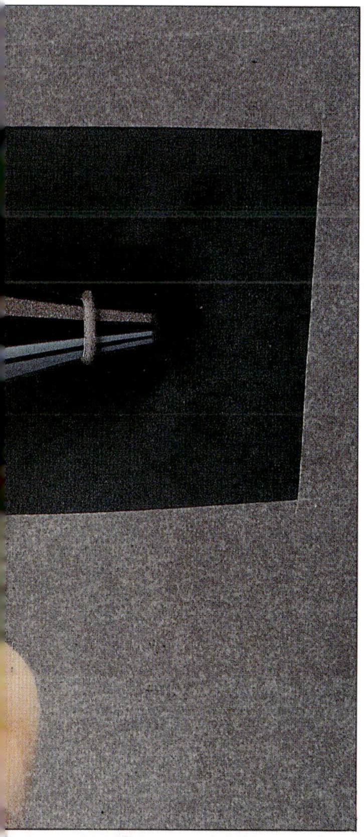

THE

ENCYCLOPEDIA OF AIRBRUSH TECHNIQUES

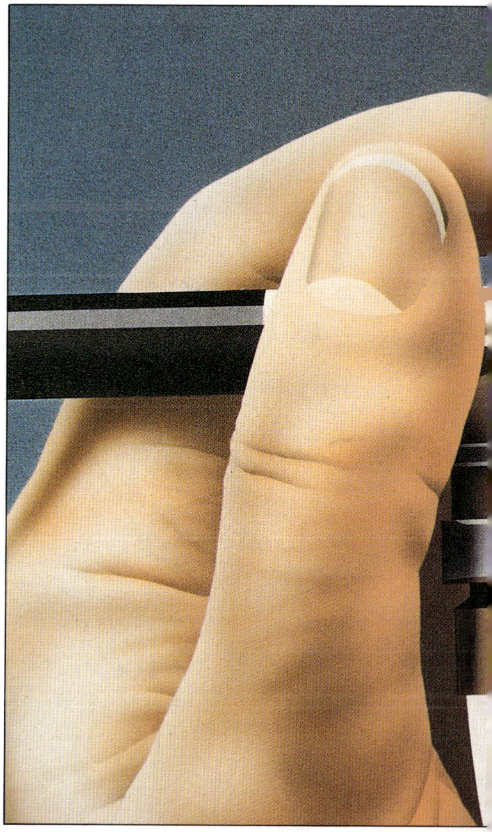

MICHAEL E. LEEK

SEARCH PRESS

A QUARTO BOOK

Published in paperback 2001 by
Search Press Ltd
Wellwood
North Farm Road
Tunbridge Wells
Kent TN2 3DR

ISBN 0 85532 986 6

This book was designed and produced by
Quarto Publishing plc
The Old Brewery
6 Blundell Street
London N7 9BH

Senior editor Kate Kirby
Copy editor Judy Martin
Senior art editors Leslie Laskarin-Hanks, Mark Stevens
Designer Karin SkÂnberg
Picture researcher Jack Buchan
Senior editor Hazel Harrison
Picture manager Giulia Hetherington
Editorial director Sophie Collins
Art director Moira Clinch

Typeset in Stone Serif by Central Southern Typesetters, Eastbourne
Manufactured in Hong Kong by Regent Publishing Services Ltd
Printed in China by Leefung-Asco Printers Ltd

CONTENTS

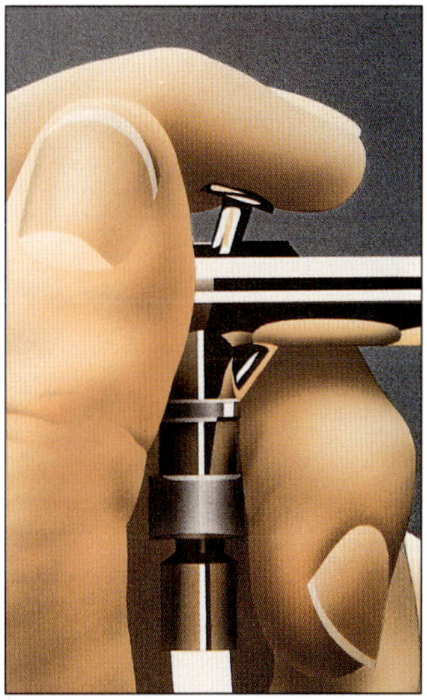

INTRODUCTION

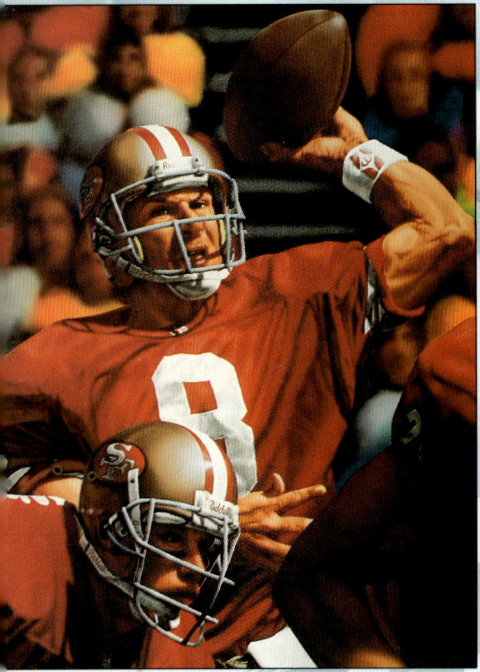

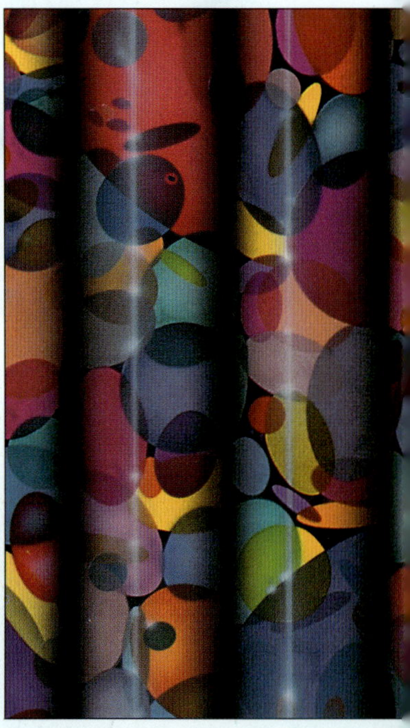

IT IS NOT SO LONG AGO that books on airbrushing were practically unobtainable simply because publishers did not think there was an adequate demand. However, the continued and increasing need for highly finished, *quality* illustrations in every area of graphic design has brought an awareness of airbrushing to a wider audience, even though the techniques themselves may still be elusive to many. Using step-by-step demonstrations and the work of professional illustrators, this book aims to cover the techniques employed. As skills improve and develop so will each illustrator introduce new approaches to his or her work, which others may find unacceptable or inappropriate, but to the illustrator using them they may become an indispensable technique in all future work. Because of this, and because there are no rules which must be adhered to, no single book on airbrushing techniques can ever be definitive.

The majority of the readers of this book, I hope, will start by studying the professional examples reproduced

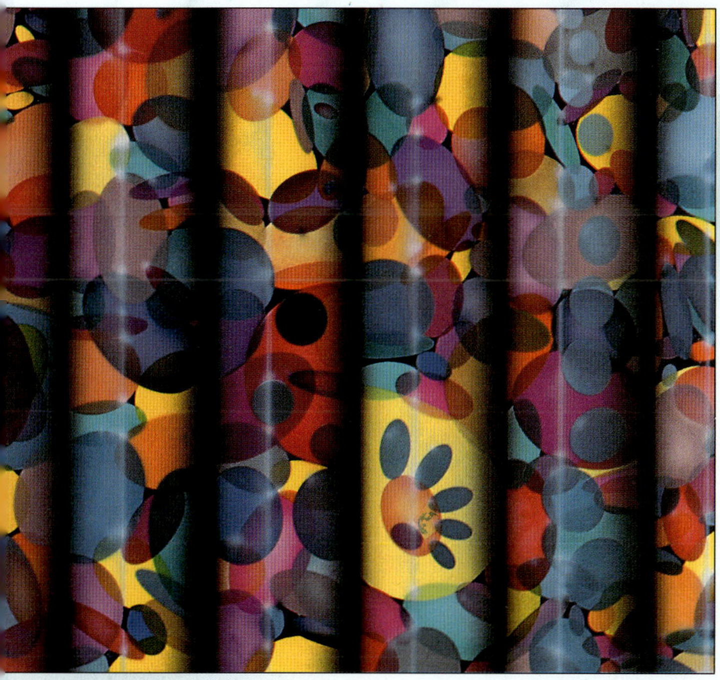

here, rather than look at the step-by-step demonstrations first. While it is undeniable that the demonstrations have played a part in the choice of techniques used, the finished examples have been selected primarily on the strength of the airbrushing. Regardless of the fact that most of the illustrations reproduced here were for a specific purpose and would therefore be seen in a context, many do stand as illustrations in their own right – such is the standard being achieved today.

My introduction to the airbrush was a by-product of lectures on the theory of perspective and shadows. These were both subjects I found fascinating and quickly developed an understanding of them. This meant I was often ahead of my colleagues and had time on my hands to take exercises to finished artwork stage. My lecturer would encourage me to render these exercises using an airbrush, Winsor Blue or Payne's Gray watercolor, and an old foot-pump with a reservoir – which was designed for use with an airbrush. Not only did this develop my skills in using a new tool, but it also taught me patience – it took a good two or three minutes to pump up the tank to the required pressure and then spray for about 30 seconds before having to start pumping again. All this after slowly and carefully cutting film masks on artwork drawn on paper which was often thinner than the film. (This explains why few of my works have survived – the majority just fell apart like jigsaws.)

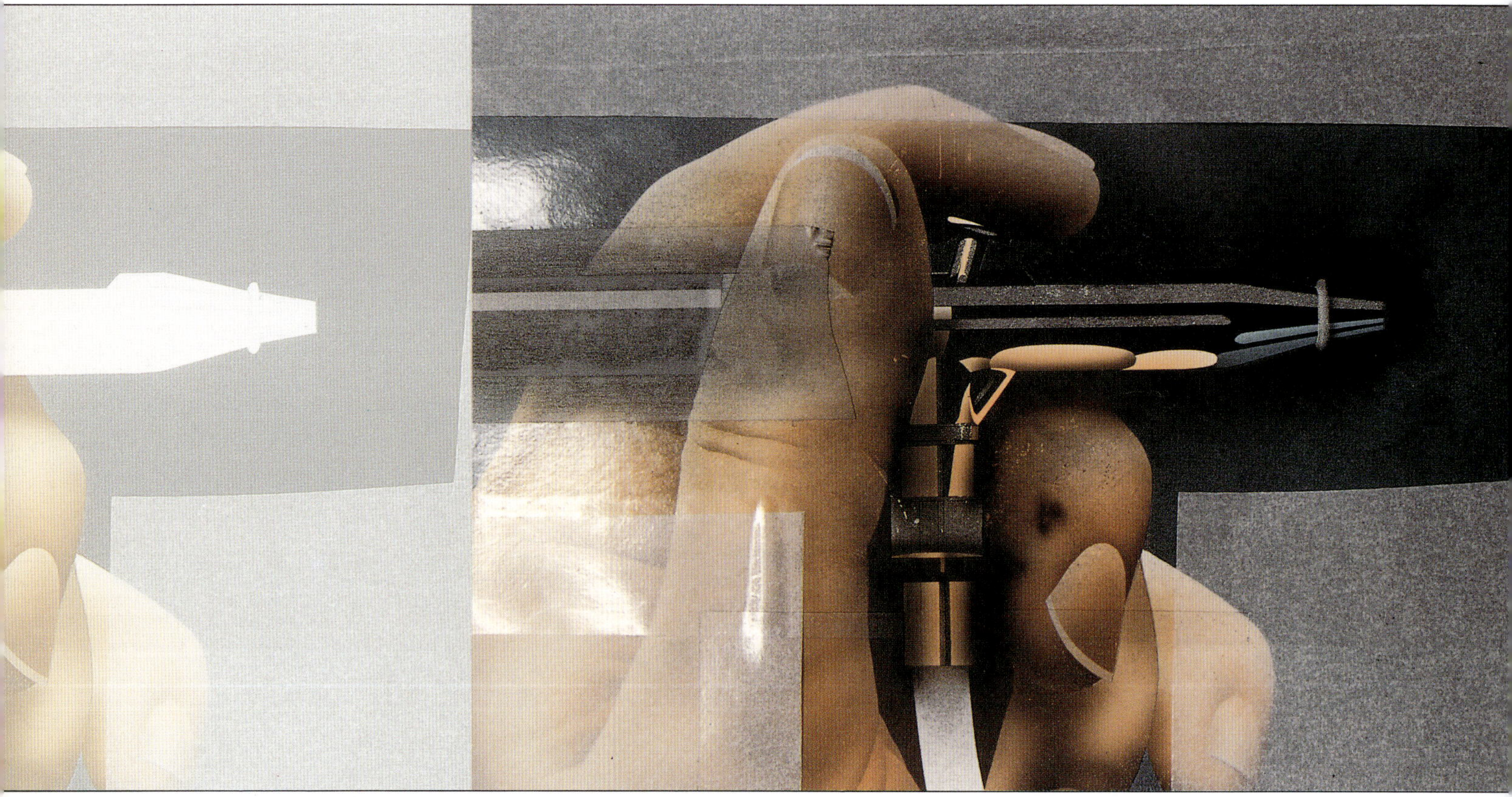

PART ONE
TECHNIQUES

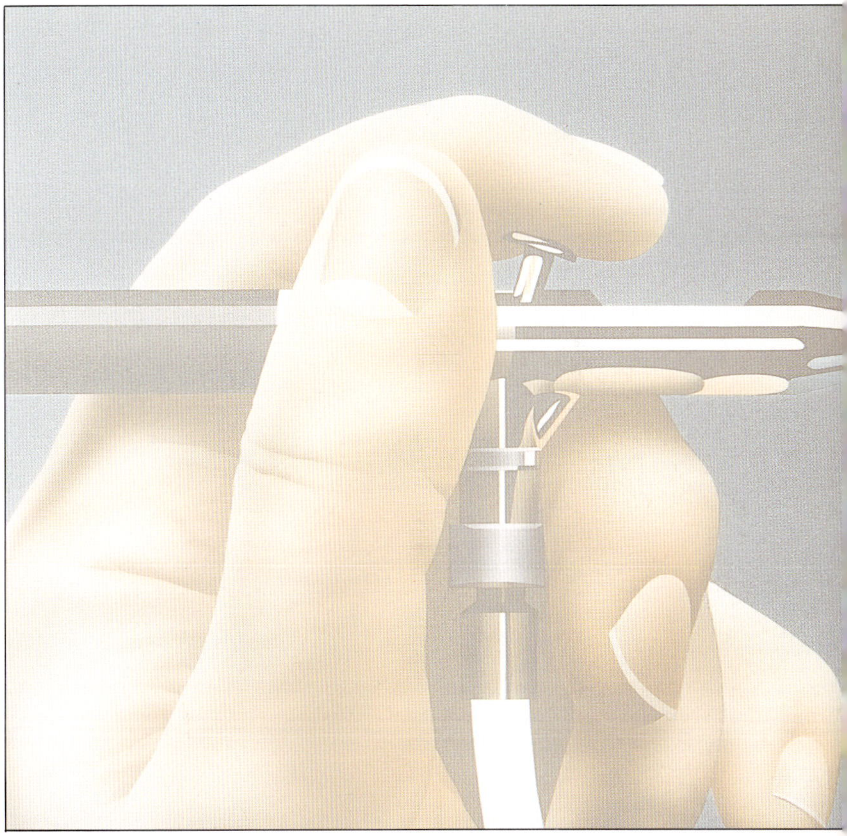

THE APPLICATION AND USE of the airbrush as a means of rendering natural, man-made, and fantasy or science fiction subjects has increased enormously over the past three decades. Illustrators have found this tool an invaluable aid either for rendering a complete illustration or in limited application to enhance detail, texture, form, or contrast on an illustration which has been primarily hand-painted.

Because of the more widespread use of the airbrush, various techniques have developed to arrive at the quickest and most effective means of achieving desired effects. Many of these techniques are peculiar to the airbrush and are the result of much experimentation by individual illustrators based on both the advantages and limitations of the airbrush. When the airbrush is in constant use, it will soon be apparent that there are techniques other than those described and illustrated here. They will be discovered or identified through a particular need and may well become essential to the illustrator who chances upon them. In this book, the purpose is to describe those techniques which have a wider and more general application in illustrative work, be it creative or technically based.

Airbrushing is an acquired skill. It requires practice, patience, careful planning, experiment, and, to produce successful work, an understanding and awareness of color, light, tone, and contrast. In addition an ability to draw is essential.

ACETATE MASKING

Acetate is a completely transparent, plastic material available in sheet or roll form and in a number of different thicknesses. It is useful in airbrushing as a substitute for, and complement to, self-adhesive masking film. Because it lacks adhesive, acetate will allow residual color to encroach underneath, creating a soft-edged effect which can be used to advantage. If this is not wanted, care must be taken to ensure that the mask is held evenly and flatly against the artwork to provide a firm edge to the sprayed area.

The cut or broken edge of a piece of acetate can be used to form a loose mask, or a whole shape can be cut out of the material corresponding to a particular part of the artwork. Because acetate is, like masking film, completely transparent, the mask can be accurately positioned in relation to previously sprayed areas of the image. When acetate is cut, especially for a mask which has sharp, hard-edged corners, it can be prone to splitting. Although a split may appear insignificant on the acetate mask, it is surprising how a small amount of sprayed paint passing through it will be sufficient to show up on the artwork.

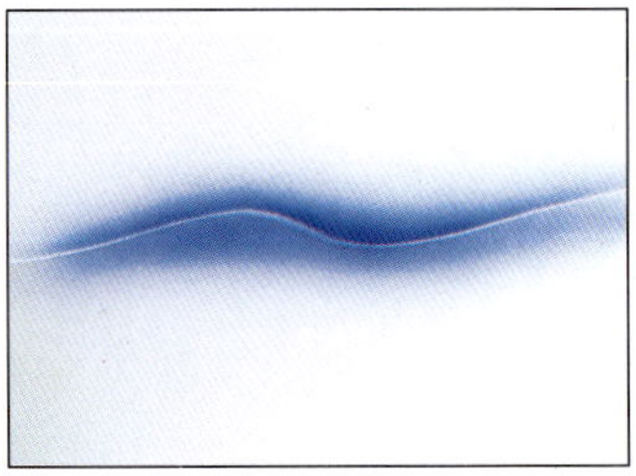

1 Sweeping curves have been cut into a piece of acetate. This has been laid flat on the illustration board and color sprayed along the curved edge.

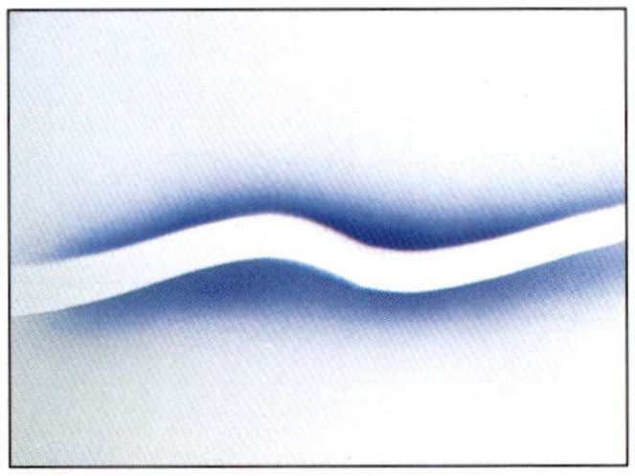

2 When the acetate is moved away from the sprayed area, it can be seen that the curve is accurately repeated by the spraying. The edge quality is slightly less crisp than would be the case if masking film had been used.

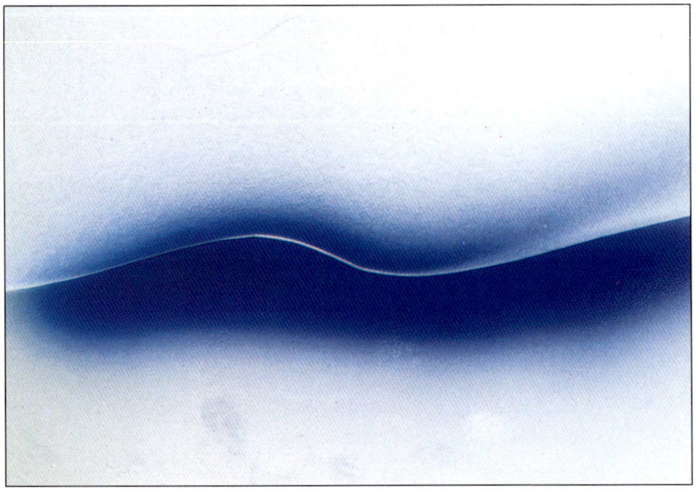

3 The same mask is used, but instead of leaving all of it flat on the artwork, one end has been lifted while spraying.

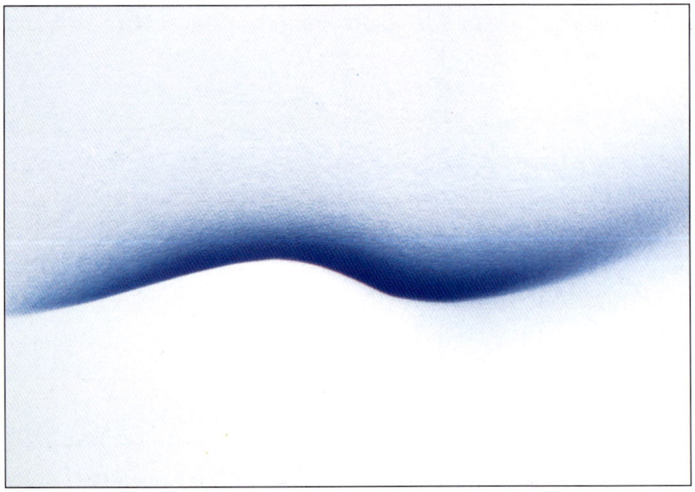

4 The removal of the mask shows that where the acetate was laid flat, the sprayed color has a firm edge, but where it was lifted, the color fades off and blends into the white of the board. This is a useful technique when both hard and soft edges are required at the same time.

ANGLED SPRAYING

This term is used to describe the technique of blending colors into each other, without having a hard, or clearly defined edge between them. It is achieved by the distance the airbrush is held away from the artwork and the angle at which the airbrush is in relation to the artwork surface. This technique may be used in conjunction with the section on GRADATED TONE.

Wide-band Blending

1 It is required to blend two colors together without an edge between the two being shown. After the overall area for the color work has been masked off, the first color is sprayed from top to bottom, holding the airbrush at an angle of 90° to the artwork to create a very soft and gentle gradation.

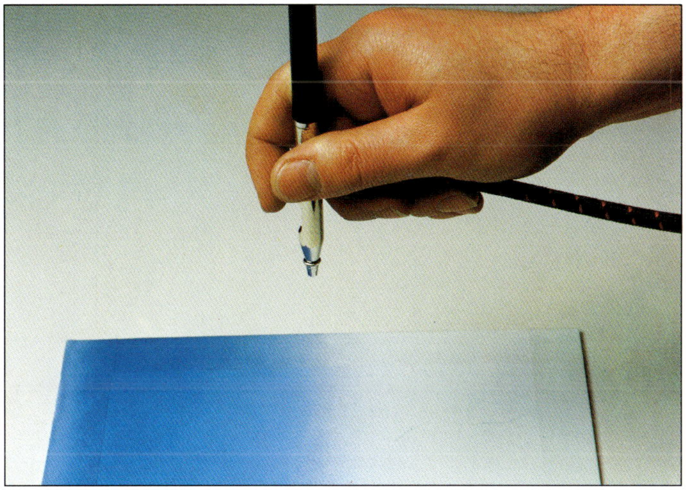

This photograph demonstrates the height and angle of the airbrush in relation to the artwork as the first color gradation is applied.

2 The second color is now sprayed at the same angle as the first, allowing the gradation to overlap and merge with the first color.

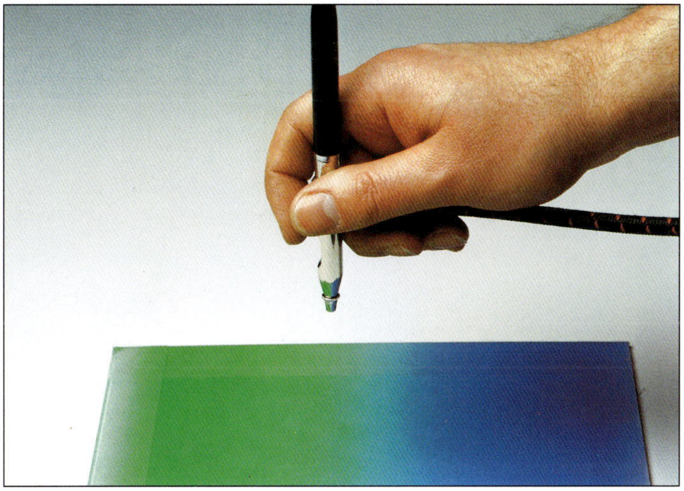

In applying the second color, the artwork has been turned 180° so that the color can again be sprayed from the top of the board, allowing greater control.

Narrow-band Blending
1 In this example a narrower band of blended color is demonstrated. At this stage the gradation from color to the white of the board is more sudden

2 The second color is applied as in stage 1. The finished result shows a clearer definition between the two colors than in the wide-band demonstration

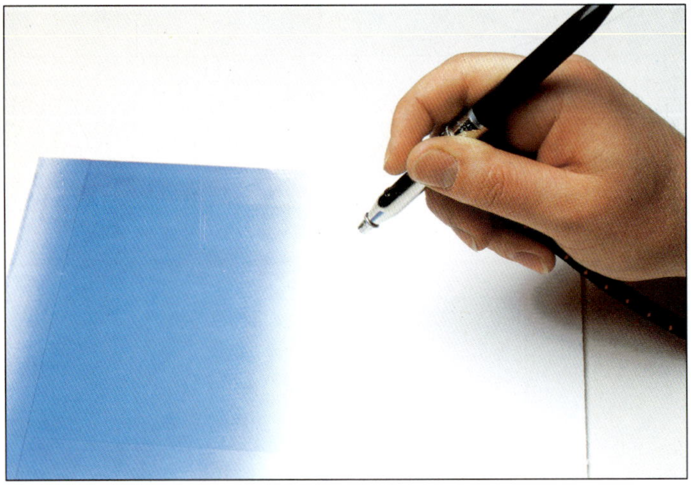

The first color is being sprayed from the top with the airbrush held at a shallow angle to the surface.

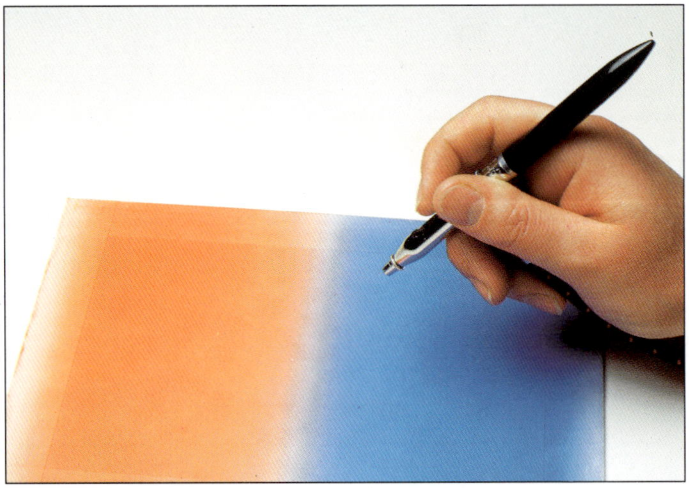

The artwork has been turned 180° for the spraying of the second color, with the airbrush being held at the same angle as in stage 1.

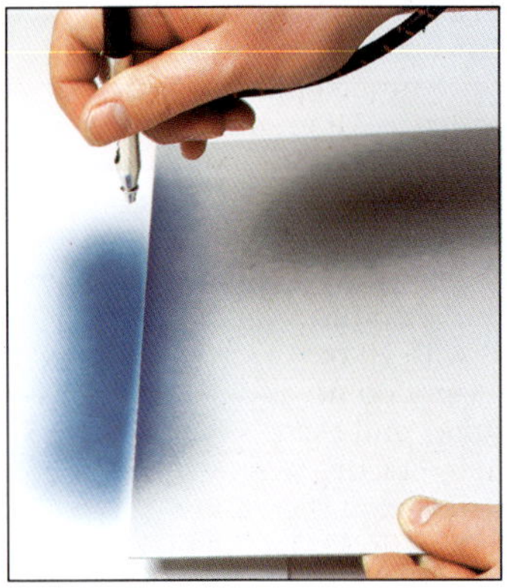

Using Cardboard in Angled Spraying
In both of the following examples, reference can also be made to CARDBOARD MASKING, LOOSE MASKING and TORN PAPER MASKING.

1 In this example the cardboard is held slightly away from the artwork and the airbrush is at an angle of 90° to the surface. This will give a fairly firm, but soft edge on completion.

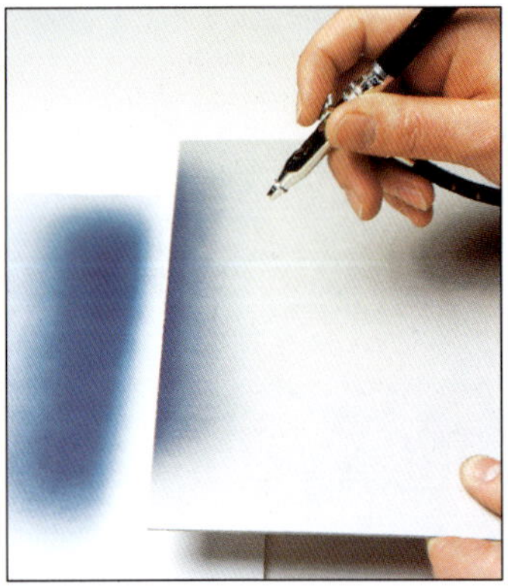

2 In this photograph the cardboard is again used as a mask, but the angle of the airbrush has been brought down toward the horizontal, which will give a much softer edge and gentler color gradation.

BASIC EXERCISES

The preparation of any type of artwork or painting requires concentrated practice and patience. Time spent here will pay dividends later and prevent unfortunate and unnecessary mistakes from being incorporated into finished artwork. The airbrush is not a difficult tool to use, but as with all others, what it can and cannot do needs to be understood, and there is no better way than practice. Having said that, this section should not be seen in isolation from the other techniques described in this book.

For the beginner, it can be difficult at first to obtain full control of the flow of paint and air through the airbrush—smooth action in starting and stopping the spray, essential for freehand work, and control of an even spread of color, even when masks will be used to define specific shapes. In addition, the height and angle of the airbrush during spraying affect the final result. Basic exercises can take any form which helps to develop the artist's understanding of the tool's capabilities.

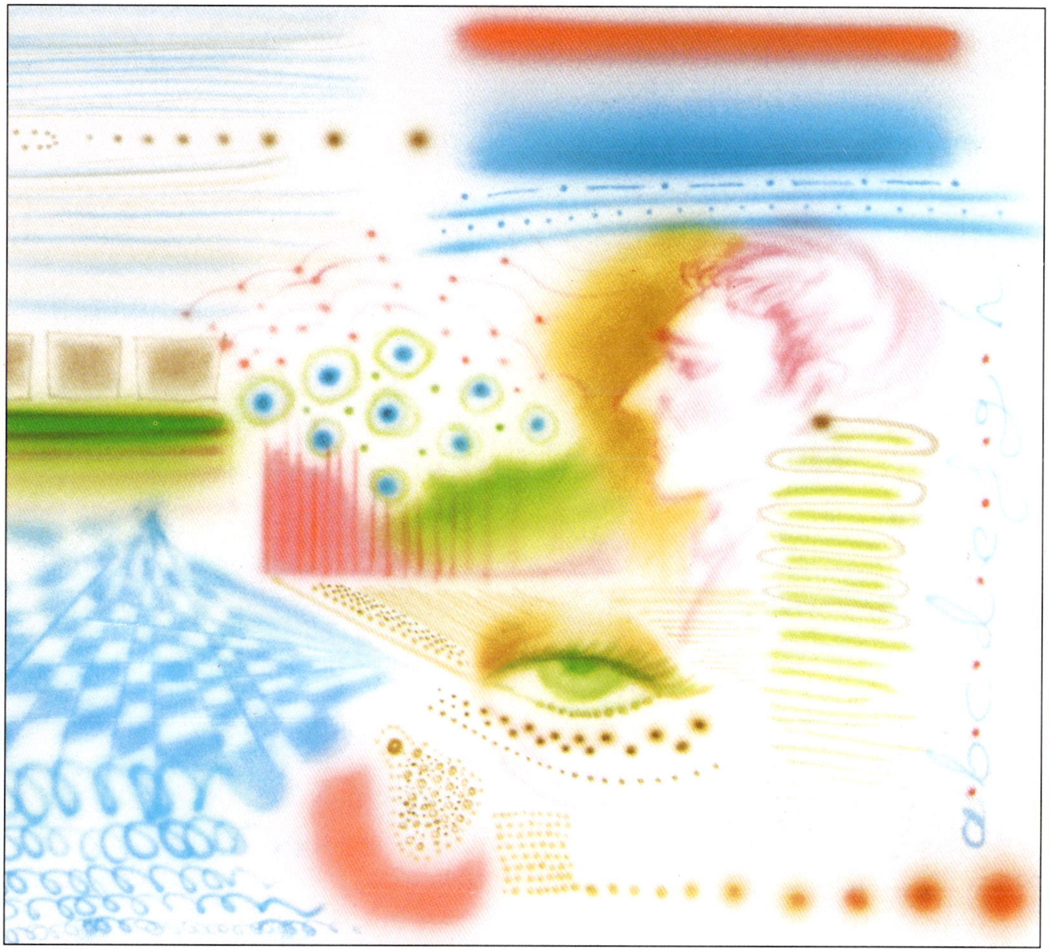

This sheet has been covered with different techniques and applications of the airbrush. All have been completed primarily without use of masks of any kind. This type of "doodle-sheet" is excellent practice, which enables the aspiring airbrush illustrator to develop skill and confidence in using the airbrush, and also in understanding the limitations of the tool.

BASIC FORMS

These exercises cover four basic shapes: a cube, cylinder, sphere and cone. They represent the principal geometric shapes which are likely to be encountered in airbrushing an incredible variety of subjects, whether taken individually, in groups or, as is more likely, parts from each in any combination. If specific and detailed areas in a large number of the finished illustrations in this book are closely examined, it will become apparent that many of the abstract shapes which make up the illustrative content are composed of surfaces such as angled planes and curves which can be extracted from these basic shapes.

Not only is practice essential in order to master the skill of handling the airbrush, but it is also useful in understanding the shapes themselves. Furthermore, if you extend the principle of these exercises by varying the colors and surface textures, you will acquire greater understanding of how light affects the shading and contrast from one surface to another, from one side to another, and from one object to another.

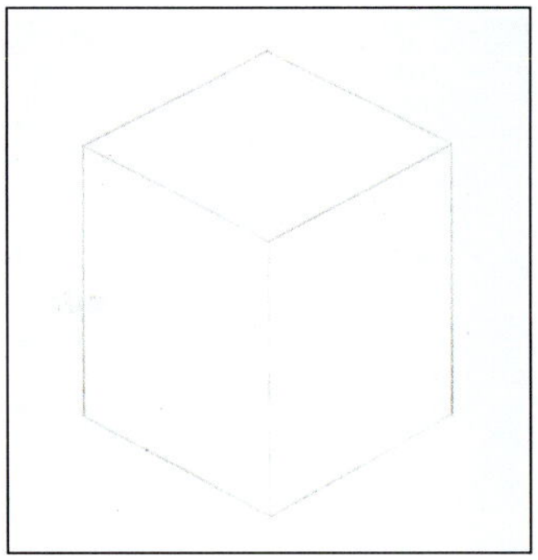

The Cube

1 The cube is drawn symmetrically with one corner directly facing the viewer. The cube and the surrounding area are covered with a single piece of masking film.

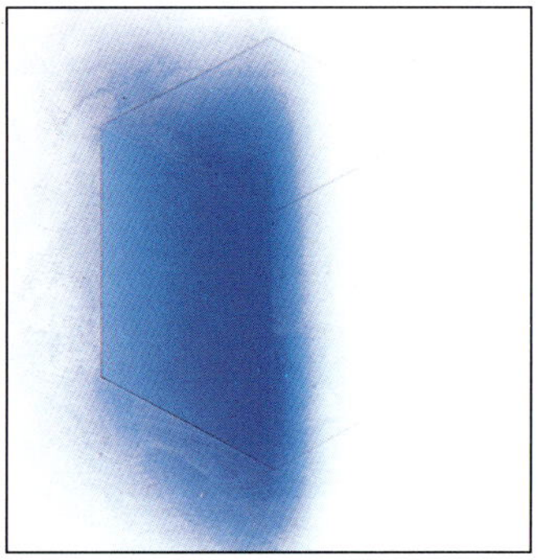

2 The film covering the left-hand face of the cube is cut and removed for the first stage in the spraying sequence.The left-hand face is sprayed with the greater depth of tone to the right and running parallel to the vertical edge. This is gradated on the left to show a subtle, reflected highlight.

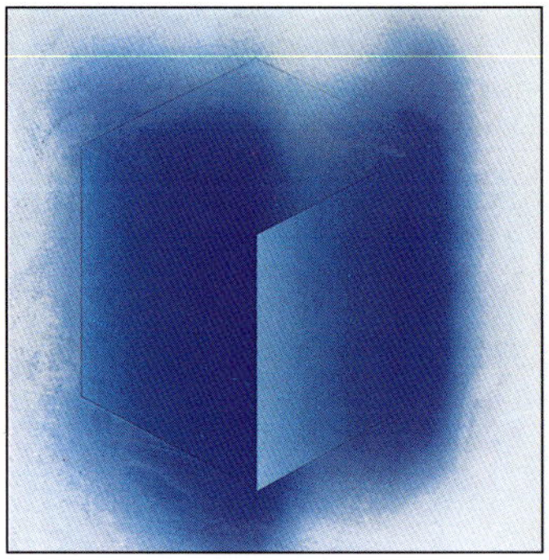

3 Leaving the left-hand face unmasked, the film masking the right-hand face of the cube is cut and removed. On this plane the depth of tone runs from right to left, but with increasing strength in the highlight toward the leading edge of the cube.

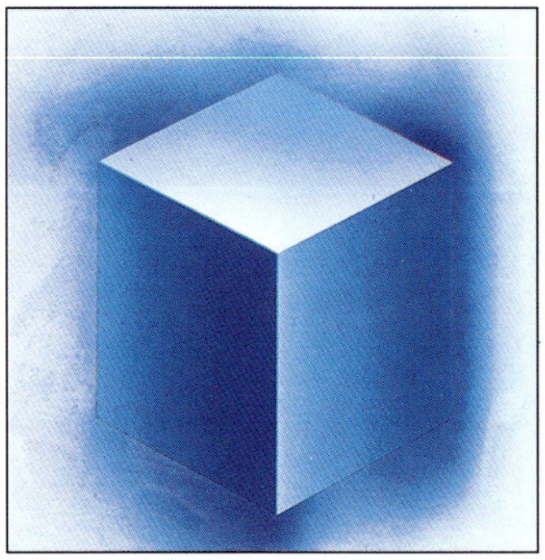

4 The horizontal surface of the cube is cut and removed, again leaving the two vertical surfaces unmasked. The depth of tone here is lighter overall than on the vertical plane and runs horizontally from the top to the bottom, with the nearest corner to the observer being almost devoid of color.

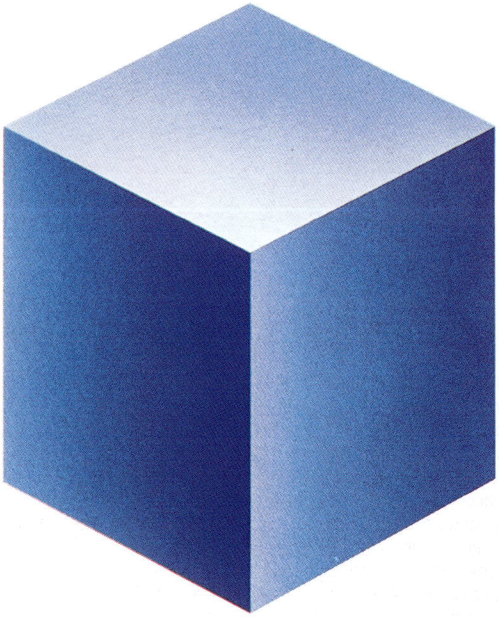

5 On completion, the remaining film is removed, showing the cube rendered in monochrome with enough depth of contrast to create a three-dimensional image.

The Cylinder

1 A straightforward drawing of a cylinder, standing vertically on one end, is covered with masking film which extends also across the background area, as for the cube.

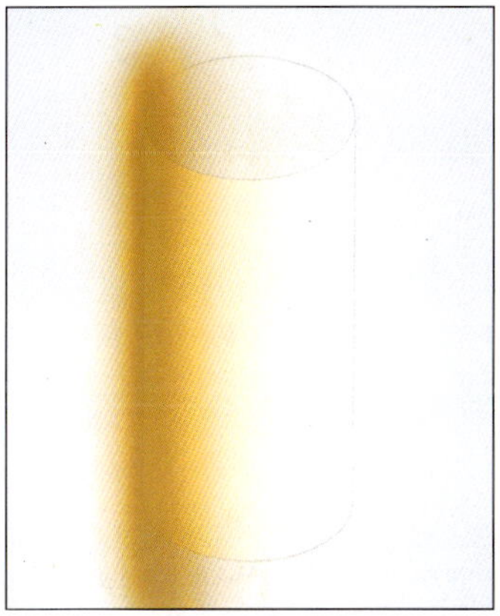

2 The body of the cylinder is cut and the film removed. The spraying begins from the left-hand edge, and the color is allowed to overlap the background masking. It is sometimes advisable to turn the artwork when spraying so that the cylinder is horizontal, with the first edge being sprayed at the top. This makes it easier to control the extent and depth of color, besides ensuring that the color runs parallel to the centerline of the cylinder.

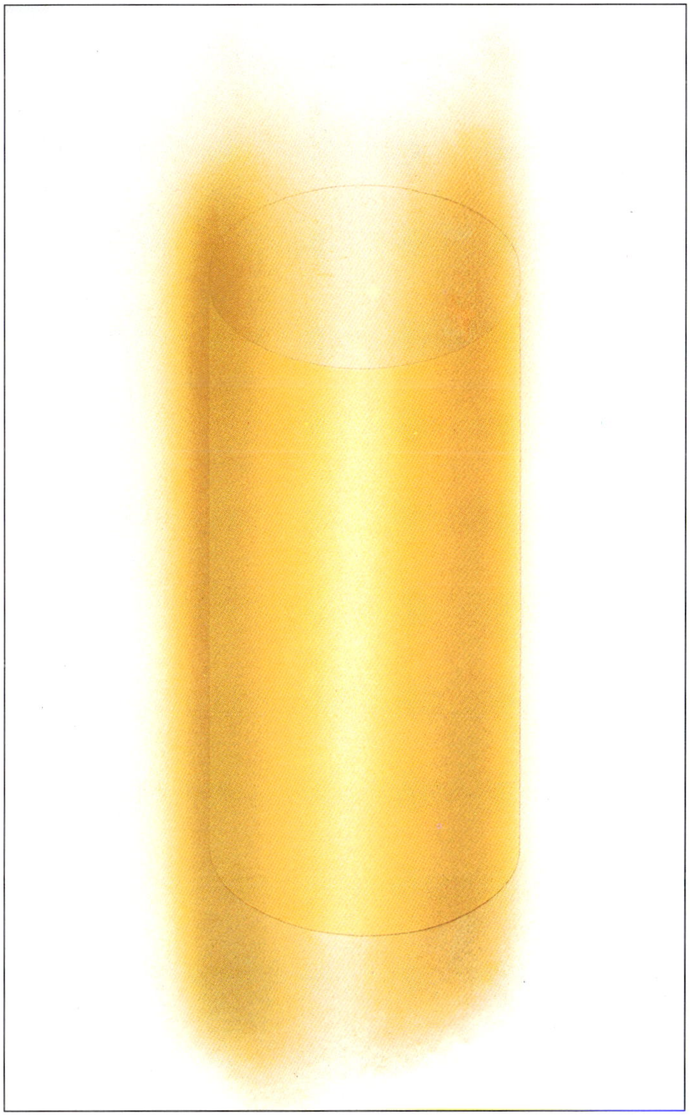

3 On the right-hand edge, the same technique is applied as in stage 2. The important difference is that the color is applied within the edge of the masked shape to create a thin, reflected highlight at the extreme right of the cylinder.

Again the color is gradated quickly as it is brought toward the center of the cylinder. This gives a strong highlight at the center, running the complete length of the cylinder and parallel to the edges.

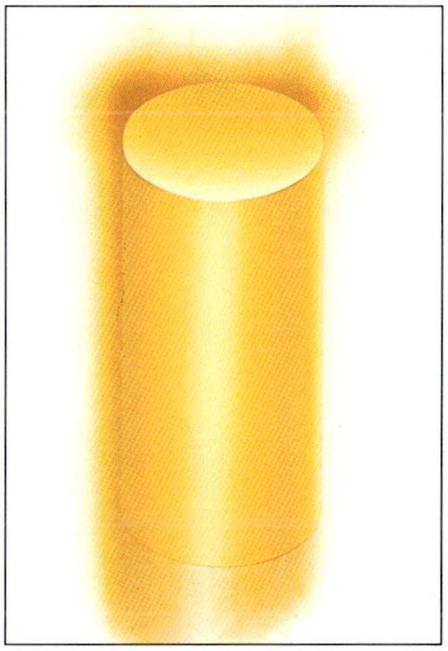

4 Finally, the top of the cylinder is sprayed. After cutting and removing the film from the elliptical plane, color is sprayed in a horizontal direction, concentrating on the outer or upper edge so that only residual color falls onto the leading edge.

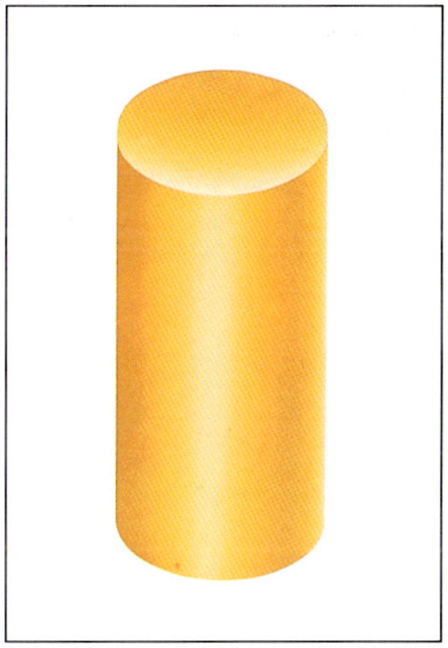

5 The masking film is removed, leaving a hard-edged cylinder illuminated by a light source immediately in front. This technique produces a simple but effective form with a "satin" finish.

The Sphere

1 A circle is cut directly into masking film which has been laid on the illustration board, using a compass cutter. A piece of masking tape is placed at the center to prevent the compass point for from marking the boardbeing marked and also to assist in removal of the mask.

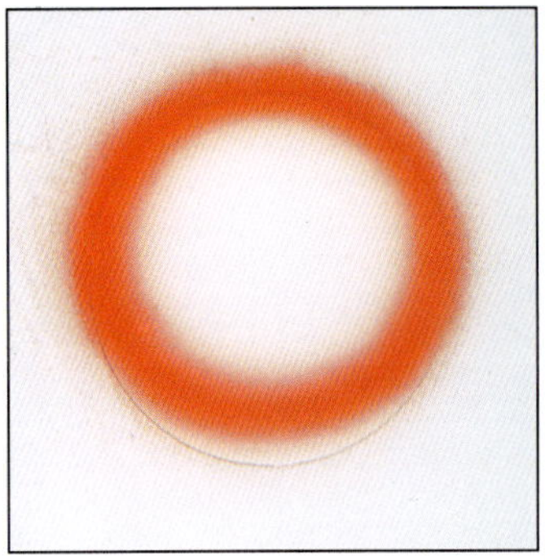

2 An oval of color is sprayed which encompasses the top and both sides of the mask, but does not extend as far as the lower edge. This gives a reflected highlight on the base of the sphere which will enhance its three-dimensional quality. This initial oval of color must be applied carefully and is best attempted after practicing with the airbrush on a freehand basis. As there are no planes within the overall shape of the sphere, the mask only defines its outline, not the internal areas of light and shadow.

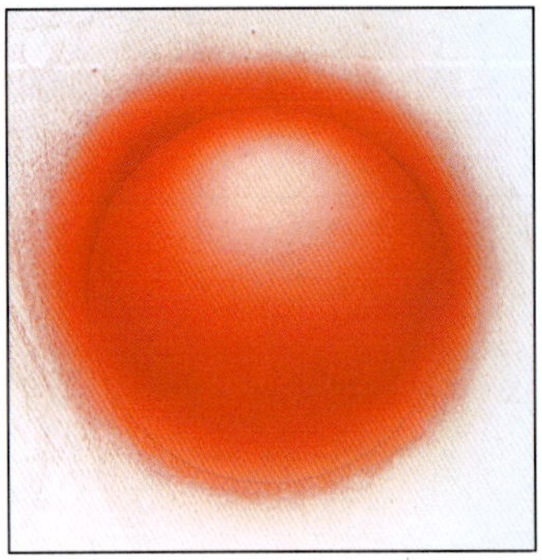

3 In the second stage of spraying, color is applied, leaving a soft-edged, roughly circular highlight near the top of the sphere. Residual color slightly softens the reflected highlight at the lower edge

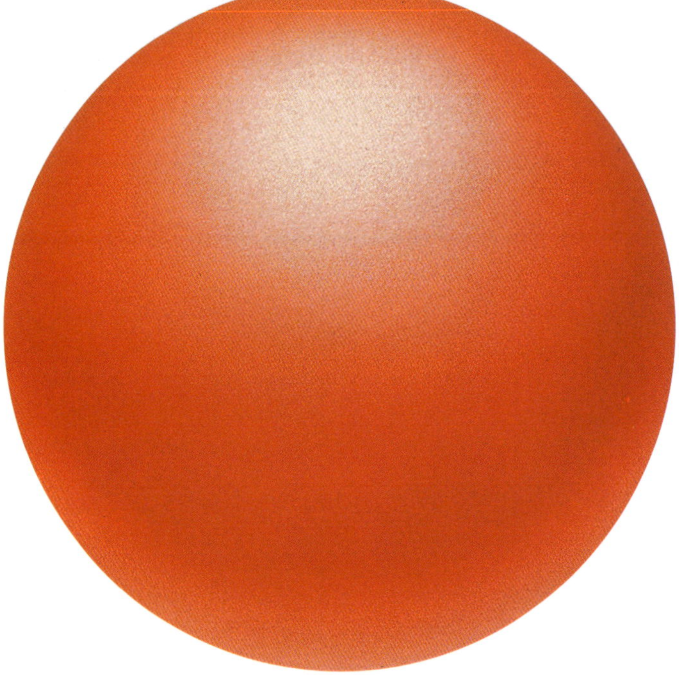

4 Once the masking film has been completely removed, the reflected highlight at the base of the sphere and the principal highlight at center top are more effectively appreciated. After practice in controlling the airbrush for freehand modeling within the masked outline, it will soon be possible to produce spheres with the light sources angled from other directions. A study of spherical objects and the way light falls on them, as well as the way in which other colors are reflected, will be of immense value for future practice and application.

The Cone

1 The cone is drawn using an ellipse template for the base to give a three-dimensional impression. The artwork is covered with masking film and the cone shape cut out.

2 In this example the illustrator has chosen the left-hand edge of the cone to be sprayed first. The color is taken over the masked edge and gradated quickly as it comes around towards the center of the cone. When spraying a cone, it is important to remember that the color should be applied from the base to the top and the area sprayed should follow the overall shape of the cone.

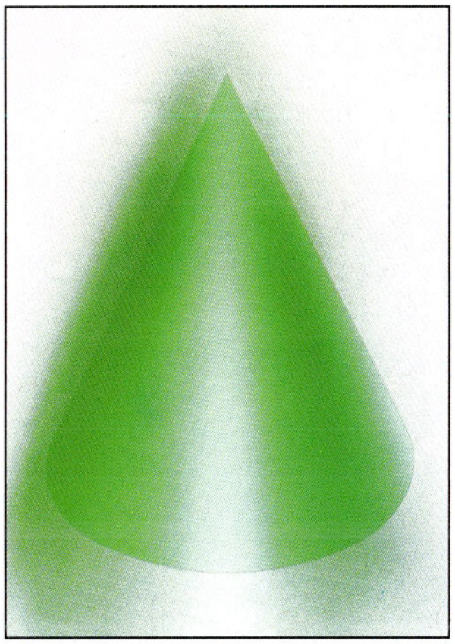

3 The same exercise is carried out on the right-hand side, but, as with the cylinder, the color is not concentrated on the masked edge; it is brought in slightly to allow a reflected highlight to be shown. Again the color is gradated quickly towards the center to create the main highlight.

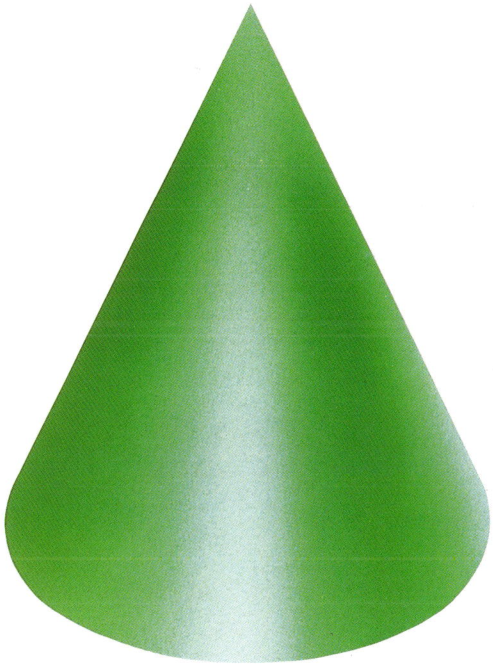

4 The final stage is the removal of the masking film. The cone is seen as a complete three-dimensional form with the central highlight and soft shading creating a "satin" finish like that of the cylinder.

CARDBOARD MASKING

This technique is on the same lines as ANGLED SPRAYING, LOOSE MASKING and TORN PAPER MASKING, and reference should also be made to them when following the sequences illustrated here.

The advantage of cardboard as a masking material is that it is readily available and inexpensive – you can use pieces left over from other studio projects. It can be used to mask particular shapes quite accurately and to create various edge qualities, but as it is opaque, it is less versatile than acetate or masking film.

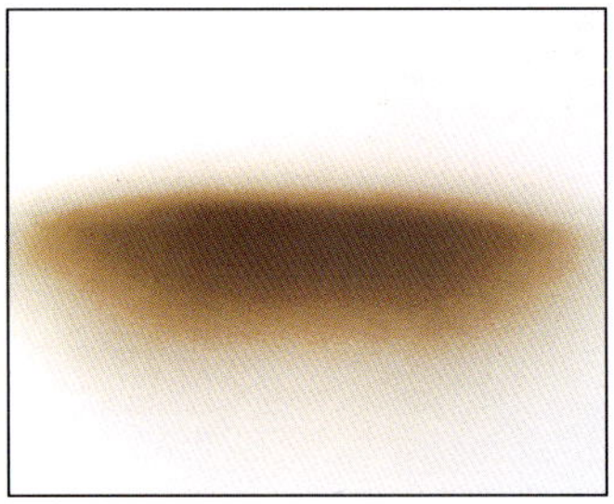

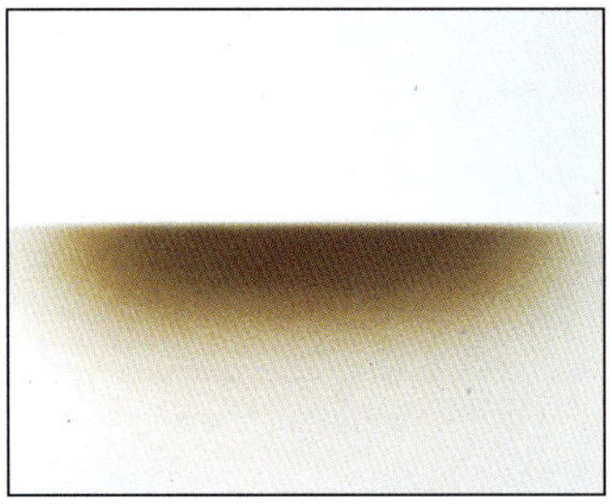

Straight Edge
A piece of straight-edged cardboard has been laid flat on the artwork; the area of color resulting from spraying over the cardboard has a soft but clearly defined edge.

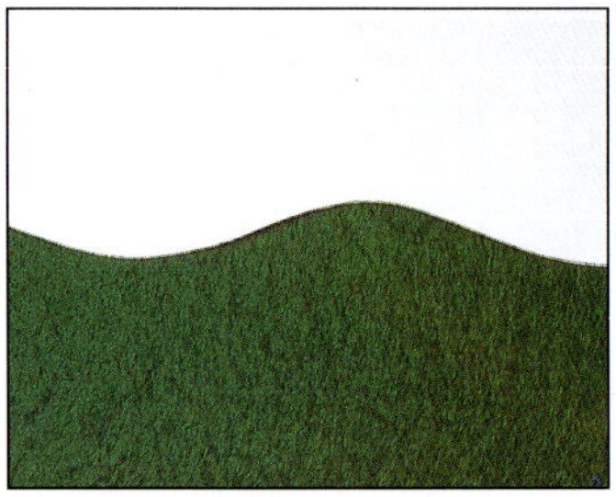

Shaped Edge
1 A piece of cardboard has been cut to a predetermined shape, in this case a gentle curve.

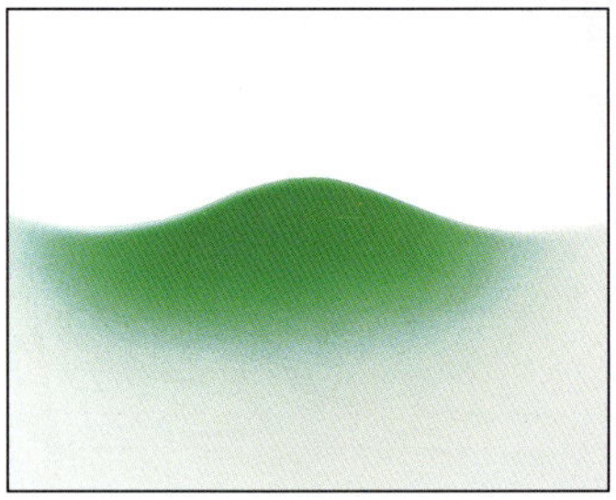

2 This is then laid on the artwork and, after spraying, shows again the clearly defined but soft edge.

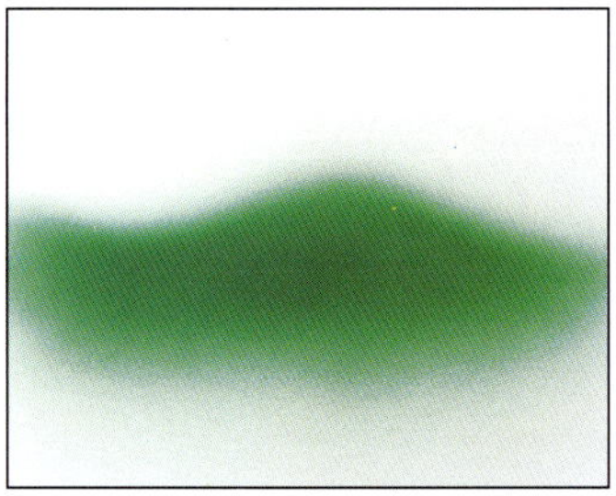

3 When the same shaped mask is used, but held above rather than on the artwork, the resulting edge is gradated and much softer, due to residual color seeping under the cardboard. The further the cardboard is held from the surface when spraying, the more diffuse the effect.

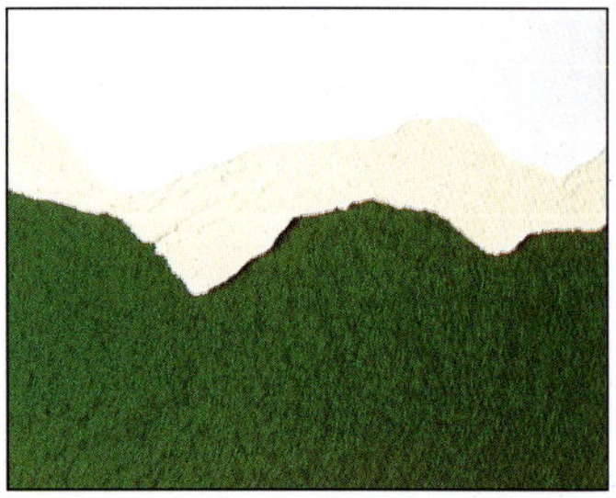

Torn Edge
1 A piece of card has been torn in half. This can be done randomly or following a pencil guide, but in the latter case, remembered that it is not possible to achieve absolute accuracy.

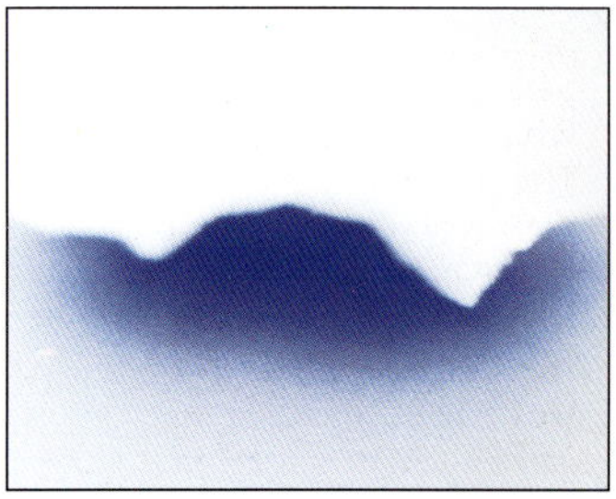

2 The effect achieved from spraying over the torn edge when the mask is laid flat on the artwork.

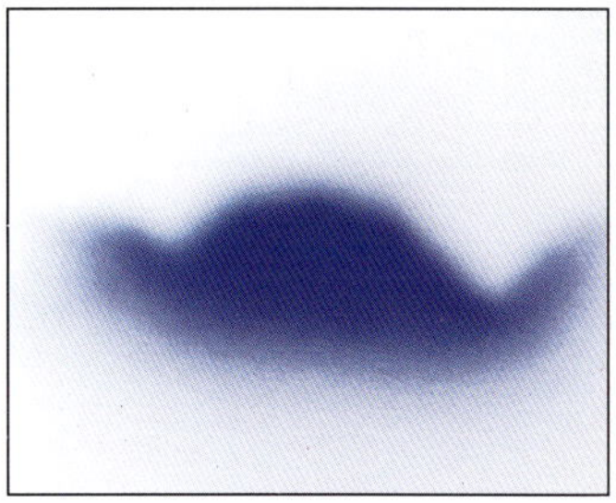

3 The effect achieved when the mask is held above the artwork, showing the more diffused, gradated edge. Again the variation in the degree of gradation can be controlled by the distance the mask is held away from the artwork.

CAST SHADOWS

Cast shadows have a variety of uses in illustration. Not only do they help in visually making the subject stand out to the front, but they are also an effective means of enhancing the three-dimensional qualities of an illustration. The demonstrations here show a soft-edged shadow effect sprayed freehand and a hard-edged shadow created with masking film.

Shadows can be generated from an artificial light source or by natural light from the sun. Each have their own set of rules. The techniques of plotting shadow areas are a subject in themselves, and those wishing to experiment further should refer to books dealing specifically with perspective, besides observing what actually happens in reality. The scope of this book does not permit an extensive explanation of the many complexities of the theory and application of perspective in relation to shadows. However, some guidance may be gained by studying the many examples of professional airbrush work reproduced in this book and recognizing where shadows have been used for a specific purpose.

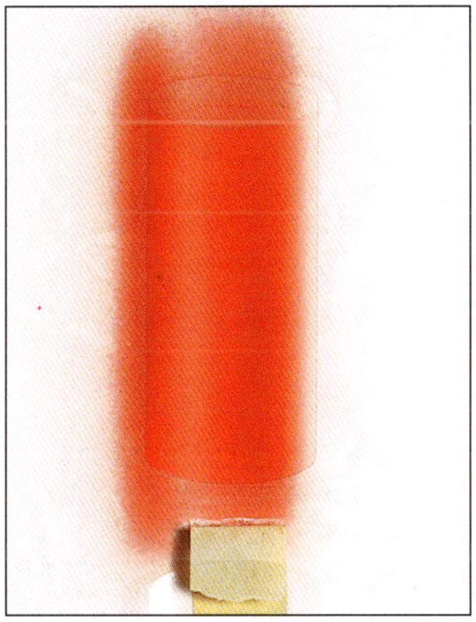

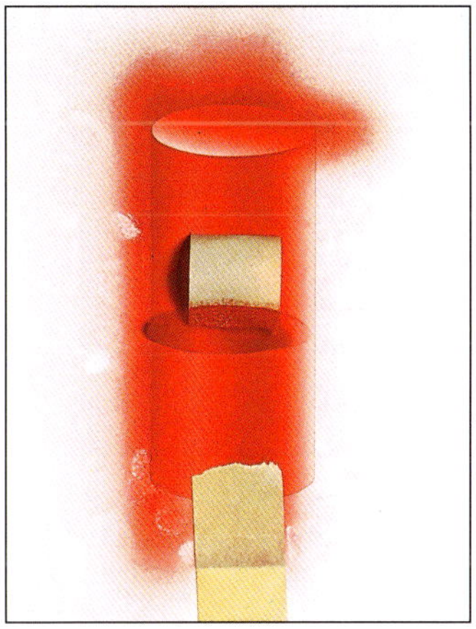

Soft-edged Shadow

1 A vertical cylinder is drawn and covered with masking film. When the outlines have been cut, masking tape is used to anchor the mask section covering the body of the cylinder to make it easy to remove and replace because this mask will be required again. Alternatively, the piece of film can be lifted and placed on the backing sheet for protection until it is re-used. The cylinder is sprayed as previously described (page 15), but with adjustments made with regard to the position of the highlights, as it is intended to cast a soft shadow to the left and toward the observer

2 The body of the cylinder is re-masked. This is essential because of the angle of spray required for the top plane as a result of the direction of the light source. The top is then exposed for spraying with due allowance being made for the leading-edge highlight, which in this example is slightly offset to the left.

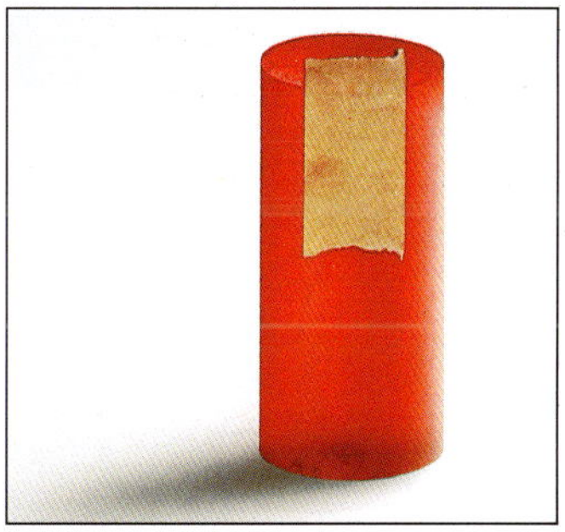

3 The masks for both the top and body of the cylinder are replaced to protect it while the shadow area is sprayed, but all background masking is removed. The shadow is sprayed from the approximate center of the base, gently bringing the color out to the extremities, but keeping well within an area relating to the width of the base. The length of the shadow should not be too long and should fade gradually and easily away from the cylinder.

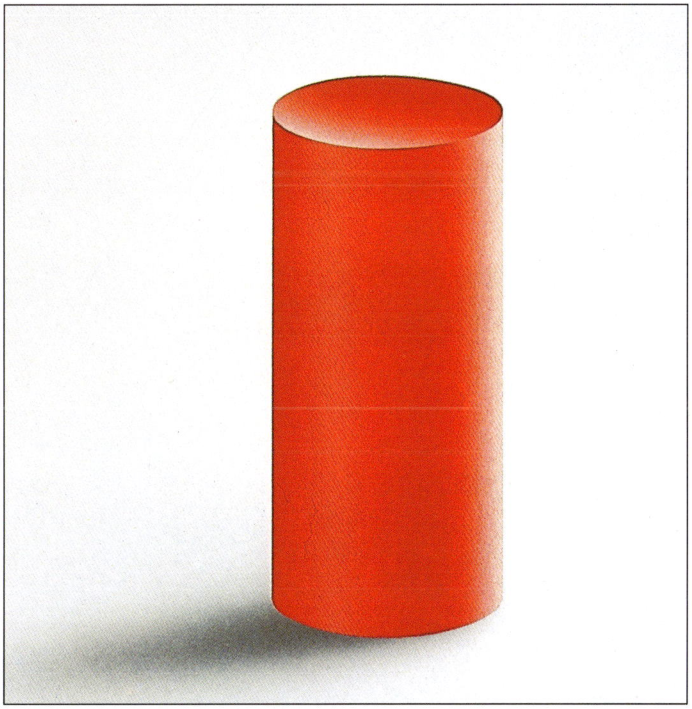

4 The final stage is the removal of the masking film from both the top and body of the cylinder.

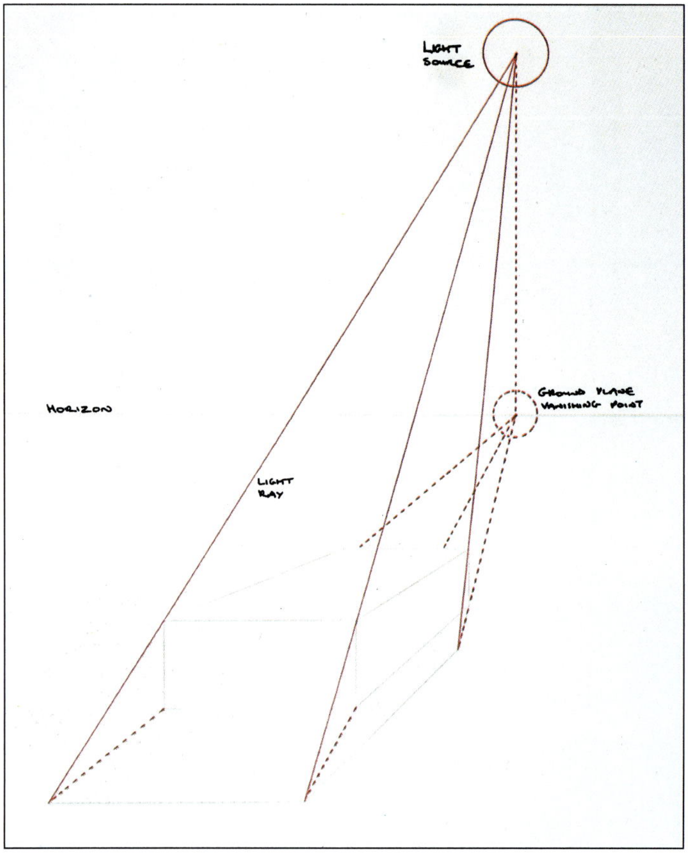

Hard-edged Shadow

1 For the purpose of expanding this exercise in cast shadow techniques, a rectangular box is shown in three dimensions with the construction of its shadow, as if cast from the sun rather than from artificial light. The terms should be self-explanatory, but it must be remembered that the vanishing point on the ground plane will always lie on the horizon and also immediately below the light source.

2 Having constructed the box and its shadow, the drawing is transferred to illustration board, but leaving out the construction lines. The whole surface is then covered with masking film.

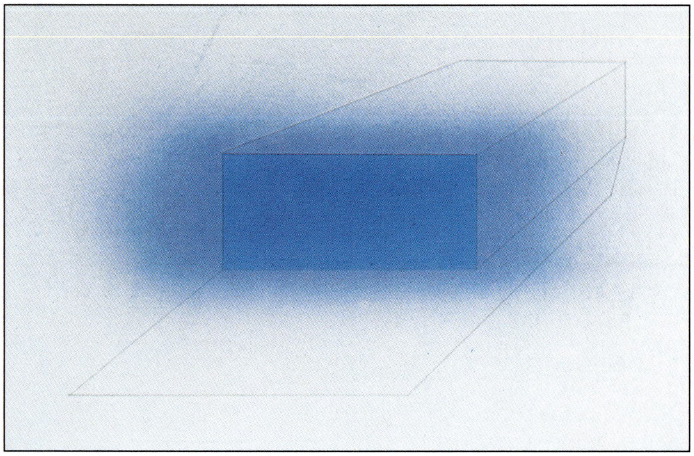

3 The side of the box nearest to the observer is sprayed first because this will be the side in complete shadow, without any reflected light. It should be sprayed with a medium-strength, flat of color.

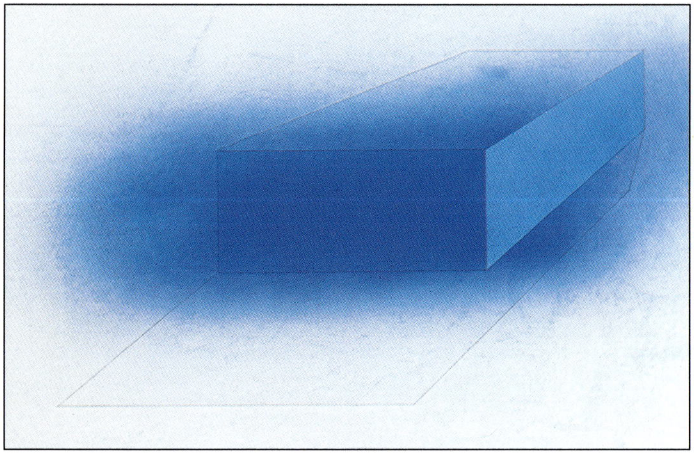

4 The right-hand side of the box is next, and the film covering this area is cut and removed. There is no need to replace the mask previously removed for stage 3, because this side needs to be the strongest in tone and leaving it exposed allows the color density to be built up in successive sprayings.

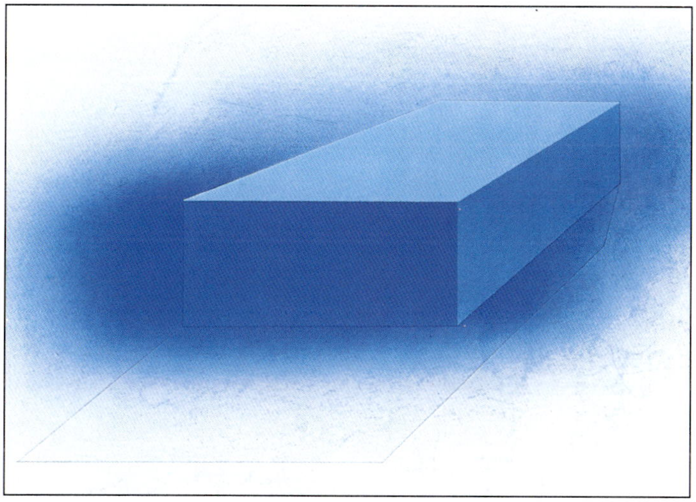

5 Next the top is sprayed, again leaving the previous stages exposed. With the viewpoint chosen, the top of the box is shown as receiving the maximum amount of light, thus having the highest overall tone, and this should be borne in mind when spraying.

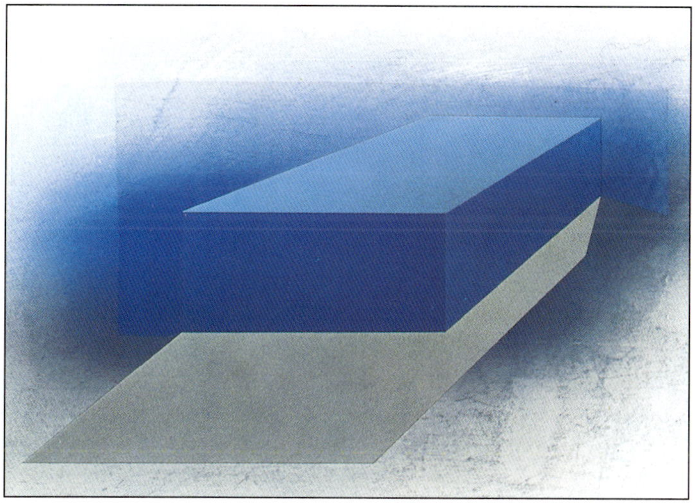

6 The box is re-covered with masking film. The masking film covering the shadow is cut and removed. In this exercise a flat tone is laid down to represent the shadow, but it is also acceptable, and in keeping with nature, to make hard-edged shadows gradated. The gradation may pass outwards from the object or inwards from the extremities of the shadow; it is all dependent on the effect and emphasis needed

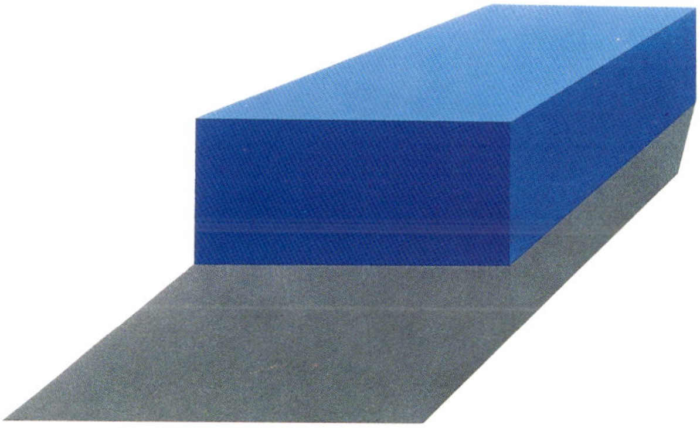

7 The final image shows the completed box and its shadow with all the masking film removed. Because of the sequence in which the box was sprayed, a certain luminosity is apparent, which assists in delineating the shape and defining the direction of the light source.

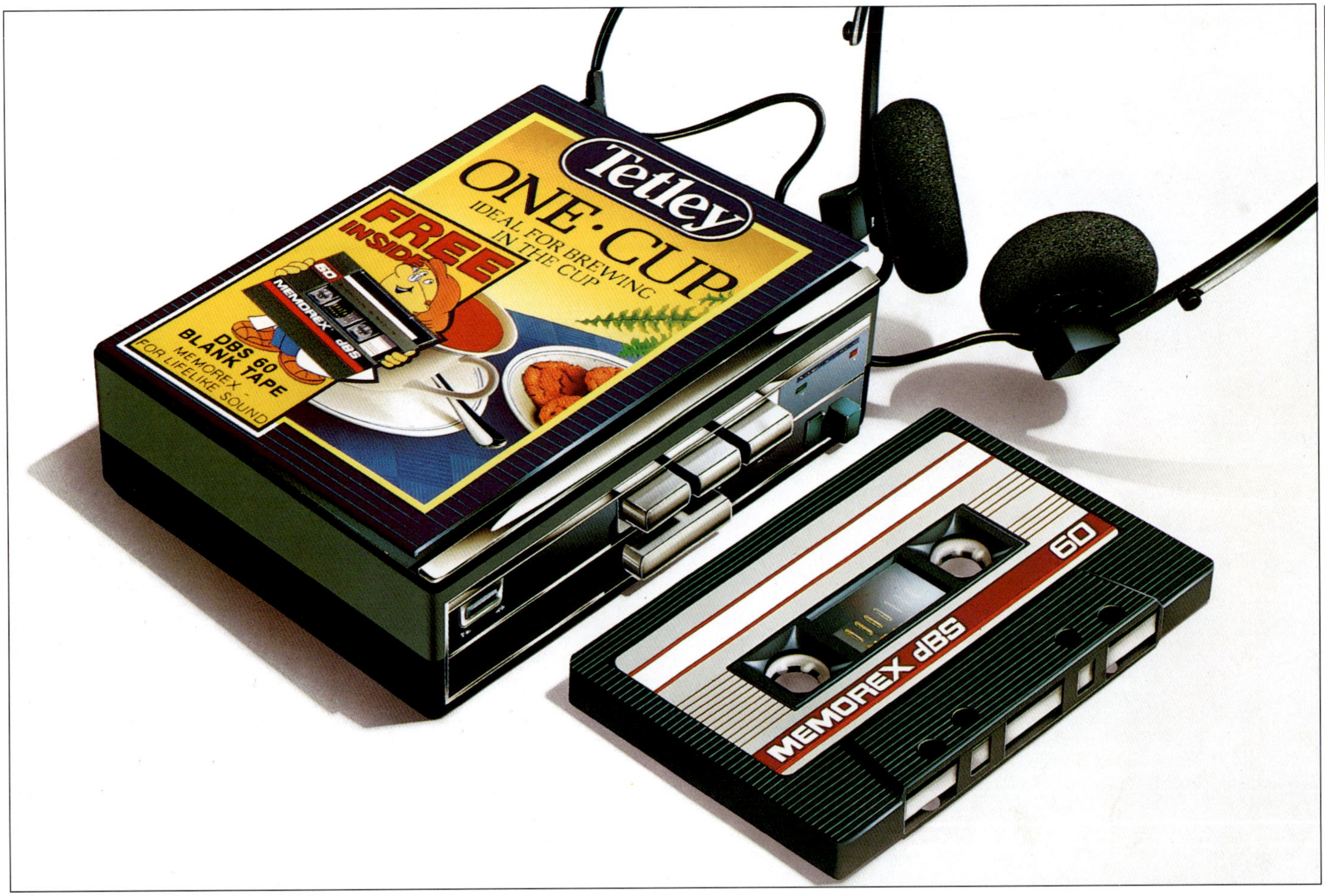

Tetley One-Cup personal stereo
John Brettoner

Modern hi-fi equipment and personal stereos are subjects which have proven popular with illustrators specializing in airbrush rendered illustrations. The subjects seem to be particularly apt, and the example reproduced here is excellent, showing the quality of overall finish which all students of airbrushing should aim to emulate. It is included in this section because it demonstrates clearly the application of GRADATED TONE to form soft-edged cast shadows. Without them, the three items would appear to float in space; as it is, the cast shadows create the impression that they are lying on a flat surface, even though no color or edges are visible on this imaginary surface.

The illustration is comparatively simple in terms of the accurate plotting of the shadows. Other subjects may not be, but all require careful observation to ensure that they at least look as if they are the true shadows of the object from which they are cast. When planning the inclusion of shadows, it is essential that their position and direction does not conflict with the direction of the light source, regardless of the material or surface of the subject being sprayed. Highlights and shadows should always be in harmony with each other.

There are two other airbrushing techniques used on this personal stereo which deserve to be mentioned here, because they represent excellent examples. First, the LETTERING TECHNIQUES, which have a quality indicating the obvious skill and care which the illustrator has applied; second, the very subtle application of SPATTERING on the speakers, which is just enough to indicate the surface texture.

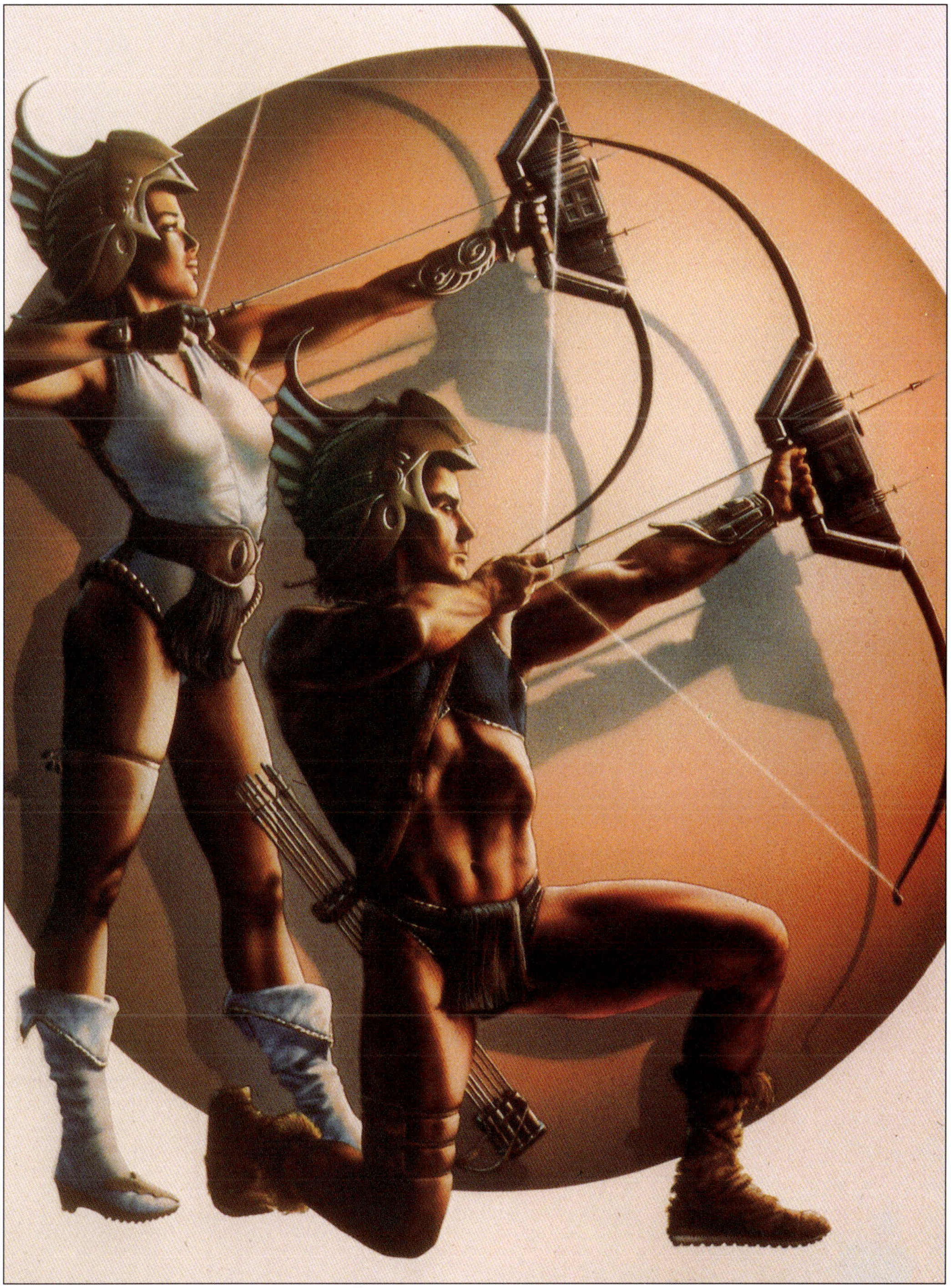

Archers
Andrew Farley

The importance of the light shadows being in harmony with the source of light is made even more apparent in this illustration. By defining the shadows and the angle of the light source, on both the sphere and the bodies of the archers, a clear impression is given of the time being at sunset. The color tones, strength and extent of the shadows on the bodies increase this impression. The cast shadows on the sphere [see BASIC FORMS], as well as the shading across its natural form indicate the direction of the light, with these shadows applied by loose masking or acetate masking.

The archers also demonstrate the degree of observation required when airbrushing the human form. Other examples may be seen in the second half of this book under the section focusing specifically on rendering HUMAN FORM with the airbrush.

CHROME EFFECTS

By its very nature, chrome, or any other highly polished or reflective surface, is difficult to reproduce convincingly in an illustration. While the airbrush is a more than useful aid, if the effect is not rendered with care and pre-planning, it can be extremely crude and simplistic. It therefore requires practice and a close study of actual examples, including the methods used in some of the illustrations reproduced in this book. This is because chrome is rarely seen without something else reflected in it, usually in close proximity.

These exercises introduce the technique of how to approach the airbrushing of chrome in both black-and-white and color. Each is demonstrated in isolation, and neither should be taken as the only method. When airbrushing chrome, the approach adopted must be judged on its merits and is dependent on such things as the location of the chrome in relation to other objects or materials, the base color of surrounding objects, and colors in the environment in which the chrome needs to be shown. All of these will obviously determine the base and reflective colors to be used when spraying.

The color exercise shown here uses a convention for creating the effect of reflected color. This is based on the assumption that the lower part of a chrome object might be reflecting earth colors from the ground, while the upper part reflects lighter tones from the sky. This ground/sky division requires the artist to establish an approximate horizon level across the chrome surface.

Finally, always ensure that the air pressure through the airbrush is correct. If it is too low, the finish will appear grainy and textured, which would take away the reflective appearance. Chrome has an extremely smooth surface.

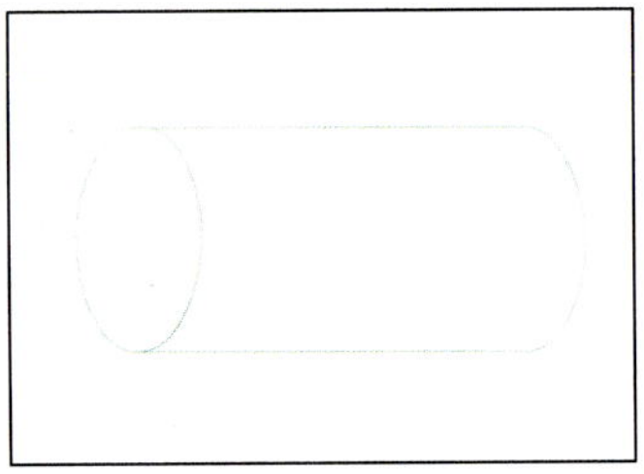

Monochromatic Effect

1 As the basis of this example, a cylinder is drawn three-dimensionally and in a horizontal position. The artwork is covered with masking film in preparation for spraying.

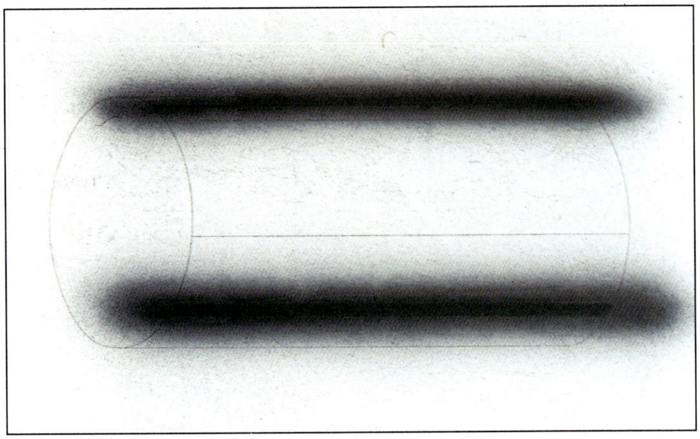

2 The body, or length, of the cylinder is divided into various shaded areas and those needing the strongest or darkest shades are cut, unmasked and sprayed first. It is important that when spraying a black-and-white object, the darkest areas are sprayed first, as this not only saves time, but also requires the minimum of mask cutting. By following this sequence, any residue from subsequent spraying which automatically encroaches on the darkest areas will merely strengthen the darkest tones and, with proper control, improve the depth of contrast in the finished artwork.

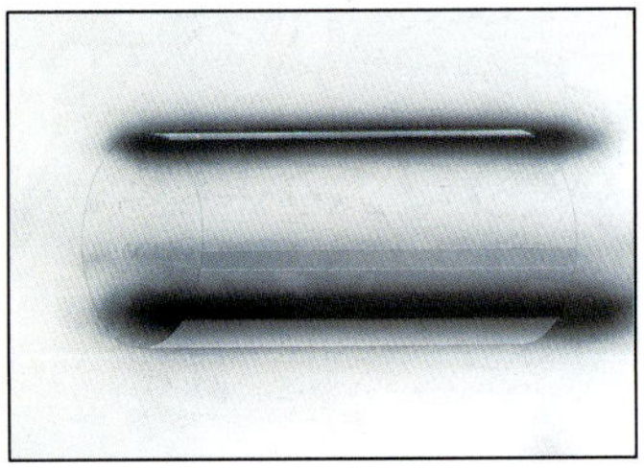

3 The areas of medium are exposed and sprayed.

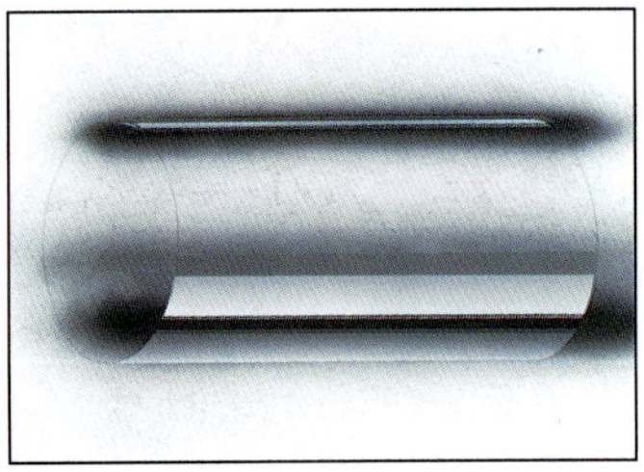

4 The first of the gradated tonal areas is now cut, removed and sprayed, making sure the color does not extend too far down and thereby diminish the strength of the highlight.

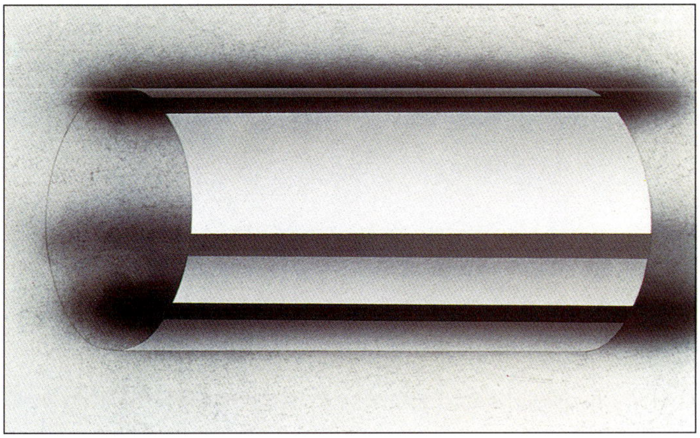

5 The second area of gradated tone is applied to the top half of the cylinder. Again, be careful not to spray too heavily as the color is brought down into the area of the white highlight.

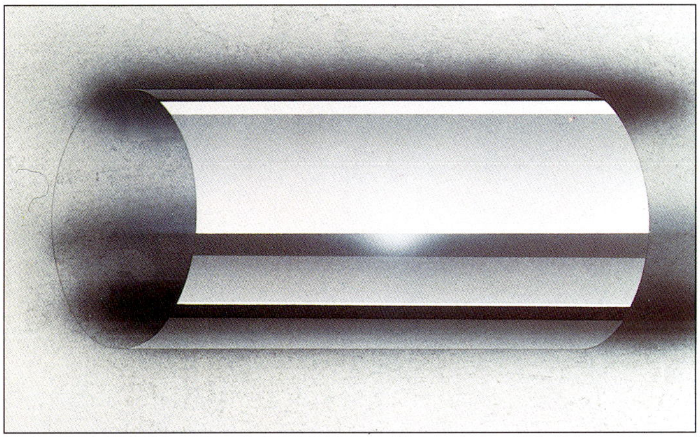

6 Using opaque white, an intense highlight is sprayed freehand and in the approximate center of the body of the cylinder.

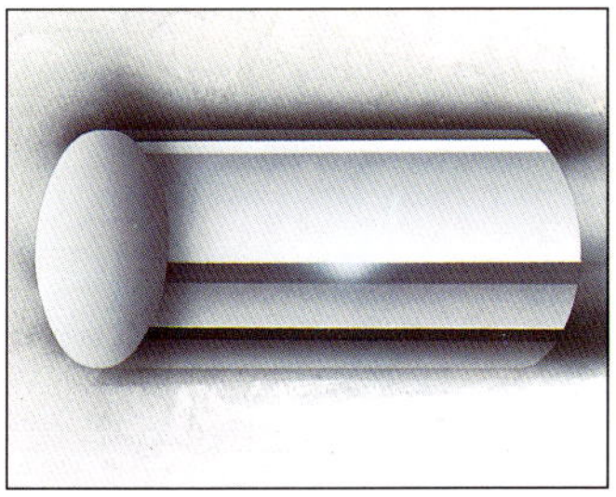

7 The body of the cylinder is now re-covered with masking film and the end of the cylinder is exposed for spraying. To emphasize the edge of the cylinder, the color is applied vertically and gradated from right to left, allowing a sufficient residue of color to extend over the complete surface of the end plane.

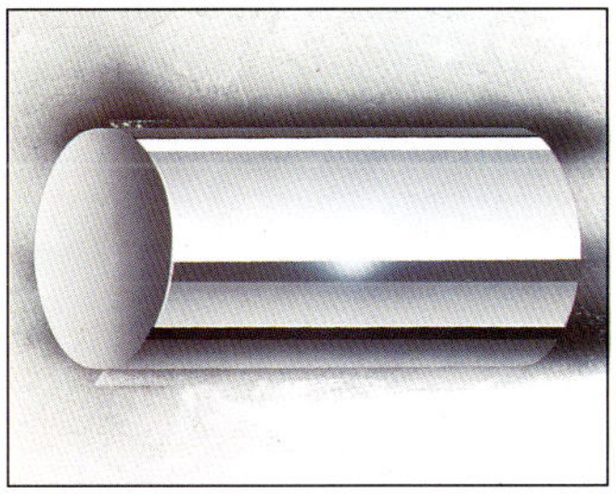

8 The masking film protecting the body of the cylinder is removed, and a thin highlight is scratched with an art knife along the curved edge between the body and the end of the cylinder.

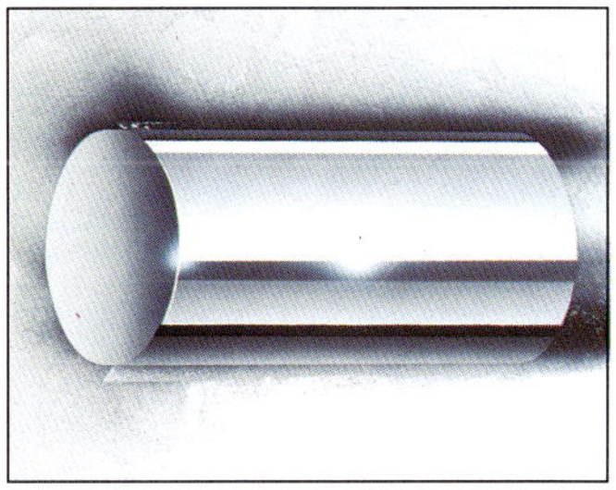

9 Another opaque white highlight is applied freehand over the linear highlight scratched back in stage 8.

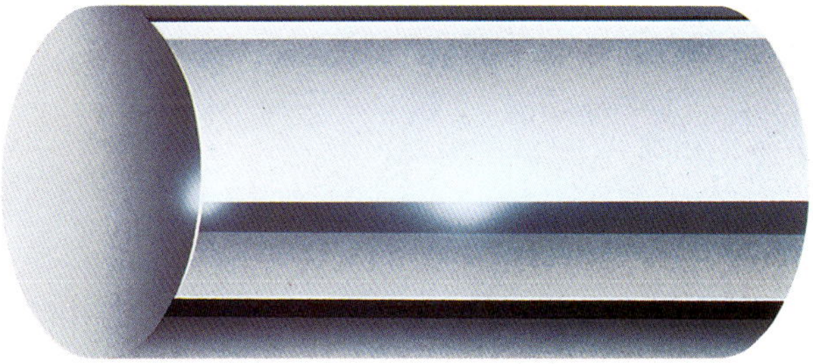

10 The surrounding masking film is removed, revealing the finished artwork. With more practice, and by observing actual examples, it will soon be apparent that there are many variations possible in rendering highly polished surfaces such as chrome.

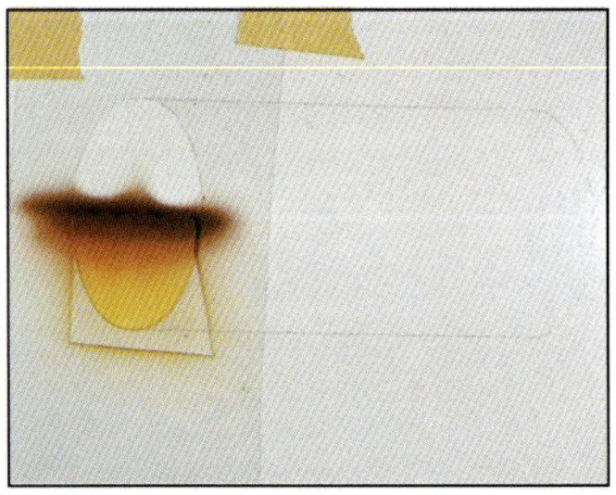

Ground/Sky Reflection

1 Using the same image, the cylinder is drawn and covered with masking film. The end of the cylinder is prepared for spraying and an acetate mask is overlaid, which has been cut to follow an approximate "horizon" level across the center of the cylinder. This exposed area is sprayed with gradated color, using yellow ochre and vandyke brown to represent the base or ground which would be reflected in the cylinder. The yellow ochre is sprayed first, covering the whole area. This is followed by an overspray of vandyke brown, but concentrating the color at the top edge of the mask, which represents the reflected "horizon." This is gradated down into the yellow ochre, but not so that it covers it.

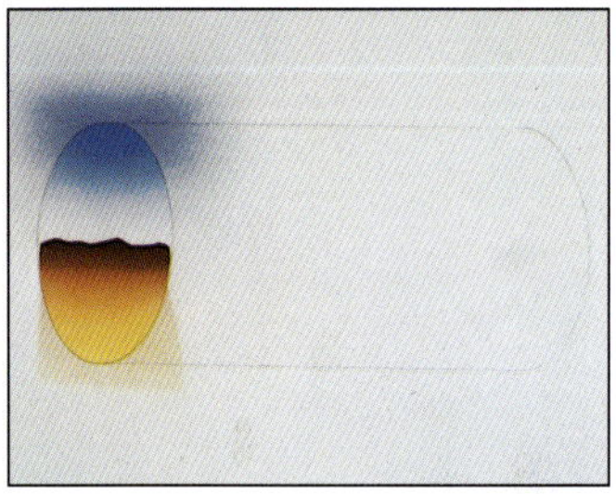

2 The acetate mask is removed, and blue is then sprayed from the top of the cylinder end, gradating downward toward the "horizon." To be effective, this color should have enough gradation to allow the white of the board to come through between the brown and the blue, as shown here. The end of the cylinder is now completed.

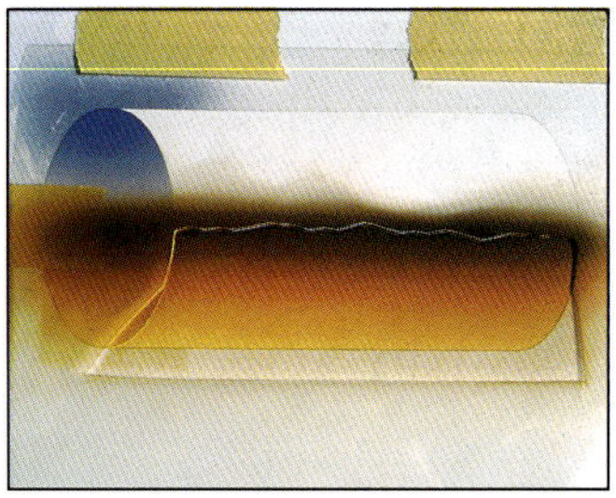

3 The masking film is replaced over the sprayed area, and the film protecting the body of the cylinder is removed. Another acetate mask is prepared to allow exposure of the area covering the ground from the "horizon" down. This is sprayed using the same colors and following the same sequence as for the end of the cylinder.

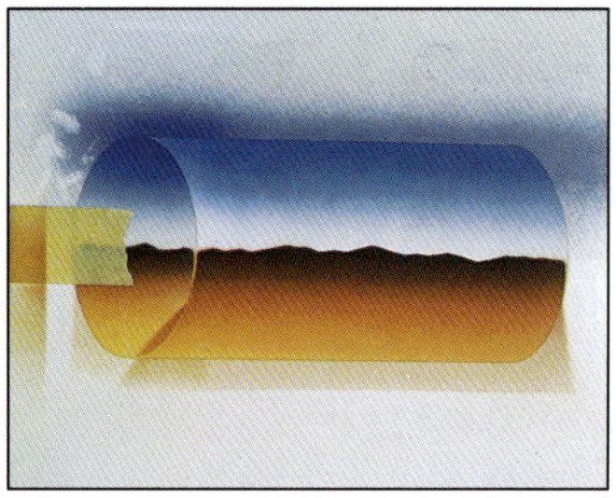

4 The acetate mask is removed and the reflected color for the sky is sprayed, again being gradated from the top to the "horizon."

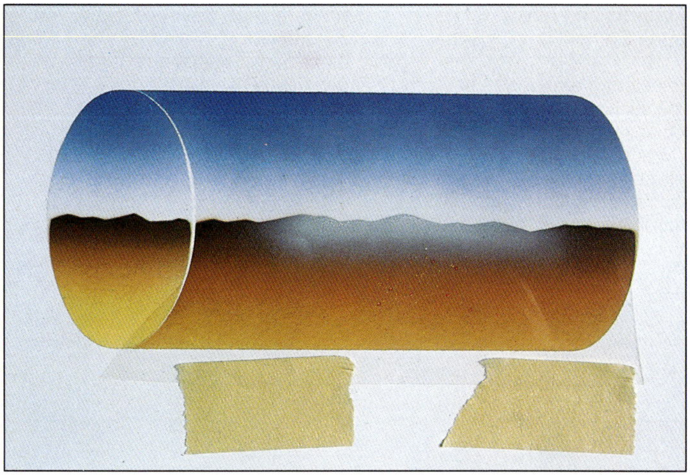

5 The linear edge between the end and the body of the cylinder is highlighted by scratching out color with an art knife. This is followed by a sprayed highlight of opaque white immediately above the "horizon" line across the body of the cylinder, using an acetate mask to protect the background color.

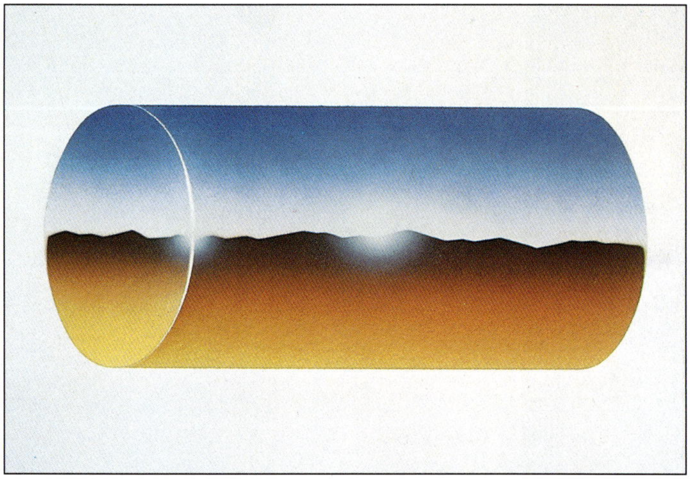

6 A highlight, again of opaque white, is sprayed freehand on both the linear highlight and approximately in the center of the body of the cylinder. Both are positioned at the level of the reflected "horizon."

Metallic tap fittings
John Brettoner

Effects similar to those appearing on the surface of chrome will be seen on any highly reflective and polished surface, such as brass, copper or stainless steel. This illustration of two single faucet flanking each side of a mixer faucet is an excellent example of how one illustrator has successfully rendered the same subject with three different metallic finishes. The faucet on the left is of brass; the mixer in the middle has a semi-gloss enameled finish and the one on the right has a chrome finish.

The majority of examples of airbrushed chrome finishes in illustrations can be found on vehicles, as demonstrated under TRANSPORT (pages 98-115). However, while vehicles spend much, if not all, of their lives in the open and therefore the rendering of their chromed surfaces lends itself to reflections of horizons and the blue of the sky, this is not appropriate to objects seen inside. A compromise is therefore necessary, especially if, as in the illustration reproduced here, no surrounding objects or surfaces are included. Under such circumstances the illustrator must resort to studio-shot photographs for reference, or, as is more likely, his or her skill and knowledge of how compound surfaces appear when reflecting nothing more than pure light and other parts of the same object. Such a technique may seem abitrary in application, but if the finished result looks as intended, then success is achieved.

Techniques used on this illustration include FILM MASKING, LOOSE MASKING, FREEHAND SPRAYING, LINING-IN and RULING. The background is a good example of ANGLED SPRAYING and GRADATED TONE. Worth special attention are the subtle reflections made by the sectioned part of the mixer faucet in the handle and body of the faucet on the right. Soft, gradated reflections of the faucets are also visible on the surface. To give contrast between the warmth of the brass and the hard coldness of the chrome, touches of dark green have been applied to the latter.

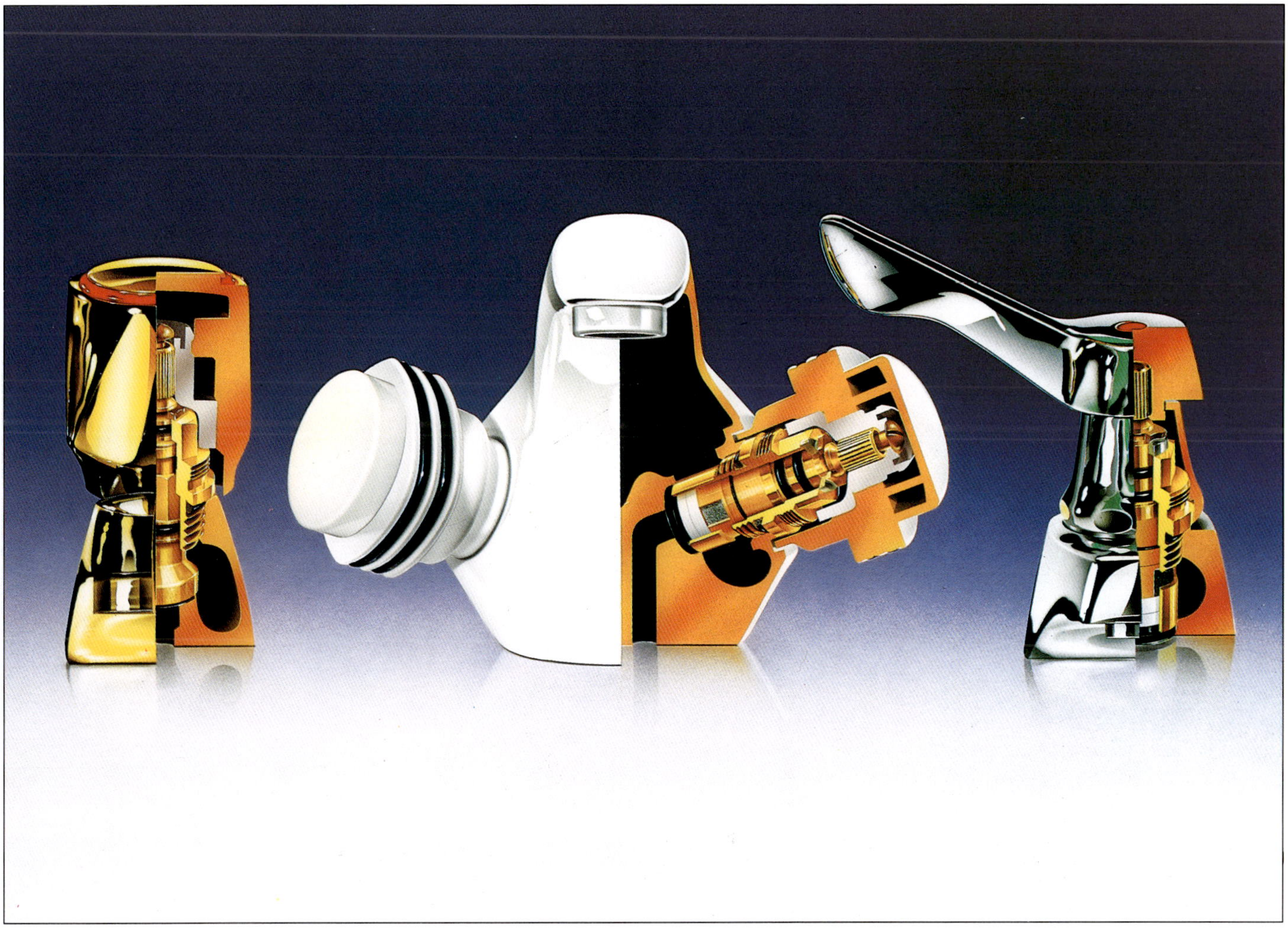

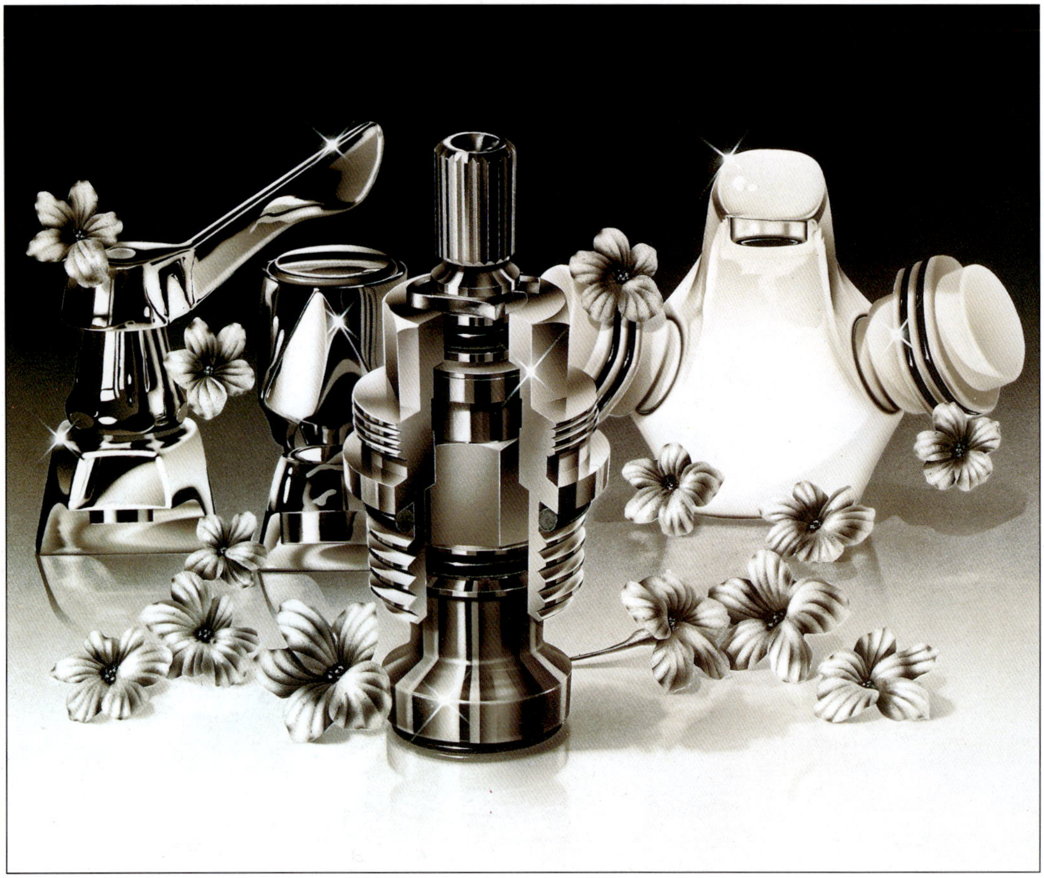

Black-and-white faucets
John Brettoner

As a contrast to the full-color rendering of faucets, an example is given here of a similar subject rendered with an airbrush in black-and-white. In the foreground is a valve assembly, with two single faucets offset to the left and behind it. To the right is an enamel-finished mixer faucet.

Because the illustrator has only black, white and the various shades of gray obtained by mixing the two base colors, the airbrushing demands a high degree of skill in the understanding of shading, contrast and light and shadow. It also requires very careful planning to prevent one area from blending in with another or the objects seeming to merge. This illustration achieves all, with not one part being illegible or vague. It has been rendered using the same techniques as the full-color illustration, including the background, but with the addition of STARBURSTS in seven selected, and carefully thought-out, places. Soft-edged CAST SHADOWS sprayed with GRADATED TONES have also been used, which adds to the impression of the faucets sitting on a surface.

Laser-cut bread
John Brettoner

Strong contrast between one material or texture and another is one of the distinct advantages of airbrush rendering as compared to hand-painting, where it can be difficult to achieve the same precision. With a considered approach and using the appropriate techniques, the effect can be quite stunning, as shown here in the definition applied to the robot's hand and a loaf of bread being cut by a laser beam. The robot's hand has been sprayed in what have become almost the traditional colors for rendering chrome, using FILM and LOOSE MASKING. In addition, reflections have been added to the hand where it is gripping the bread, and also from the laser beam. The addition of such reflections always makes an illustration look complete, but the illustrator must take care not to overdo them or place them in the wrong position.

Hand-painted and sprayed DOT HIGHLIGHTS have been placed on the hand and metallic base in positions reflecting the most intense light. These have not been used excessively, but just enough to add to the dramatic effect in the chromed finish of the hand and smooth surface of the base.

The loaf of bread combines brushwork with SPATTERING, which has also been used, in varying densities, to represent the starlit night. One star has been highlighted by the use of a STARBURST, DOT HIGHLIGHT and HALO. The laser beam is composed of a wide band of pink which has been LOOSE MASKED to give it soft edges, and then OVERSPRAYED with two thinner red lines within the pink. Between the two red lines, an opaque white line has been drawn in, ending at the metallic surface with a large, freehand dot highlight. The final touches to this illustration are the ruled lines representing both highlights and linear detail [see RULING and LINING-IN].

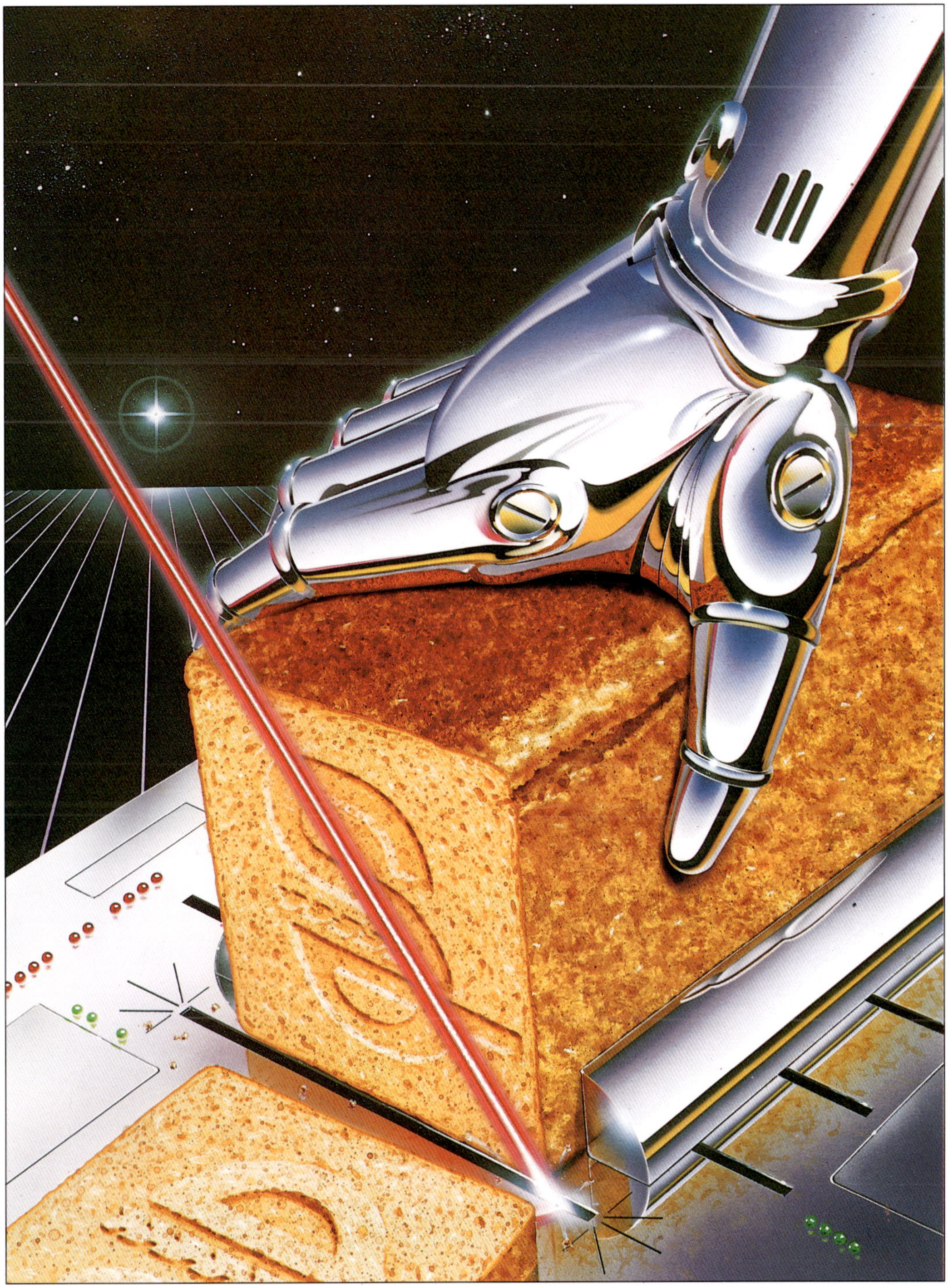

CORRECTION TECHNIQUES

Errors and accidents are unavoidable; it is therefore necessary to devise quick and effective techniques which can rectify the situation without having to resort to a complete re-start. The example illustrated here, an irregularity in the spray quality, is a common mistake, usually the result of lack of control. Sometimes it is caused by dried paint particles being blown onto the artwork through poor cleaning of the airbrush.

Over-spraying with White
1 It was intended to produce a piece of artwork with smoothly gradated color running from maximum strength of color at the top to a very soft and subtle strength at the bottom. However, it can be seen that a small but noticeable error has unfortunately been made in the lighter area of the spraying.

2 To rectify this mistake, opaque white is sprayed across the complete width of the colored area containing the irregularity, but gradating from the bottom to approximately the middle to maintain the original gradation.

3 To retrieve the required density of the tonal gradation, the area is resprayed with the original color after the white paint has dried.

4 When the mask is removed, the effect is of a clean area of gradated color.

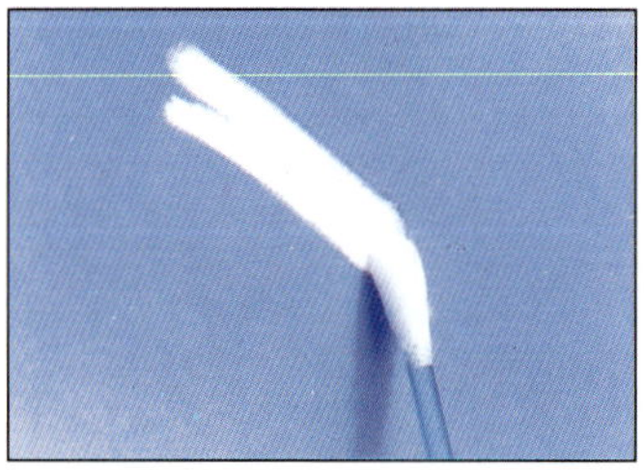

Lifting Watercolor
When correcting small watercolor-based areas of the artwork, cotton buds may be used to remove paint. If the color is fairly strong, it may be necessary to use quite a few buds, especially if the area requiring correction must be brought back to the white of the original surface. This method is not always effective when used on a textured surface, such as rough board-mounted paper, because the pigments become ingrained in the surface. It is best restricted to smooth, china-clay coated boards.

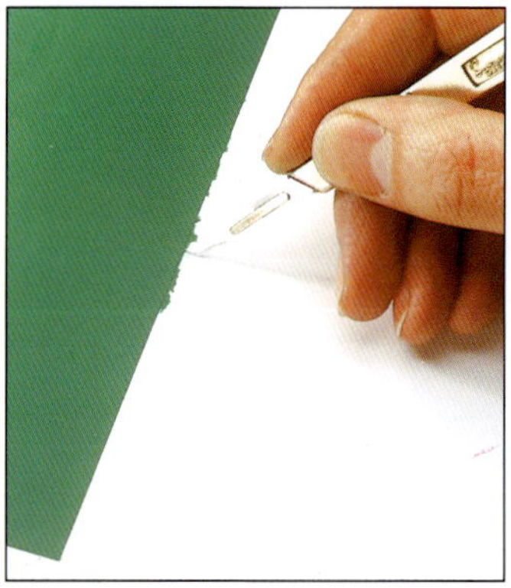

Removing Color Bleed
In this example the paint was sprayed on too wet. Consequently, color has run under the mask, resulting in an unsightly, ragged edge. On a smooth, hard coated surface, such errors are best removed with an art knife when the paint is thoroughly dry. Reference should also be made to the technique of SCRATCHING BACK.

DOT CONTROL

Many people, when first introduced to the airbrush, believe it is only capable of spraying medium or large areas and is not suitable for fine, detailed work. Plenty of dot control exercises will not only prove them wrong, but will also build up confidence and skill in using the airbrush. It is also good practice for applying sprayed dots as highlights to give sparkle to the finish of a detailed illustration. This technique is covered under DOT HIGHLIGHTS in the following section.

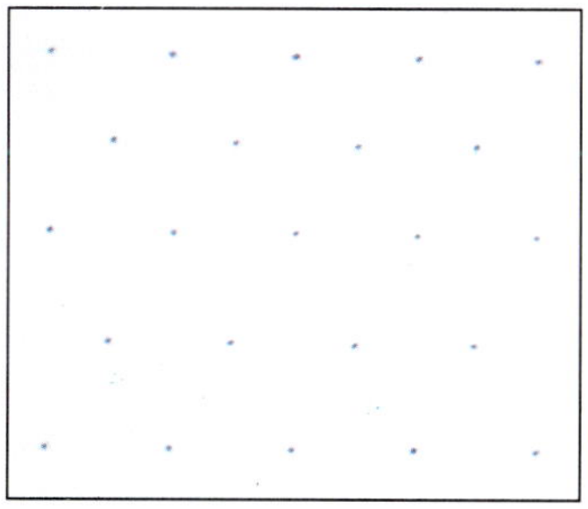

1 This shows a sheet of same-sized dots laid out in five horizontal rows. The control lies in attempting to achieve the same size and color intensity in each sprayed dot.

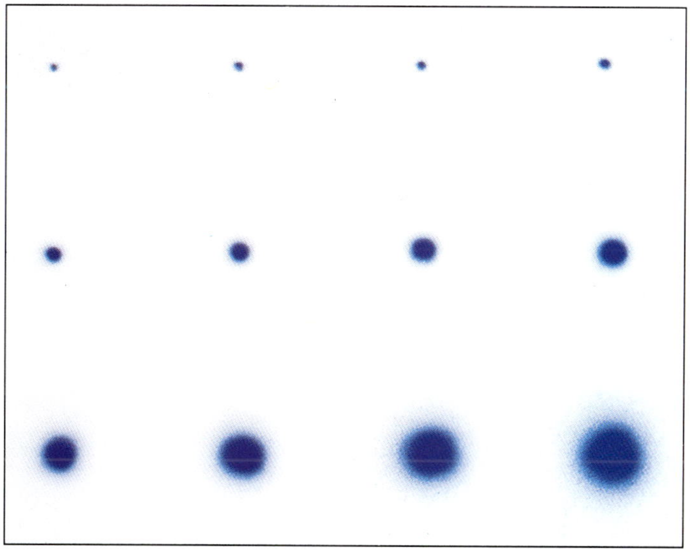

2 Here three rows of dots have been sprayed progressively from small to medium to large. As every dot in the sequence varies, this extends your control of the flow of medium and the distance of the airbrush nozzle from the board surface to achieve the right size of dot.

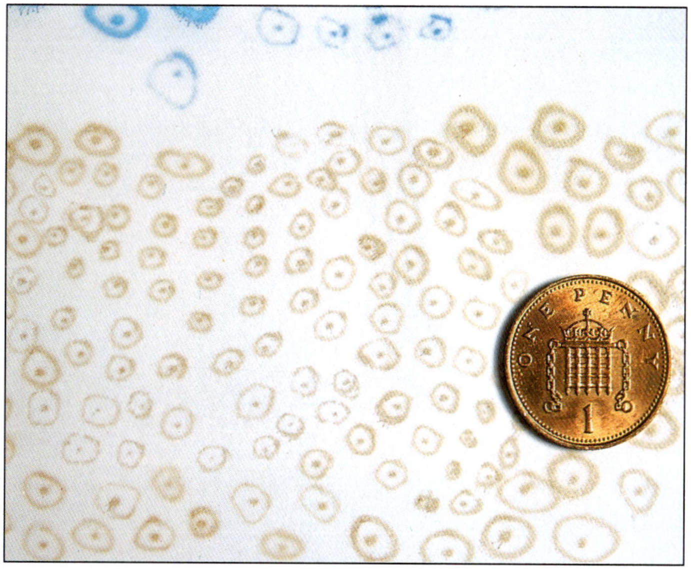

3 To increase control of the airbrush and both the air pressure and amount of paint allowed through it, these dots have been sprayed individually and encompassed in sprayed circles. The small penny coin gives a good indication of the scale of the original exercise.

DOT HIGHLIGHTS

The use of dot highlights is a particularly valuable means of adding that final, finishing touch to an illustration. Highlights must obviously be used only on those surfaces and on edges which would normally reflect light in such a concentrated way. They should appear as an integral part of the object and must always conform to the chosen direction of the light source.

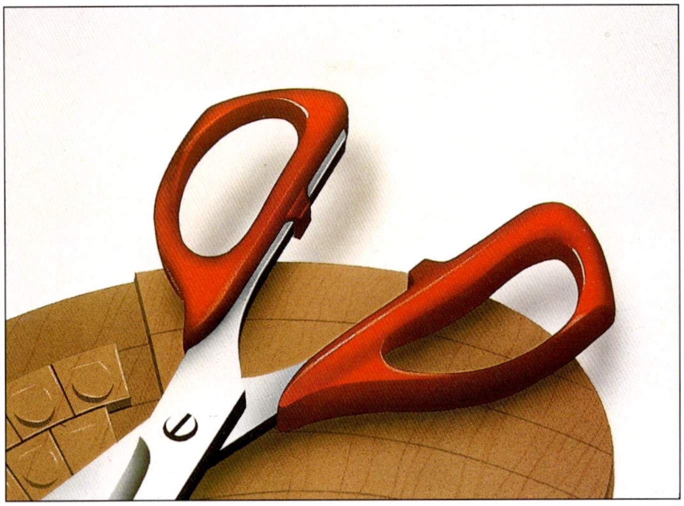

On a Curved Edge

1 To pick out the edges on which light would be intensely reflected and also to enhance the contrast and three-dimensional quality of the scissors in this illustration, white lines have been scratched onto the handles. It should be noted that these highlights are not short, blunt lines, but taper off toward the narrower part of the handles. This is important, because the highlights must appear to be on and part of the same surface, and not some distance away.

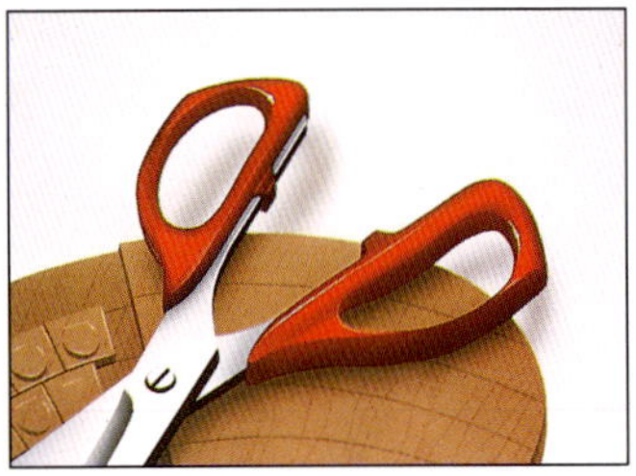

2 Opaque white dots have been applied with a brush in selected places on top of the scratched highlights. These are positioned at the point of the greatest light reflection.

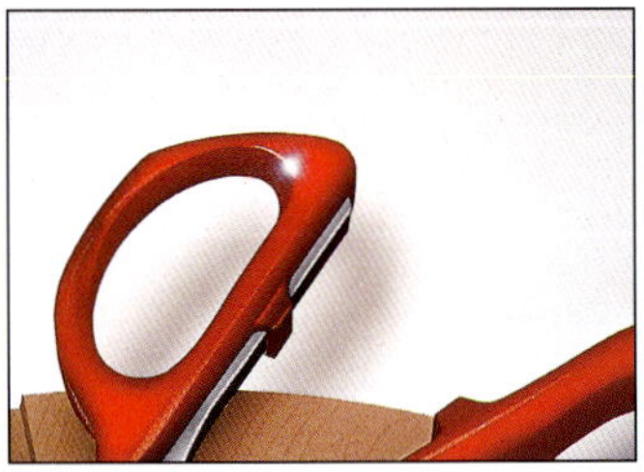

3 Opaque white is then sprayed directly over the dots to diffuse the edges, although in some cases this may not be necessary.

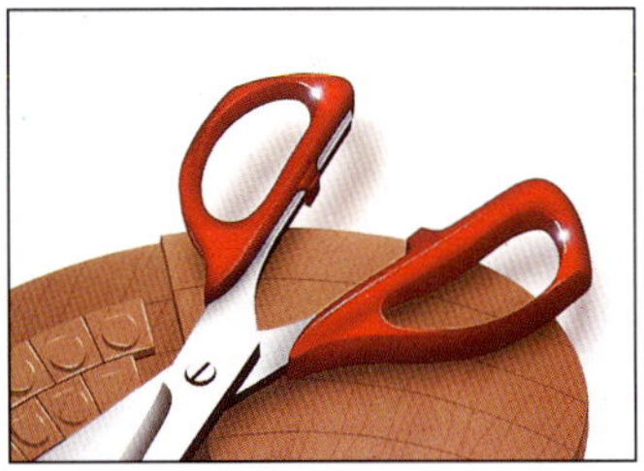

4 The completed image, by comparison with the first stage in this sequence, shows how the more complex highlight detail adds luster to the finished image.

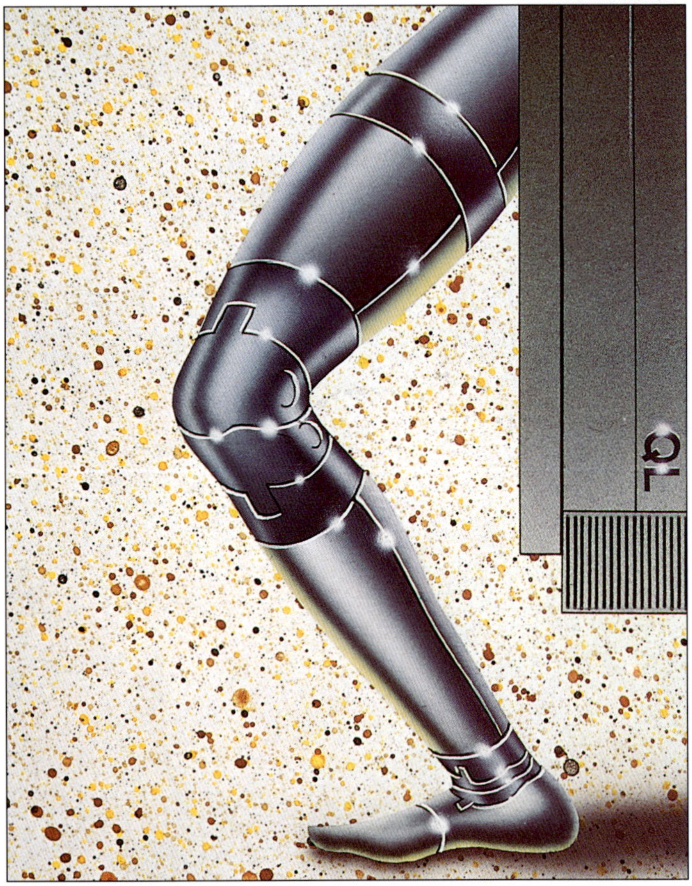

On a Metallic Surface

This example shows the application of dot highlights to the leg of a robot. These highlights are simply small bursts of opaque white spray which give extra sparkle to the effect of polished metal.

Porsche and tanker
John Spiers

Dot highlights are most commonly used on static subjects, but this illustration demonstrates an application when speed and movement are to be shown. STARBURSTS would be effective highlights on those areas where intense light would be reflected, but might tend to conflict with the sense of movement. In this example dot highlights have been used in the center of linear highlights, with soft-edged and loose-masked lines of opaque white leading from them in the opposite direction to that in which the vehicles are traveling. Not only does this intensify the surface reflection, but the combination accentuates the feeling of speed. This makes an interesting comparison to the racing car shown on page 99. The body of the tanker is an interesting variation on the full-color chrome effects technique, with the addition of a reflection of the car passing it. The sky is an example of FREEHAND SPRAYING, while LOOSE MASKING has been used on the distant mountain ranges. SPATTERING has been used to establish texture to the ground surface and on the road.

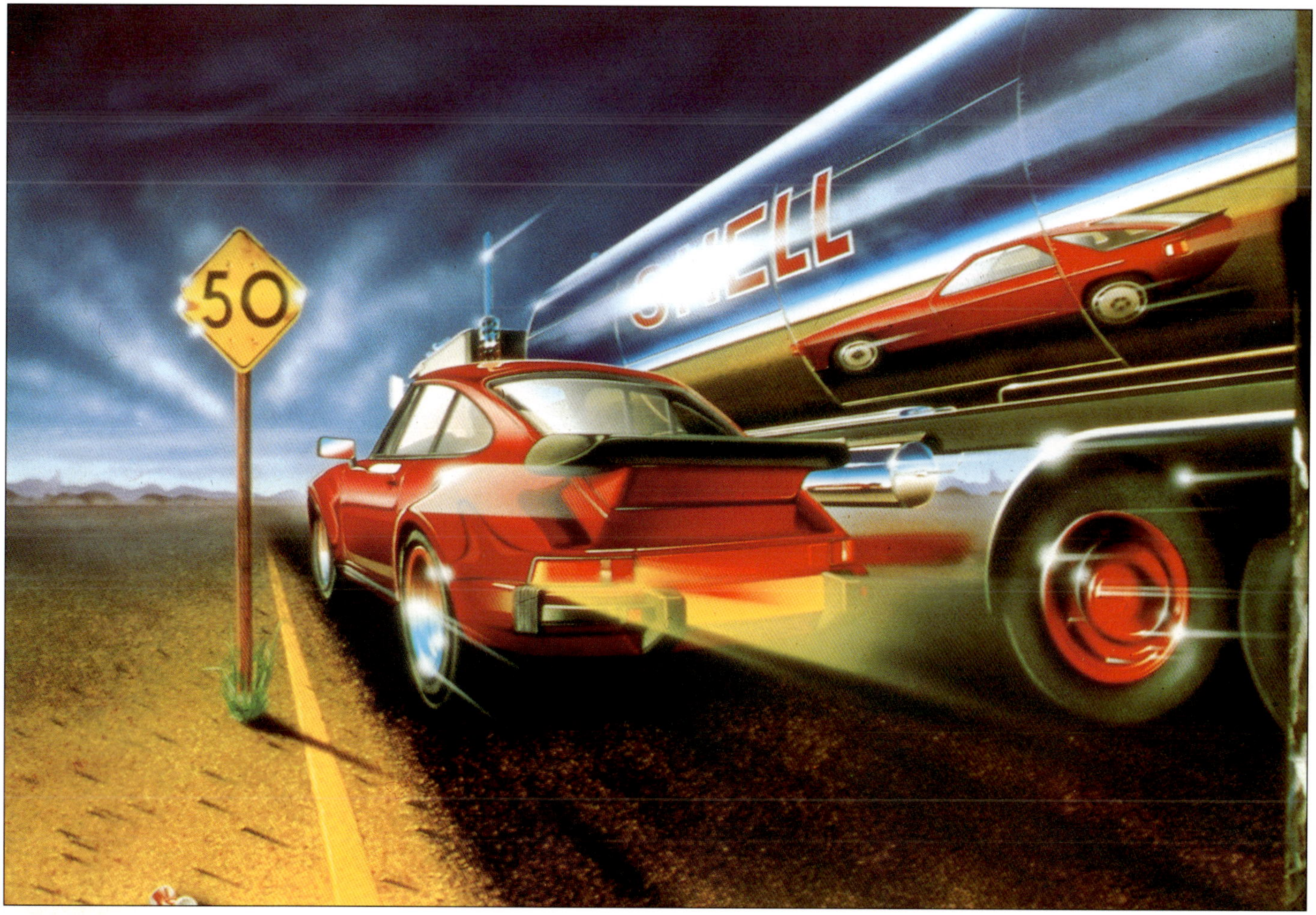

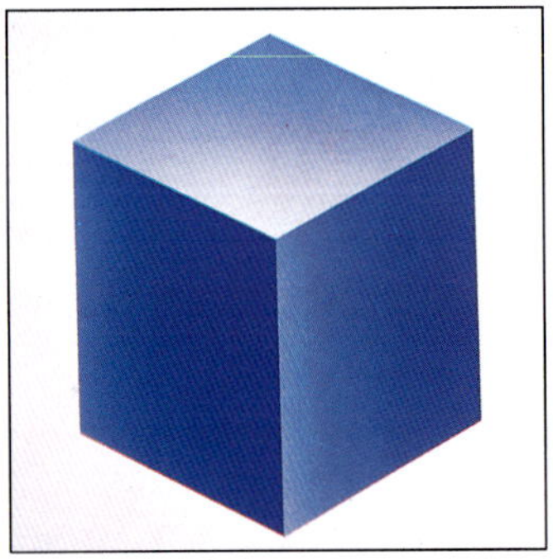

On an Angled Edge

1 The basic cube has been sprayed with a high degree of contrast shading.

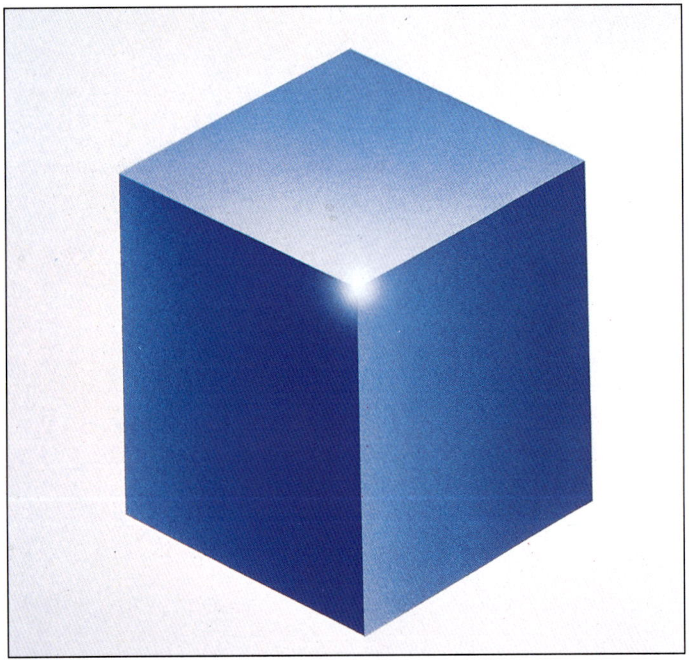

2 To enhance the contrast and to add glare, a dot highlight has been sprayed freehand on the nearest corner of the cube. The effect immediately makes the cube appear to be finished with a more reflective and brighter surface.

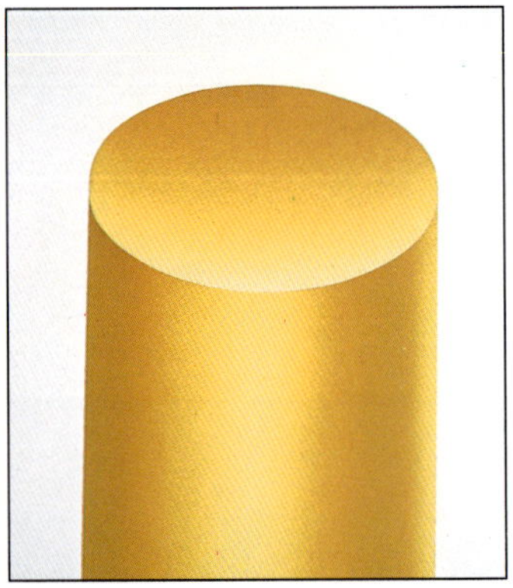

Multiple Dots

1 The upper part of a cylinder is shown before applying the highlights.

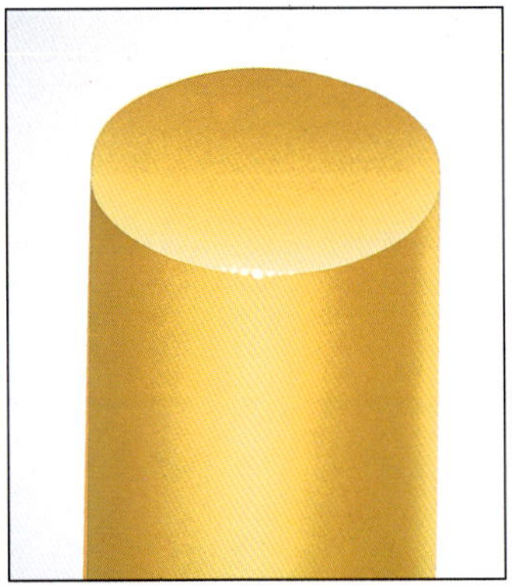

2 A number of opaque white dots have been brush-painted onto the leading edge; they are reduced in size as they get further away from the center of the highlight.

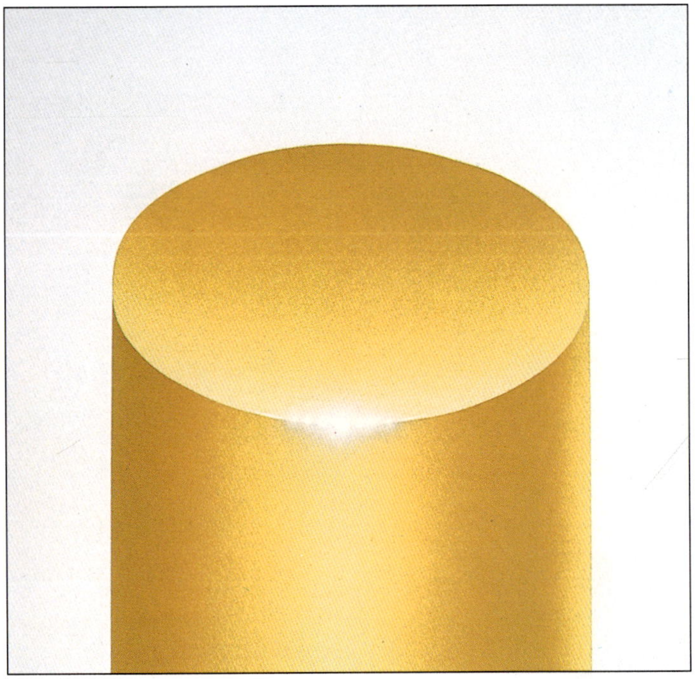

3 To diffuse the edges of the dots, the highlight is oversprayed with opaque white.

DROP SHADOW

Drop shadow is a method of using cast shadow to emphasize the principal object in an illustration, either in part or to throw the whole object into relief. The shadow areas can also be used to create the illusion of different levels. Refer also to CAST SHADOWS.

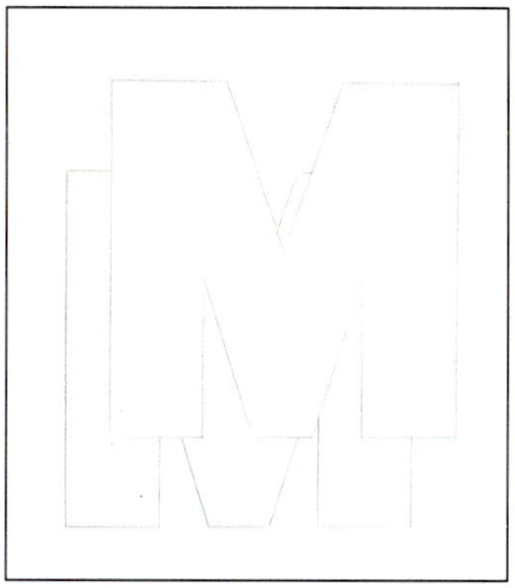

Using Masking Film

1 A sans-serif character "M" is used to demonstrate the drop shadow effect, and both the character and its shadow are drawn together in the required position.

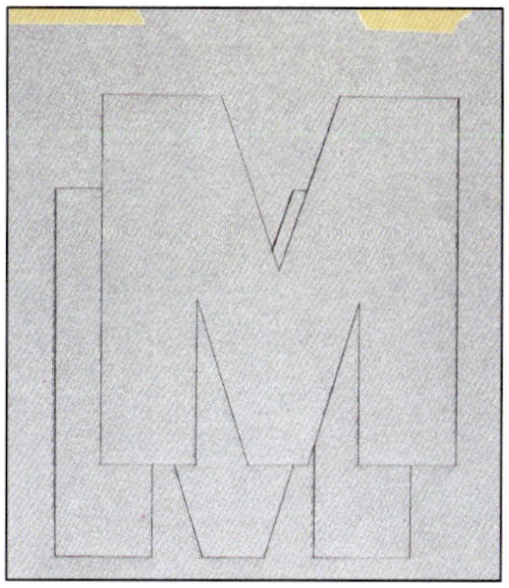

2 The drawing is then transferred to the illustration board.

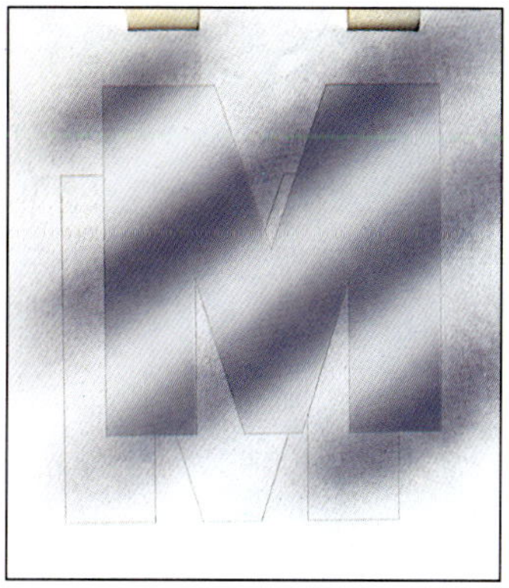

3 After covering the board with masking film, the character is cut out, the mask section hinged with drafting tape and pulled back to the top of the artwork. The exposed character is then sprayed using diagonally gradated, soft-edged stripes, to give a metallic effect.

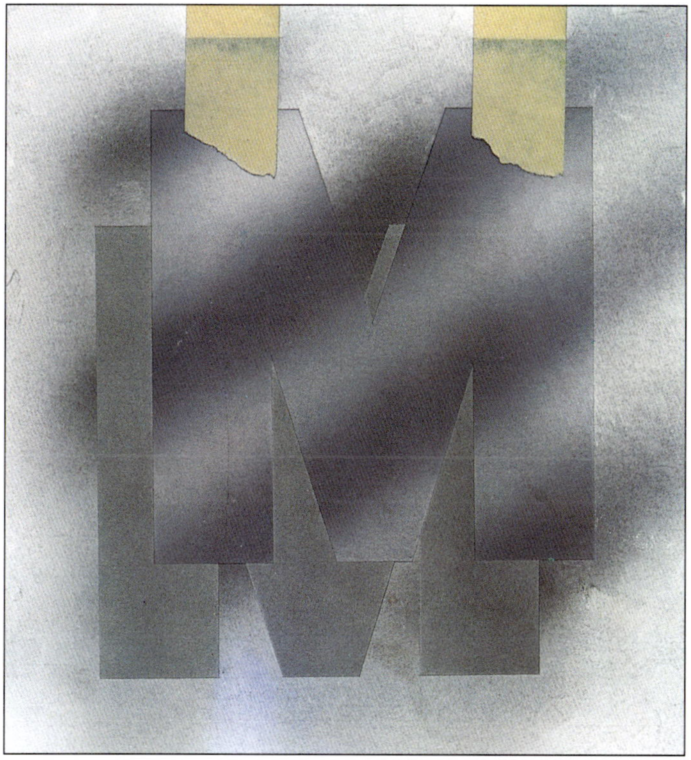

4 The hinged mask for the character is repositioned and the shadow cut out. This is sprayed with a flat, even color to add contrast between the character and the shadow.

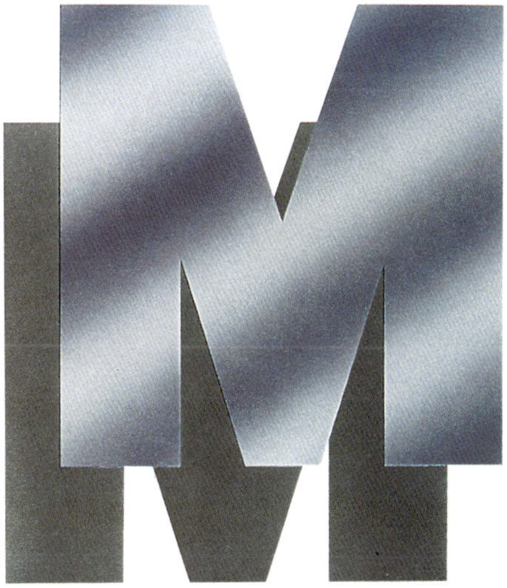

5 When the required depth of tone has been achieved, the masking film is completely removed, revealing the crisp, hard-edged character and solid area of shadow.

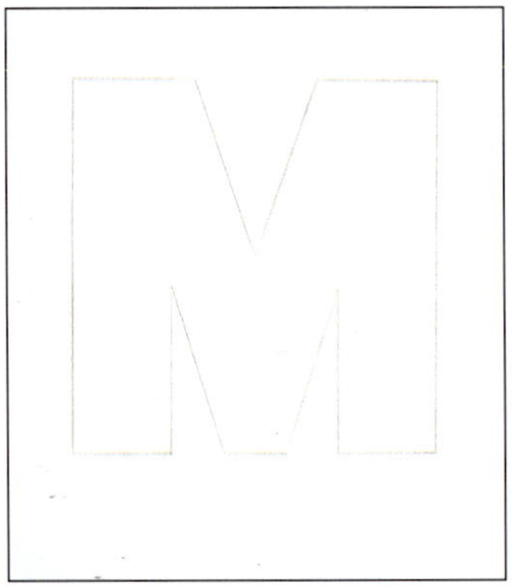

Using Acetate

1 The same character "M'" is used, but this time acetate is used as the masking medium.

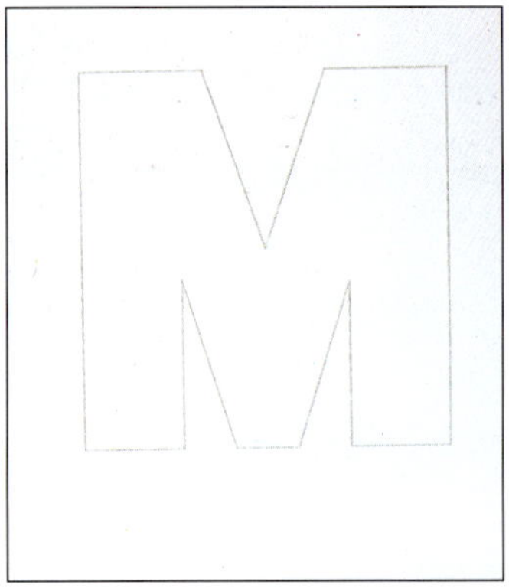

2 To maintain the exact shape in shadow form, an acetate mask is firmly placed over the drawn character and the shape accurately cut out.

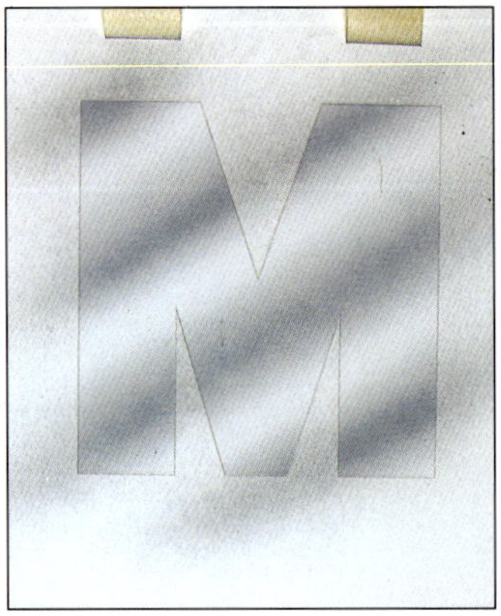

3 The main part of the acetate mask protects the area surrounding the character, which is exposed for spraying, while the acetate mask of the character, after correct positioning, is hinged to the top of the artwork awaiting further use. The character is sprayed, following the same style as the masking film example (pages 40-47).

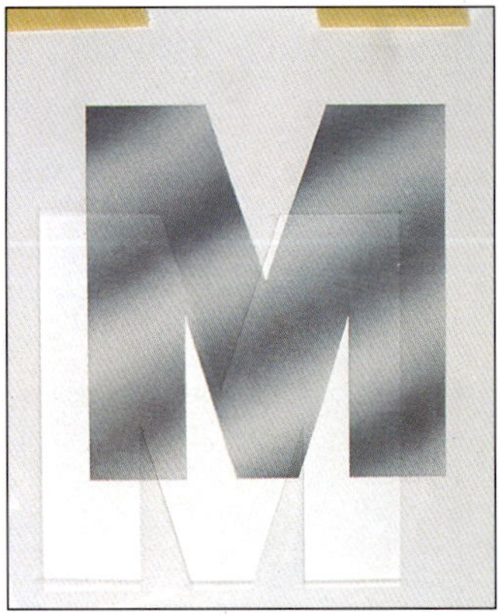

4 On completion of the spraying of the character, the larger part of the acetate mask is removed and repositioned downward and to the left for the spraying of the shadow.

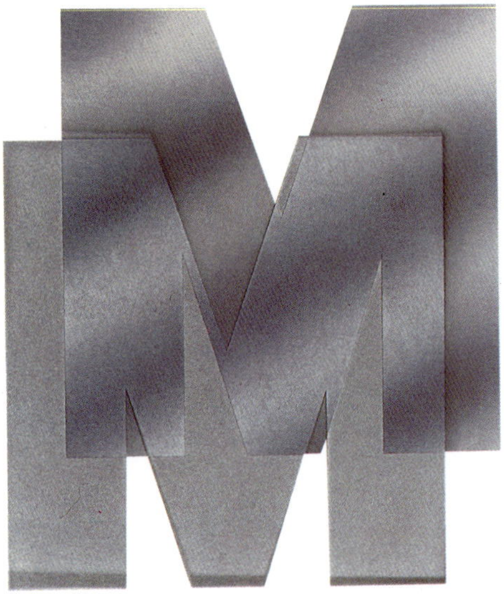

5 The hinged copy of the character is repositioned to protect the exposed areas of the sprayed character, and the drop shadow area is sprayed with an even tone.

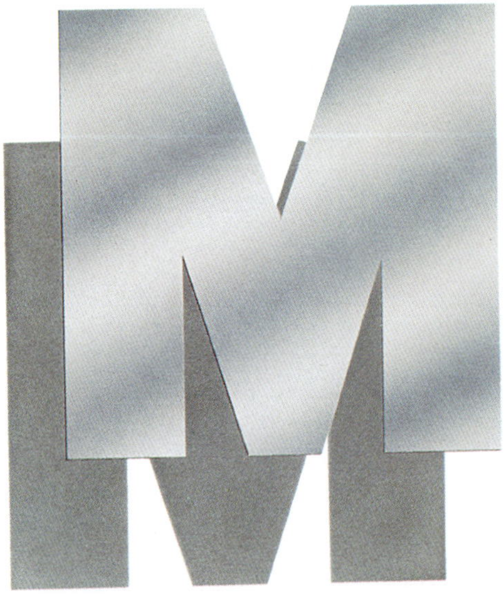

6 When both acetate masks have been removed from the artwork, it will be noticed that because acetate is non-adhesive, the drop shadow has acquired slightly soft edges. In some cases this effect may be preferred to the hard-edged finish obtained by using masking film.

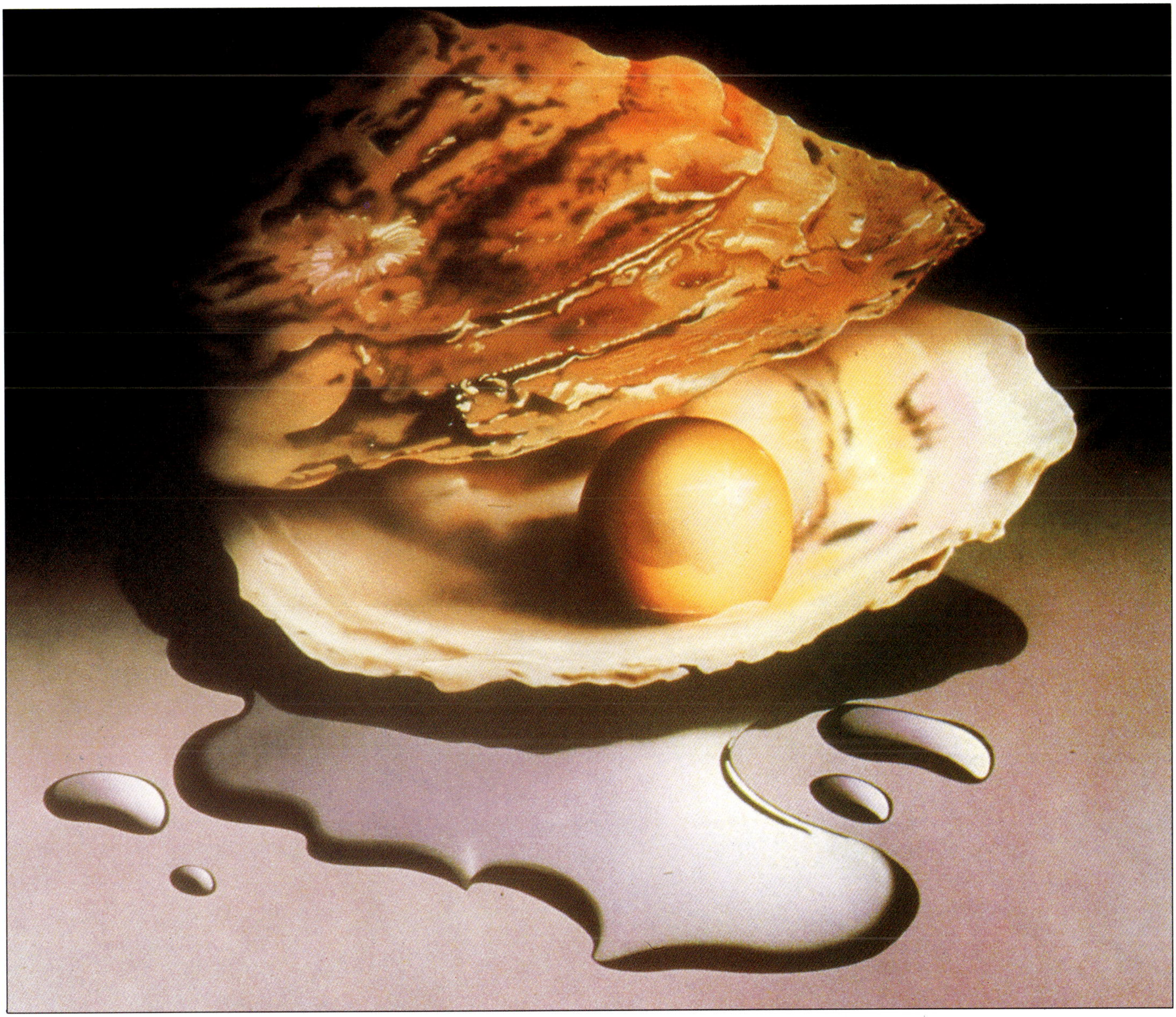

Oyster
Pete Kelly

An effective drop shadow has been included here. It serves to increase the contrast between the lower half of the shell and the GRADATED TONE of the backdrop.

ERASURE

This is a general heading referring to the use of erasers, both solid and the pencil type, which may be used for corrections and for applying highlights to specific areas of the artwork. This technique is usually only successful when applied to illustrations which have been sprayed onto a hard, smooth-coated board, of the type commonly used in the preparation of ink-line drawings. Furthermore, it is best applied to illustrations which have been sprayed with watercolors. This is because the surface layer of sprayed watercolor paint is extremely thin. On gouache and acrylic sprayed surfaces, there is more chance of damaging the surrounding color, and therefore overspraying with opaque white is far better and less risky.

As a correction technique, erasure should be limited to small areas. When used to create highlights, a hard, pencil-type eraser is by far the best, because it is possible to maintain a reasonably sharp point on the rubber core which will give greater control. The finish varies according to the amount of paint removed. This could range from complete exposure of the white of the board, to very subtle highlights such as would be seen on matte or unmachined surfaces. With care, the pencil eraser could also be used to enhance contrast, especially when much of the difference between the lights and the darks has been lost by excessive color application.

1 In this example a sphere has been sprayed, with a dull highlight to represent a non-polished surface.

2 At the natural position of the highlight, the color has been erased with a circular motion using a pencil eraser. It will be noted that the amount of paint removed at the extremities of the highlight is decreased, so that the highlight fades into the base color.

FABRIC MASKING

There are occasions when traditional methods of rendering textured surfaces with an airbrush are not as effective as one would hope. The use of medium- to coarse fabric opens up additional opportunities which, when applied to an illustration, will give a surface texture not neccessarily identifiable with the fabric used. Some do reproduce the distinct fabric weave, and therefore experimentation is advisable before applying a fabric mask to finished artwork, unless, of course, the intention is to represent the specific effect. Besides testing a piece before use, it is also worth keeping samples of both the fabric and the spray effect from it for future reference.

Types of fabric suitable as masking materials are those which have an open weave to allow the sprayed color to pass through and between the fibers. The texture may be applied over large or small areas, which in themselves can produce additional variations of form and contrast. The material need not be used just because of its texture, for the frayed edge of torn fabric also offers a characteristic result. A form of repeat pattern could be applied using, for example, a figured open-weave as seen in old fashioned glass curtains, or indeed the many types of lace which are available.

A background texture can be applied over the artwork before the object or subject itself is sprayed. Naturally this requires the principal part of the illustration to be sprayed in an opaque medium in order to prevent the base texture from showing through. Small, controlled areas may be sprayed by overlaying the fabric on top of a previously cut piece of masking film.

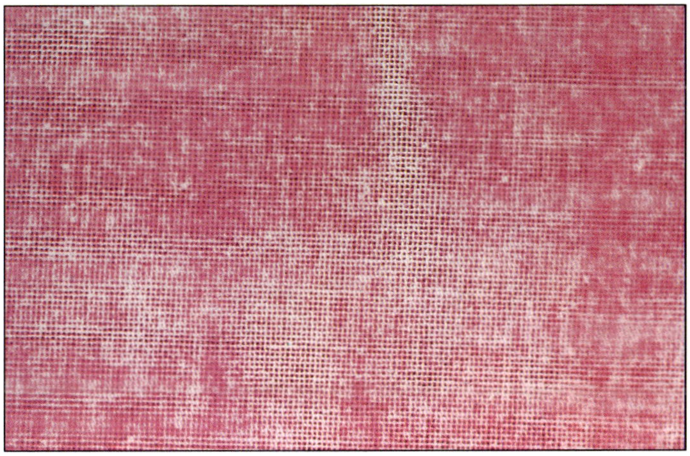

1 In this demonstration of fabric masking, a piece of fine-weave embroidery fabric has been used. The resulting sprayed texture is a fine-grained, but even finish.

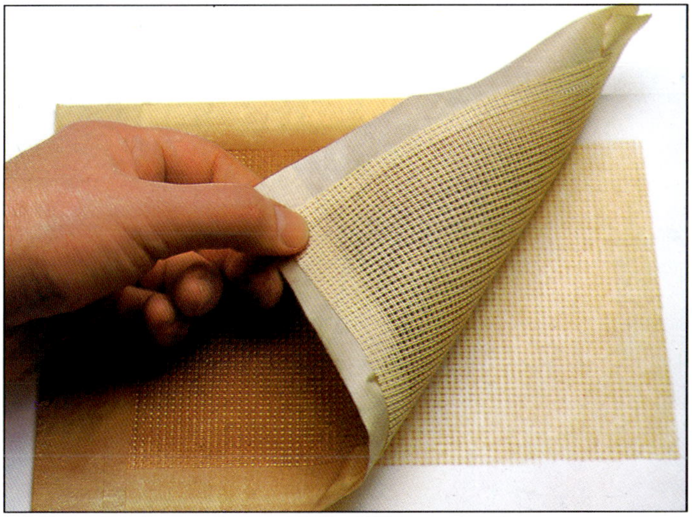

2 Masking tape is used to secure the fabric around all four edges, which also allows the finished artwork to be contained within straight, hard-edged borders. Here a piece of needlepoint canvas has been used, giving a more open and coarser-grained finish.

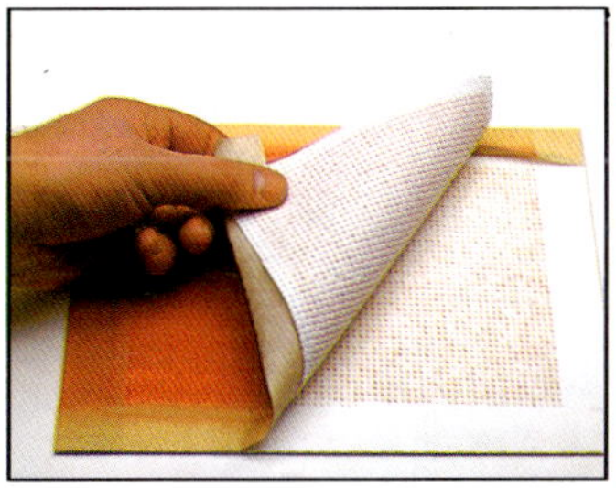

3 This example shows the effect using a tighter embroidery canvas, which on a large area remains even and regular. When used on small irregular shapes, with the spraying restricted to specified areas, it will appear more random and have a less obvious connection with the original fabric texture.

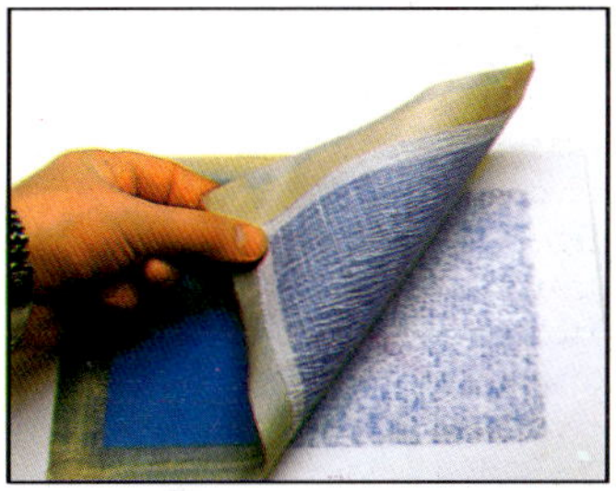

4 Loose cotton scrim has been used here, giving a more random effect.

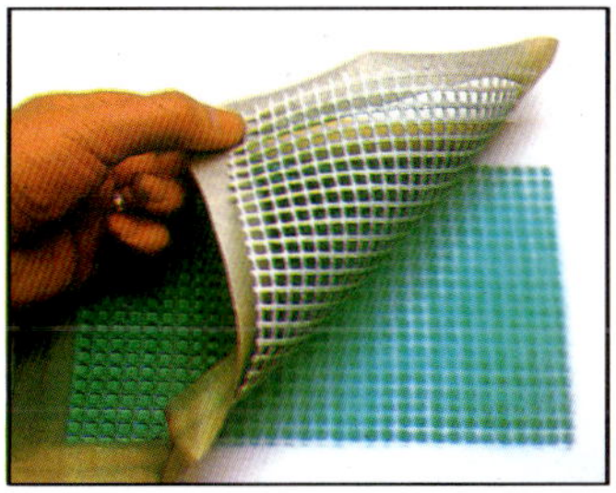

5 A simplified checked or grid pattern is the result when spraying through rug canvas over a large area.

FILM MASKING

The use of transparent, self-adhesive masking film in airbrushing is the most popular method of protecting areas of the artwork which are not currently being worked on. Masking film is available with either a matte or a gloss finish and is supplied on a protective backing sheet, which can be used to save cut masks likely to be needed again. The adhesive on the film is low-tack, allowing masks to be placed over a clean or previously sprayed surface and subsequently lifted without damage to the underlying material.

Because the film is transparent, it allows those areas covered to remain visible, which is extremely useful when judging the strength of color and shading against those areas already sprayed. It is also possible to remove excess and residual paint from the film by carefully wiping over it with a damp cloth, tissue or absorbent cotton, without damaging the artwork or the area exposed for spraying (this of course applies to paints which remain water-soluble after drying).

When using masking film, always cut it with sharp, new blades, as old ones quickly lose their edge and tend to tear the film rather than cut cleanly through it. Gentle but even pressure is required when cutting, to avoid scoring the artwork.

In the two examples given here, particular note should be taken of the sequence used in applying the tonal ranges; they are not the same for transparent watercolor and opaque gouache. With a transparent medium, the depth of shade and color is built from dark to light by overspraying transparent layers; with the opaque medium, color mixes are made independently, and light colors can be sprayed over dark if required.

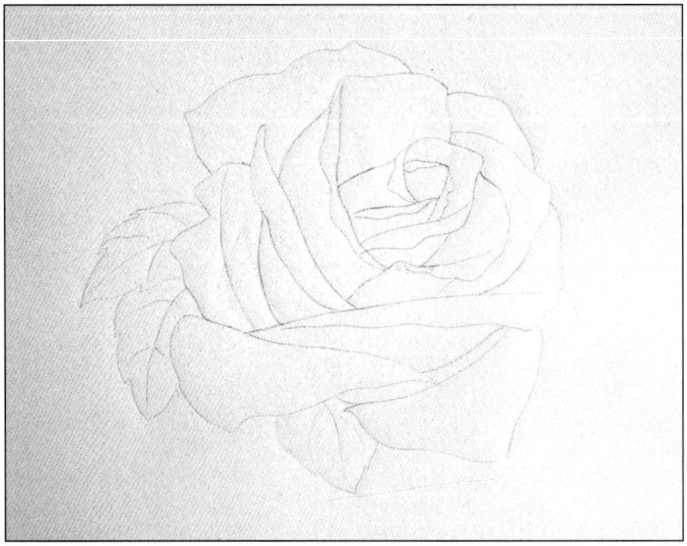

Watercolor Medium

1 To demonstrate a reasonably complex example, a rose is used as the subject matter. First, a drawing is prepared on detail paper, as shown.

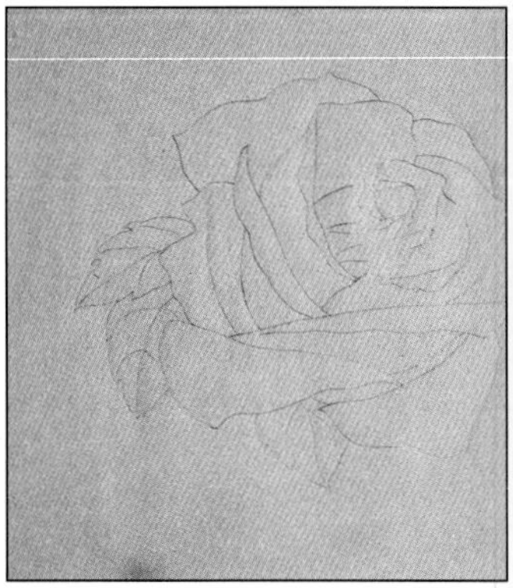

2 The drawing is then transferred to board using graphite paper or jeweler's rouge.

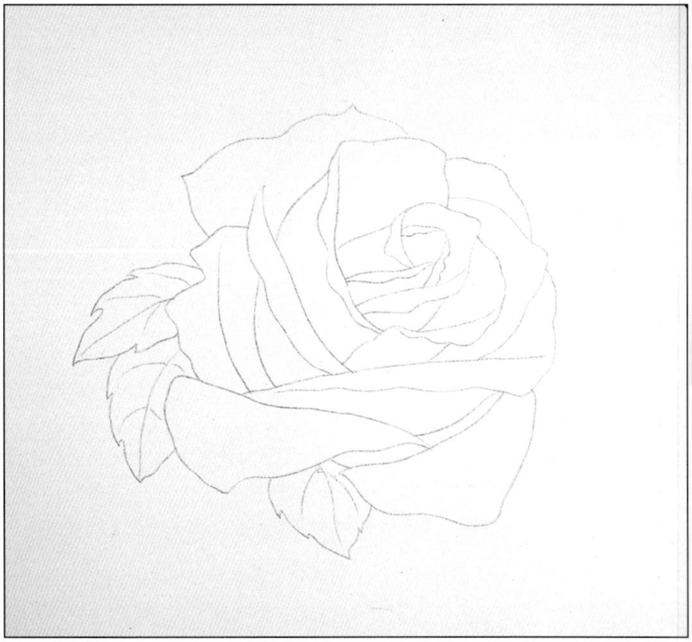

3 The transferred drawing on the board must consist of very faint guidelines, as they will not be completely obliterated when a transparent medium is used.

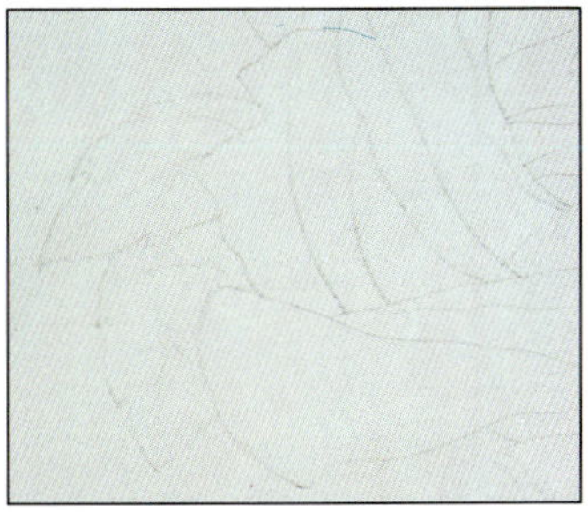

4 The artwork is covered with masking film and all lines describing the leaves are cut into the film.

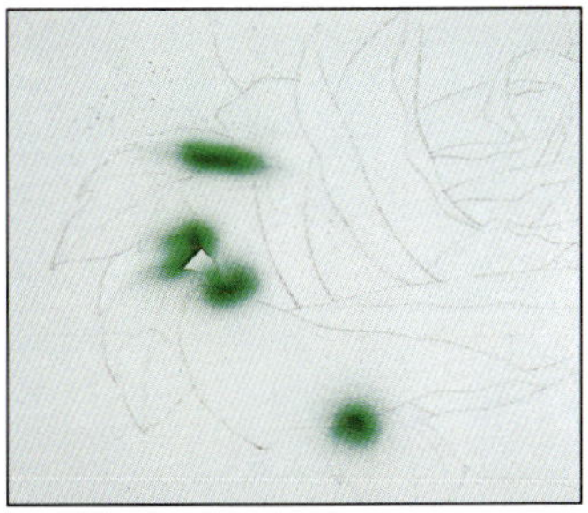

5 The spraying sequence begins with removal of film from the leaf sections which will have the darkest shade.

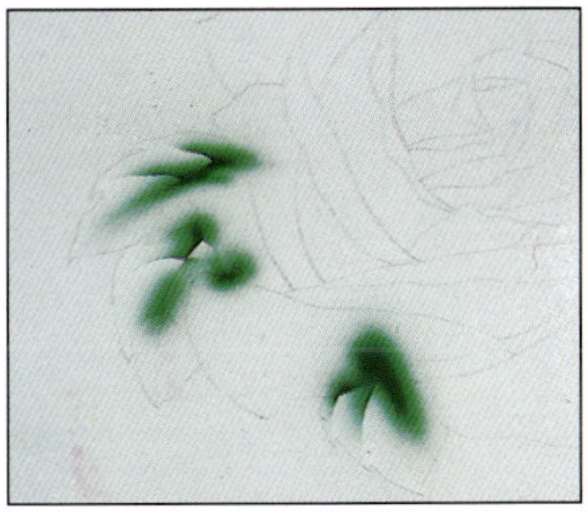

6 The medium tones of the leaves are now sprayed. Mask sections cut along the lines of the leaf veins are removed in sequence to give hard-edged areas of tonal gradation.

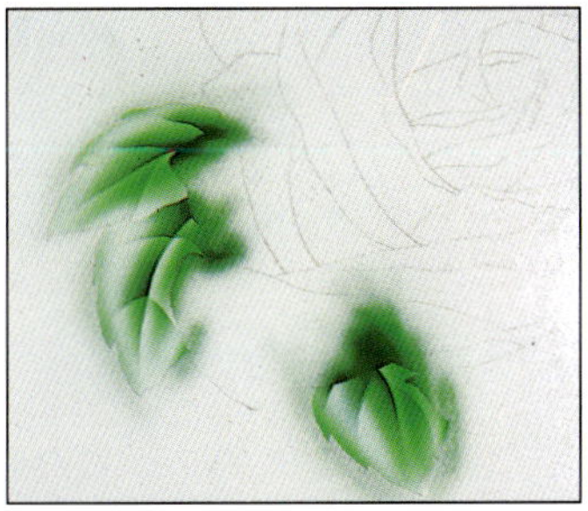

7 The final parts of the leaves to be sprayed are the lighter shades. At this stage, all the masking on the leaves has been removed and the lighter tonal gradations are executed freehand.

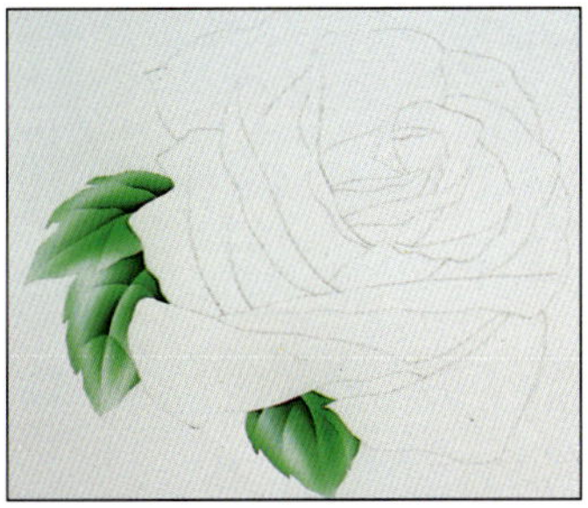

8 On completion of the leaves, all masking film is removed and a new piece is laid over the whole of the artwork. All lines surrounding the petals of the rose are then cut into the film.

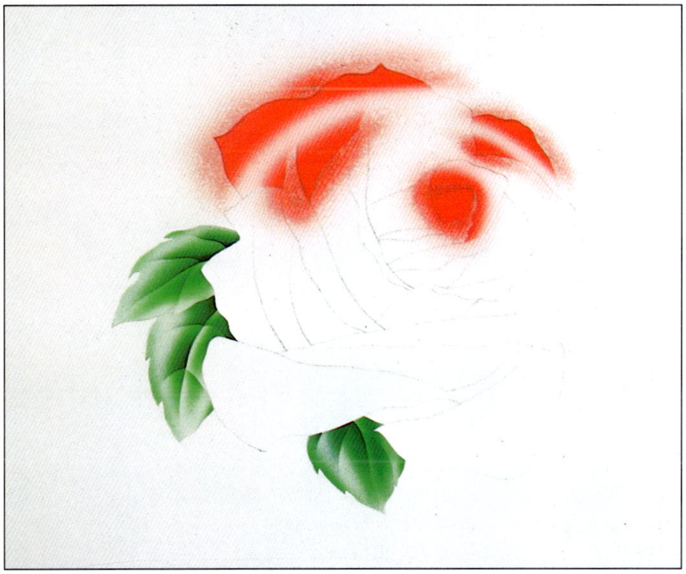

9 The sequence for the rose follows the same pattern applied to the leaves, working from the darkest shades first, followed by the medium and then the lighter ones. In the first stage, dark shades are sprayed in the upper part of the flower.

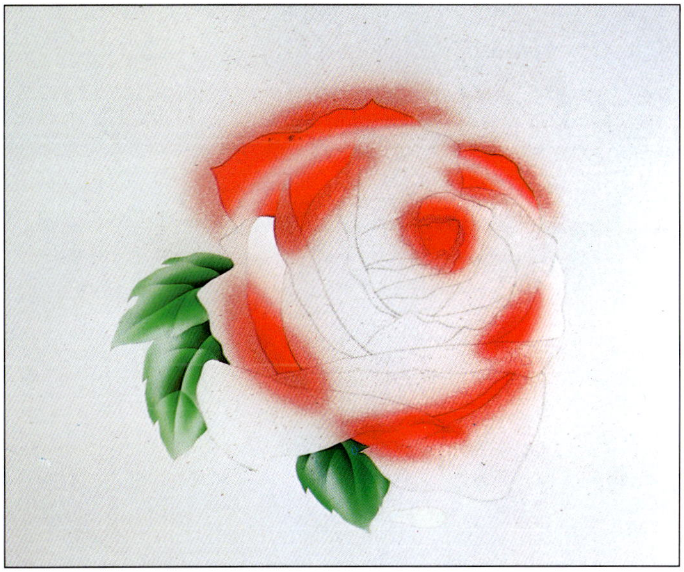

10 The tonal values and form are built up with the spraying progressing from the furthest petals to those in the foreground.

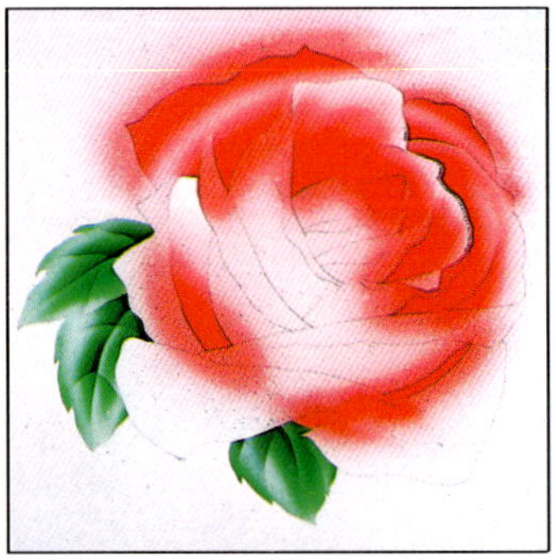

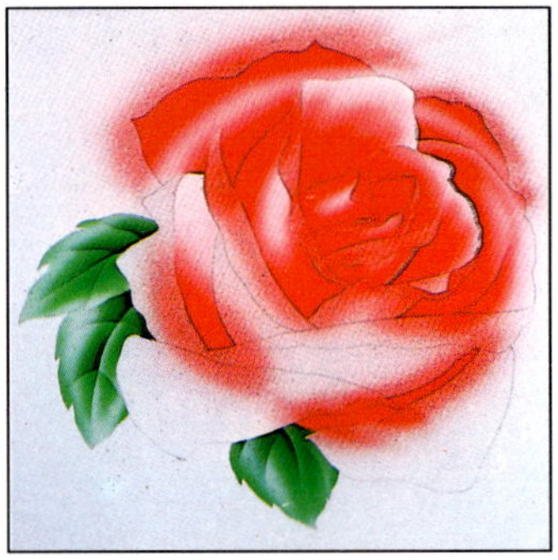

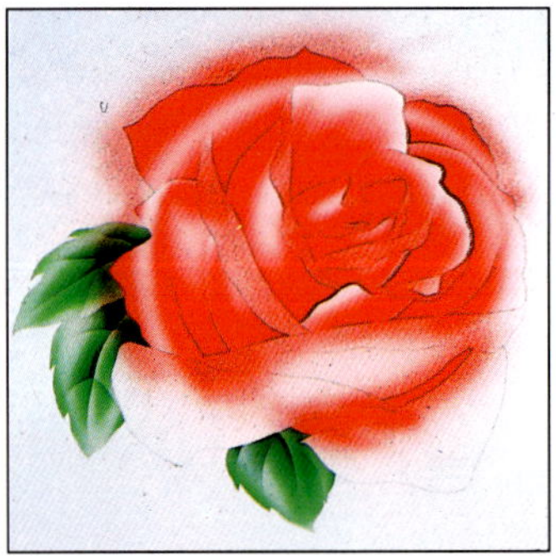

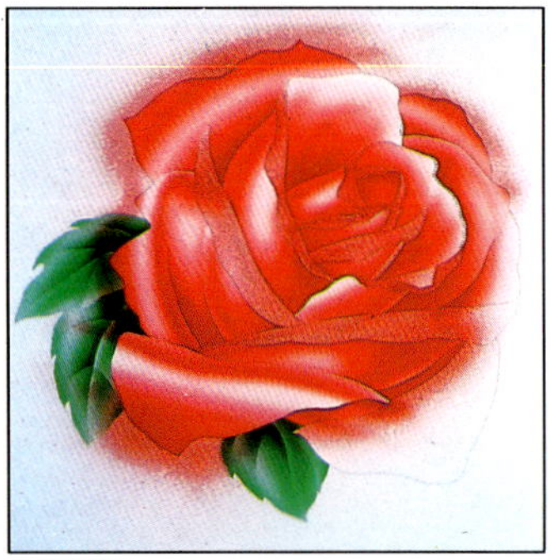

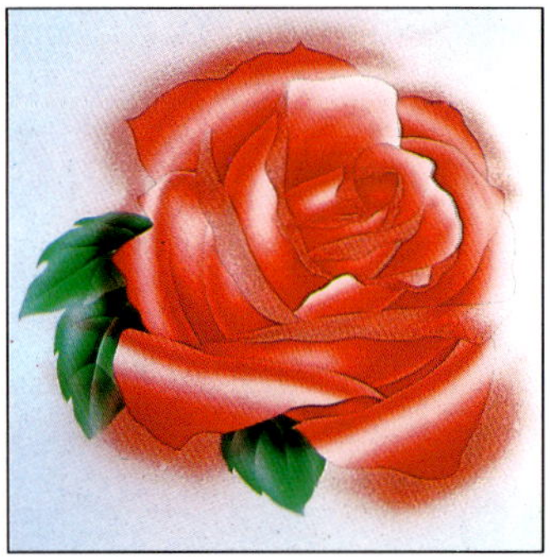

11-15 The process is continued, with the mask sections lifted in sequence to allow development of the medium and light shades.

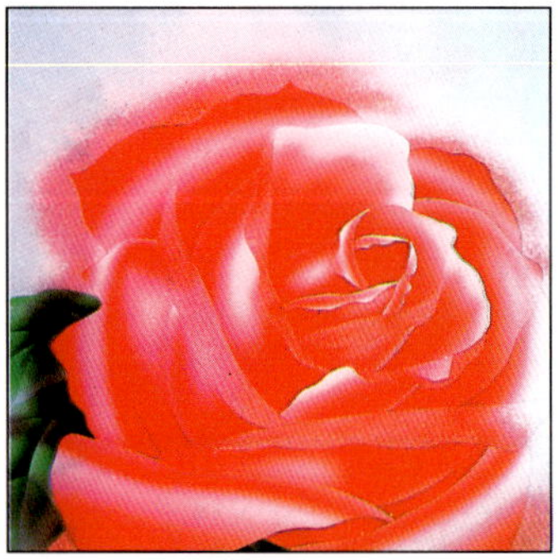

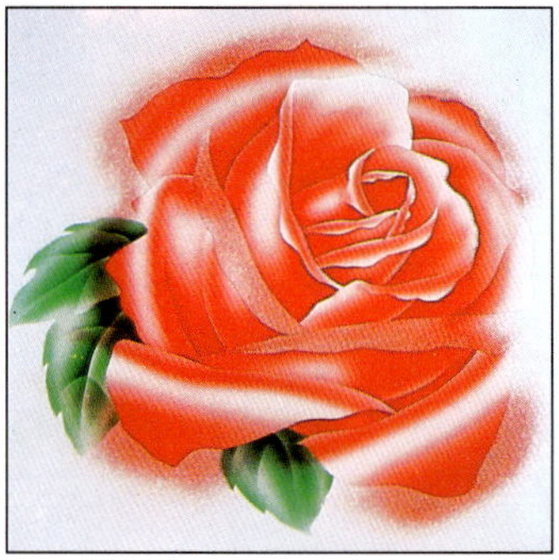

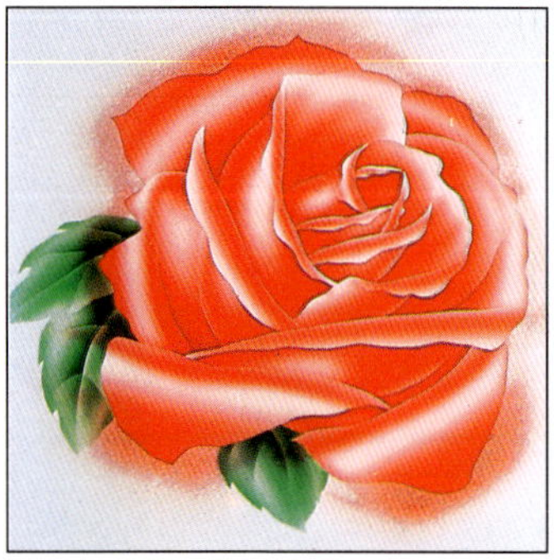

16-18 The curled edges of the petals are sprayed, also following the sequence dark to medium to light, and working from the center outward.

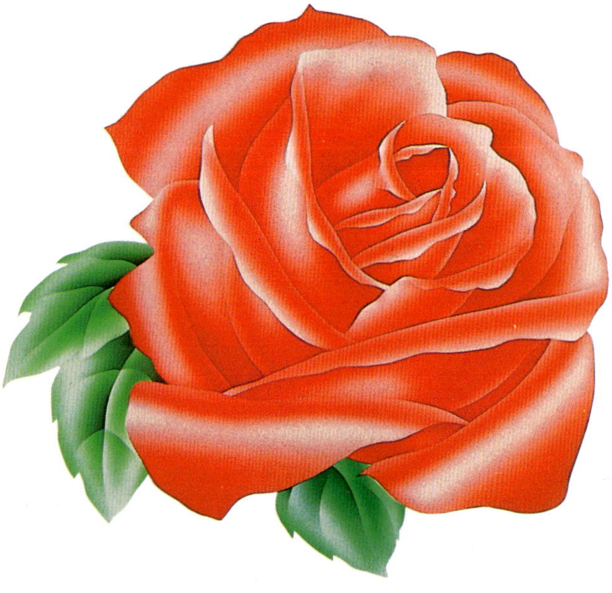

19 Finally, the remaining masking film is removed from the artwork, revealing a crisply defined rose.

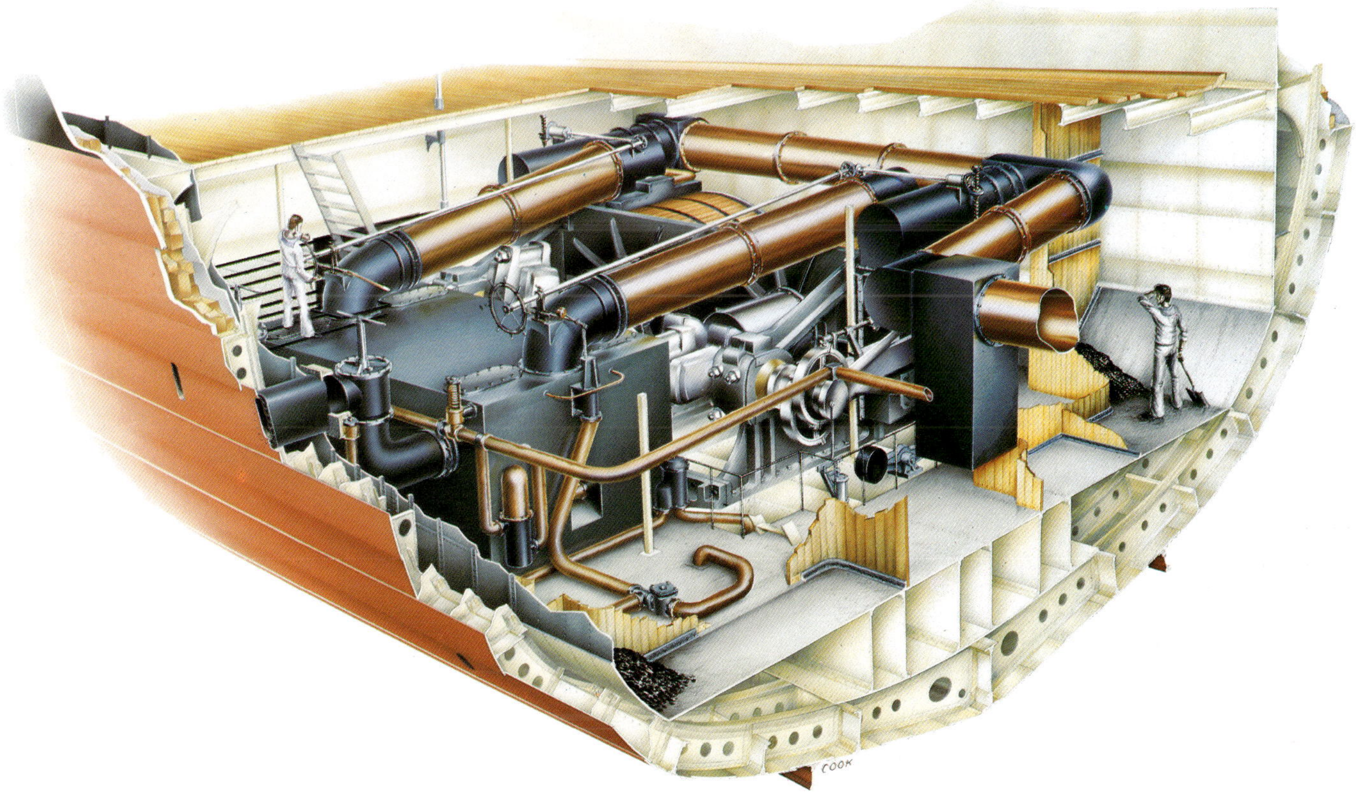

HMS *Warrior*'s engine room, 1861
Gary Cook

This three-point perspective illustration is a reconstruction of the engine room of the world's first iron-built warship, HMS *Warrior*, and was commissioned for the book *The Immortal Warrior*. The purpose of the illustration was to explain the layout and arrangement of the engine and condenser in relation to that part of the ship's hull structure which contained them.

The drawing was constructed on tracing paper using copies of the original Admiralty as-fitted drafts from the British National Maritime Museum as reference. It was then transferred onto CS10 board, which is a hard, china-clay-surfaced board ideally suited to both airbrush and ink- line work. The illustration was rendered primarily with the airbrush using transparent and opaque watercolor. Self-adhesive masking film was used throughout, with the exception of the bands of tone running along the copper steam pipes, for which cut paper [see LOOSE MASKING] masks were used. LINING-IN was completed using a ruling pen and a fine sable brush.

Because of the limited number of colors used to paint the engine room itself, great care was needed when spraying to maintain both the contrast and the different planes of the casings for many of the engine components, and the white structural details. These two important areas are basically black and white respectively. It was therefore decided to omit strong cast shadows, using darker shades only to aid legibility. In addition, enough contrast had to be shown between the matte or rough-surfaced casings, painted black on the original, and the polished copper steampipes. For the former, subtle GRADATED TONES of blue-black were used, while for the pipes the white of the board was allowed to show through the transparent color, increasing the strength of the highlights.

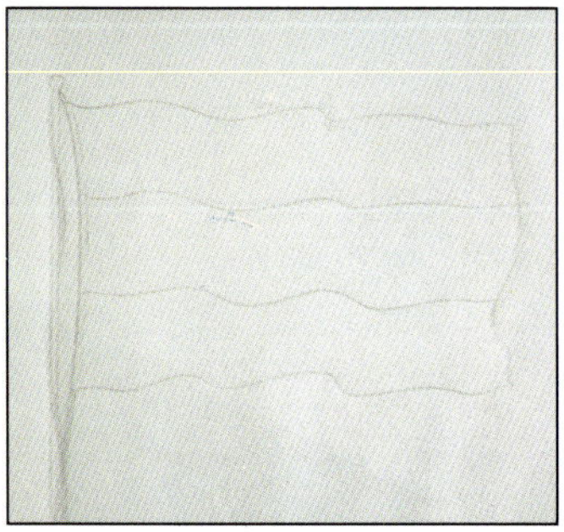

Gouache Medium

1 The intention here is to produce a piece of artwork showing a flag with movement. This is drawn first in pencil on detail paper.

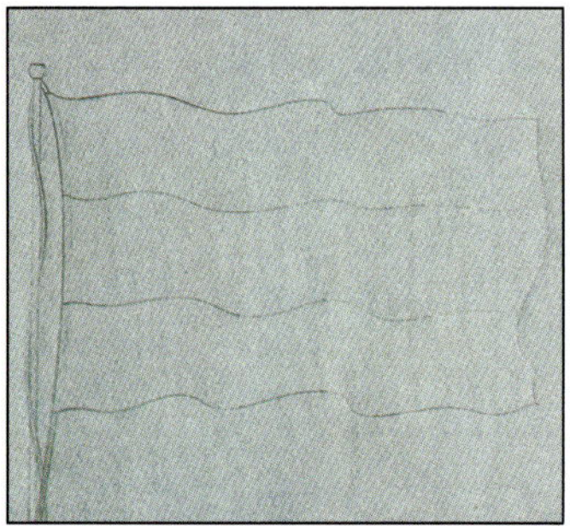

2 The drawing is transferred to board using graphite paper.

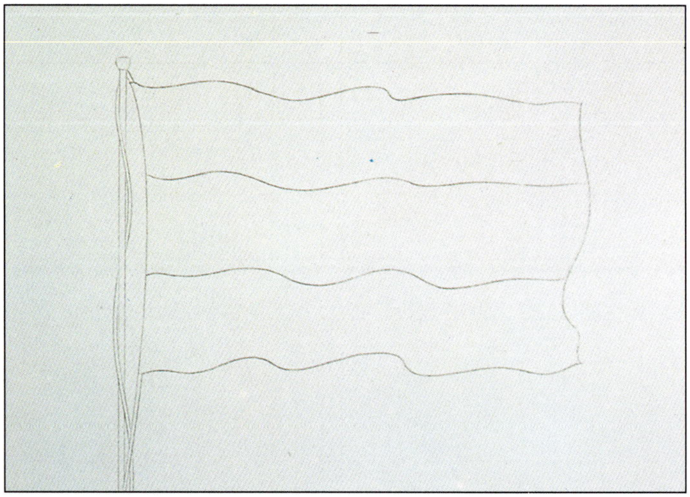

3 Both the detail paper drawing and the graphite paper are removed, showing the transferred drawing of the flag. The lines in this drawing will be gradually concealed by the spraying, due to the opaque quality of gouache.

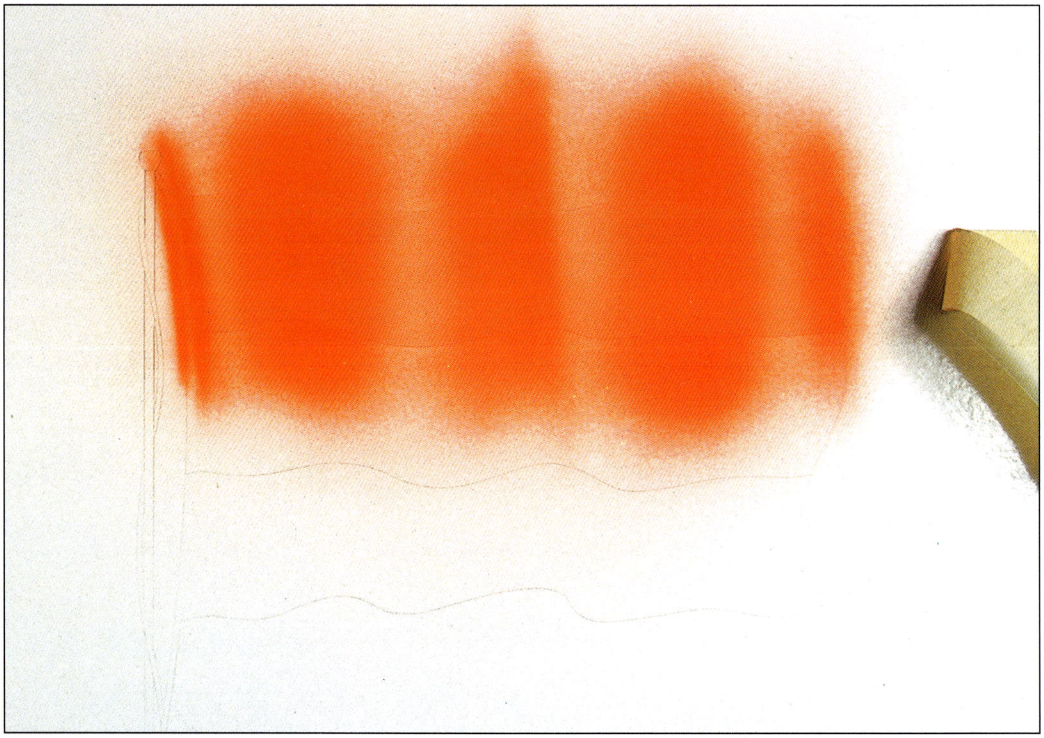

4 A piece of masking film, sufficient to cover the image and surrounding area, is placed over the artwork, followed by cutting of all lines of both the flag and staff. The mask section on the topmost horizontal stripe of the flag is hinged with drafting tape, lifted off and pulled back to the right. The exposed area is sprayed in a medium shade of red. This is worked as vertical bands of color, allowing residual spray to create areas of lighter shades.

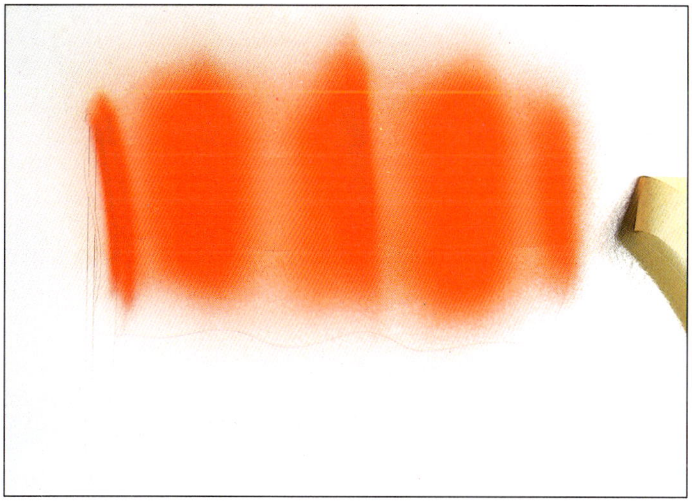

5 A darker shade of red is over-sprayed next, increasing the contrast.

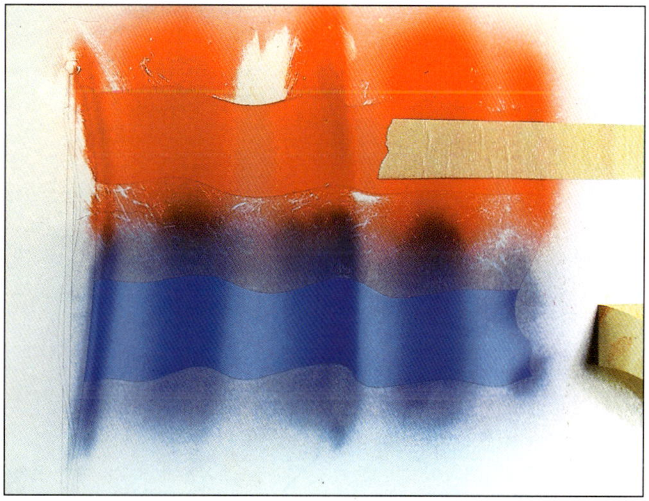

6 The mask for the first stripe of color is replaced, and the lowest stripe is hinged, lifted off and pulled back to the right. This is then sprayed in blue to create the medium-strength and pale tones.

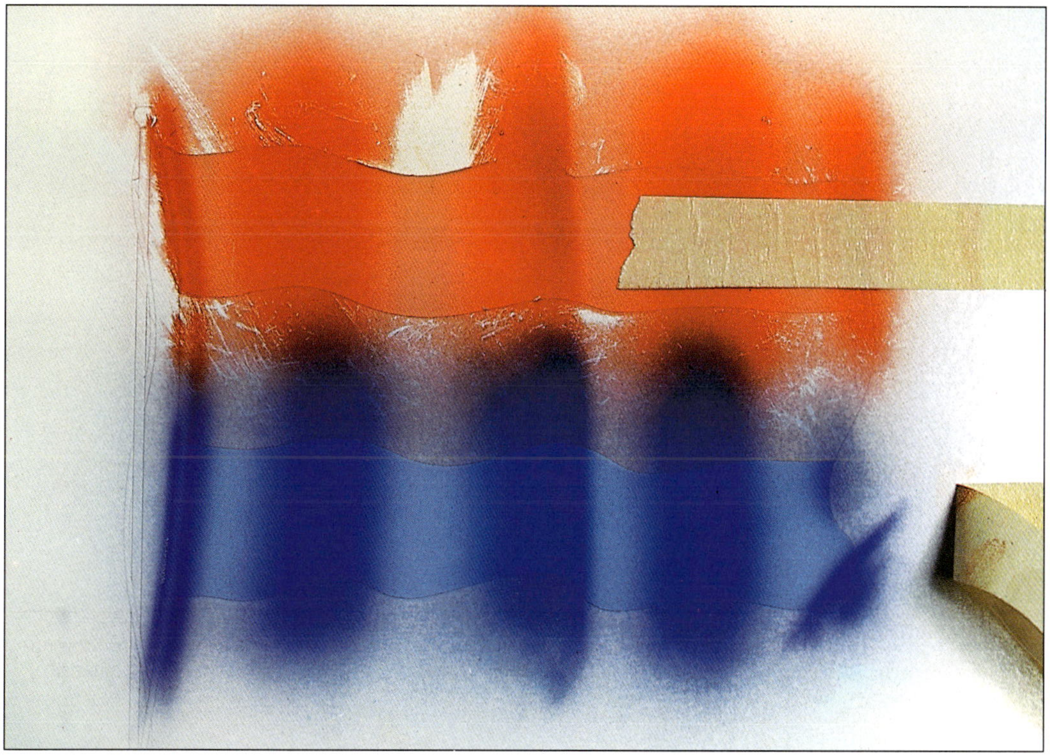

7 The darker shades are over-sprayed, following closely the pattern established with the first stripe.

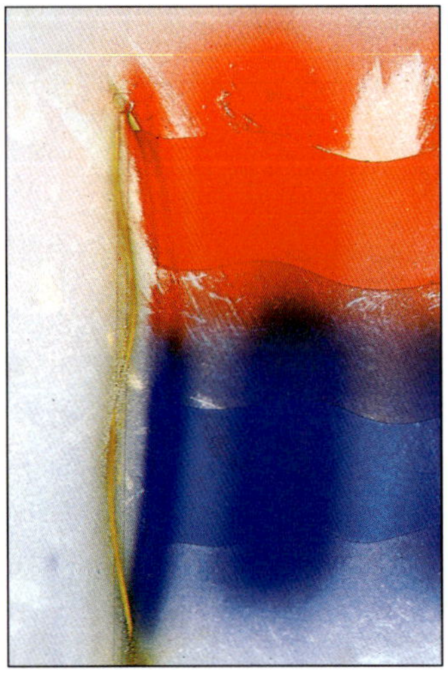

8 The hinged mask for the lower stripe is replaced, and the first part of the rope halliard is exposed and sprayed.

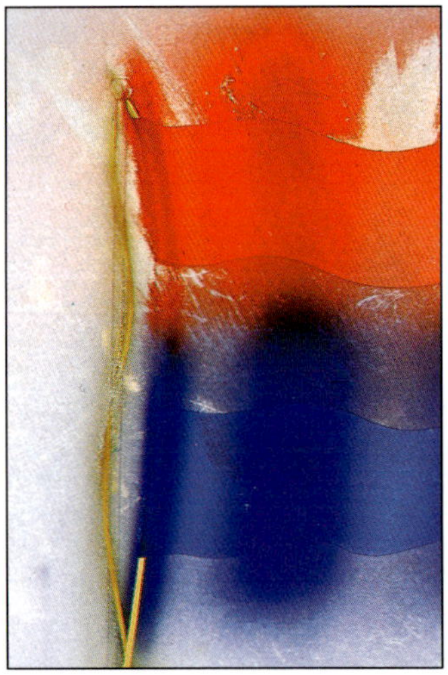

9 The second part of the rope, nearest the observer, is next to be sprayed.

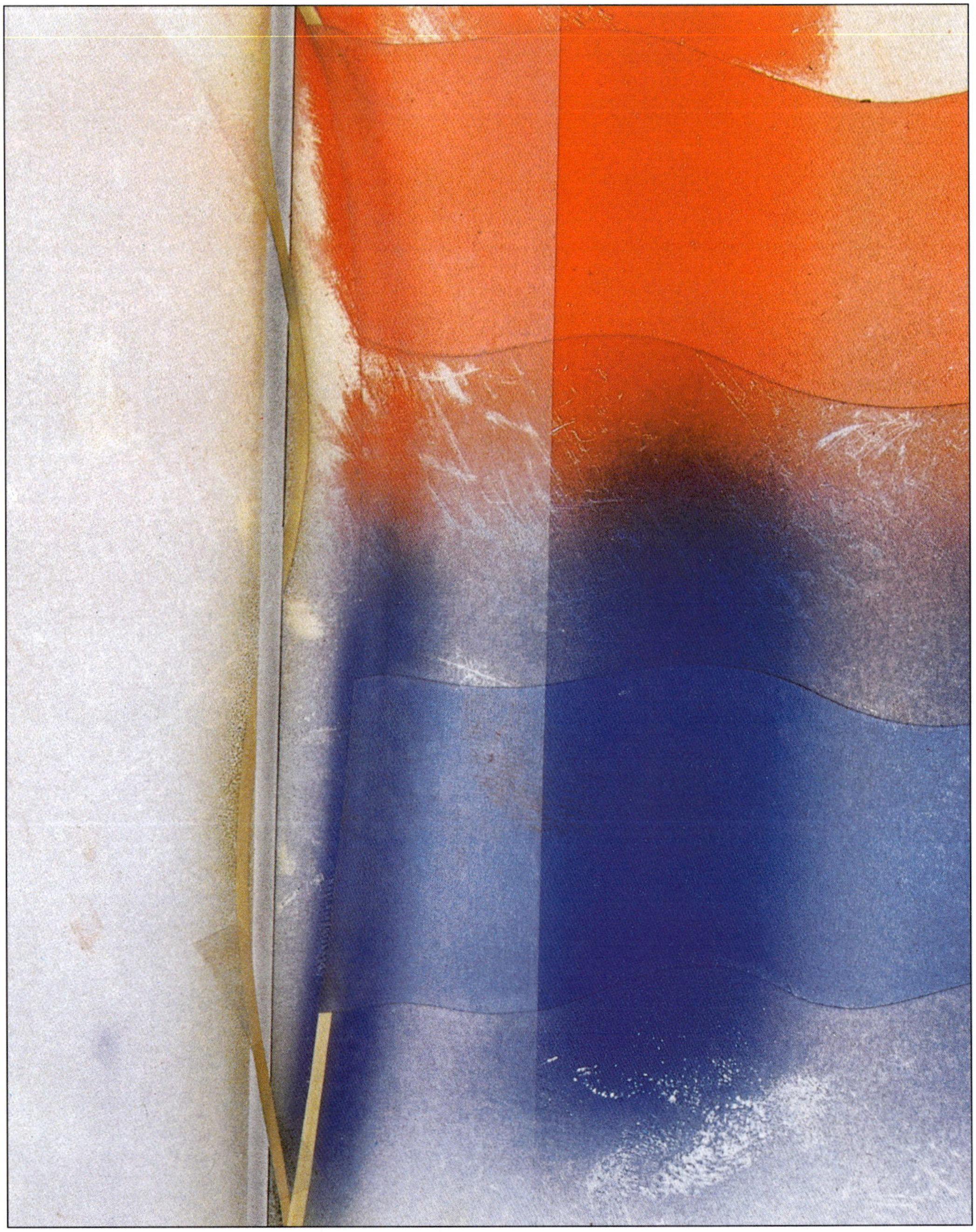

10 All of the rope is now re-masked with transparent tape, following which the flagpole is unmasked and sprayed in the appropriate color.

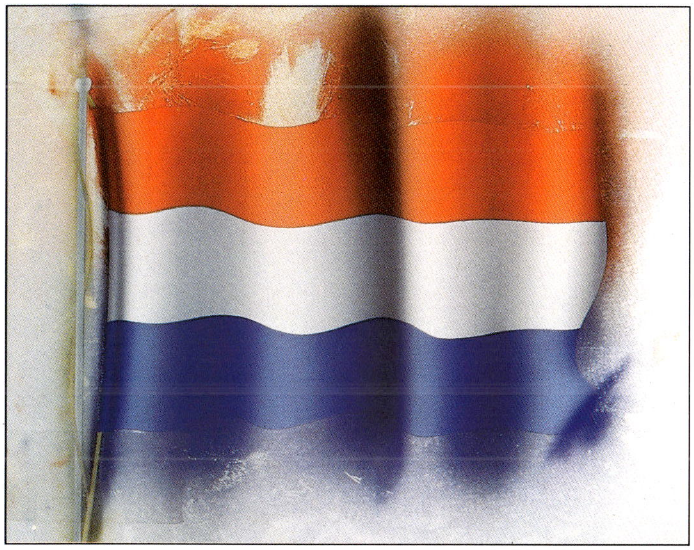

11 The pole is re-masked with transparent tape and the white, middle stripe of the flag is exposed, together with the red and blue stripes. A blue-gray gouache mixture is now sprayed over all three stripes in vertical bands, bringing the three colors together and adding a continuous depth of tone to the whole flag.

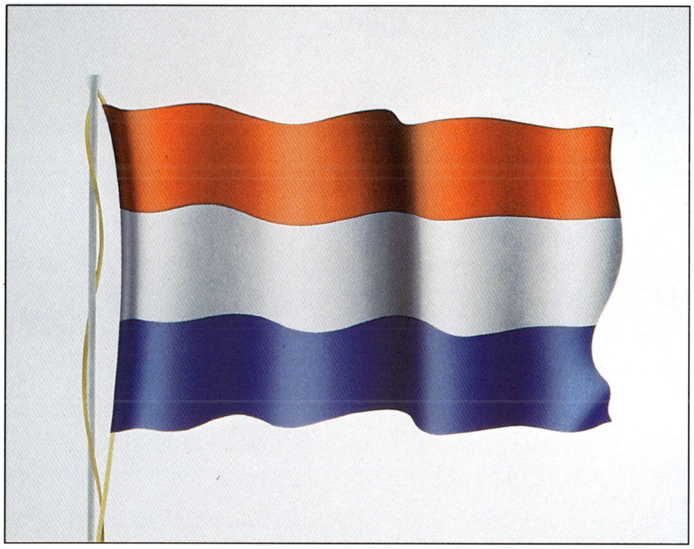

12 The masking film is removed, exposing the finished artwork.

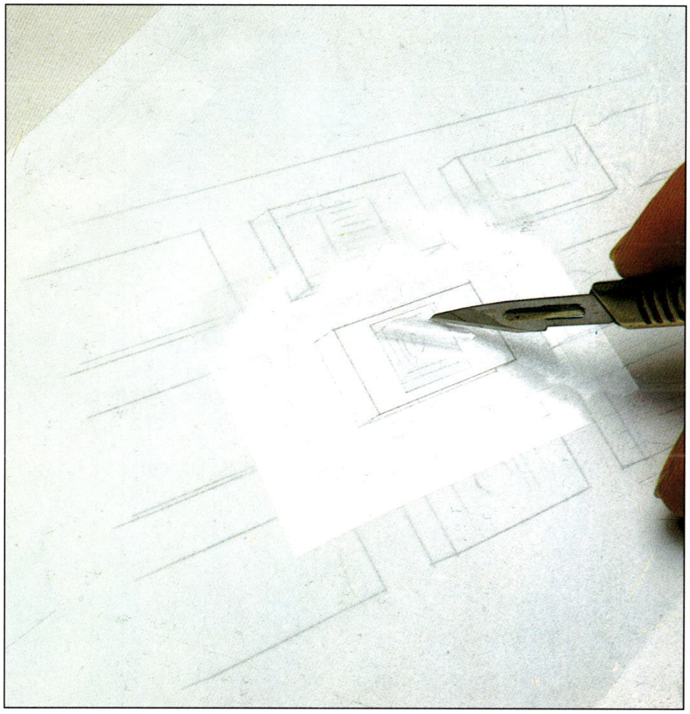

Double Masking

Self-adhesive masking film is expensive. It can be wasteful to use film to cover a large, extensive area of the artwork, especially if the section being worked on is only a small part of the whole. To avoid wastage, detail paper or cartridge paper can be used to protect the majority of the artwork from residual spray, with film being applied only to the relevant area of detail. It is important to cut a hole in the paper larger than the area to be sprayed, because sufficient space must be given to allow the masking film to stick to the artwork. It is a widely used technique and may be applied to many of the other techniques of masking and spraying described elsewhere in the book.

This photograph shows the application of double masking. A small square section is to be sprayed. The artwork has been covered with paper with a rectangular hole cut in the appropriate place. Masking film has then been overlaid and the required shape cut out.

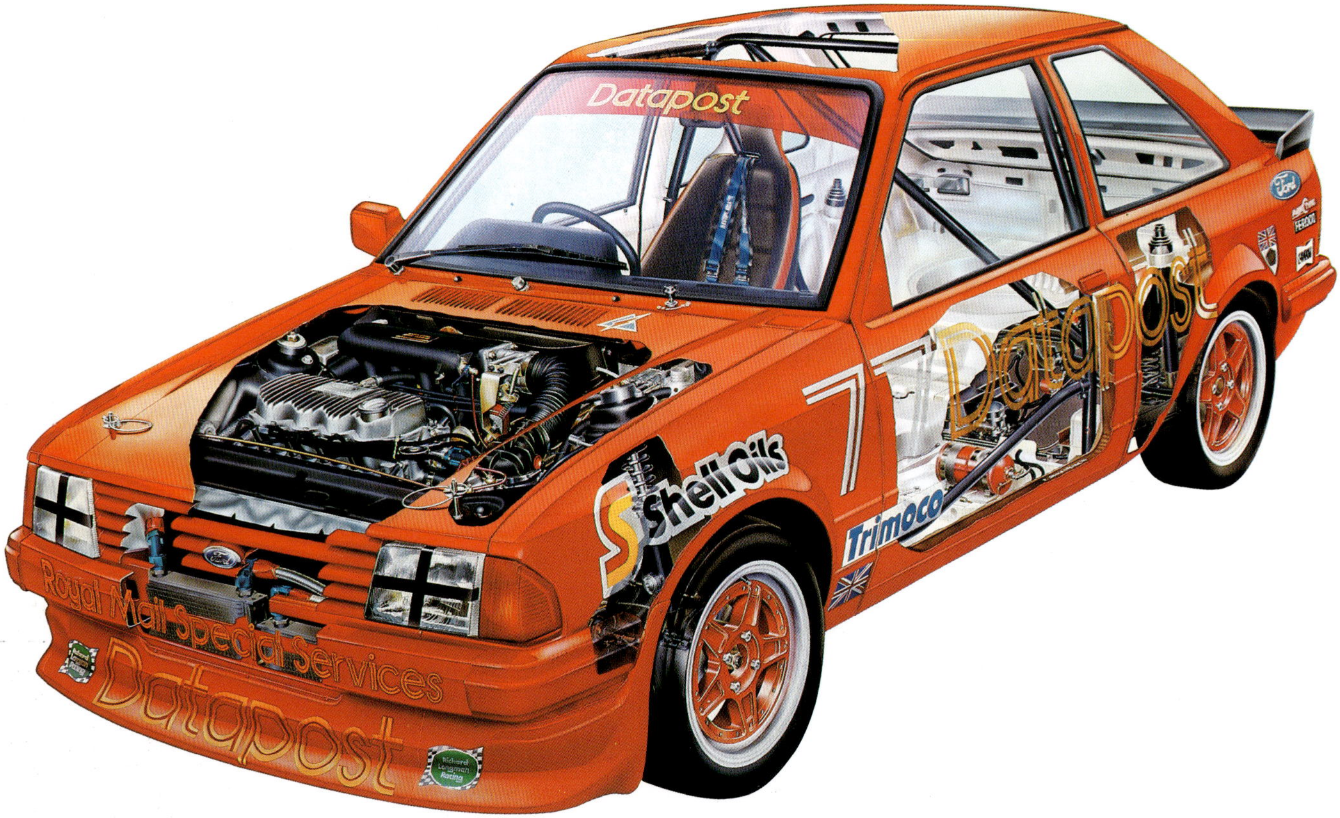

Datapost Ford Escort RS 1600i
Paul Shakespeare

This large illustration, measuring approximately 71 in x 59 in (178 cm x148 cm) was originally commissioned by Datapost to advertise both the British postal service and its racing team. It was produced with the close cooperation of the racing team managers, the Ford Motor Co. Ltd. and Richard Longman Racing, the organization responsible for converting the basic Escort model into a racing car. The brief specified that the illustration should show those areas of the car which did not conform to a standard production model, which explains why only limited areas have been cut away. The illustration was eventually purchased by The Patrick Collection, Birmingham, England, where it is now on display in this privately-run museum.

Once the pencil drawing was completed, it was transferred to a semi-smooth surfaced watercolor paper which had been dry-mounted on masonite. This proved unsatisfactory as a vehicle for airbrush rendering, because the fibers of the paper would lift whenever the masking film was removed. It was finally decided to photograph the original pencil drawing, from which a large, grayline print was made and dry-mounted on masonite. This gave a sound and smooth surface on which to airbrush, although great care was needed when cutting masks to prevent the knife from cutting too deep and thereby damaging the lamination of the photographic paper. A particular advantage of spraying on photographic paper was the ease with which it was possible to remove any color that had run or small mistakes [see CORRECTION TECHNIQUES]. Because gouache, which is water-based, was the principal medium, the surface could be cleaned using surgical cotton. This left the surface in its original condition for respraying.

No particular problems were encountered in the spraying process, which began with those areas furthest away from the observer and within the cutaway sections. The body of the car, with the exception of the lettering, numbers and stickers, became, to all intents and purposes, a black-and-white study. This meant that when applying color, greater control was required to ensure the shape was not lost and the contrast was maintained, with reference being constantly made to areas already sprayed. The tonal values on the body of the car and the lettering had also to be kept in relation to each other, especially where they changed direction and were therefore affected by changes in the amount of light reflected on them.

The areas normally visible through the windows were sprayed with the same strength of color as the rest of the car. When completed, the windows were oversprayed using opaque white, but keeping the density light so the effect is semi-transparent. This has had the effect of KNOCKING BACK what is seen through the windows.

FLAT TONE

While it is perfectly possible to apply an even, flat shade of color by hand, much practice is necessary before the results are acceptable and without blemish, especially when using watercolor on gouache. The airbrush simplifies this process, although it still requires practice when applying flat shades of color which need to be trans-parent or translucent. When applying transparent watercolors with the airbrush, it is essential that the air pressure and amount of paint allowed through the airbrush remain constant, to prevent stripes from appearing. The distance the airbrush is held away from the artwork must also remain constant to avoid variations in tonal value. However, the advantage of being able to overspray any imperfections does give the airbrush the edge over hand-painting. As a technique, the application of flat tone is directly related to GRADATED TONE and as an exercise should come before it.

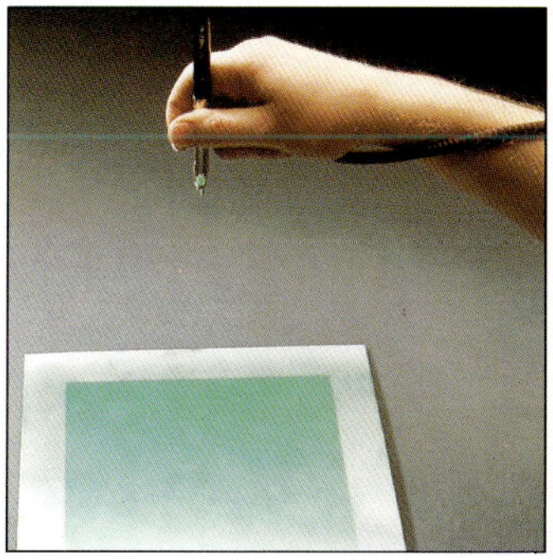

1 The area to be sprayed with a flat tone has been masked and the spraying proceeds from the top to the bottom, passing the airbrush from side to side over the masked area. It is always advisable to start and finish the spraying on the masking film, as this ensures that the color is laid evenly at the edges of the masked shape.

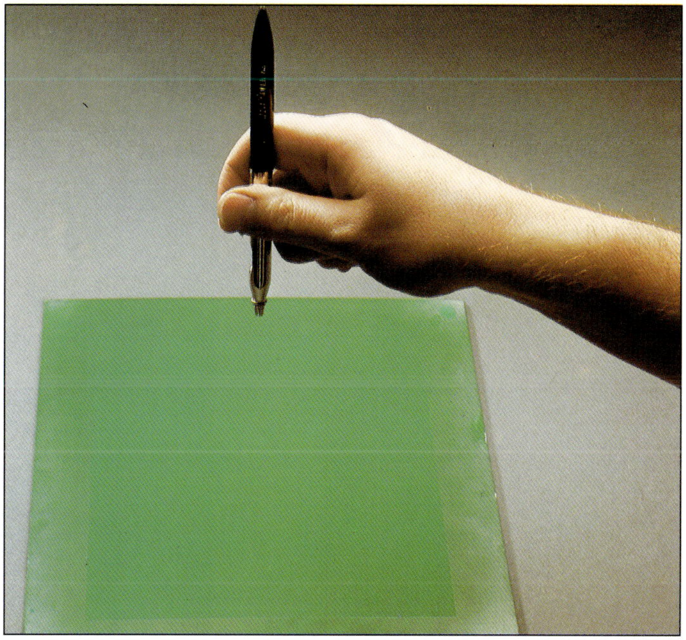

2 Color is gradually built up following the same process until the required density has been achieved. A useful method of maintaining an even, flat color is to turn the artwork 90° after each layer of color has been sprayed. This also helps to avoid or cover up any stripes which may appear due to irregular spraying.

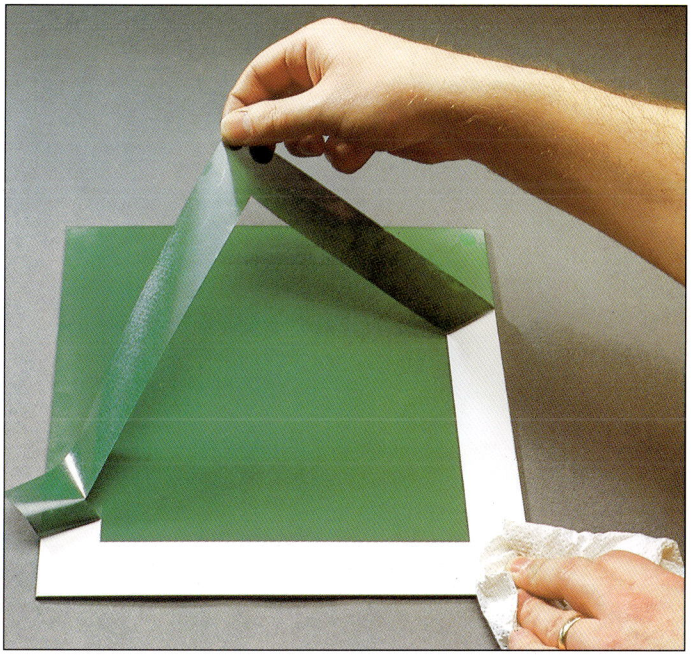

3 On completion, carefully remove the masking film.

FOUND OBJECT MASKING

The function of all techniques in airbrushing is to arrive at a given result. The technical means of achieving these results is unimportant if the illustration itself is successful. It may therefore come as a surprise to some to find natural and indeed manmade objects being used as masks for spraying. They open up an incredible variety of textures and images which can be put to good use in illustration. The following demonstrations are just a small sample.

When collecting sample objects, especially natural ones, always make sure they do not hold dirt or dust. Besides damaging and marking the surface of the artwork, some dirt might get ingrained, which would deaden the freshness and vitality of the finished artwork.

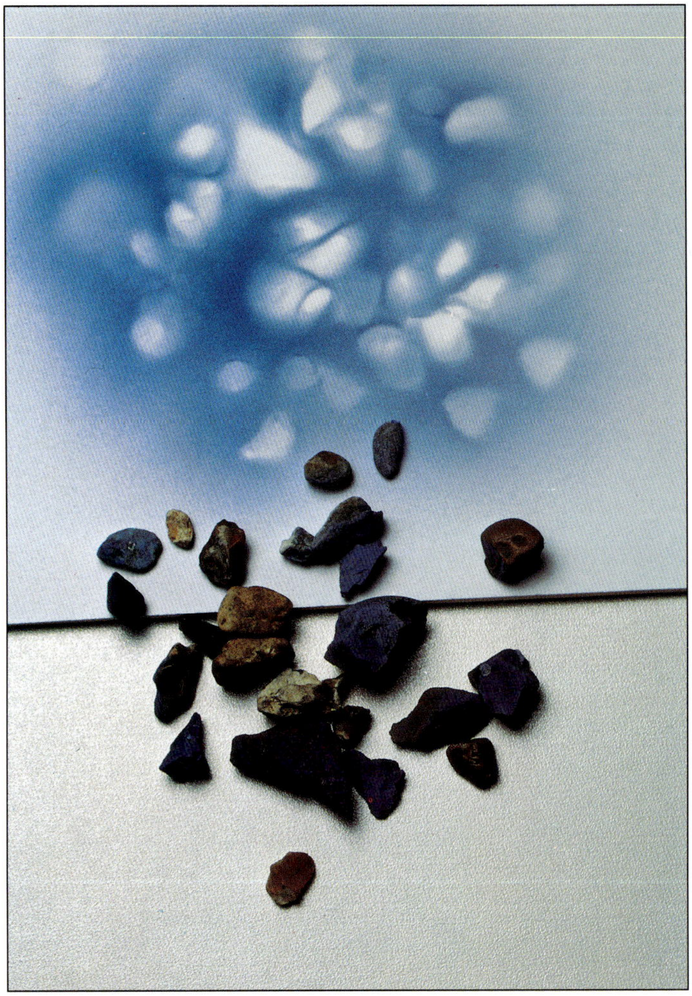

Stones
A collection of stones has been laid on the artwork and then oversprayed. The photograph shows the stones after they have been removed, with the effect on the artwork being apparent at the top of the picture. With practice, and possibly by making a test sheet first, you may find that the stones can be placed in set positions to achieve a particular pattern or texture.

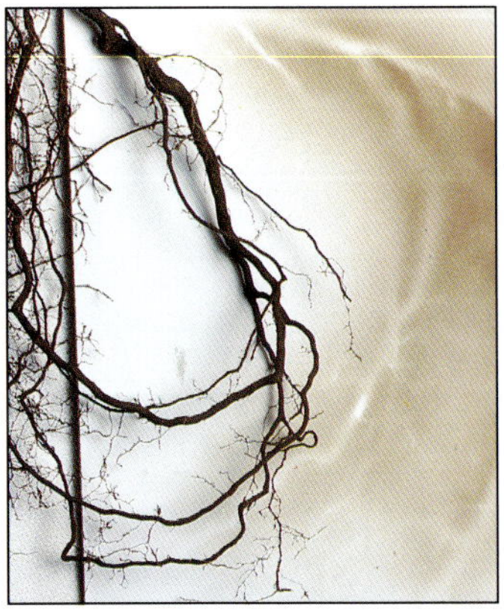

Twigs
The use of this twig as a mask has produced an effect similar to old leather or, possibly, marble veining. It would be impossible to simulate this effect by more conventional means.

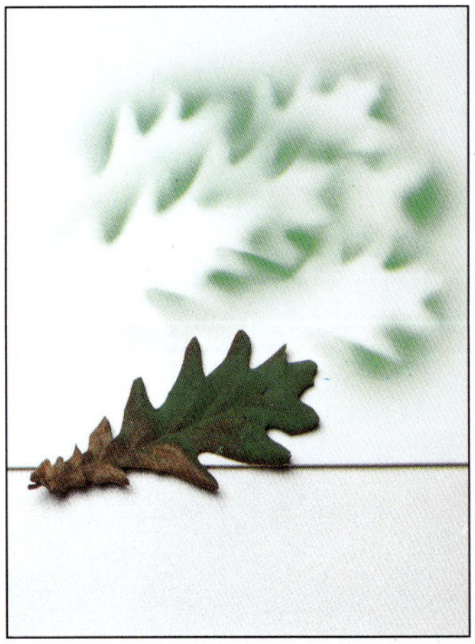

Leaves
In this photograph a leaf has been used as a mask. Its jagged outline produces a random repeat pattern.

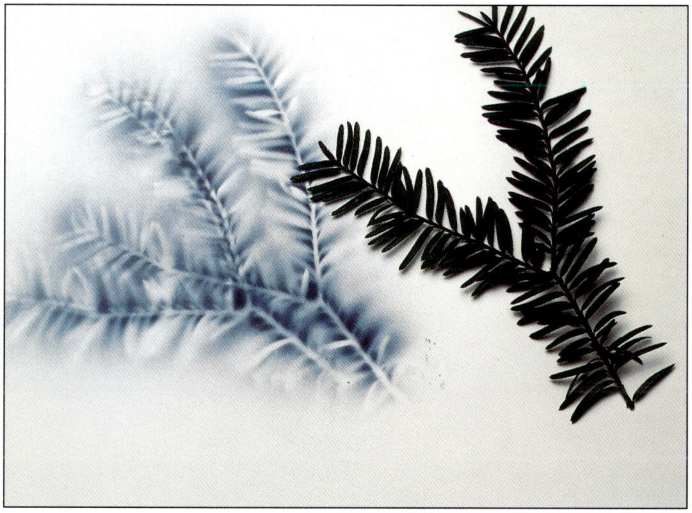

Branches

A piece of pine branch is shown with the repeat pattern achieved by moving it across the board and over-spraying to build up the texture.

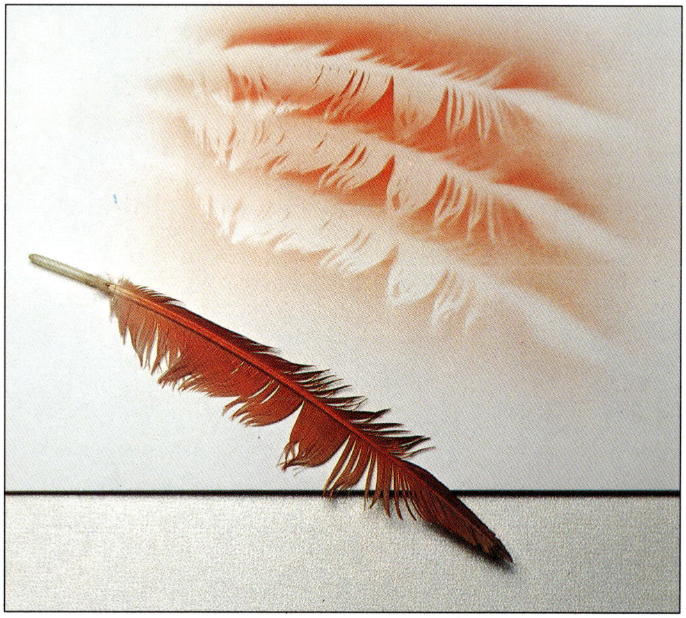

Feathers

A subtle and delicate effect has been achieved with a feather. Because of the light touch of the airbrush spray, it is possible to reproduce even such a fine texture quite accurately.

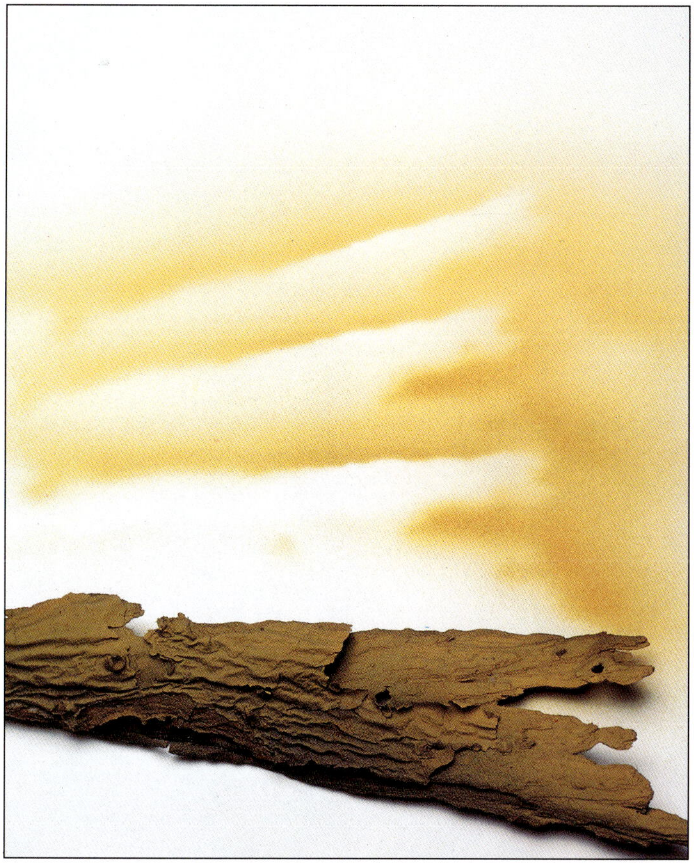

Bark

A strip of tree bark has been used here, and by slightly moving it on a pivot from the left, a repeat pattern is achieved which appears to fan out gradually. The spraying has been restricted in this example to the top edge of the bark, which gives a more interesting silhouette.

FREEHAND SPRAYING

This is a technique requiring much practice before it can be used effectively on finished artwork, because, as the title suggests, no masks are used to aid the illustrator and all control lies in the hand. It is a skill which should be acquired because there are very few occasions in illustration when some application of freehand spraying is not needed. Some illustrators have developed freehand spraying to such a high degree that all of their work is produced this way. However, freehand spraying will always give a soft edge which is not necessarily compatible with all subjects, and it is more general practice to work with masks which define individual shapes, but to use freehand spraying to develop form and detail within the masked areas.

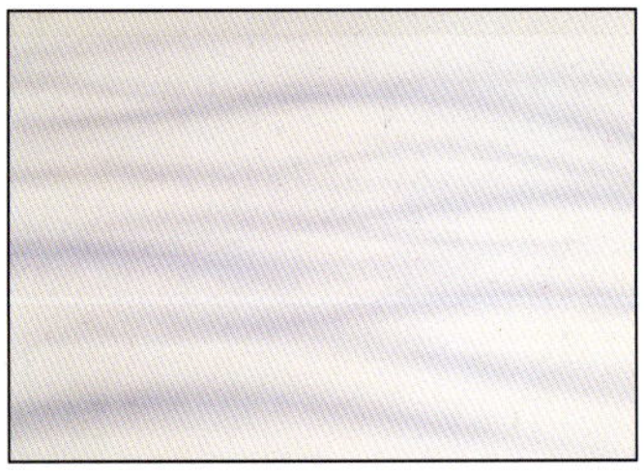

1 Here the illustrator is demonstrating a wave effect by freehand spraying. The initial spraying is light and it is essential that the control of the airbrush flows easily in the required general direction, in this case horizontally.

2 The depth of color is gradually built up evenly from top to bottom.

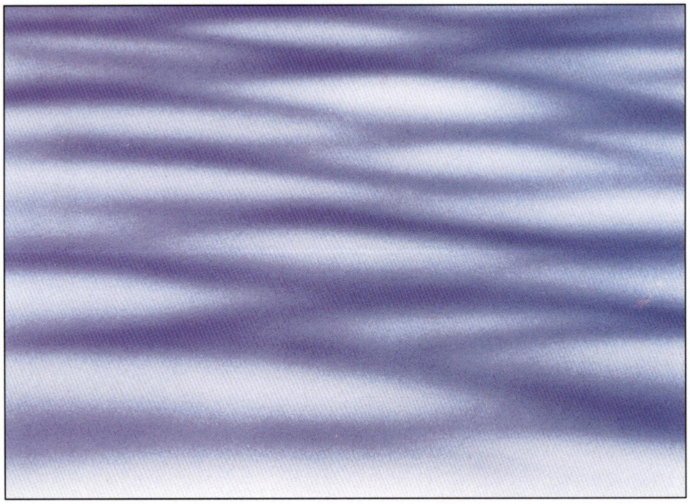

3 The completed example shows how the interwoven lines have built up a complex tonal effect.

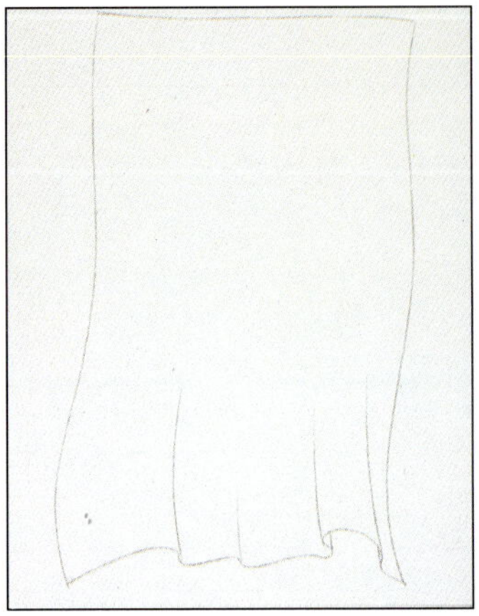

Freehand Spraying Within a Masked Shape

1 A neat and clean pencil drawing representing fabric is prepared, keeping the detail to a minimum. This could be drawn on detail paper first, which allows for corrections to be made so that the shape looks convincing, or, as here, straight onto the board for spraying. Whichever approach is used and after the drawing is completed, the board is covered with masking film.

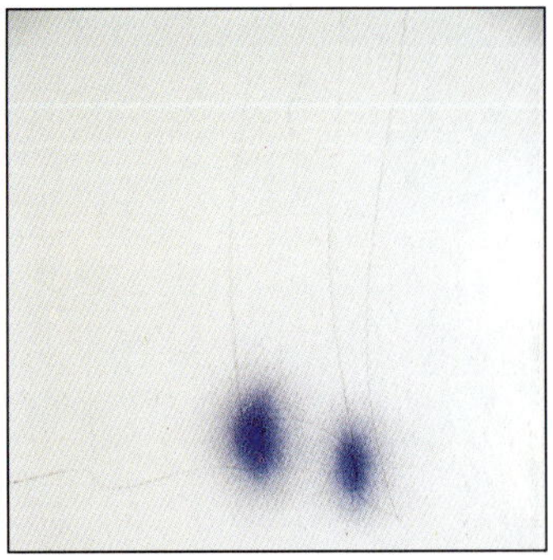

2 The first stage in the spraying sequence is to remove film from the two hard-edged shadow areas formed by the deep inner fold of the fabric. These two shapes are sprayed with dark shades.

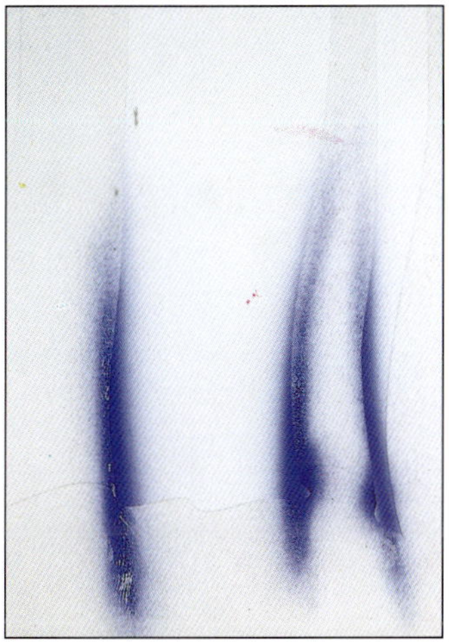

3 The masking film is then partly cut and removed in order to spray those areas of the fabric which require part hard-edged shadows, but which do not extend to the full depth of the drawing. It should also be noticed that in these areas and opposite the hard edges, the shadows gradate quickly to the white of the board.

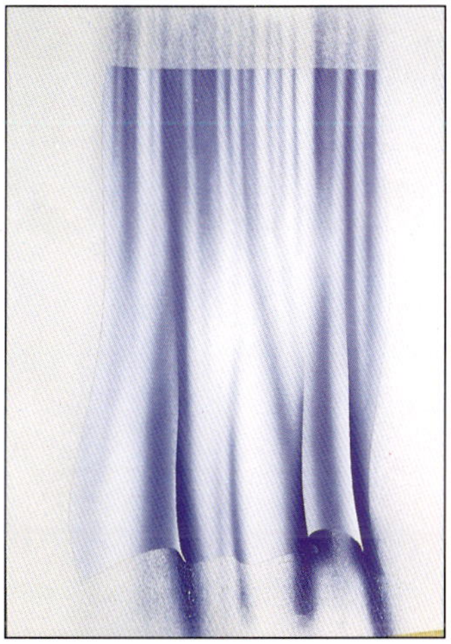

4 The remainder of the masking film covering the fabric is now removed, and the freehand spraying begins by building up the soft tonal areas. As this progresses, the impression of flowing fabric will slowly increase. Because of the very nature of manipulating and controlling an airbrush, it may well prove easier if the artwork is turned 90°. This is because a directional spray running from left to right allows more natural movement of hand and arm than from top to bottom. When following this exercise, great care should be taken to ensure that the tonal gradations soften at the appropriate points; otherwise, the completed image will lack subtlety.

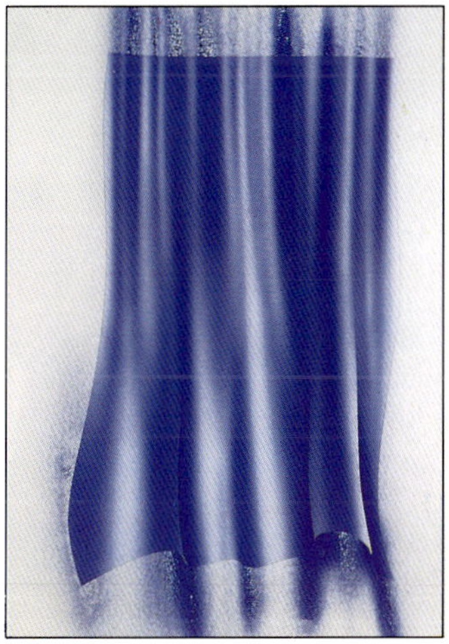

5 The tones and shadows to accentuate the "feel" of the fabric are built up in a freehand style.

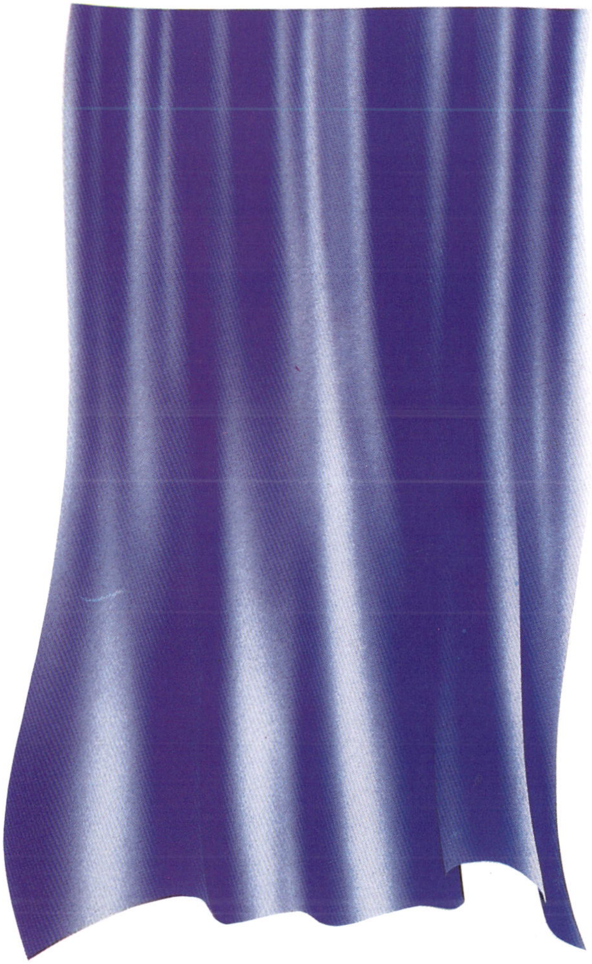

6 When the required depth of shade and strength of color have been reached, it is then necessary just to remove the surrounding masking film to reveal the finished artwork.

GHOSTING

When it is important to show the complete exterior shape of an object, but also selected internal shapes within it or behind it, ghosting is used. It is particularly used in technical illustration when descriptive three-dimensional drawings are being prepared. For example, a brief might require a complete cutaway view of a complex new four-stroke engine, but because of the compound form of the cylinder head, cylinder block and sump casing, the engine would be unrecognizable unless enough information was included of the exterior; it would therefore be practical and desirable to include ghosting. This would enable the engine as a whole to be understood, as well as the workings and design of the interior, or those areas not normally visible.

In application, ghosting relies on subtle color and shading changes which will not adversely affect the exterior in preference to the interior, or hidden object, and vice versa. Careful planning in the sequence of spraying is also a necessity, both to prevent unnecessary extra work and to avoid creating an image that is almost illegible on completion.

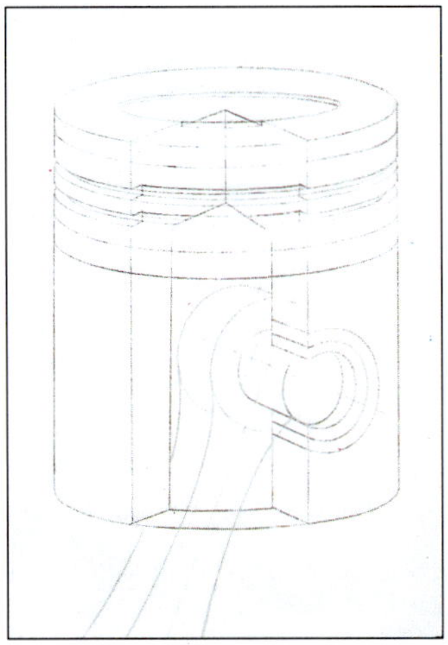

Ghosting Over a Section Cutaway

1 The form of a piston, its gudgeon-pin and part of the connecting rod is drawn on detail paper, with the location and shape of the cutaway area clearly indicated.

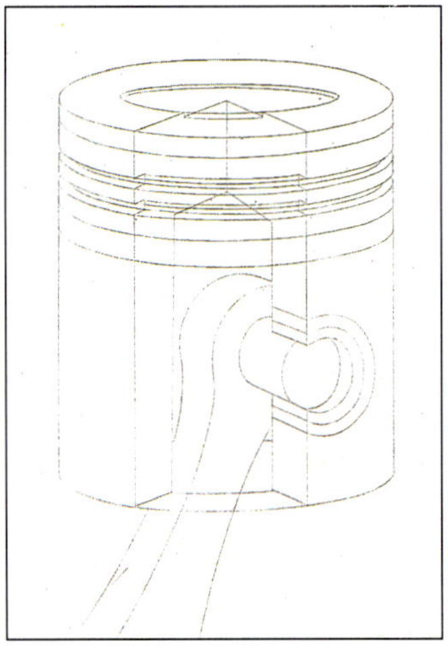

2 The drawing is transferred to illustration board and covered with masking film.

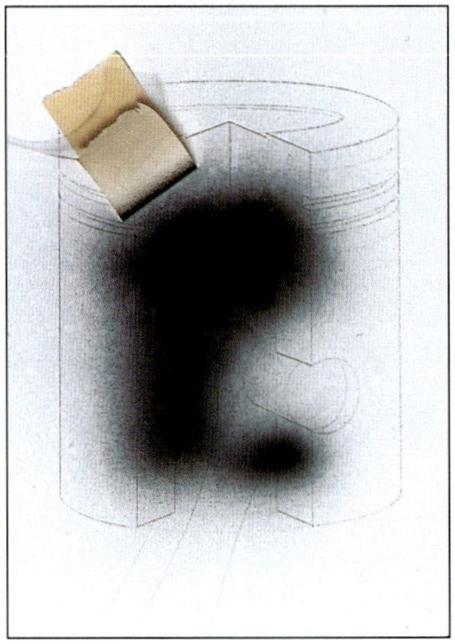

3 The masking film covering the inside surface of the piston, made visible by the angle and position of the section cutaway, is cut and hinged to allow for these areas to be sprayed first, as they are represented in heavy shadow, and therefore contain the darkest shades.

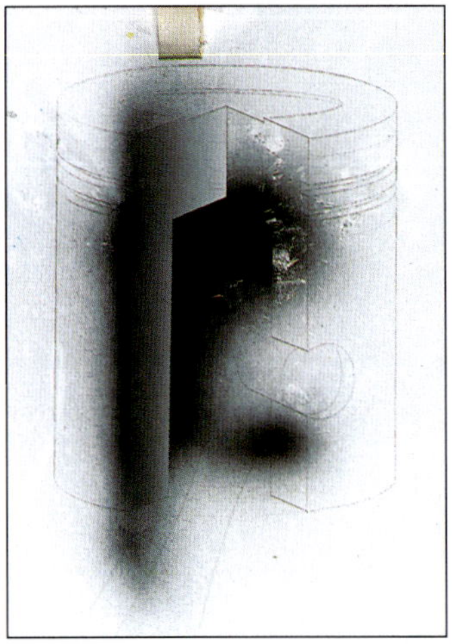

4 After cutting the mask to expose areas of the medium shades, these are sprayed, allowing for a reflected highlight to remain toward the inner edge. This represents the left-hand face of the cutaway. When spraying vertical sections, it may be easier to turn the artwork 90° so the airbrush can pass horizontally across the surface.

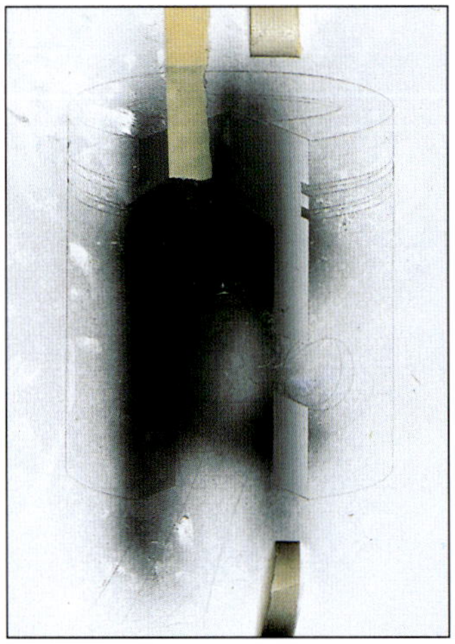

5 The same process is completed for the right-hand face, but now the reflected highlight is toward the outer edge of the piston.

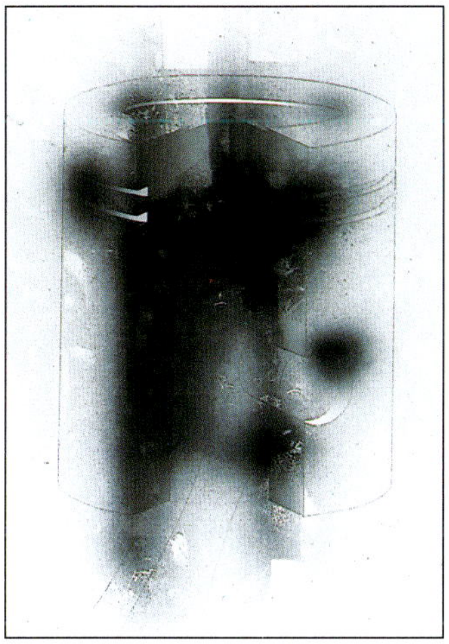

6 Other areas of the drawing are sprayed in medium shade to build up the form and shape of the piston. The areas concentrated on here are the recess to the top of the piston, the shadow and form within the grooves for the piston rings (which are not included in this example), and the form on the hole into which the gudgeon-pin is fitted.

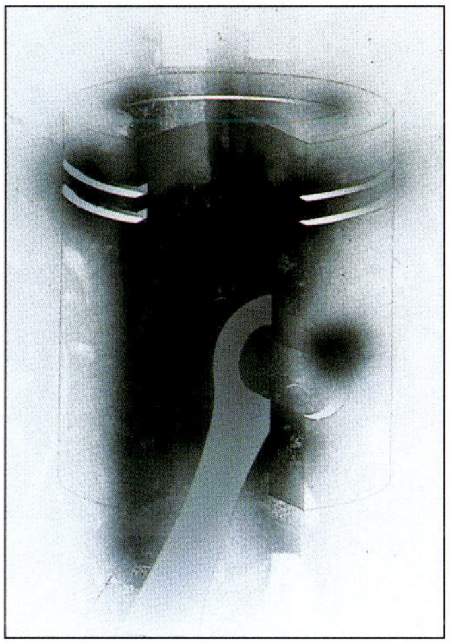

7 The process started in stage 6 is continued, varying the depth of tone according to the direction of the light source and the location of the area being sprayed. Here the facing side of the connecting rod, the vertical surface to the top recess and the horizontal surfaces on the grooves for the piston rings are sprayed.

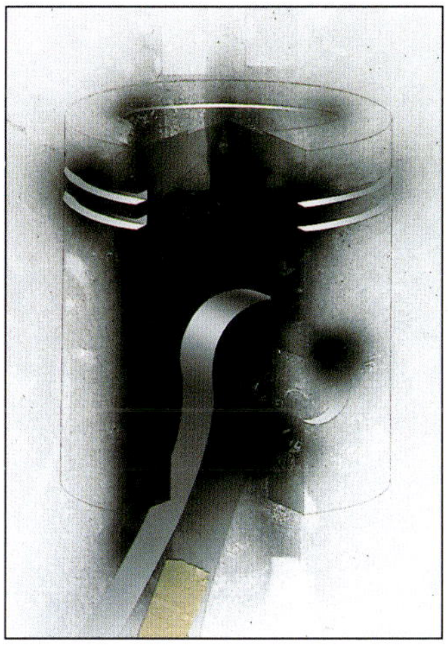

8 This stage shows the thickness or depth of the connecting rod sprayed up, with sufficient contrast and form to indicate the shape clearly. Notice should be taken of the use of hinged mask sections, which not only allow for accurate repositioning but prevent accidental or damage loss.

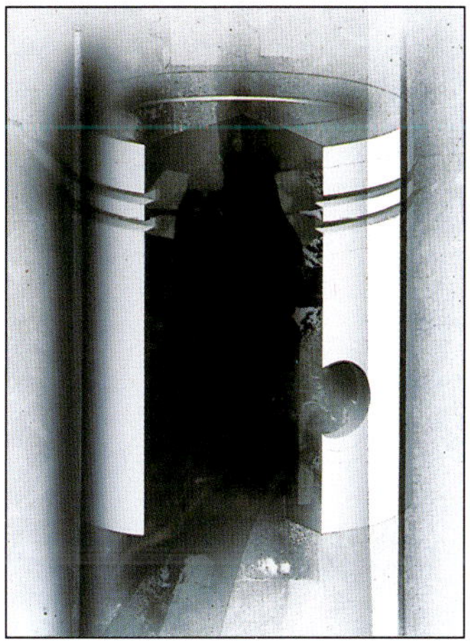

9 Replacing all previous masks, the body of the piston is sprayed using acetate to mask the vertical bands of color. This part of the work involves spraying the darkest shades and hard-edged areas first, then developing the medium and light shades and gradated areas.

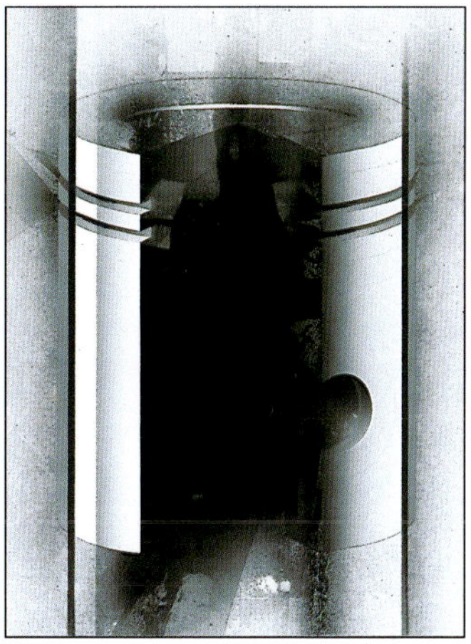

10 The gradated shades have been sprayed at this stage to model the cylindrical form of the piston.

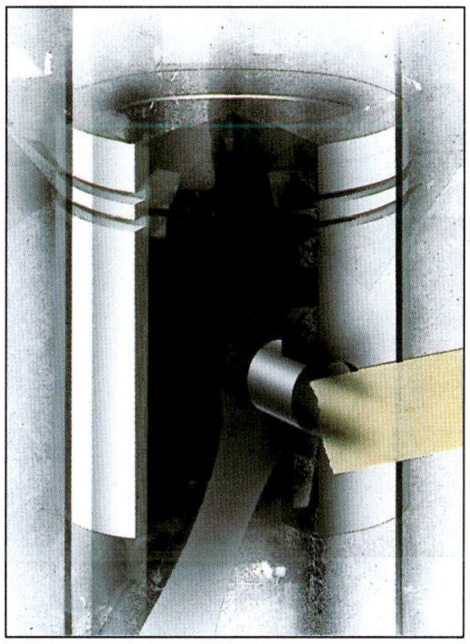

11 The central section of the exterior of the piston is the last stage to complete the body of the piston. Also shown completed is the cylindrical head of the gudgeon-pin, with a principal highlight across the center and reflected highlight at the base.

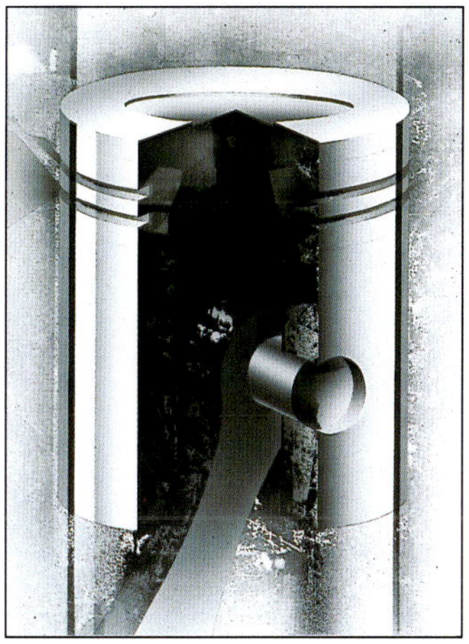

12 The top of the piston has been sprayed with enough variety to differentiate between the recess and the body of the piston. At the same time, the end of the gudgeon pin is unmasked and sprayed with gradated tone.

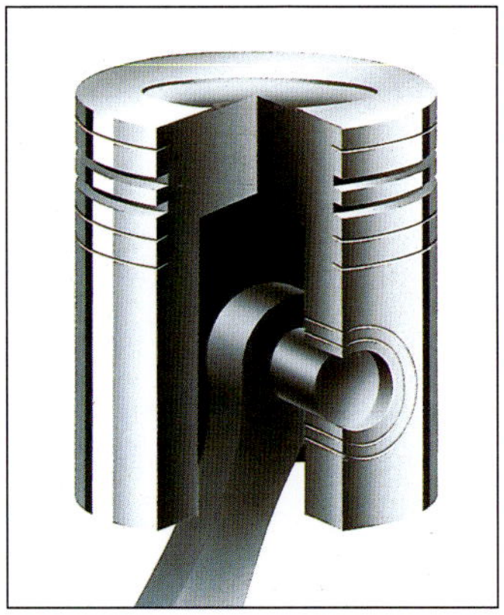

13 The solid, cutaway rendering of the piston is completed and the remaining masking film removed prior to detail work being applied by hand with pencil and brush. Highlights are scratched in using a sharp art blade.

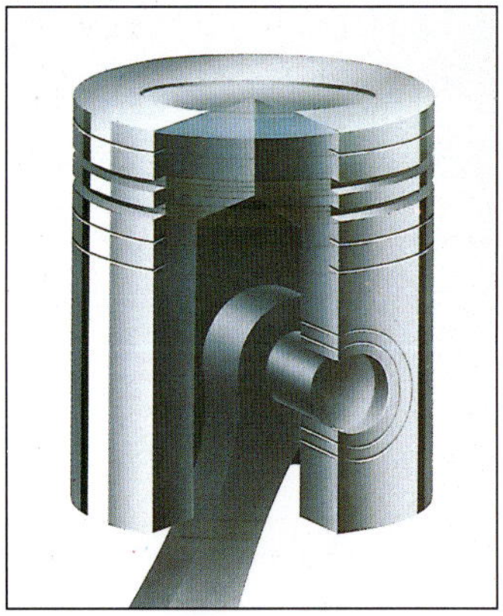

14 The artwork is completely re-covered with new masking film in preparation for the ghosting to be sprayed. Those areas which are to be the lightest are cut and removed first. In this example these areas include the top of the piston. Light-shaded ghosting is sprayed using opaque white.

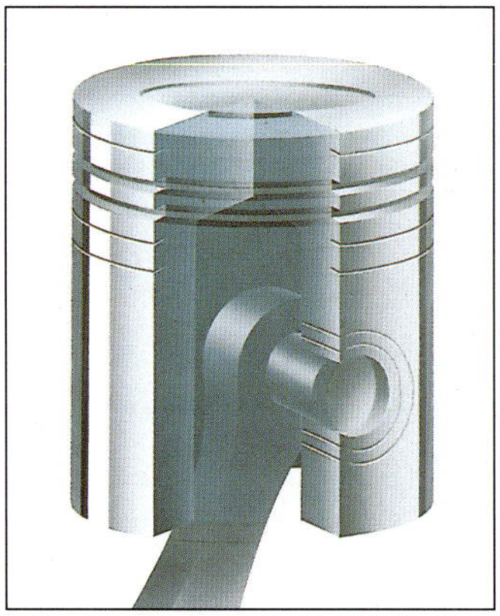

15 Next the medium shades of ghosting are sprayed, which include the continuation of the grooves for the piston rings.

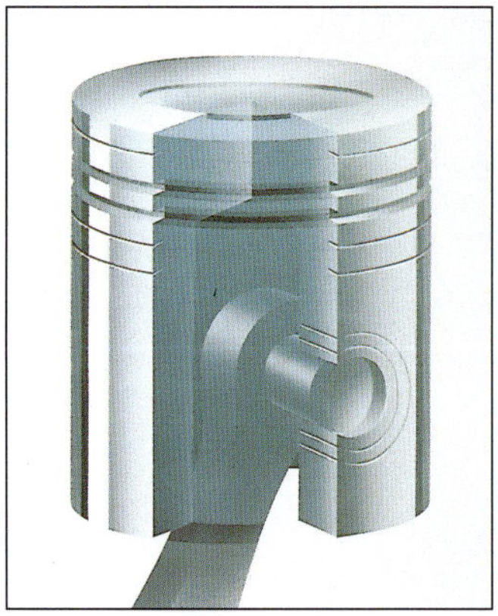

16 The darkest shades are the last to be applied, giving emphasis to the depths of the top recess, the grooves for the piston rings and the thickness of the piston base.

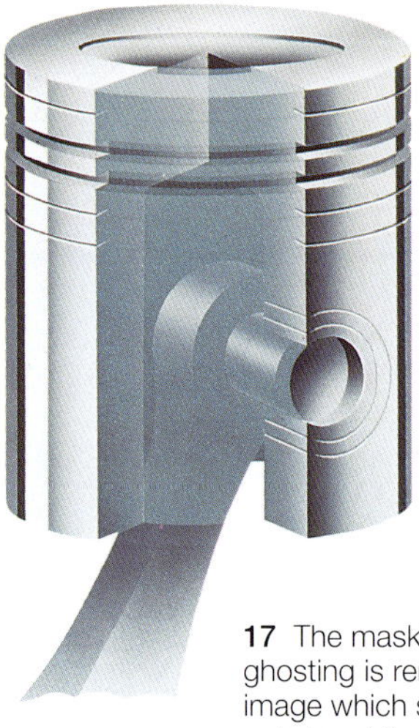

17 The masking film laid on for the ghosting is removed, leaving an image which shows the complete exterior of the piston as well as the cutaway section, revealing the connecting rod and gudgeon-pin.

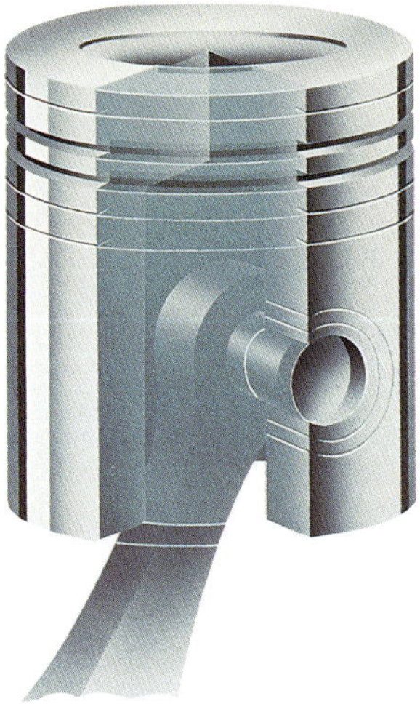

18 To improve the depth of contrast and detail, it is necessary to line-in the ghosted areas of the illustration using pencil and brush-painted opaque white. This also improves the quality and finish. Great care must always be taken when ghosting, because it is so easy to lose detail and contrast, which would defeat the exercise and make for a flat illustration. It is advisable to practice with a black-and-white piece first, as the tonal values are relatively controllable, before moving on to more complex color work.

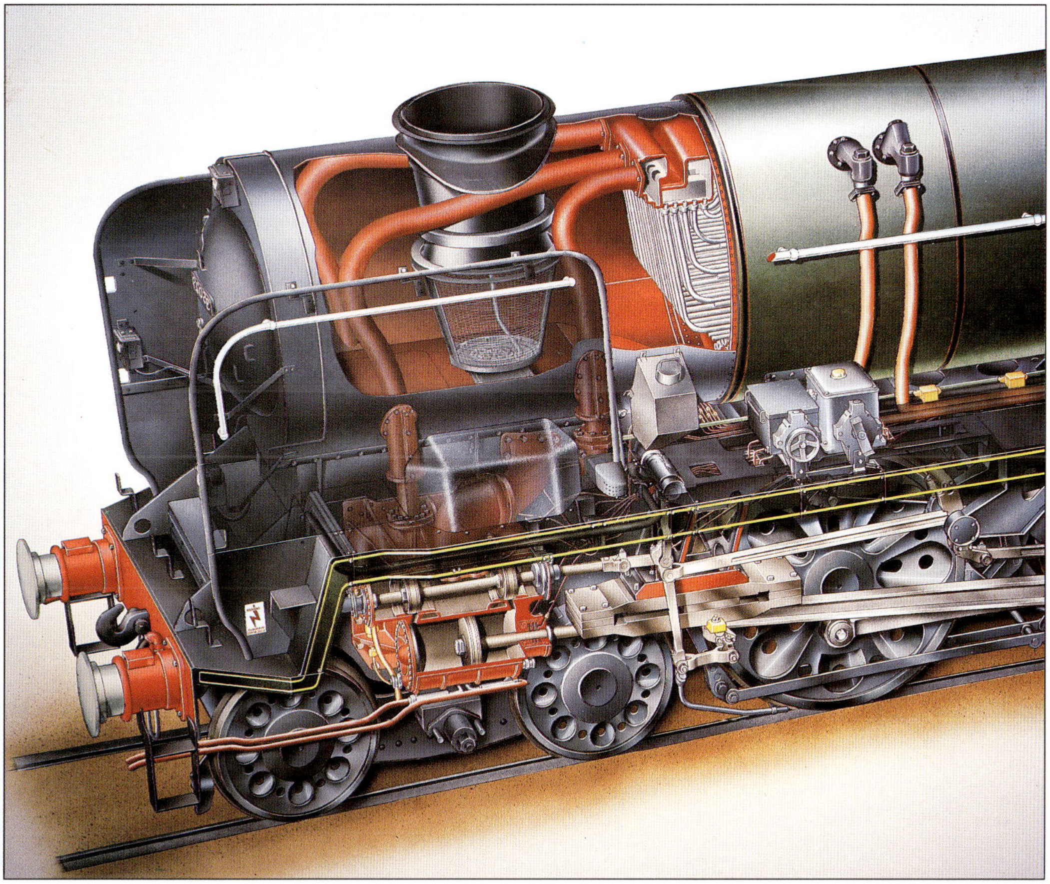

Southern Railway Merchant Navy Class 4-6-2 locomotive *Ellerman Lines* (detail)
Mark Franklin

Complex, three-dimensional cutaway perspective illustration in full color presents difficulties when it is required to show as much detail as possible without confusing the viewer. In this example, a detail taken from a large airbrushed illustration commissioned by the Science Museum, London, every aspect of the working parts of a particular steam locomotive had to be clearly shown. The part of the illustration reproduced includes the fire box, smoke deflectors, boiler casing, running-board, bogies and part of the driving wheels with motion gear. As with most steam locomotives, the fire box includes a blast pipe and ash filter, as well as steampipes leading from the front of the boiler down into the valve chests. The exhaust steam is also fed through pipes which lead into the fire box. On this particular locomotive, smoke deflectors were fitted immediately alongside and projecting slightly in front of the fire box.

Without the nearest smoke deflector, there would have been no problem in showing the area described with a conventional cutaway. However, with the deflector, an integral and important part of this locomotive, in position, the problem arose as to how to show both the deflector and the interior of the fire box. The solution, as shown here, was to render the fire box and its contents as solid objects, while spraying the deflector as if made of tinted glass, that is, ghosting its form, with the exception of the rim and handrail which remain solid to enhance the shape and location of the deflector.

To a lesser extent, the running board has also been shown ghosted, revealing detail through it.

GRADATED TONE

Gradated tone means the application of color which changes gradually from dark to light, either fading into the white of the board, or blending into another color. When the contrast is controlled, a gradated tone can eliminate the need for oversprayed highlights. If sprayed with transparent watercolor over a previously applied color, a translucent effect is possible in which the first color appears to shine through the second. Tonal gradation is the principal means of modeling three-dimensional form in an illustration, and broad areas of gradated tones and colors make atmospheric backgrounds.

Gradated tones are particularly effective in creating skies. If, for example, a midday sky is desired, the first gradated tone would be a soft base of yellow ochre or Naples yellow running from the horizon up, and blending in with the white of the artwork about a third of the way into the sky area. A second gradated tone is then oversprayed, but with a weaker mix of cadmium red, also blending in at about the same point. Finally, a gradated tone of cerulean or cobalt blue is sprayed from the top of the artwork to blend with the previous two colors, but further down towards the horizon.

The facility which the airbrush gives in producing gradated tones, whether on a large or small scale, is one of the distinct advantages of this tool. While it is possible to achieve the same result by hand, it becomes increasingly difficult to manipulate within areas which restrict the free flow of a brush and keep within predetermined boundaries. In this, the control provided by masking techniques and the delicate quality of the airbrush spray enable the illustrator to produce flawless gradations.

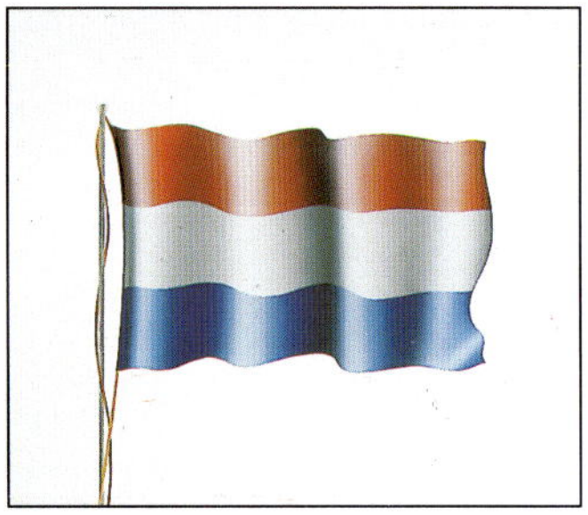

Background Gradation
1 A gradated tone is to be applied as a backdrop to the flag. The complete working area is covered with masking film, and the background area is cut and removed, leaving only the flag protected prior to spraying.

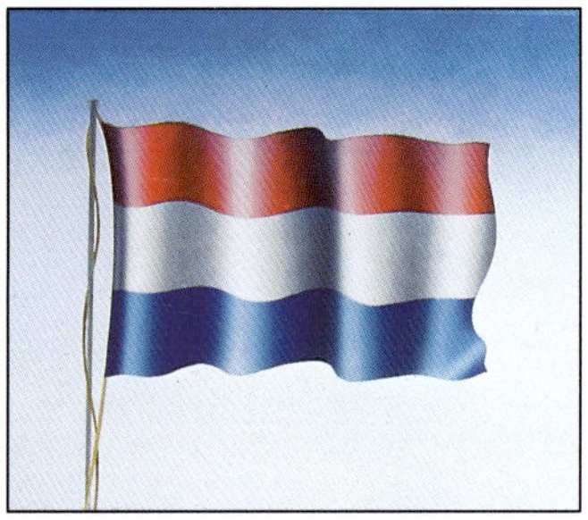

2 The color is applied by spraying from dark to light, building up the deeper shaded area first, avoiding the spraying of an excessive and concentrated strength of color too quickly.

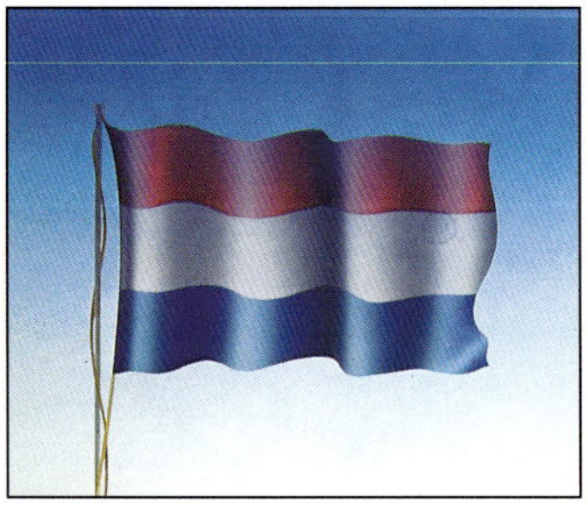

3 The process is continued and the color slowly increased in depth as it is also brought further down toward the lower edge of the artwork.

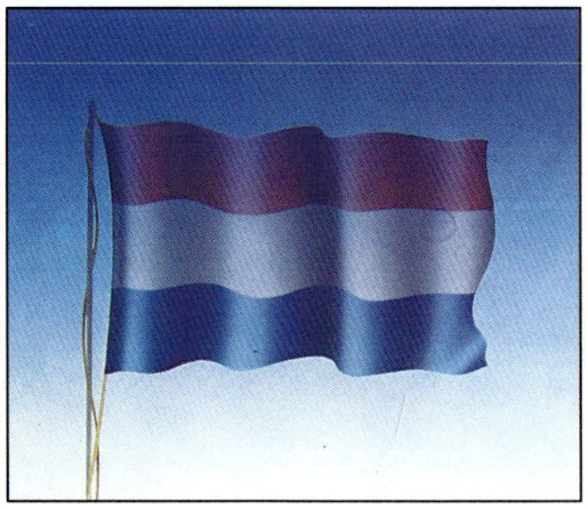

4 The final stage in spraying is to strengthen the shading of the color, again working from top to bottom

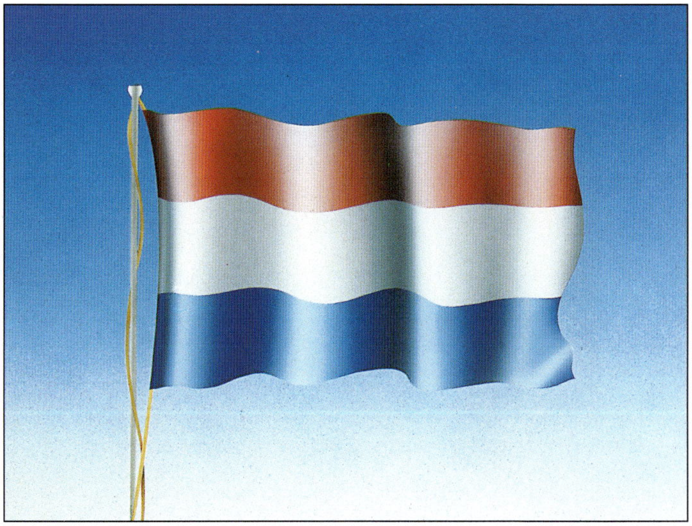

5 Finally, the masking film is removed from the flag and border, revealing the gradated backdrop in relation to the three-dimensional image of the flag. The overall effect is to throw the flag even more to the fore.

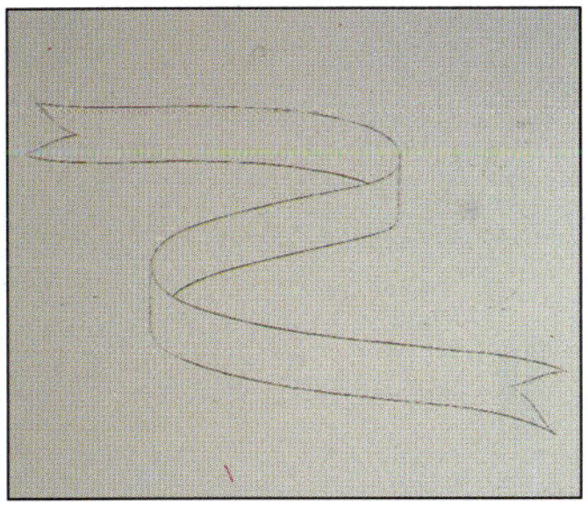

Gradation Within an Object

1 A drawing of a ribbon making a flowing S-shaped curve has been prepared on illustration board and the whole artwork covered with masking film. All of the lines making up the ribbon are then cut into the masking film, including those which make the transitions from inner to outer curves.

2 The film covering the top part of the ribbon is removed and hinged back with a piece of masking tape. This section is then sprayed vertically with bands of gradated color following the shape of the curve.

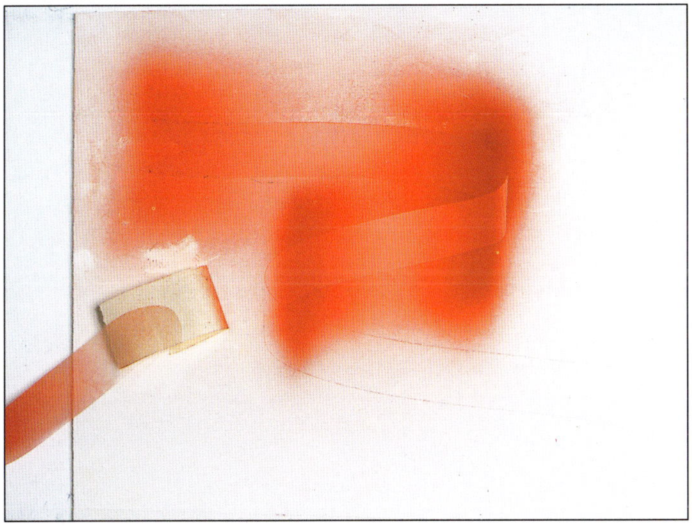

3 The hinged mask from stage 2 is replaced. The second mask, which is also hinged, is pulled back to expose the central curve of the S-shape. The gradations on this section are formed in the same way as on the first.

4 The final stage is spraying is the lower part of the ribbon, after replacing the previous mask and hinging back the last one.

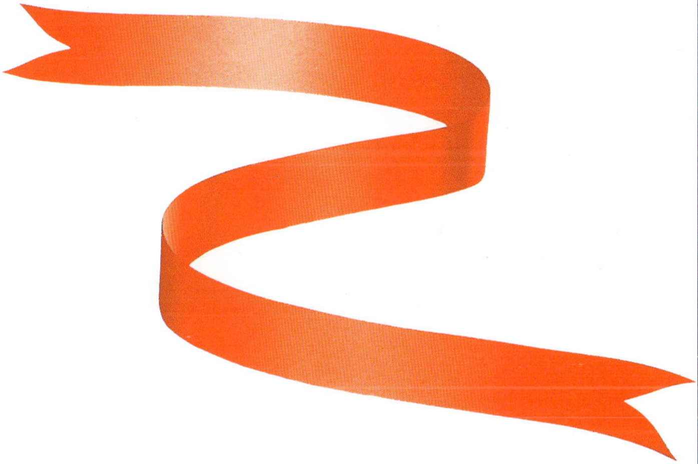

5 All masking film has been removed, showing the ribbon airbrushed with three-dimensional form, relying only on gradated tones of color. No dark shades or white highlights have been added.

HALOING

Haloing, as its name implies, is the application of a circle of light and should appear as a soft, gentle glow, fading away outward from the circumference. The technique can be used to create an effect of distant radiance, as in the "galaxy" example shown here, or to soften and diffuse highlights in closer objects.

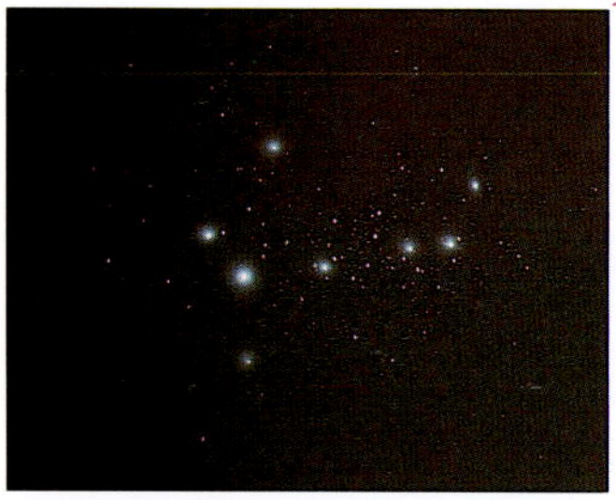

1 Various-sized stars have been painted as white dots and over-sprayed to diffuse the edges; others have been sprayed with a splatter-cap as dots of various sizes to give an illusion of immense depth.

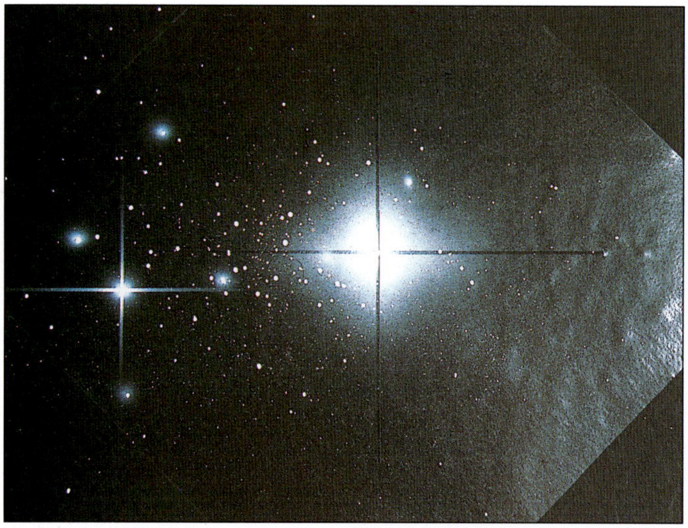

2 Starburst shapes have been cut into masking film (acetate could also have been used) and positioned over certain stars. These are sprayed using opaque white, which is applied in each case to the center of the mask.

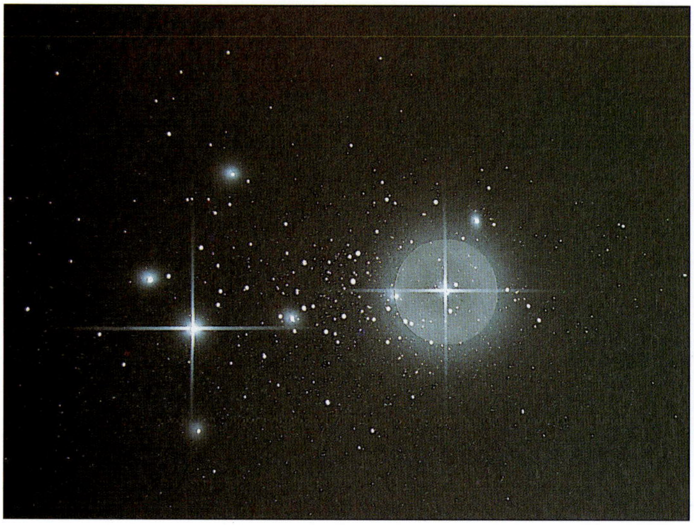

3 A circle cut from masking film is placed over the center of a starburst and gently sprayed around the edge with opaque white. It is important not to apply too much white when spraying the halo to maintain the effect of diffusing light.

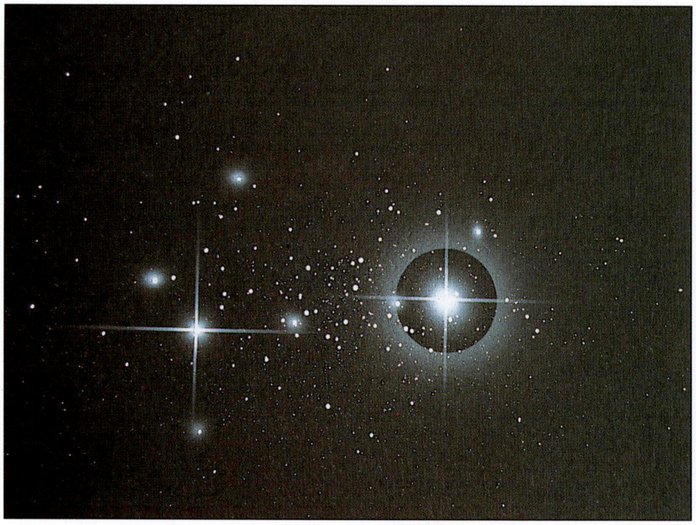

4 When the masking film is removed, the effect can be quite subtle, as demonstrated here.

HIGHLIGHTING

There are various techniques for adding light, form and contrast to a shape, to prevent the subject from looking flat. Highlights draw the viewer's attention and can be used to excellent effect to emphasize the points of visual focus in an image.

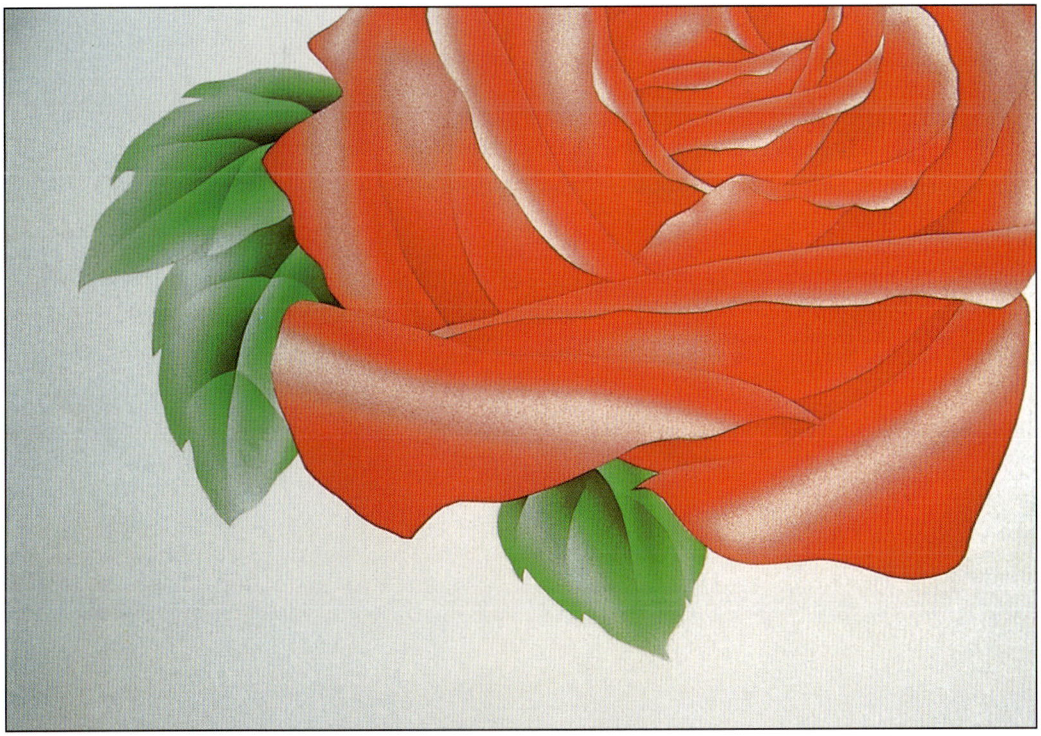

Using the White of the Board
This is an example of leaving the white of the board to form a natural highlight in an area of color. It is achieved by carefully controlling the amount of gradation and strength of shading when spraying the color.

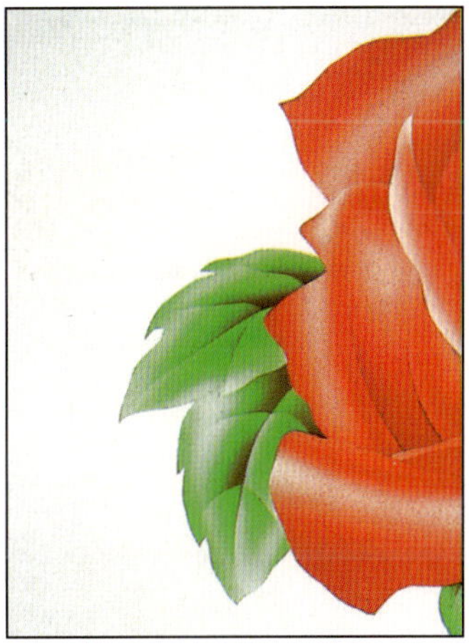

Using an Art Knife Blade
1 Although the leaves are shown here with sufficient contrast and form, they lack the surface texture and highlights which would enhance their appearance.

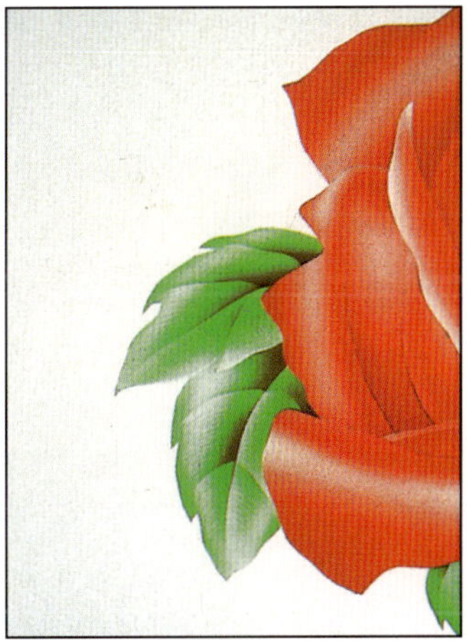

2 By using an art knife blade to scratch into the sprayed colour, the highlights in the leaves are defined as fine white lines.

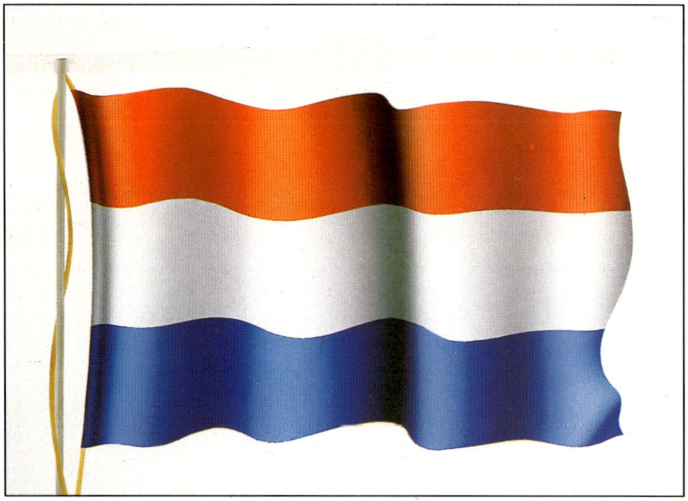

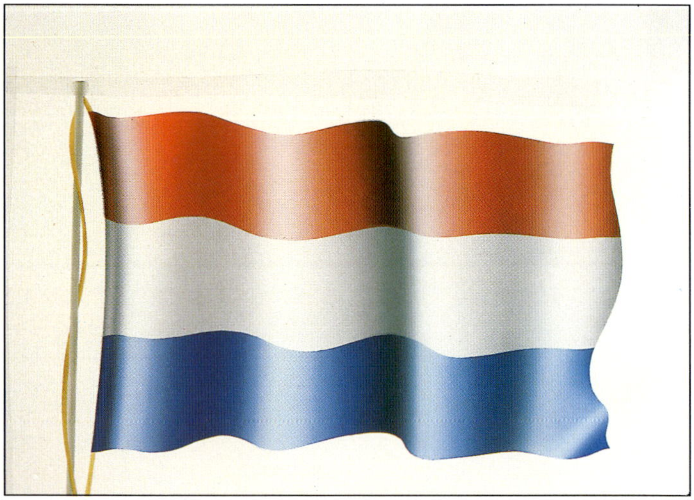

Using Opaque White
1 The artwork has been covered with masking film and the complete flag exposed for spraying, as it is intended to increase the contrast by overspraying highlights.

2 Opaque white is now sprayed freehand in the appropriate places, bearing in mind the chosen direction of the light source.

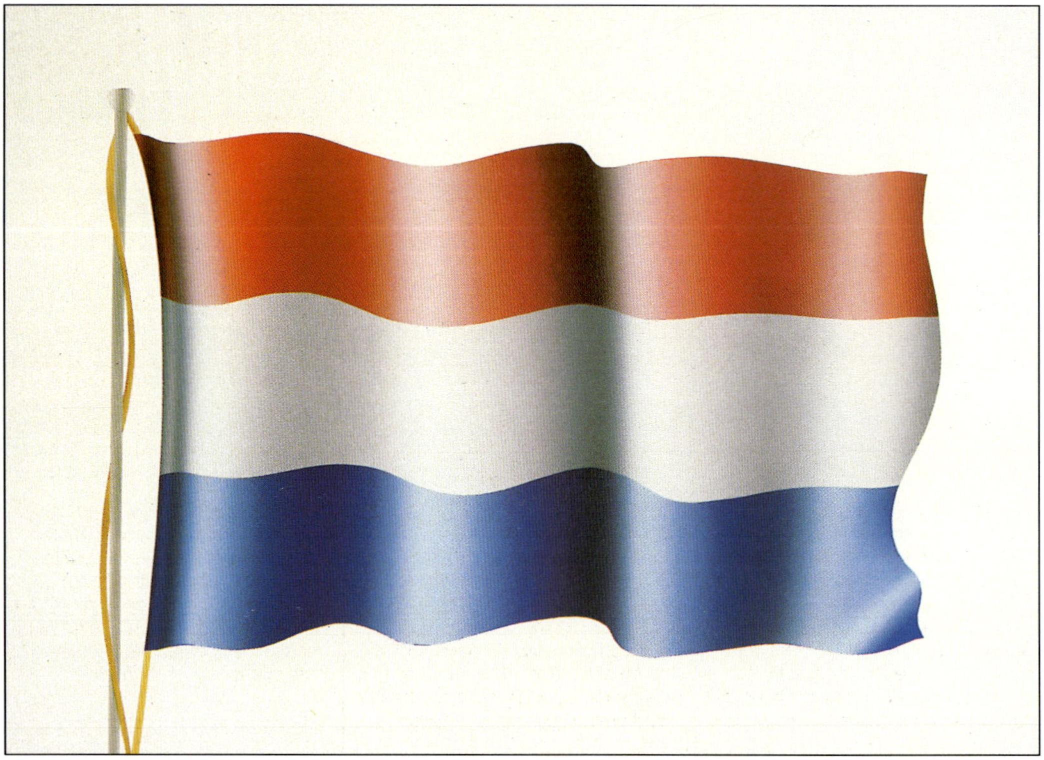

3 When the required depth of contrast has been achieved, the masking film is removed, revealing a more pronounced image.

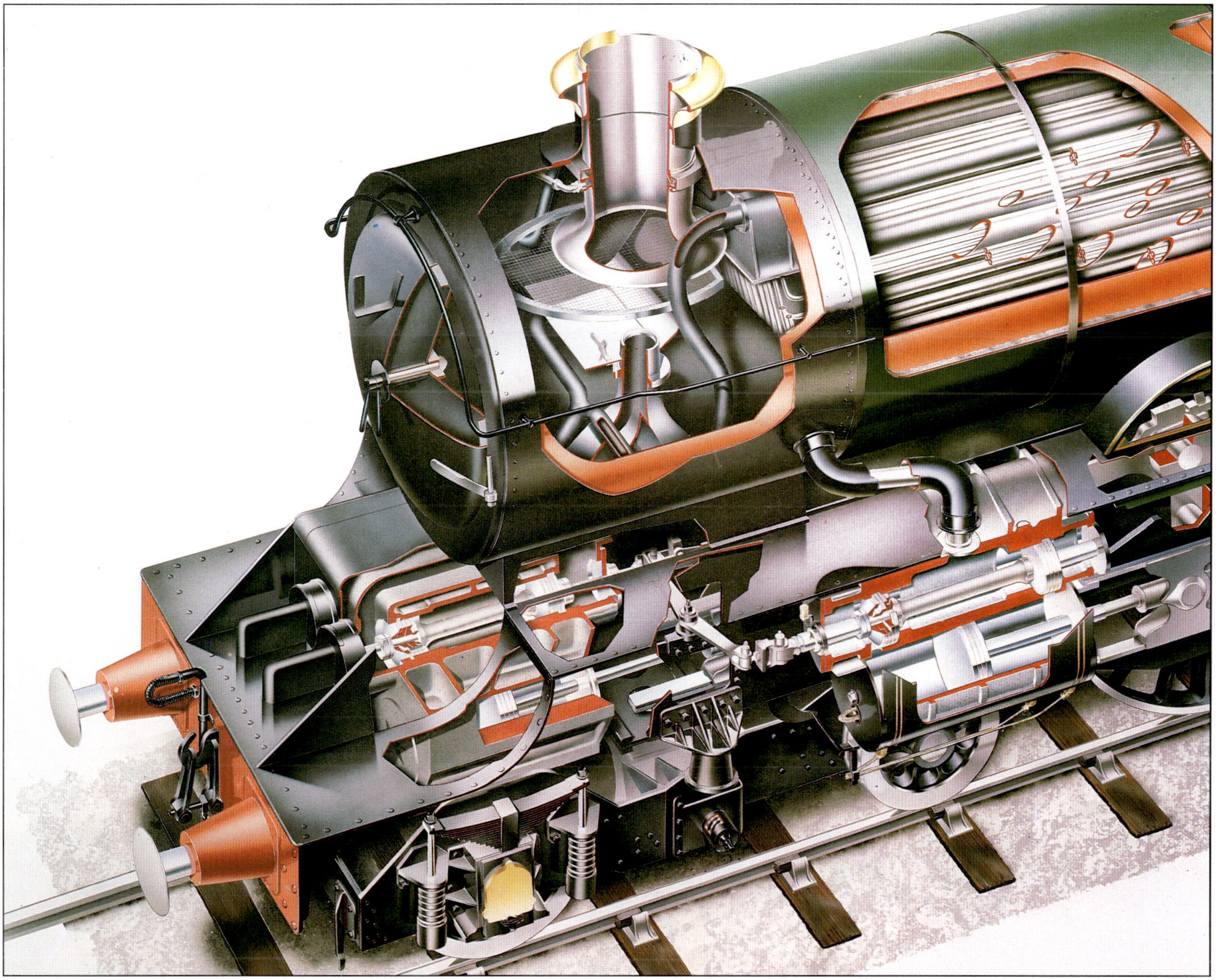

Great Western Railway King Class 4-6-0 locomotive *King Edward II* (detail)
James Weston

Without highlighting, most illustrations would look bare and unfinished. They would lack that final quality which enhances, complements and clarifies the image portrayed.

Highlighting is, therefore, along with RULING and LINING-IN, an important and integral part of an airbrushed illustration.

The example shown here is a detail of the complete illustration reproduced on page 102. All techniques described in the practical demonstrations of highlighting have been used on this illustration, with the exception of scratching out with an art knife blade, because this is not suited to the surface quality of the paper on which the illustration was drawn. The underlying white of the paper is evident on the highlight to the smoke box and boiler,and in the polished steel of the pistons and valve rods. Opaque white has been used on the suspension springs to the bogie axle, the lightening holes of the bogie wheels, some of the pipework and the running boards.

To appreciate fully the techniques of highlighting, reference should also be made to the various effects to be seen in many of the other finished illustrations.

KNOCKING BACK

When it is not possible to take a photograph of a subject in the exact conditions required to show it off to advantage, it is usual to resort to the technique of knocking back the less appropriate areas of the image by overspraying with either dark or light shades. To maintain interest and visual impact, it is not necessary to eliminate these areas completely.

This technique is used extensively in photo-retouching and can also be applied to airbrushed artwork when, for example, the background detail of an illustration appears to compete too strongly with the subject.

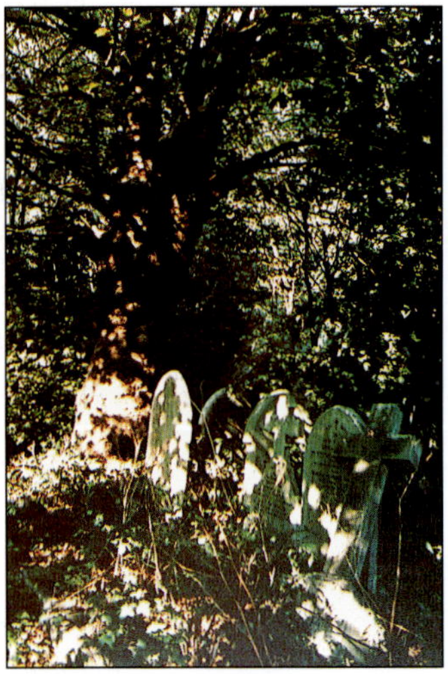

Darkening an Obtrusive Background

1 In this photograph the primary subjects are the headstones in the foreground. However, the intensity of the light is such that the highlights on the tree compete with those on the ground and on the headstones. To overcome this, it is necessary to knock back the tonal contrast in the tree. Prior to spraying, the photographic print is dry-mounted onto board.

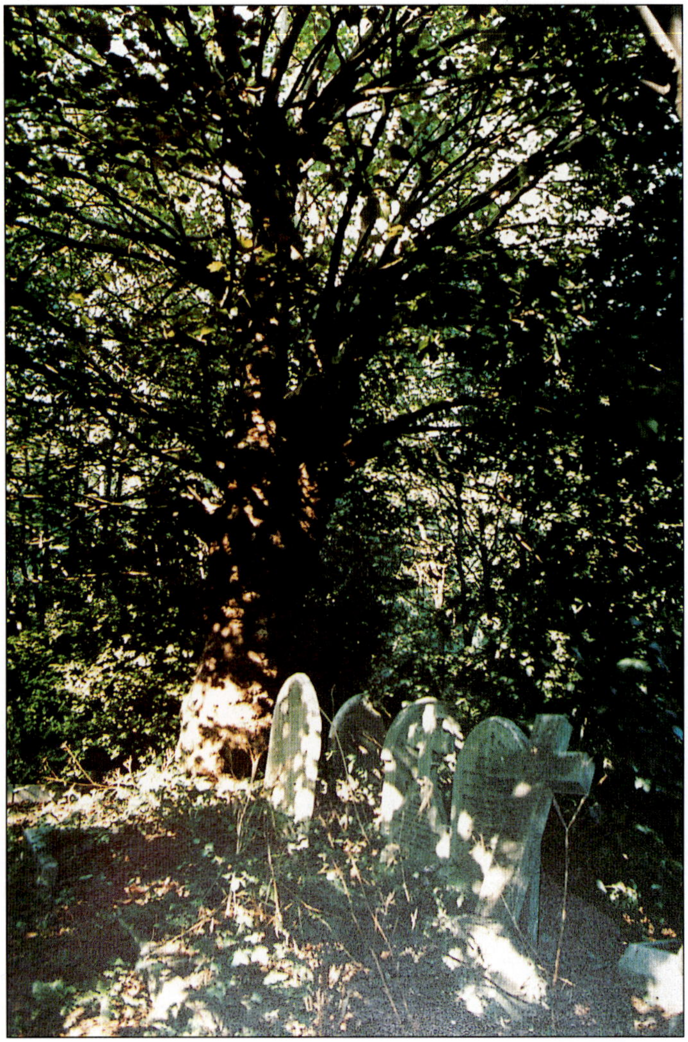

2 The whole print is covered with masking film, and the area of film covering the tree trunk is cut out and removed.

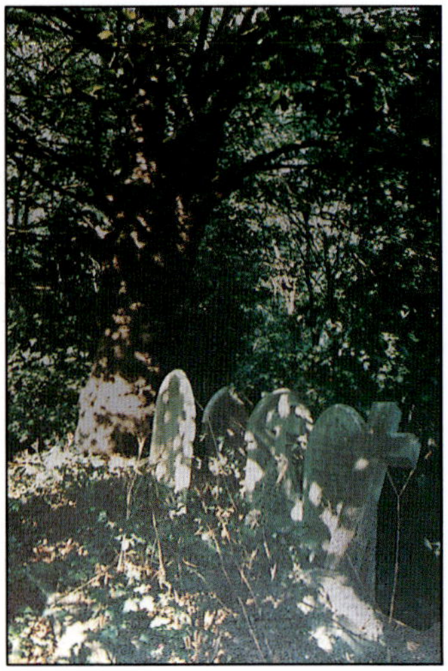

3 A dark tone of transparent color is sprayed over the exposed surface of the print.

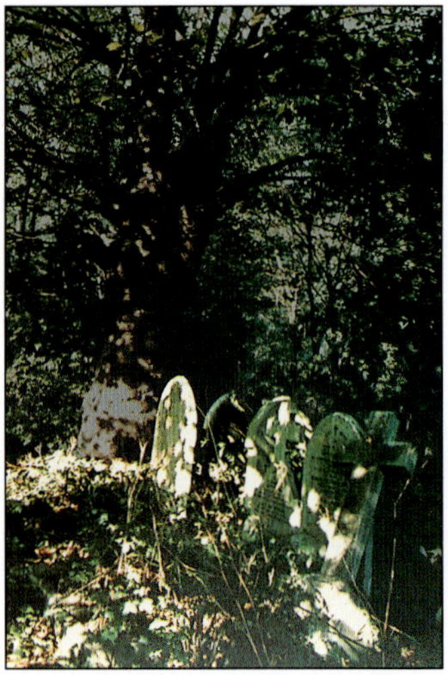

4 When the required depth of shading has been applied, the masking film is removed, leaving the foreground untouched and the tree trunk now appearing to be set back, but without losing its natural contrast.

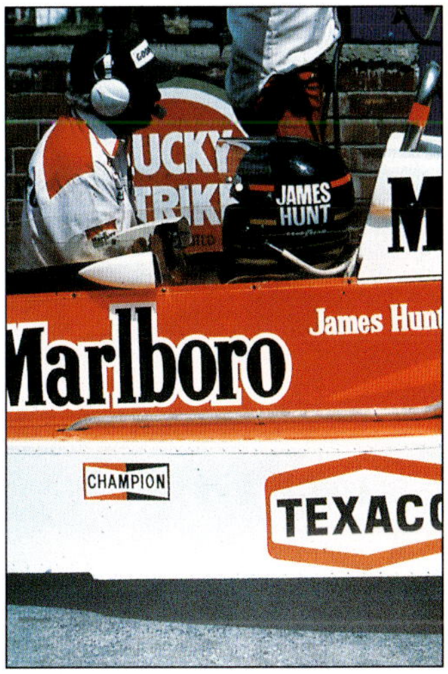

Weakening Background Tones and Contrast

1 This photograph shows a racing car with figures and details in the background. The latter appear, because of their close proximity, to be on the same plane as the car and therefore it is not absolutely clear where one ends and the other begins. To rectify this, the background must be knocked back. The first stage is to dry-mount the print onto board.

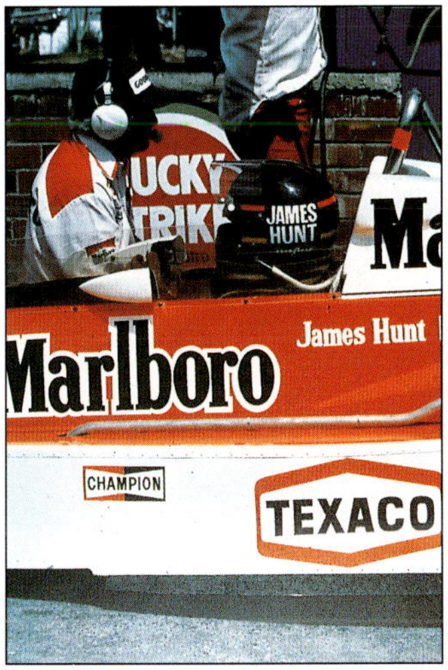

2 Masking film is placed over the whole print area and the sections covering the background and track are cut and removed for spraying.

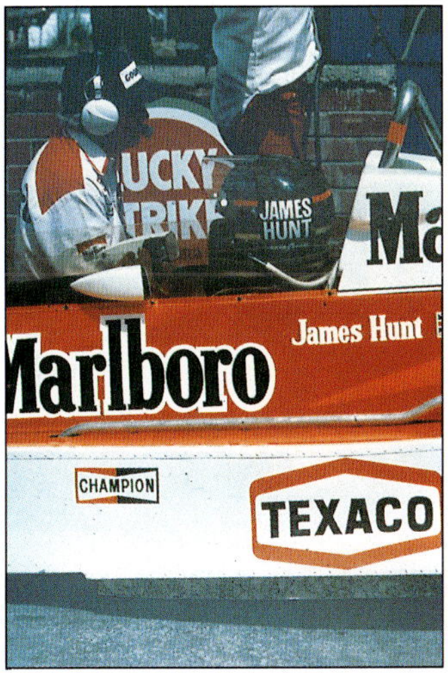

3 The exposed areas are over-sprayed with white. This is not so opaque as to destroy the definition, but it causes a surface effect of light "veiling" over these parts of the image.

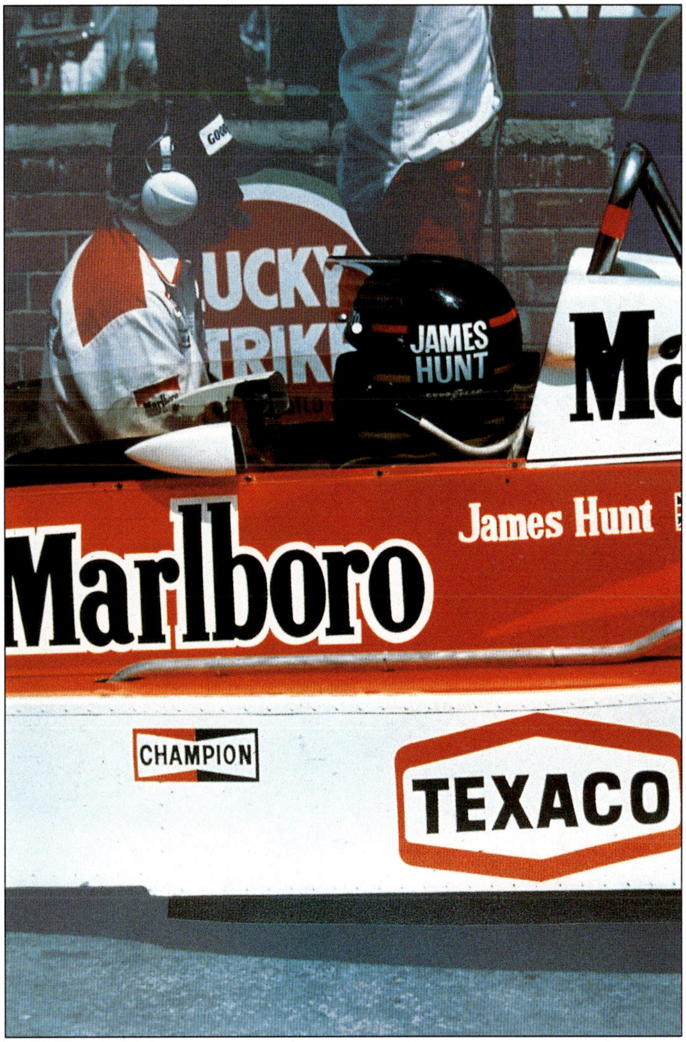

4 Once the revised shading clearly separates the background from the principal subject, the masking film is removed. The difference in clarity and emphasis between stage 1 and the completed image is obvious, and it has improved the impact of the picture.

LETTERING TECHNIQUES

The use of an airbrush in lettering is helpful when flat or gradated color is required as a backdrop, or when a characters or words are to be treated as objects and sprayed to give form. This is often seen in advertising, a typical example being the rendering of words and letters to create the impression that they are made of chrome, or some other highly reflective material.

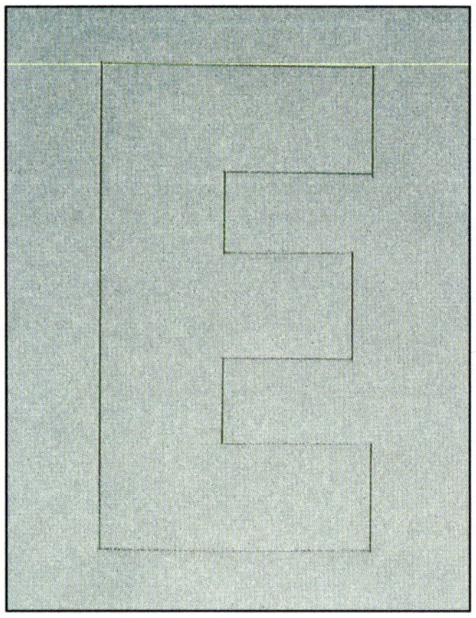

Using Self-adhesive Masking Film
1 The sans serif character "E" has been drawn on detail paper and transferred to board. A sheet of masking film is applied and the character cut out.

2 The film covering the character is removed, and the exposed shape is then sprayed in the required color and style of finish; here the paint has been gradated leaving a reflected highlight, or glow, to the lower part of the character.

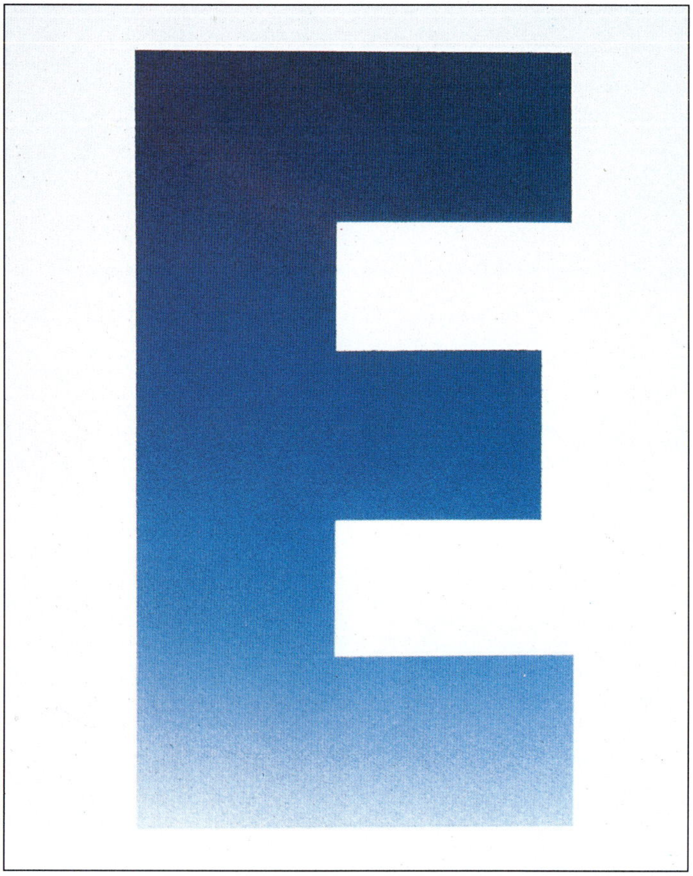

3 The masking film is removed, leaving a strong, hard-edged finish.

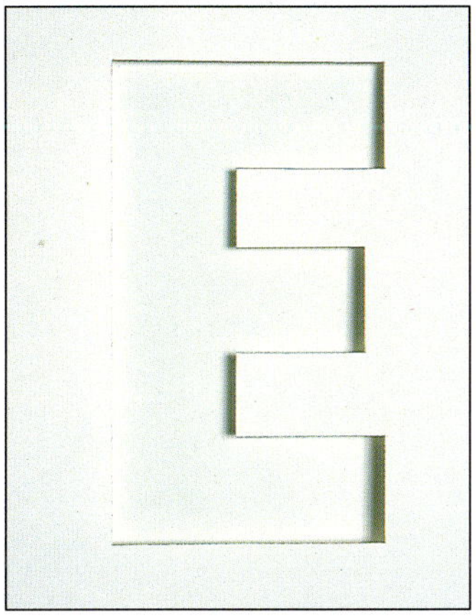

Using a Stencil

1 The same style of letter form is now drawn on stiff cardboard and the shape cut out. In the example shown, the character is comparatively easy to work with, having only straight lines and right angles. Others which incorporate curves and acute angles may appear neat and accurate at the stencil stage, but any slight imperfections in cutting will be more than noticeable on the finished artwork. Practice in cutting is therefore recommended.

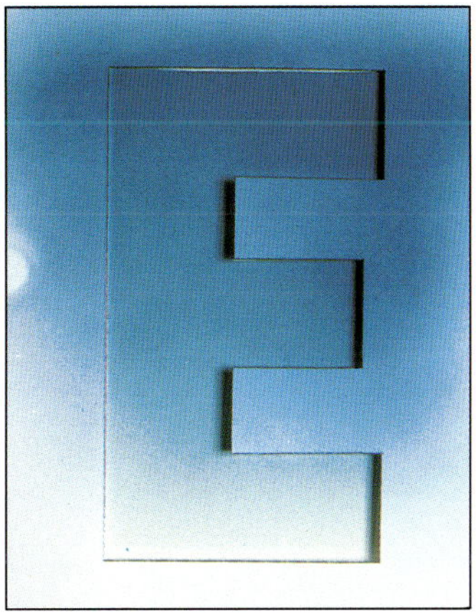

3 Removing the cardboard shows that the character has slightly soft edges as a result of residual color seeping under the edges of the stencil.

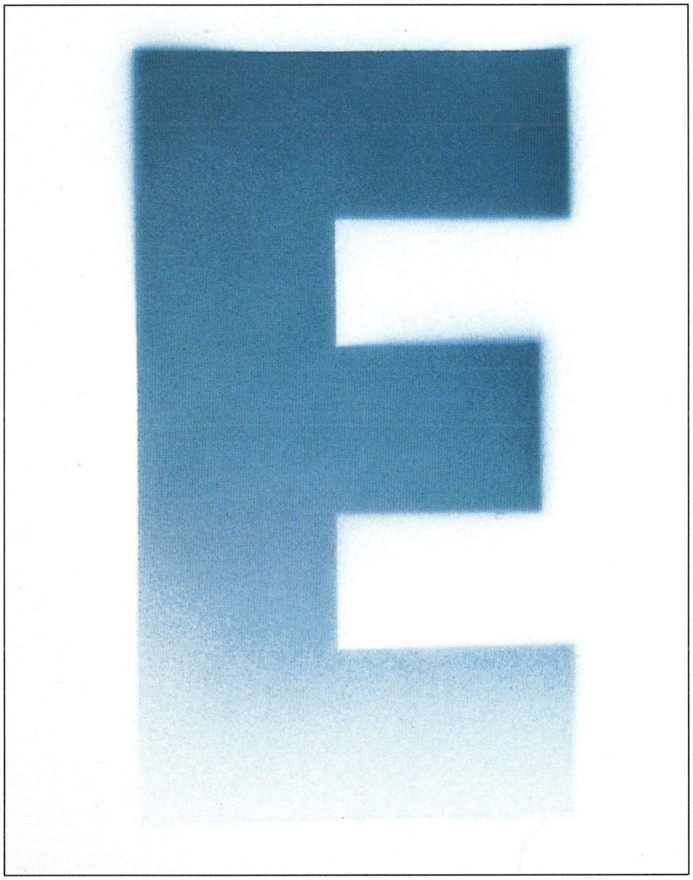

2 The cardboard stencil is held close to the board on which the finished artwork is to appear. It is then sprayed as required.

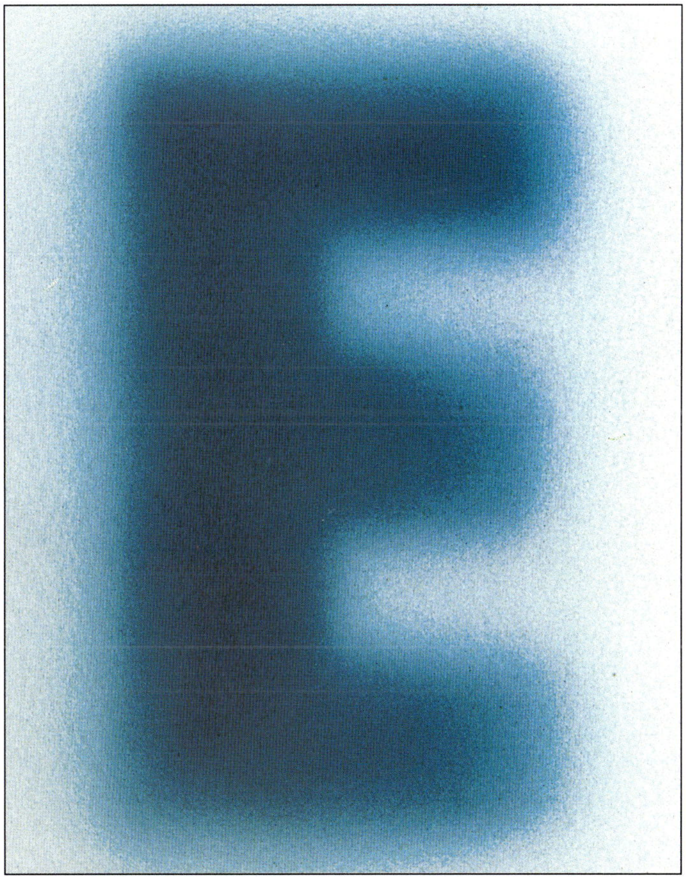

4 In this example the card stencil was held further away from the board, giving even softer and more blurred edges to the character.

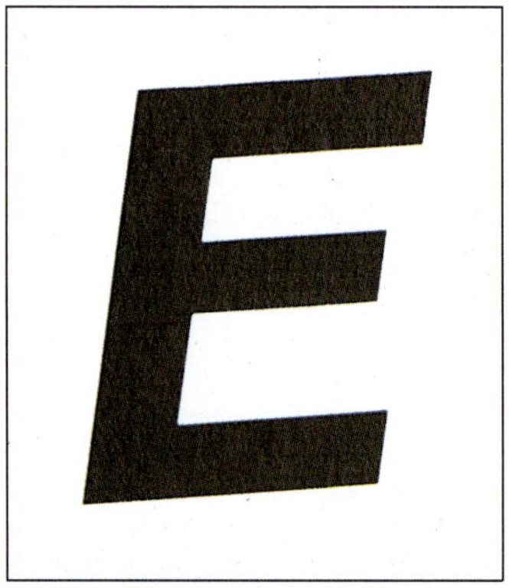

Using Dry-transfer Lettering

1 An italic character "E" has been rubbed down on board.

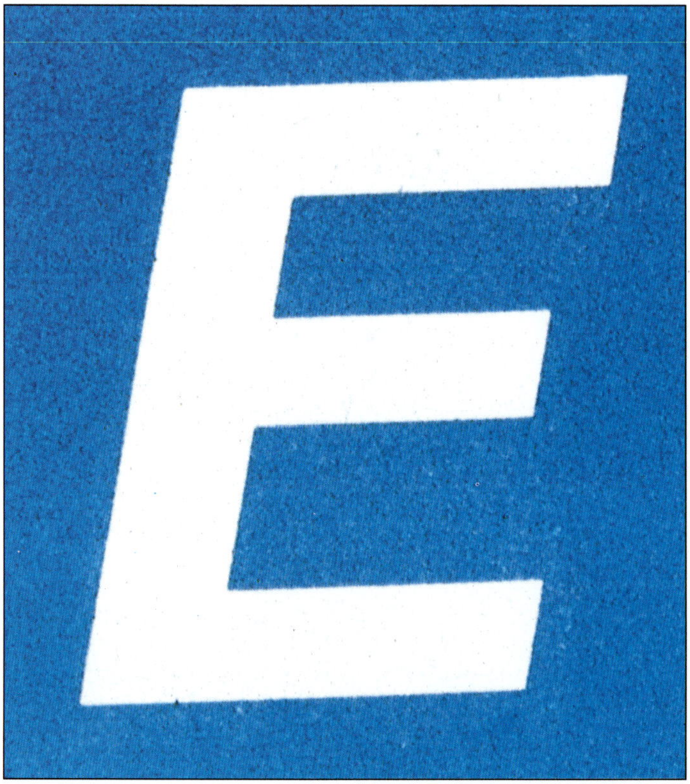

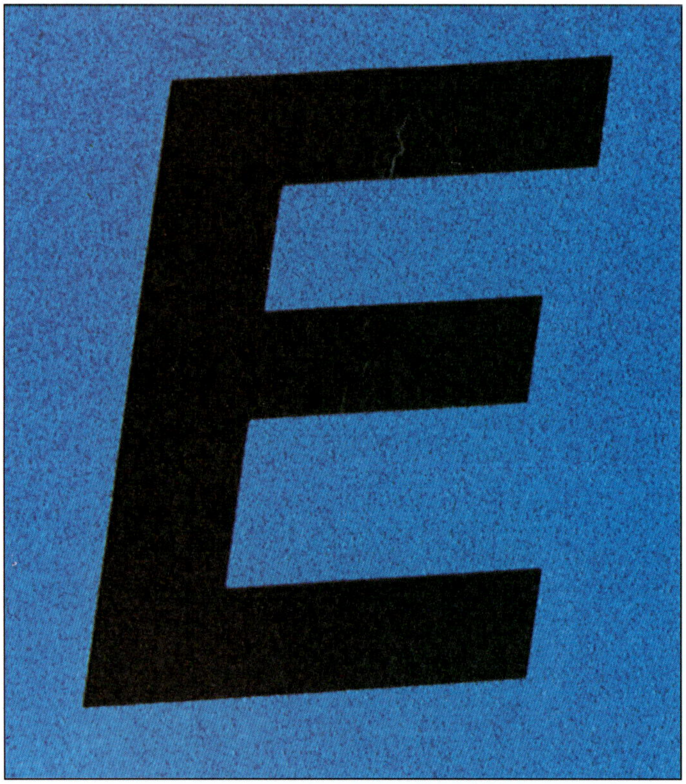

2 What will become the background or base color is then sprayed over the character and surrounding area.

3 The dry-transfer character is removed by using low-tack drafting tape to pick it up. Although not shown in this example, it is obviously possible to spray a second color over both the character and existing base color. Further characters may also be laid on top of the base color; when the area is re-sprayed and the characters removed, they would appear on the artwork in the original base color. However, extreme care is needed in removing the dry-transfer lettering so as not to damage the sprayed color underneath or, indeed, the surrounding color.

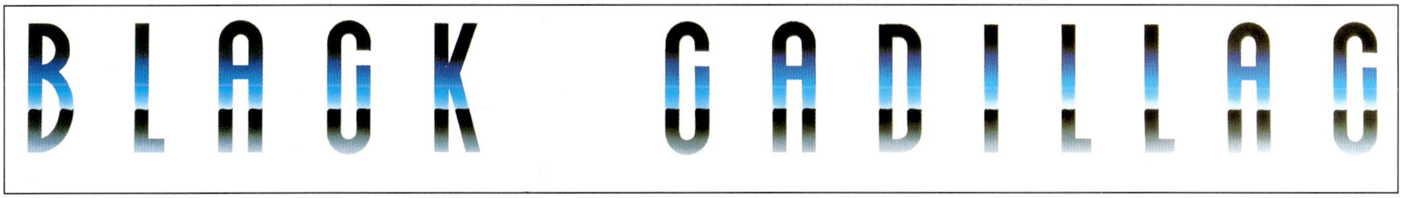

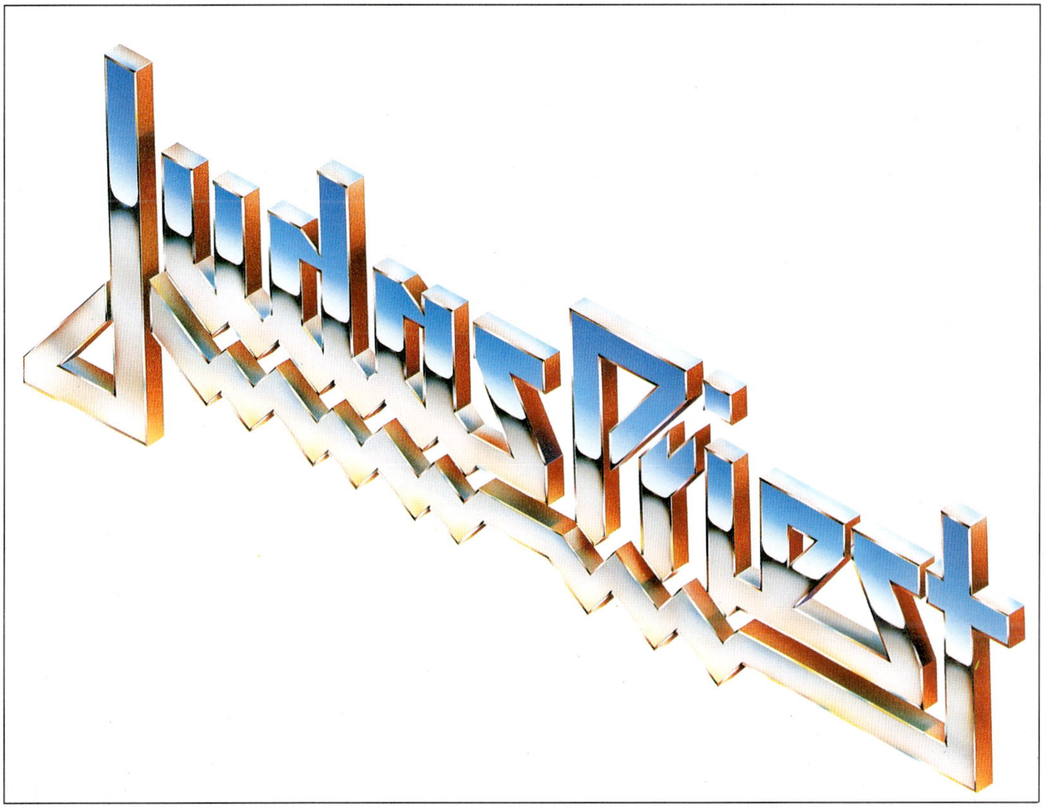

Black Cadillac
Dave Bull

This is the title from a poster illustration which has been hand-drawn in a style befitting the period of the car. The rendering has been executed to make the lettering appear black and shiny. Again, as with the body of the car, pure black has not been used – you rarely see a pure black with no color bias – but blue and blue-black have been chosen. The top half of the lettering, down to the hard-edged mask representing the reflection of an imaginary horizon line, starts with an opaque blue-black gradated into deep blue which in turn gradates into a very pale blue just above the horizon. From the horizon line down, gray-black has been sprayed in a GRADATED TONE toward the base of each character. To guarantee an equal and even number of gradated tones, all lettering would have been masked and sprayed at the same time.

The complete illustration from which this title was taken can be seen on pages 108 and 109.

Judas Priest
Mark Wilkinson

The lettering reproduced above is a classic example of how two words have been rendered with an airbrush which almost makes them an illustration on their own. It is representative of a trend which started in the 1960s and shows little sign of abating. As a style, it is very popular in advertising and the music world; the example above is the name of a group airbrushed for the tour posters.

The approach has been to create an impression of a highly polished and smooth-surfaced, metallic logo. As a technique, it follows closely with that described for CHROME EFFECTS, except that an intentionally exaggerated choice of colors has been used. Hard-edged FILM MASKING has been used throughout, with an extensive use of reflected colors. The whole image relies solely on the color and shading to hold it together, as no lining-in has been used. In masking letterforms which are shown with beveled edges, accurate and neat mask cutting is essential, for a slight imperfection would soon "jump" out and spoil the illustration.

LINE CONTROL

Line control techniques develop, with practice, the skills needed in controlling and handling the airbrush. In application, any of the techniques shown can be used as part of the general process of arriving at a finished piece of artwork and, more often, in adding the finishing touches which enhance the detail of an illustration.

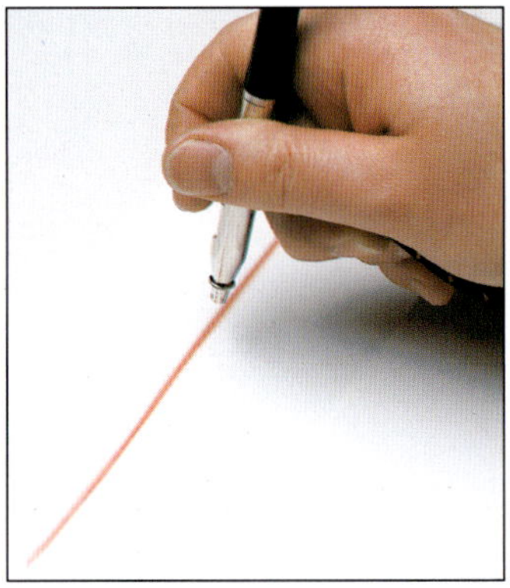

Freehand Spraying
This photograph demonstrates a vital element in the ability to control an airbrush. It shows the freehand use of an airbrush to produce fine, straight lines. The initial problem when first attempting this is the tendency to spray lines which curve toward the ends; this is because of the natural, flowing movement of the hand and a conscious effort is required to prevent it.

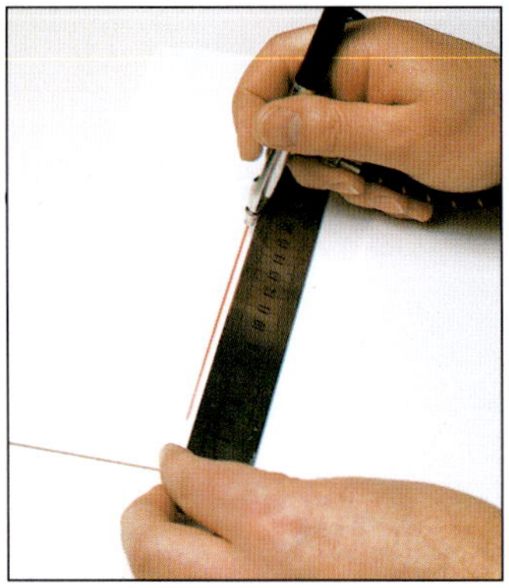

Using a Ruler
This photograph shows a line being sprayed with the aid of a ruler. The ruler must be held at an angle until the line is completed with the correct air pressure. When using this technique on finished artwork and with a mask to protect the ends of the line, it is always advisable to start and finish the line on the masking film rather than at the edges of the masked shape, to avoid including any irregularity caused by starting and stopping the flow of medium through the airbrush.

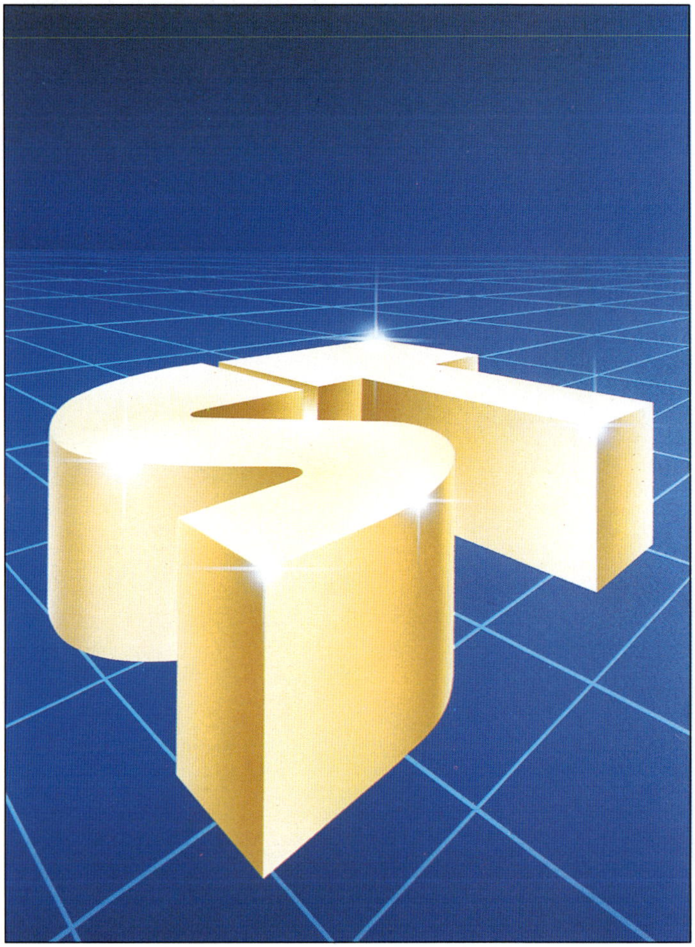

Using Masking Film
This illustration shows a magazine cover, on which the initials ST have been drawn three-dimensionally on a base representing a two-point perspective grid. The technique involved covering the artwork with masking film and cutting along each of the grid lines: these lines were left covered while the base color of dark blue was sprayed. When the color was the right density, the film was removed and a paler blue was oversprayed to tint the grid lines.

LINING-IN

While the major part of an illustration may be completed with an airbrush, it is unlikely to be left without any drawn or hand-painted lining-in. The reason is to establish and delineate detail which could not successfully be applied with the airbrush, regardless of the skill of the illustrator. Lining-in becomes, therefore, a very important part of the process of completing an illustration and should be applied with the same care as that given to the airbrushing. So often, beginners to airbrushing techniques see lining-in as a boring chore–the final stages in completing their artwork–with the consequence that a good piece of airbrushing can easily be ruined by rushed and poorly applied hand-work.

Lining-in may be completed using pencil, paint, crayon or ink, or a combination of media and with any of the wide range of drawing aids available to illustrators such as ellipse templates or French curves.

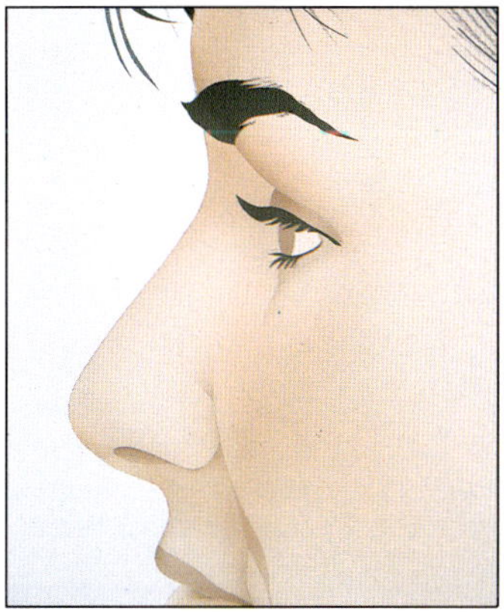

1 The basic details and form for a face profile have been sprayed in using various masks and stencils as appropriate.

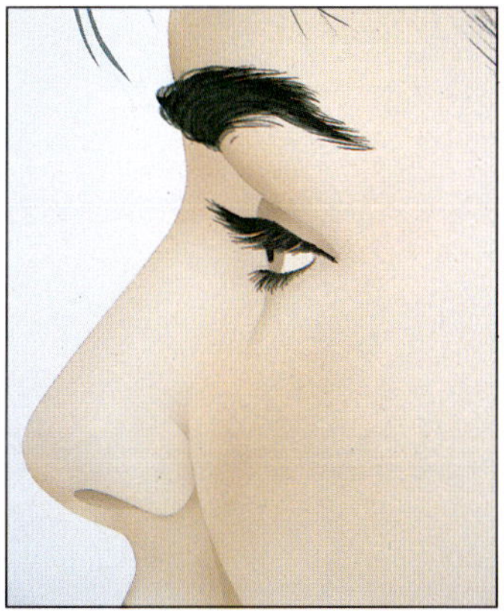

2 Freehand brushwork is now applied to bring out the finer details such as the eyelashes, the iris, and the eyebrows.

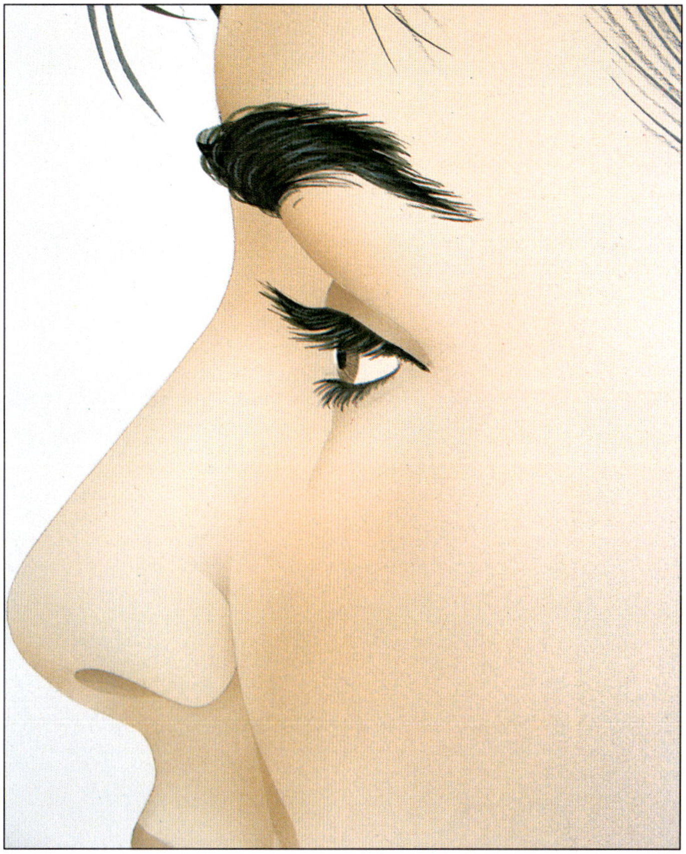

3 Finally, using a sharpened white pencil, highlights have been drawn in to complete the picture.

LIQUID MASKING

Liquid masking is achieved by using a rubber-based solution which is applied to the surface with a technical pen. The commercially available varieties of liquid masking, also known as masking fluid, are usually tinted to assist in their application. When dry, they leave a water- and paint-repellent film. Color can be sprayed over and around this rubbery skin formed by the dried masking, and the mask is subsequently peeled or rubbed away, taking care not to damage the surface color.

Masking fluid is particularly useful for covering small and intricate details, when more conventional methods of masking become cumbersome and difficult to cut accurately. It can be laid on a clean, unsprayed surface or overlaid on areas previously sprayed. However, on certain surfaces such as rough-finished boards and papers, extreme care is needed when removing the masking to avoid surface fibers being damaged. If in doubt, it is advisable to test the fluid on a sample of the paper or board to be used.

On completion of each stage in using masking fluid, the brush used to apply it should be thoroughly cleaned in fresh water, never the same water which is used to mix the colours for spraying or cleaning the airbrush. Before proceeding with successive stages of spraying, it is essential that each application of masking fluid is allowed to dry thoroughly.

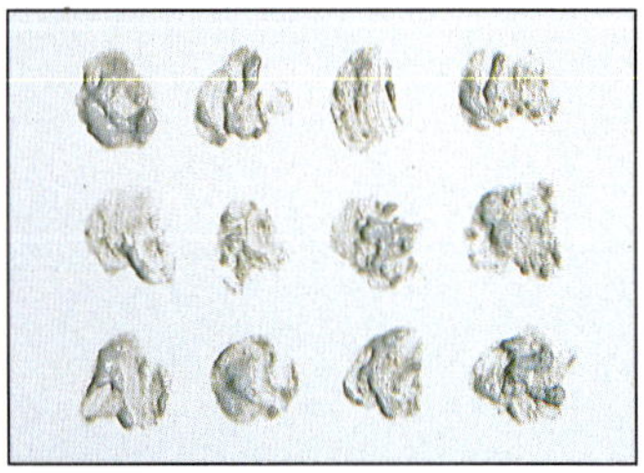

Dot Pattern Sample

1 In this example, liquid masking is used to create a layered dot pattern in selected colors. In the first stage, twelve roughly equal spots of fluid are laid down in three horizontal rows.

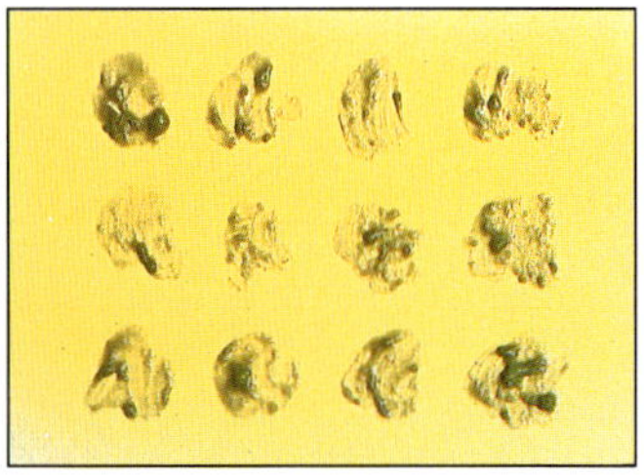

2 Here the first glaze of transparent watercolor has been sprayed over and around the masking fluid.

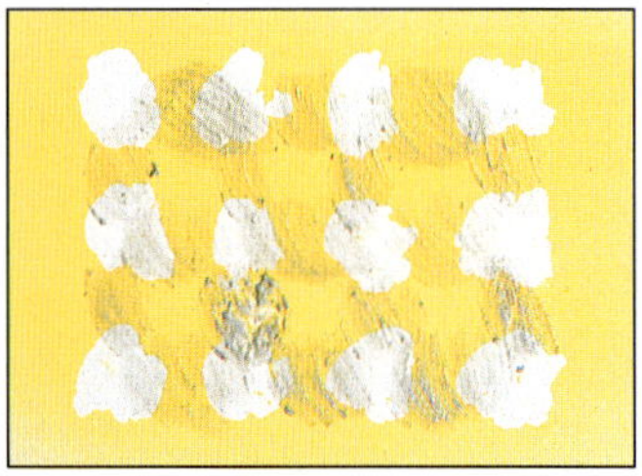

3 The original twelve spots of masking fluid have been removed by careful rubbing with a finger, leaving the white of the board showing in their place. A second pattern of masking fluid dots is then applied and allowed to dry.

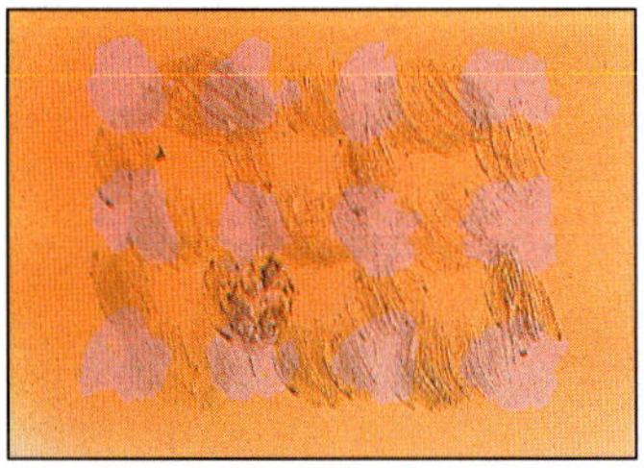

4 A second glaze of color is sprayed over the first. The true color is apparent where it covers the white spaces left by the first application of masking fluid.

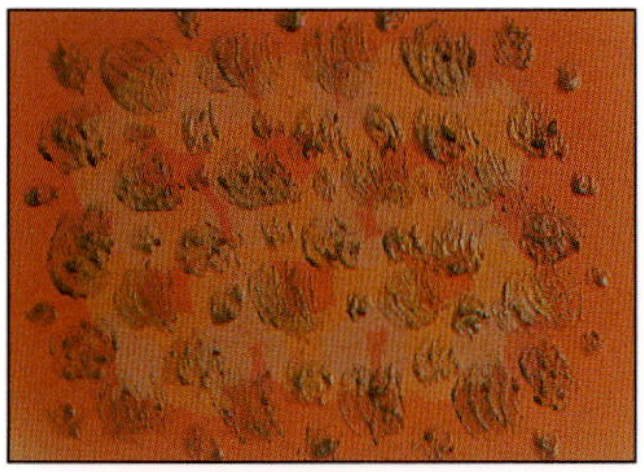

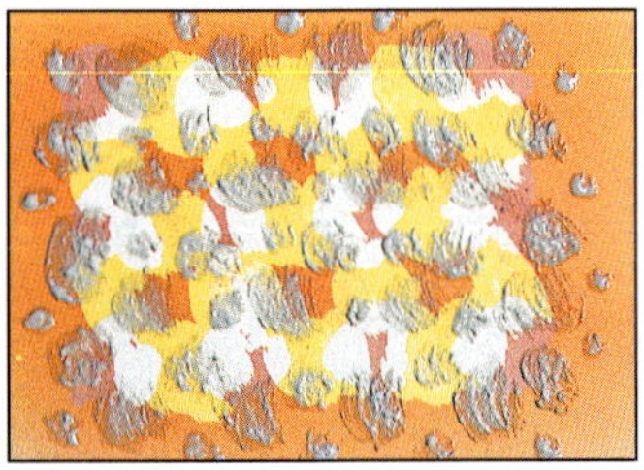

5 The second layer of masking fluid is removed and a third applied. The white areas of the board which are visible are the result of the second layer of masking fluid overlapping the first.

6 A third glaze of color is sprayed over the whole area.

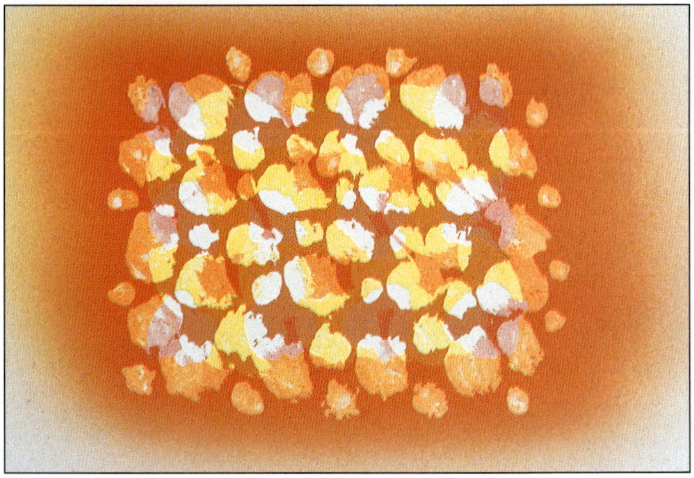

7 The final result is visible on the removal of the third layer of masking fluid. Naturally it is possible to add several layers of masking fluid and an equal number of glazes as desired. It is also possible to apply the masking fluid within clearly defined parameters on occasions when self-adhesive masking film or any other type of mask is inappropriate. Its use depends very much on what is to be achieved.

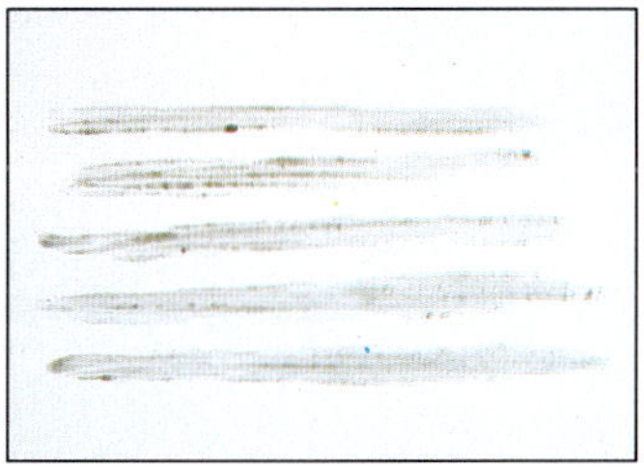

Partial Removal of Liquid Masking

1 Five horizontal stripes of masking fluid are applied to the board.

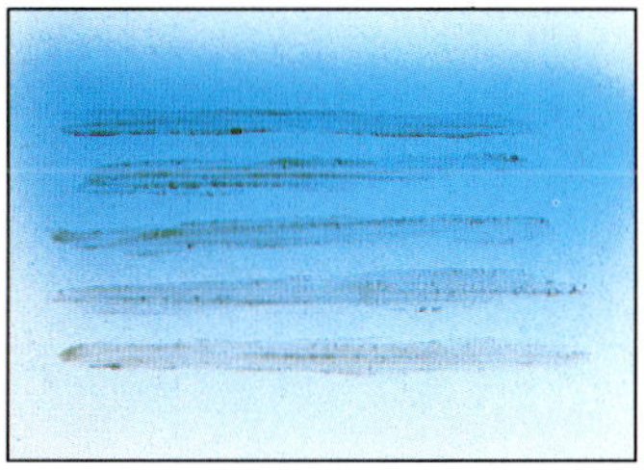

2 The first glaze of transparent watercolor has been sprayed.

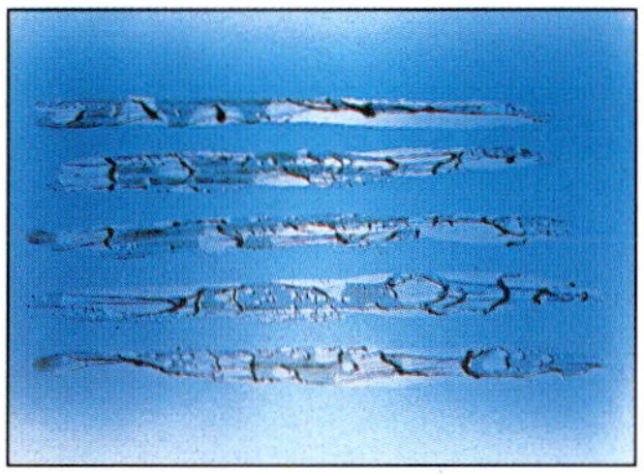

3 In this stage the first layer of masking fluid has not been completely removed. This is deliberate and is achieved by rubbing a finger unevenly over the surface. When the required amount of white surface is visible, a second glaze of color is sprayed.

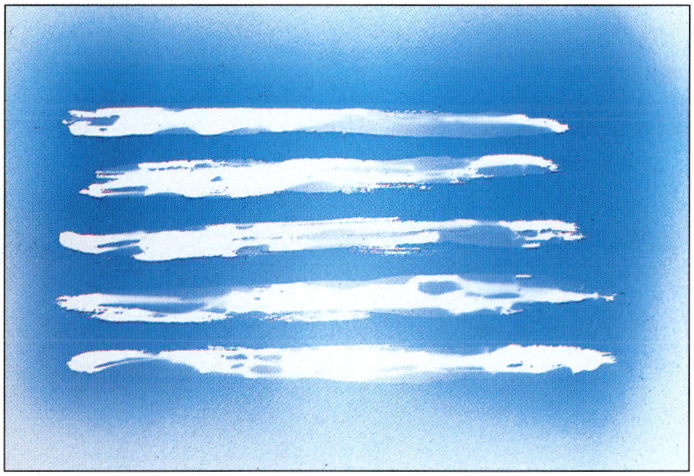

4 The remaining masking fluid is finally removed, with the first glaze showing clearly on the stripes and appearing visually at the front, while the second glaze appears as a backdrop. Again, as in the first example, additional layers of both liquid masking and glazes could be added if desired.

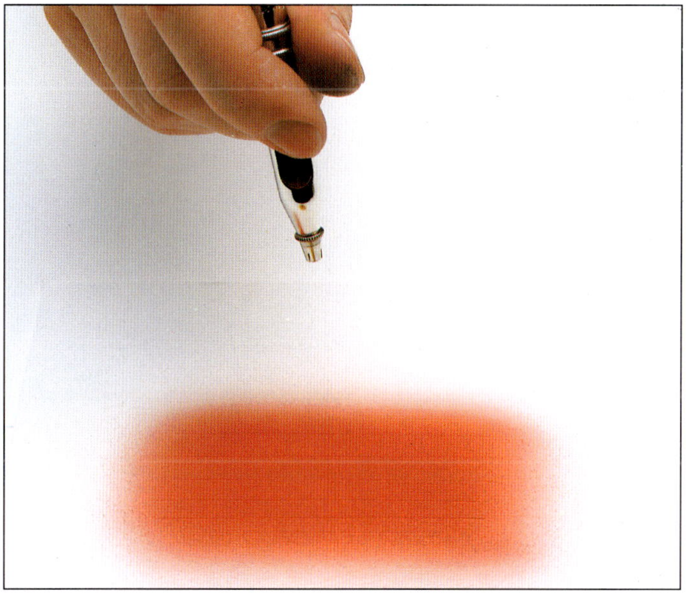

Using a Ruling Pen

Liquid masking applied with a ruling pen allows for fine linear detail to be drawn where the white of the artwork or a previously sprayed base color shows through after spraying. In all cases the masking fluid must be allowed to dry thoroughly before spraying, just as the sprayed color must also be allowed to dry before removing the fluid.

This particular technique requires extreme care in the removal of the masking fluid because the sprayed color is easily damaged. While it is possible to draw straight lines with masking fluid on a rough-surfaced board, a hard china-clay surface is preferable, as the fibers of the board are less likely to be damaged by "furring" and removal of all of the masking

1 In this example, a series of horizontal lines have been ruled using masking fluid. These are then oversprayed.

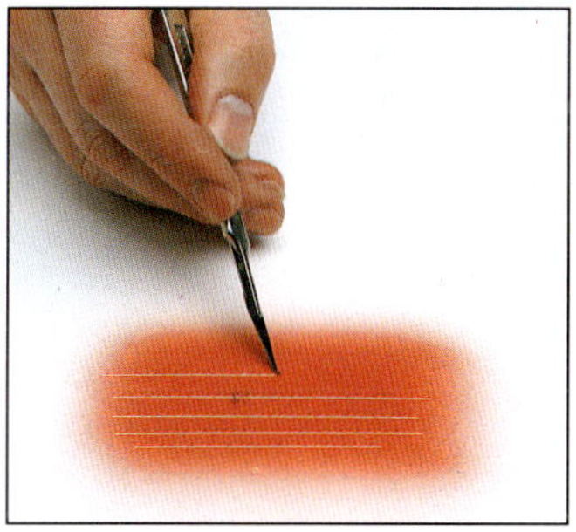

2 When spraying with watercolor or gouache, it is advisable to remove the dried masking fluid with the tip of an art knife blade, as shown here. With waterproof acrylics, it is possible to remove the mask with a fingertip, although care is required when spraying to prevent a build-up of paint that binds the fluid permanently to the artwork.

LOOSE MASKING

This refers to the use of paper and cardboard masks which, depending on use, give a clear but soft delineation to the sprayed edge. Besides giving specific effects, loose masking is a quick method of spraying areas without having to resort to masking film, as long as care is taken with the direction of residual spraying. Reference should also be made to ANGLED SPRAYING, CARDBOARD MASKING and TORN PAPER MASKING.

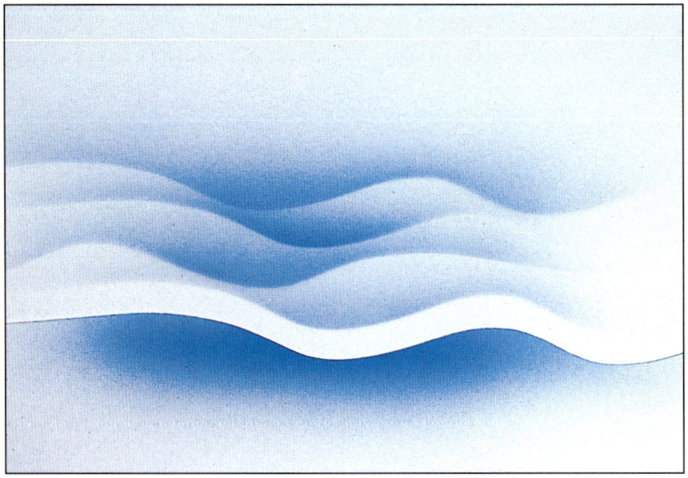

Using Paper Masks
1 Paper masks cut accurately to a pre-determined shape are laid directly on the artwork and sprayed over with a variety of different shades. Because the paper is directly in contact with the artwork, the edges are fairly well defined, with only a small amount of residual paint seeping underneath.

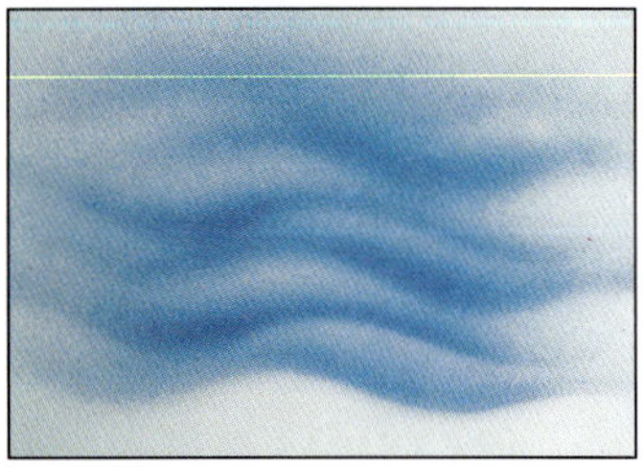

2 In this example the paper masks are held a distance away from the artwork, which allows for more color to spread under the mask. This gives a much softer finish to the edges; this softness naturally increases the further away the paper mask is from the artwork.

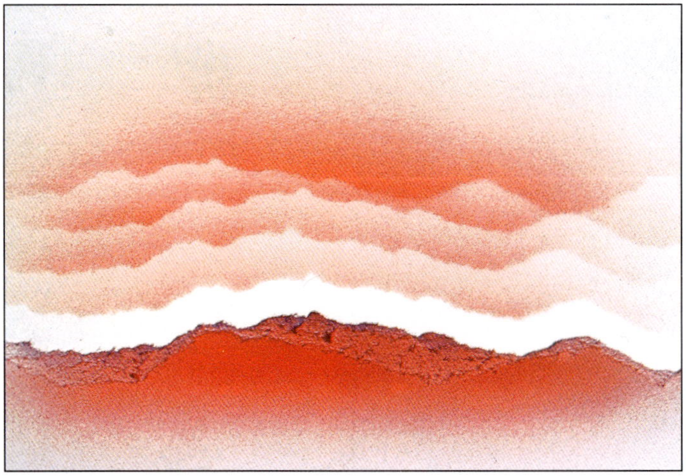

3 Here paper masks are used again, but on this occasion the paper is torn rather than cut. This example shows the effect when the mask is laid directly on the artwork. The irregular texture of the torn edge is accurately reproduced.

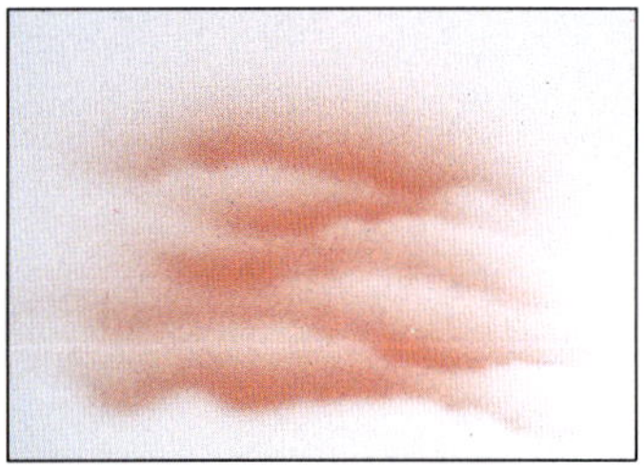

4 The same torn paper masks are used here, but held away from the artwork, giving the softer effect.

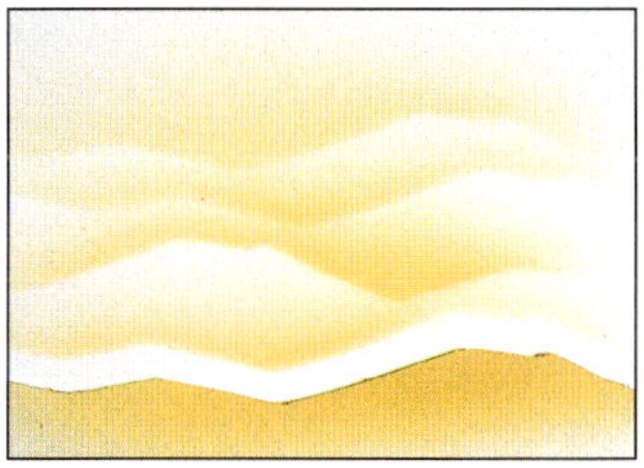

Using Cardboard
1 Cut cardboard, as shown here, gives very much the same effect as cut paper, although it is possible because of the increased thickness to limit the amount of residual color seeping under the mask.

2 The cut cardboard is used again, but held away from the artwork, giving softer edges.

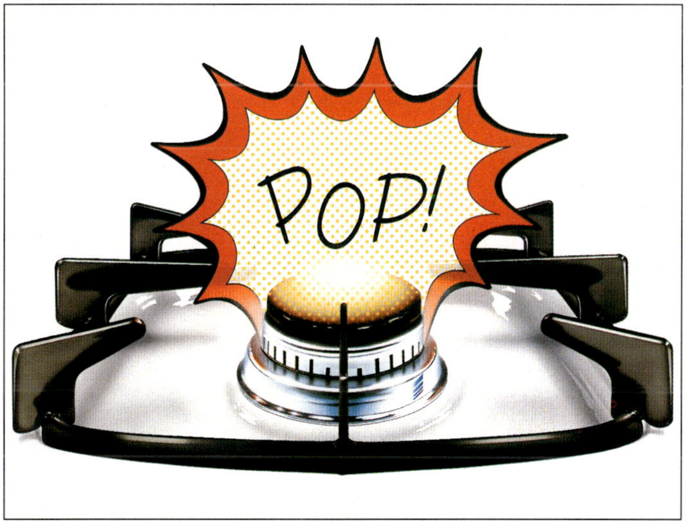

Pop!
Brian Robson

An airbrushed illustration will often show the use of many different techniques. Although the effect is often heavily dependent on FILM MASKING, it is unlikely that an illustration will be completed without recourse to more than one masking or spraying technique. The above illustration is a case in point: it shows the use of loose masking to achieve a particular finish. While the majority of the color has been sprayed with hard-edged masks, the darker shades on the cast-iron saucepan supports have been sprayed with a loose mask, held slightly away from the surface of the artwork. This gives the impression of representing the glossy enameled finish of the real thing, without appearing too severe, as harder contrasts would make them look chromed.

When assessing which technique should be used, film masking or loose masking, consideration needs to be given to the desired finish and, as important, the materials and surface finishes to be rendered in other parts of the illustration. Yet again, pre-planning is useful.

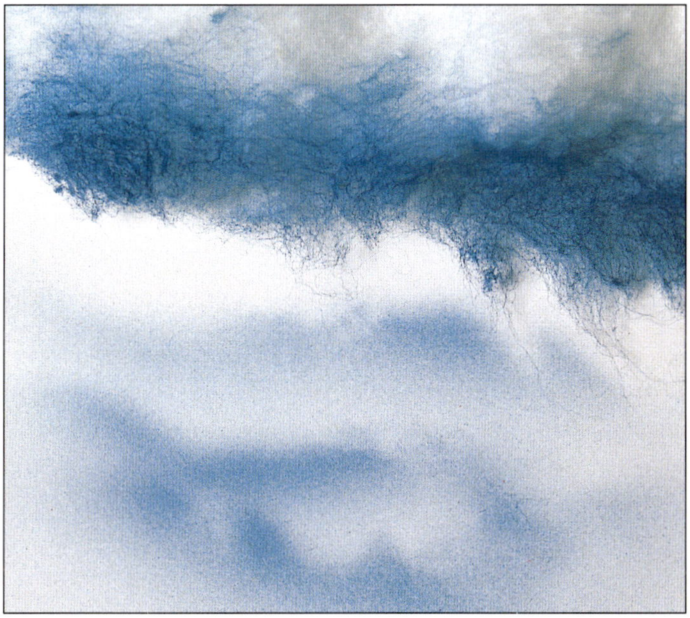

Using Absorbent Cotton
To enable even more hazy, abstract shapes to be sprayed, cotton is taped in place on the artwork and oversprayed. This can be extremely effective when, for example, stylized skies with soft clouds are needed, although care is required not to spray over the tape as well as the cotton, or to allow residual spray to encroach and cause the silhouette of the tape to become visible.

OVERSPRAYING

Keen observation of the range of values in color, light and shade will make it apparent that the base color of an object is rarely seen by itself. The reflective nature of light means that other colors will be included, usually from objects or colors immediately surrounding the principal object. Additionally, the composition of some subjects means that the colors and shades cannot be separated and sprayed in isolation from each other. This then requires the application of overspraying to model shape and form. The use of overspraying when airbrushing is similar to overpainting and gives depth and body to a subject.

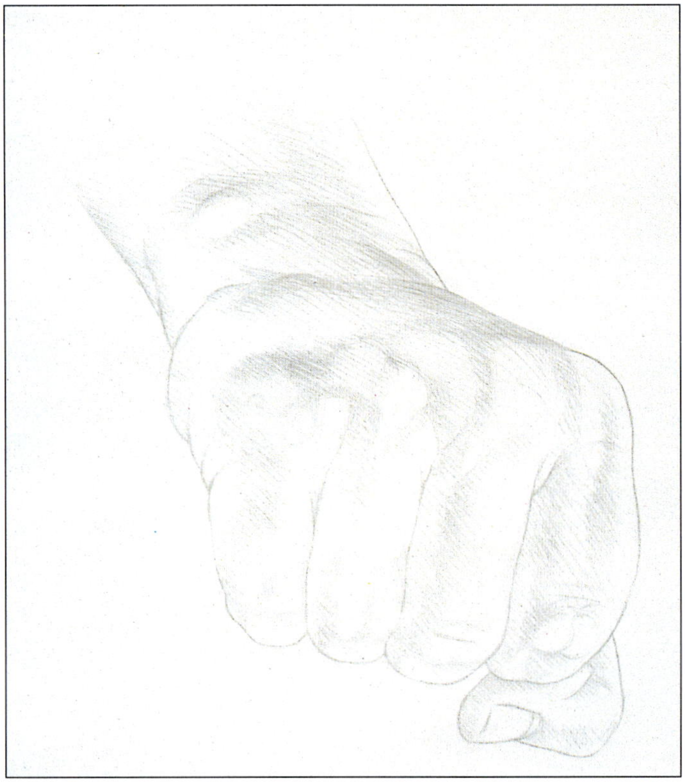

1 The preliminary drawing of a clenched fist has been drawn in pencil on detail paper, with the tonal values shaded in. These will be a useful reference when spraying the image.

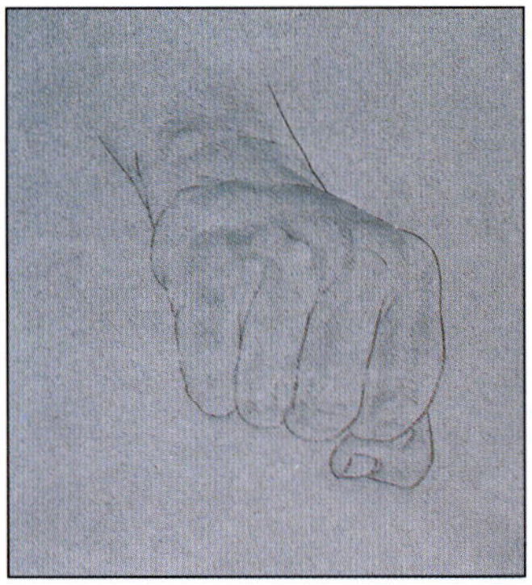

2 Once the drawing has been corrected, the outlines are transferred to illustration board.

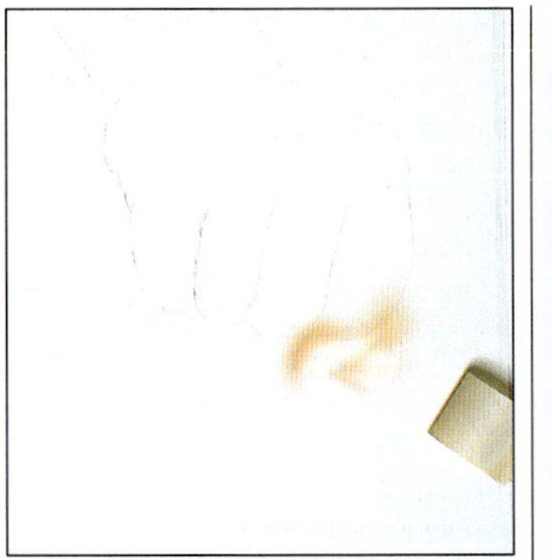

3 The drawing is covered with masking film and the complete exterior shape of the fist and the finger joints are cut in the film. Starting with the thumb, the mask is removed and hinged; the spraying is carried out with a medium shade using an appropriate color in gouache.

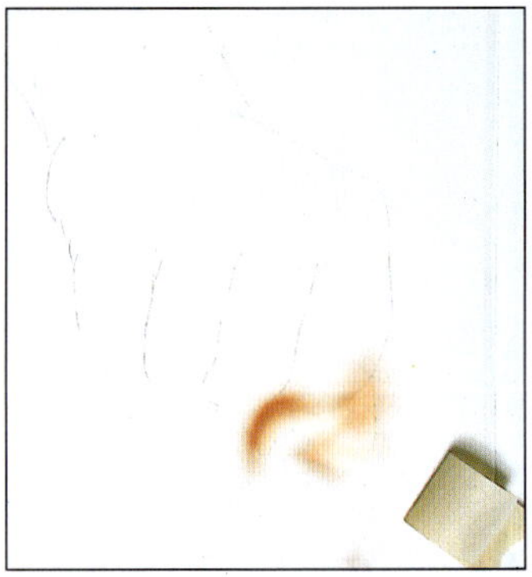

4 Darker shades are added over the medium ones, thus increasing the apparent depth of the subject.

5-8 The spraying sequence now proceeds with each individual finger until all have been modeled with the airbrush using the medium shades. At all times the separate mask pieces are cut and hinged to allow for accurate repositioning. In a subject such as this, good control of the airbrush is essential due to some areas requiring a hard-edged finish, where one finger is touching its neighbor, but where a finger joins the back of the hand, a subtle freehand technique is required. The depth of contrast must also be carefully controlled, so that on completion of the modeling of the form, there is no evidence of the sequence followed.

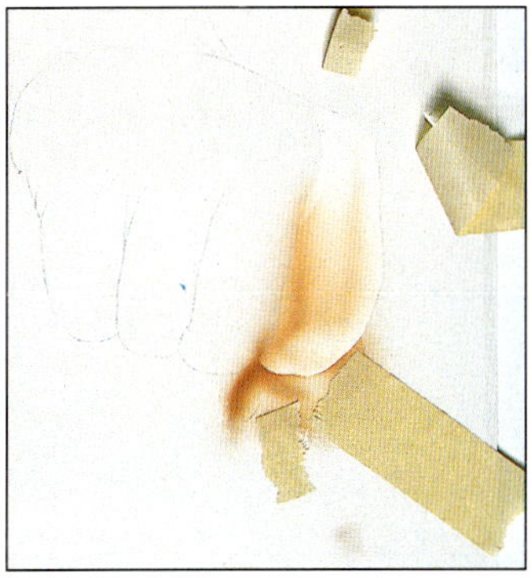

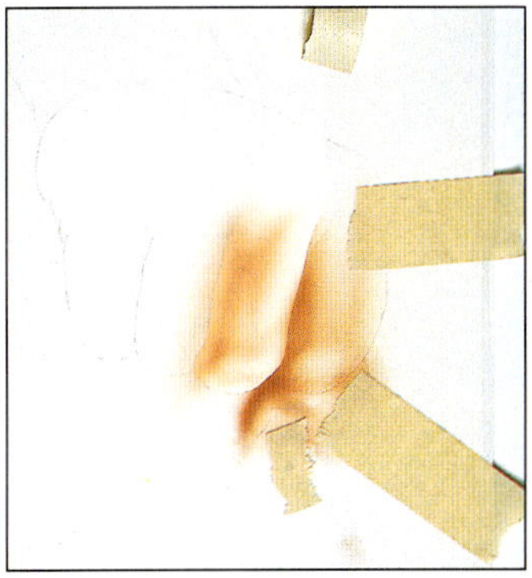

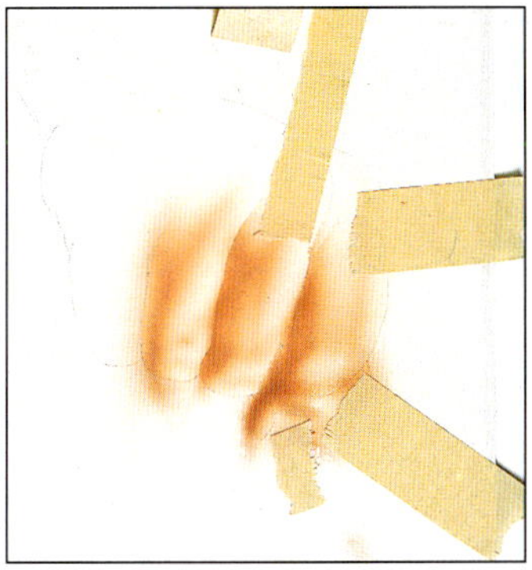

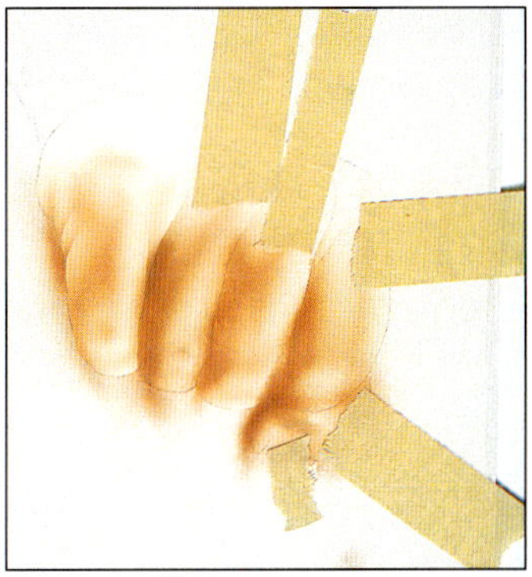

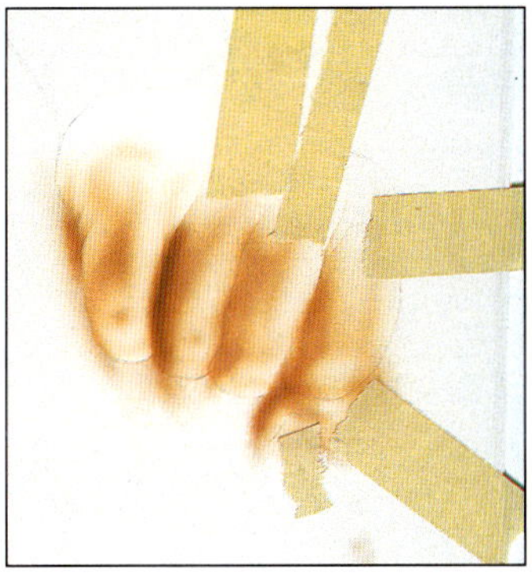

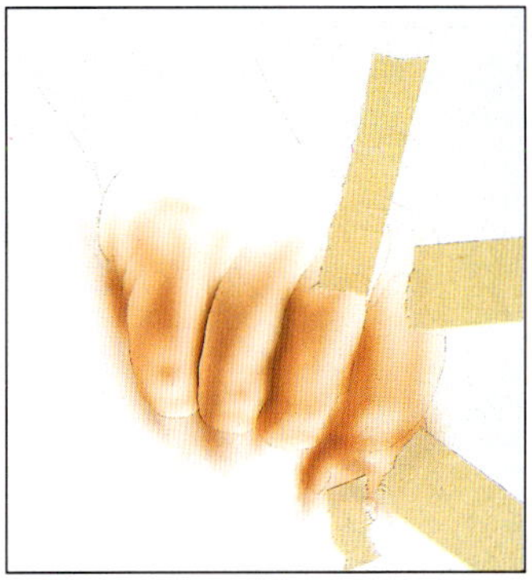

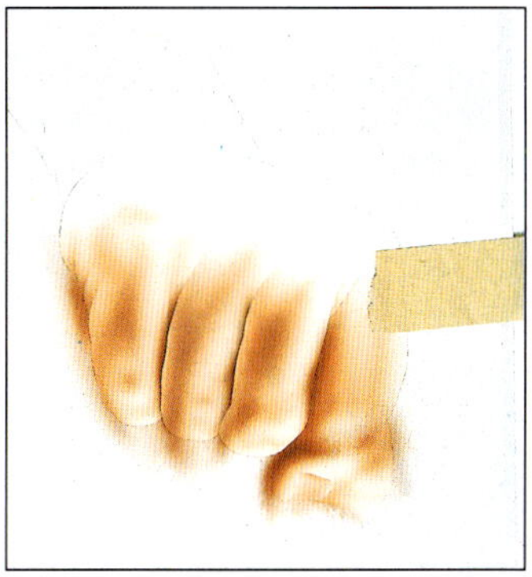

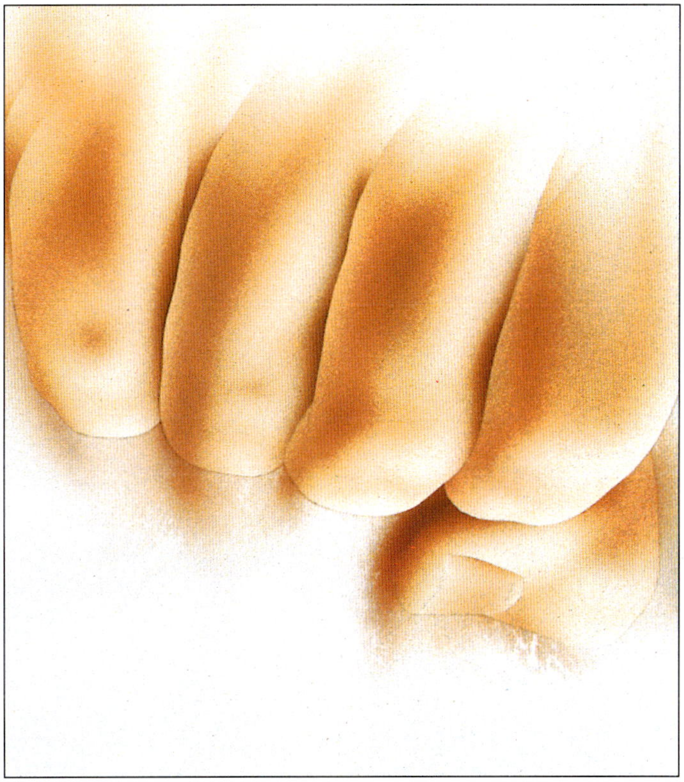

9-12 The process is repeated re-using the previously hinged masks, but this time each finger is over-sprayed with the darker shade.

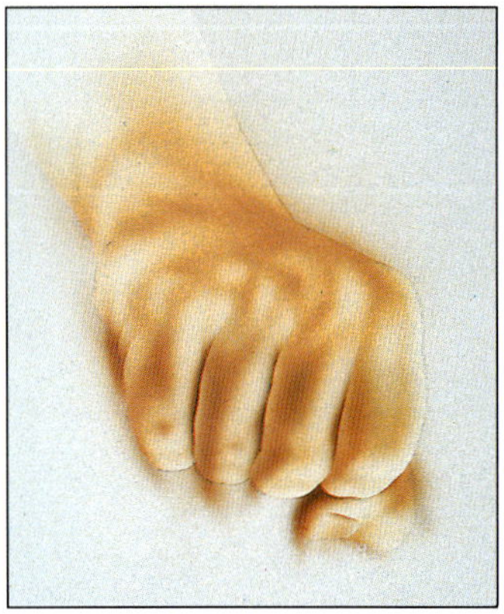

13 When both tonal values have been sprayed onto the fingers, all separately hinged masks are completely removed from the artwork. The medium shade is then sprayed freehand to model the back of the hand and the wrist.

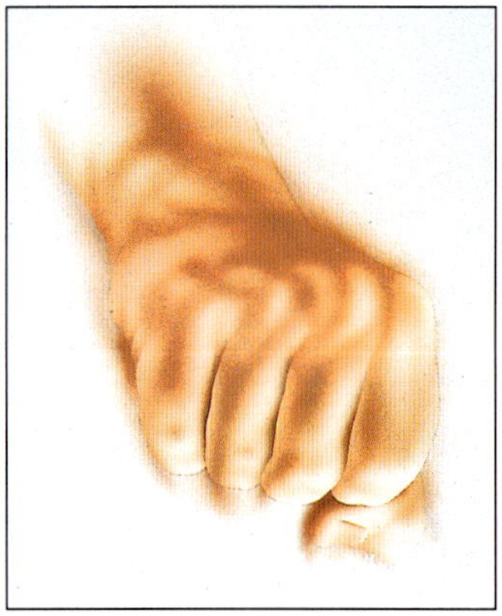

14 A medium-dark shade is now oversprayed to increase contrast and to indicate natural shadow.

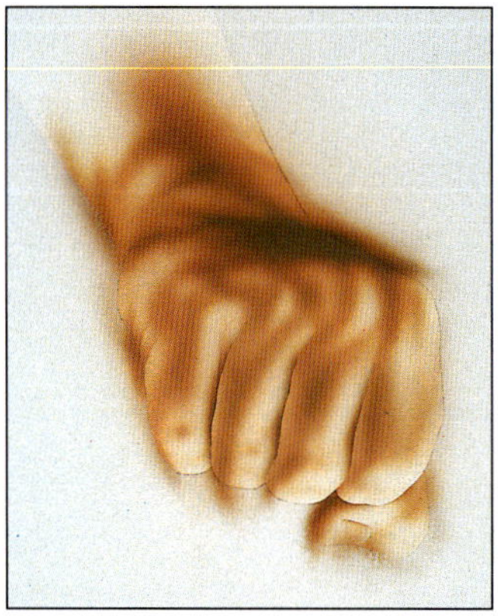

15 The darkest shade is added, primarily over the shadow area on the back of the hand.

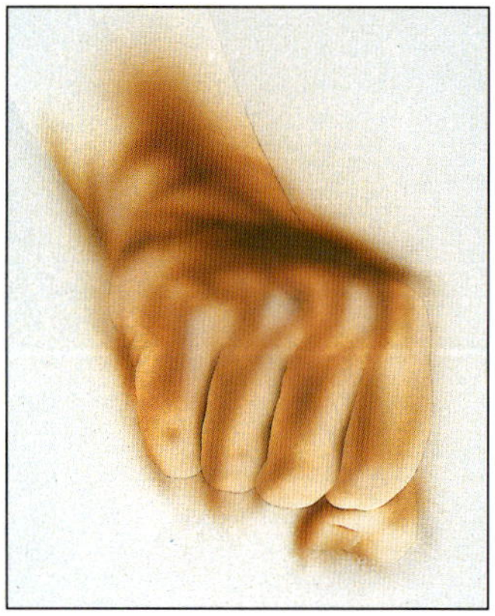

16 Finally, a very light shade, which is almost pure white, is oversprayed to add highlights to the fingers and knuckles.

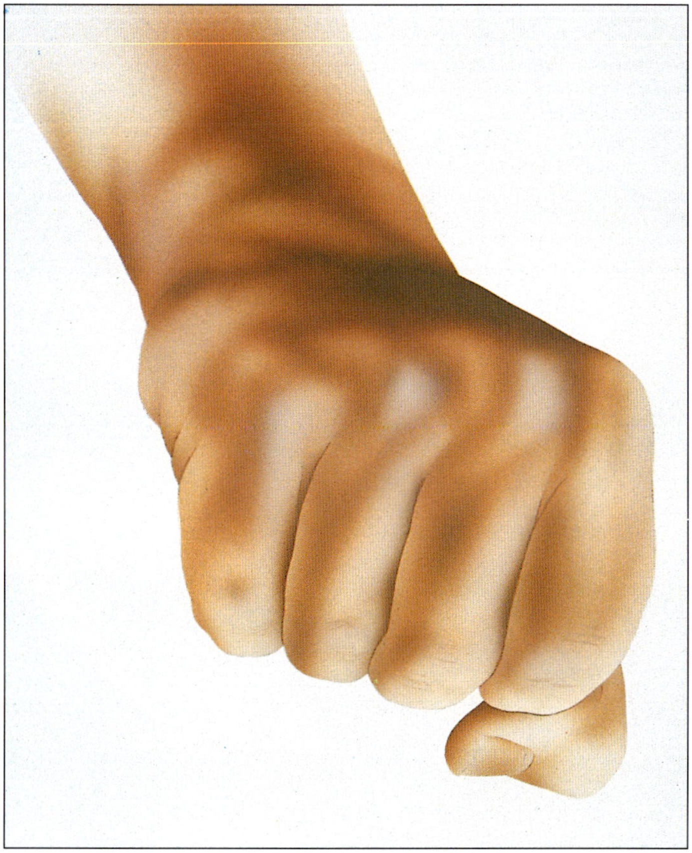

17 The artwork is completed on the removal of the final piece of masking film. Depending on the size and purpose of the illustration, additional detail could be added with pencil and brush.

RULING

Together with LINE CONTROL and LINING-IN, drawing straight lines with a ruler is an essential technique for adding detail and finish to an airbrushed illustration. It must never be rushed, as it could so easily make or mar the finished work.

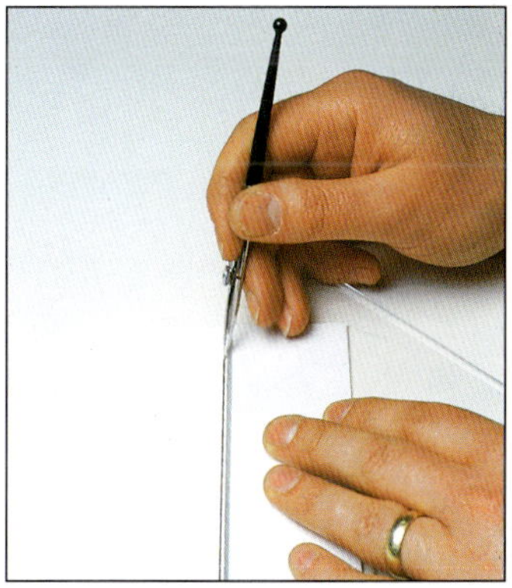

Using a Ruling Pen
The traditional and indispensable ruling pen is shown being used against a T-square. When using a ruling pen, care must be taken to maintain the same angle throughout the length of the line. It is also important to hold the pen at a slight angle to the T-square or ruler to prevent paint or ink from flooding underneath the edge.

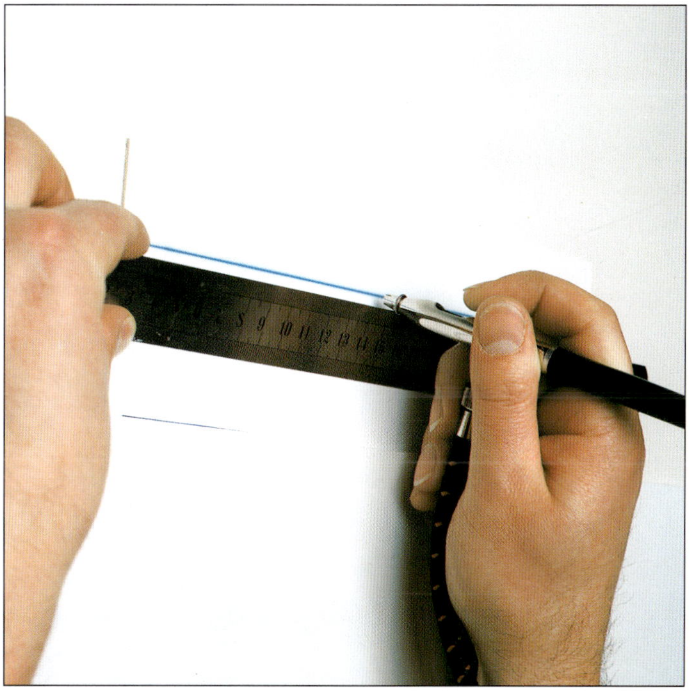

Using the Airbrush
A line is being sprayed using a ruler, held at an angle, as an aid. This gives a clean finish with varying degrees of gradated shade extending from the edges of the line, depending on the strength of medium and the air pressure allowed through the airbrush. With less pressure, the line would appear grainy.

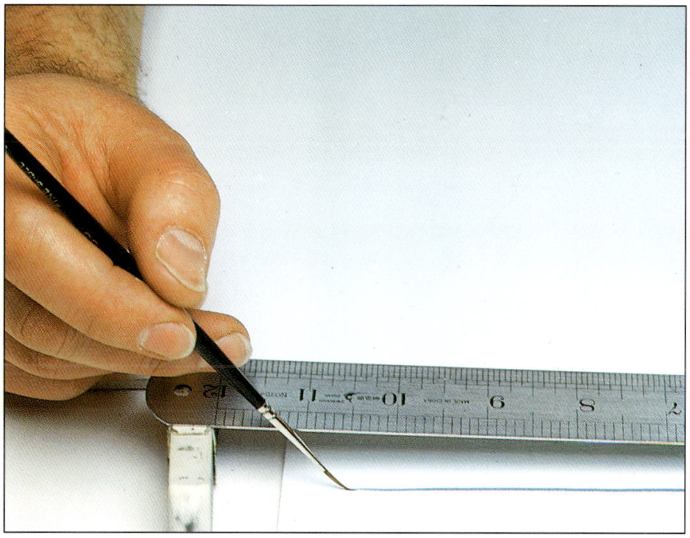

Using a Paintbrush
This photograph shows the illustrator drawing a clean, even line with a brush, using a ruler to ensure straightness. This technique requires steady pressure to maintain even thickness along the required length of the line.

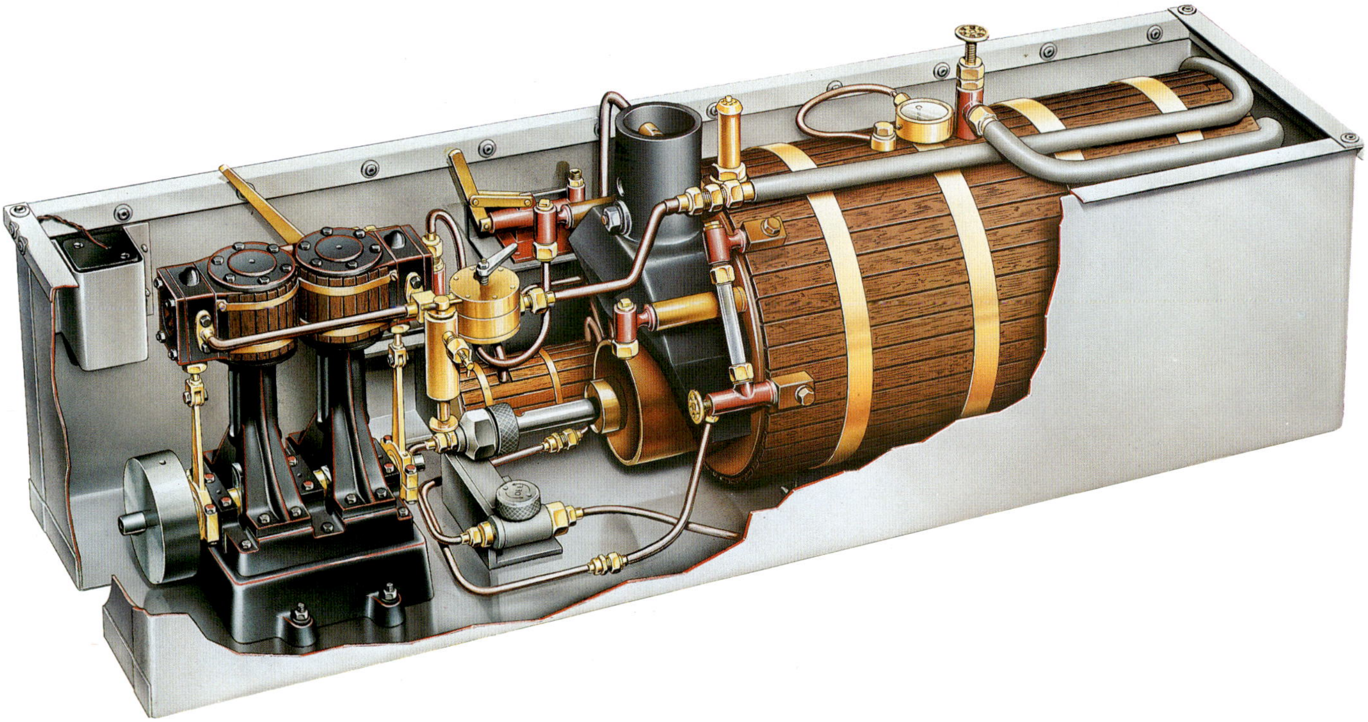

A self-contained model steam power plant
Peter Jarvis

This three-quarter view perspective illustration was commissioned by Argus Books Ltd for the book *SS Great Britain: the Model Ship*, and it clearly demonstrates the application of RULING and LINING-IN with a ruling pen and a fine sable brush. The technique adopted followed conventional methods for the preparation of full-color, airbrushed artwork for reproduction, using masking film.

However, the subject is made up of many small components which could not be airbrushed and which required extensive hand-painted work. In addition, it was decided to present the subject in a new, unused state which would enhance the various components and the materials from which they were made, but which would also add contrast between the different surfaces and the way they had been machined or finished. To create some of this contrast, a ruling pen was used.

The aluminum casing which contains the boiler, pumps and twin-cylinder steam engine has straight lines on those edges which would show a shadow. Edges facing the light source have been highlighted with a straight line which is a much lighter mix of the base color. The detail, HIGHLIGHTS and contrast on the rivets have been applied with a brush, as have the edges of the cuts. These are rendered in two shades of red, to show the thickness of the aluminum, with the leading edge picked out in a very light gray, while the shadow edge has been picked out with a dark gray. The red castings forming part of the boiler fittings were first sprayed; semi-opaque white highlights and shadow lines were applied afterwards by hand. The brass nuts also have a sprayed base color, with shadows and highlights subsequently added. This approach has been adopted throughout the illustration.

An airbrushed illustration such as this, composed as it is of so many small details, requires an extensive use of hand-rendered ruling and lining-in. As much, if not more, patience is needed at this stage of an illustration to ensure that the finish is compatible with the quality of the airbrushing. Inexperienced artists should be wary of rushing the work.

SCRATCHING BACK

The point of a new on an art knife blade is an effective and indispensable tool for adding fine highlights and texture to illustrations; this kind of detail sharpens the finish of an illustration and adds crispness to it. To achieve the effect, the surface of the artwork is scratched back to expose the white of the board.

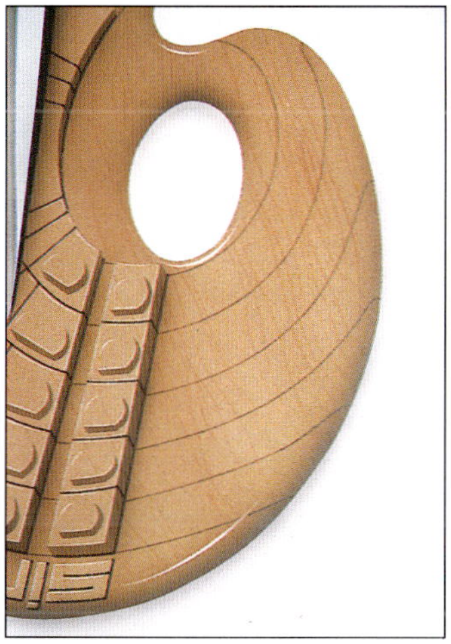

Thin Highlights
The illustration of part of a palette shows one use of a an art blade to scratch back thin, white highlights on the straight and curved edges. Although not very wide or pronounced, they are enough to add to the quality of the finished illustration.

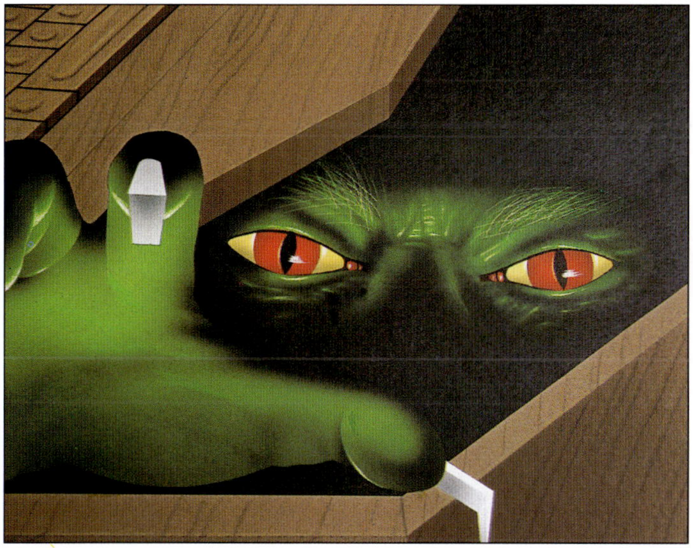

Thick Highlights
In this example, highlights in the eyes, eyebrows and lines surrounding the eyes have been subtly scratched out, giving emphasis to these features.

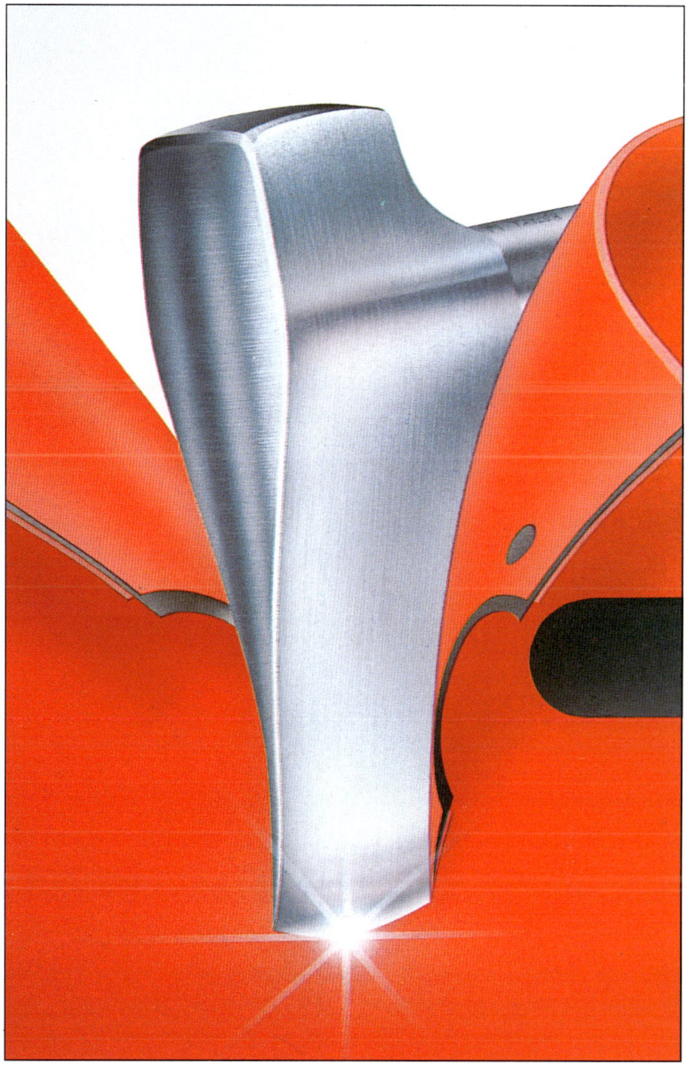

Sprayed Highlights
In this artwork of an axehead slicing through material, scratching back is used to enhance the machine surface finish of the blade and to create a sprayed highlight which emphasizes the cutting edge of the blade.

SPATTERING

Spattering can be achieved either by lowering the air pressure allowed through the airbrush, or by fitting a splatter cap in place of the usual nozzle. Additional control is achieved by varying the distance the airbrush is held away from the artwork and adjusting the combined amount of air and medium which is allowed through the airbrush. The effect is to give a stippled or grained finish with varying densities and sizes of dots.

Because a splatter cap can create quite a crude finish, practice is required before attempting to use this technique on serious illustration work. However, the use of a splatter cap does have practical applications. It can be used to represent the ground and thereby add interest and contrast, especially when the principal subject is of a polished nature; it can also be used to represent unmachined castings or the surface of a section in a cutaway illustration, to name but three examples. The use of spattering to create texture, and the finish achieved from it, does not preclude its use in adding, in a controlled manner, form and tone to a shape or object.

Two practical demonstrations are included here which illustrate how spattering can be used to simulate specific textures.

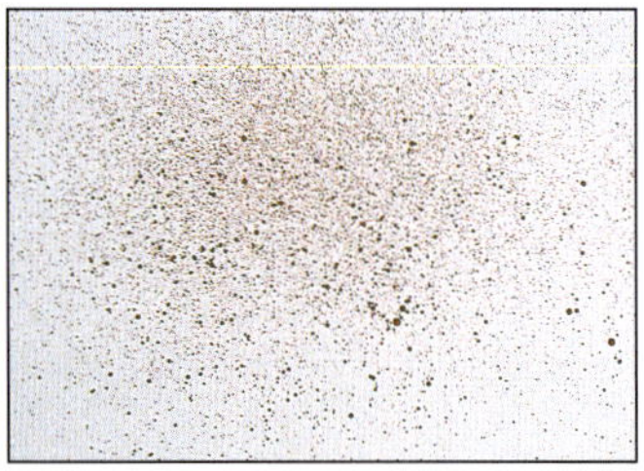

1 The above demonstrates the basic effect obtained when using a splatter cap fitted to an airbrush. The variety in density and size of dots is achieved by controlling the distance the airbrush is held away from the artwork. Not all makes of airbrush include the splatter cap as an accessory.

2 This example shows a fine spatter effect which has been sprayed from a standard nozzle by using decreased air pressure.

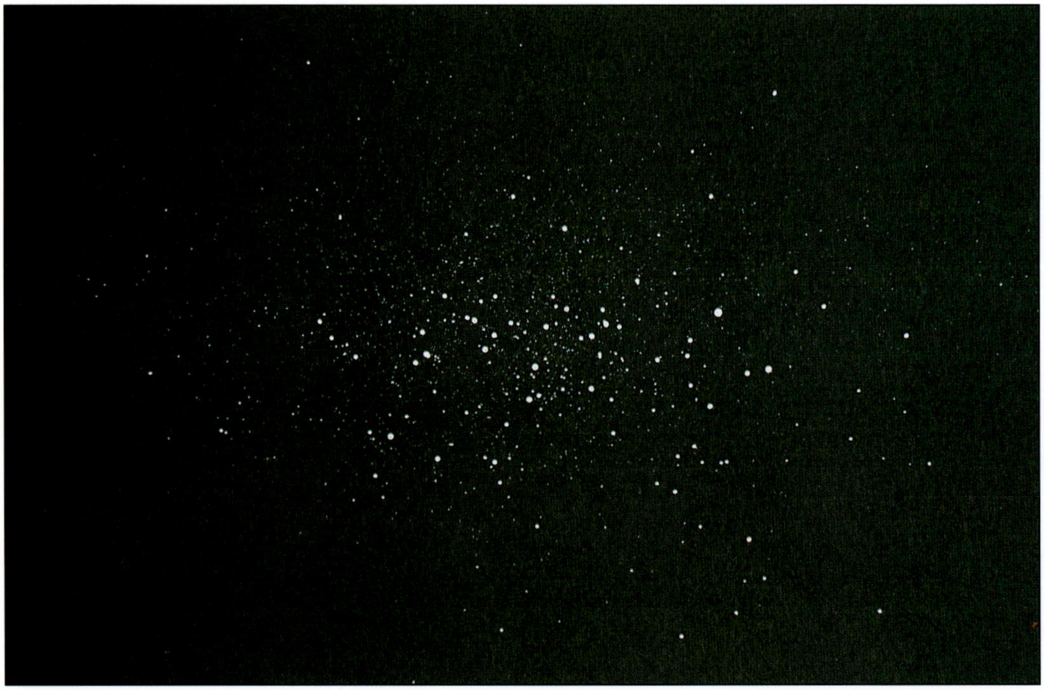

Galaxy Effect
Using a solid black or blue-black base to the artwork, opaque white is oversprayed through a splatter cap to give an impression of a galaxy of stars. This could be further worked on by applying hand-painted or sprayed "starbursts." The base spraying and the initial stars could also be sprayed with a variety of shades and colors.

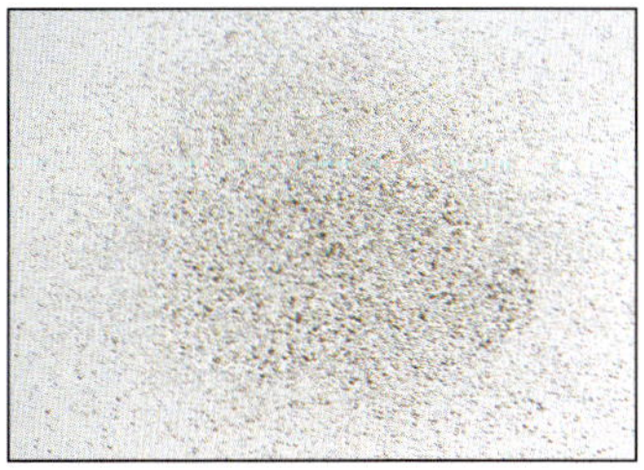

Stone Finish

1 This shows one method of spraying a stone. The shape of the stone is first drawn on board and the whole area is covered with masking film, with the shape of the stone cut out. Gouache is sprayed through a splatter cap.

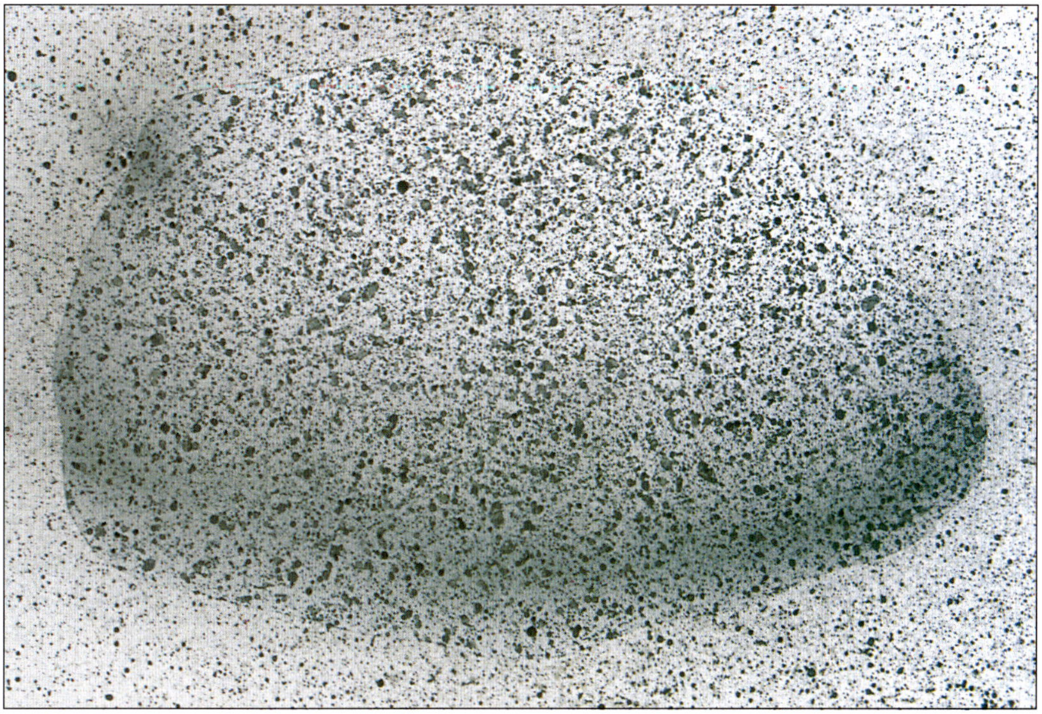

3 The form of the stone is modeled by overspraying the shadow tone using a standard nozzle.

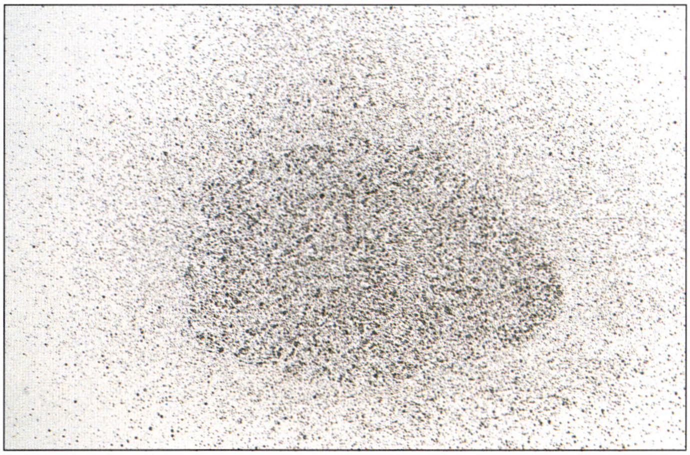

2 A second color, slightly lighter in shade, is now sprayed, again using the splatter cap.

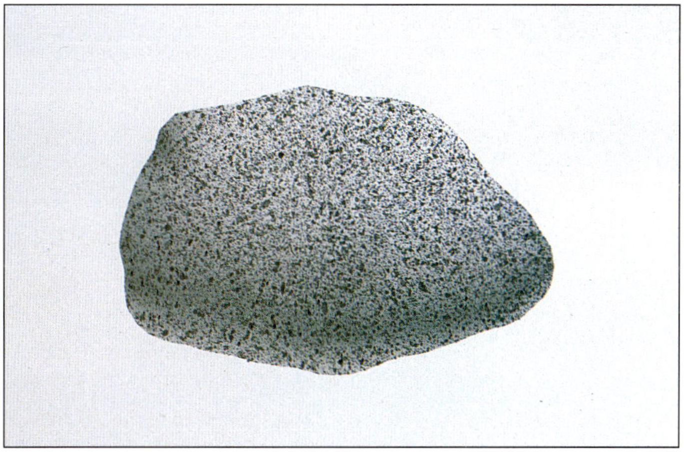

4 The masking film is removed from the artwork, revealing a simple but effective rendering of a stone. With further practice it is possible to increase the variety of shades and the number of colors, even to the point of using the splatter cap

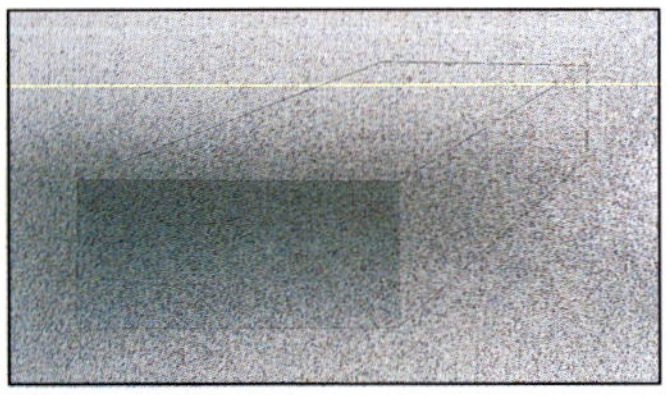

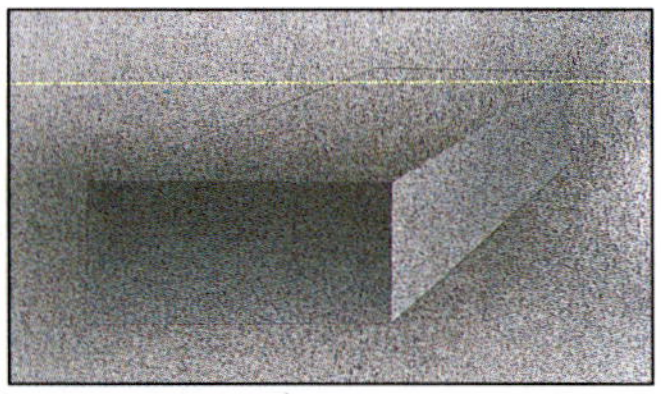

Rubber Texture

1 The second illustration demonstrating the application of a splatter cap is a rectangular box which is sprayed using watercolor to resemble a piece of rubber. This example again uses both the standard nozzle and the splatter cap. In the first instance, the shape is drawn and the artwork covered with masking film. The basic shades are sprayed using very low air pressure, beginning with the face nearest to the observer.

2 The side of the box is exposed and sprayed, again using both the standard nozzle and the splatter cap to develop the texture.

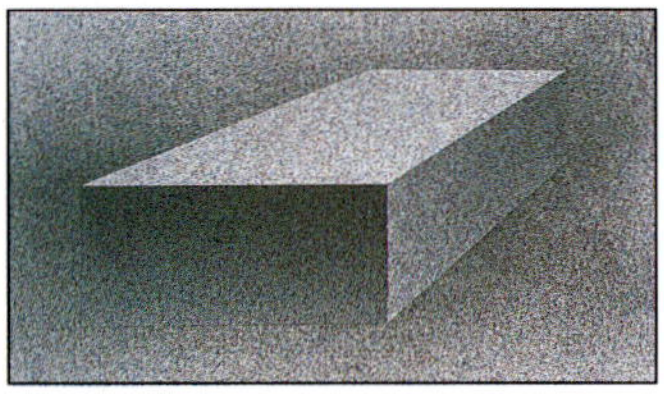

3 The top is the final surface to be sprayed. By following the sequence illustrated, there is no need to recover the previous stages with masking film: successive sprayings increase the tonal depth. Not only does this speed up the process, but it prevents errors which can be made by repositioning the film inaccurately, which tends to create unsightly double edges on the finished artwork.

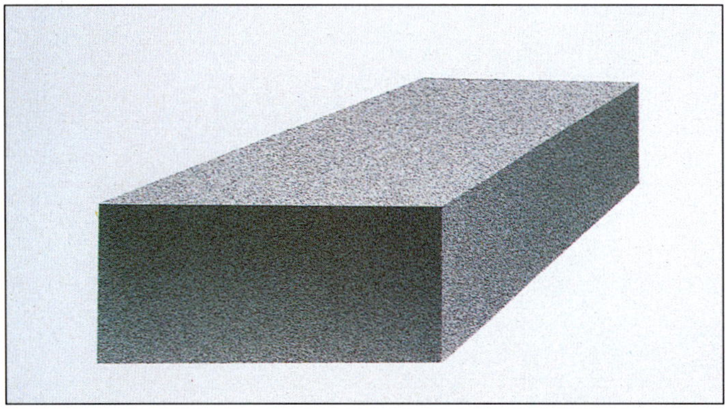

4 When the required tonal values and depth of contrast have been achieved, the masking film is finally removed.

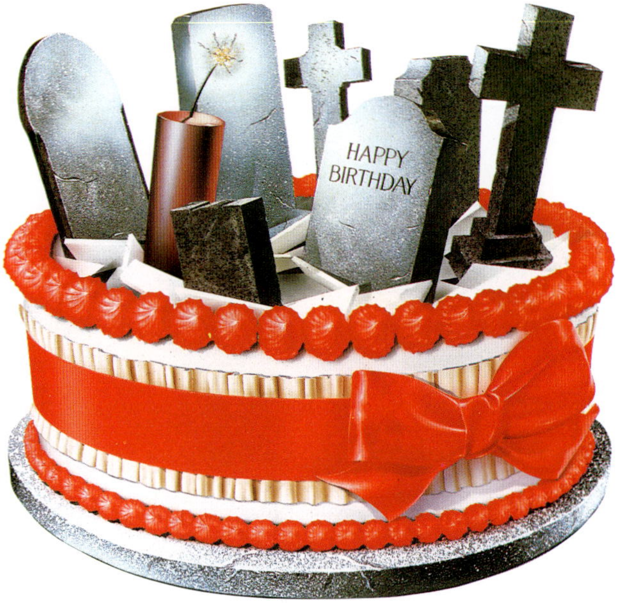

Birthday cake
John Brettoner

This illustration demonstrates an excellent application of the use of SPATTERING, although close study will reveal that it also includes many other techniques described in this book. Interesting contrasts have been made between the cake, which has been sprayed without a splatter cap, and the headstones and the foil-covered base, which are spattered. This has created a strong visual image, which emphasizes differences in the surface textures and the various materials.

The headstones were conventionally sprayed with a base color to establish the general shades and the color variations between the different types of stone. Following this, the shadow edges to the chipped and damaged areas of the stones were added by brush. Spattering was then oversprayed on the base color using a mixture of whites, grays and blacks. Next the HIGHLIGHTS to the chipped edges were applied with opaque white, with LINING-IN by brush completing the headstones.

The cake base followed much the same sequence as the headstones, with the base color and form being applied first, without a splatter cap. The spattering was then oversprayed using a mixture of opaque white and blue-black, the latter in varying densities depending on the direction of the light source. Handpainted crease marks and highlights were added, with shadows on the crease marks being applied with transparent watercolor, allowing the spattered effect to show through.

STARBURSTS

This is a particularly effective airbrush technique which can be used in many different ways. Besides the obvious use in rendering realistic impressions of stars in a night-sky or descriptive detail in fantasy or science-fiction illustrations, starbursts are also applicable in showing diffused reflections or dazzling highlights, as in the headlights of vehicles seen photographed with a long exposure.

The following sequence demonstrates the most effective method of applying starbursts, using an acetate mask. The reason is twofold, in that the artwork is always clearly visible, allowing for accurate positioning, and that a certain amount of residue color will seep under the mask, softening the edges slightly. Self-adhesive masking film can be used, but this will give a very hard-edged finish which, unless oversprayed color for the starburst is subtly applied, will be less convincing.

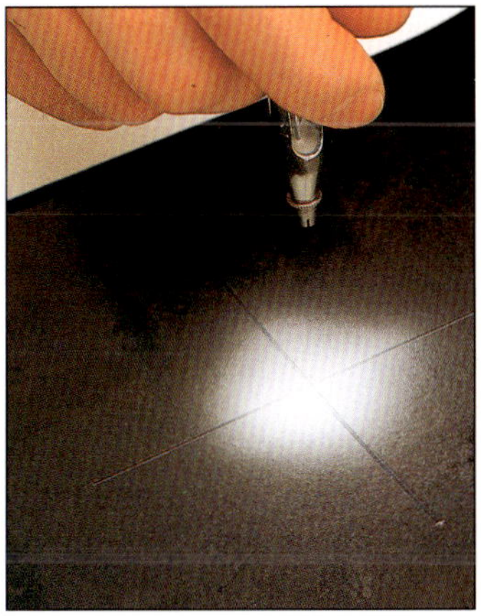

1 This stage shows the acetate mask with a simple cross cut into it. The lengths of the arms of the cross are cut much longer than required to avoid even the slightest hint of an edge appearing after spraying. Opaque white is sprayed through the mask, concentrating on the center of the cross and allowing the residual spray to find its own limits.

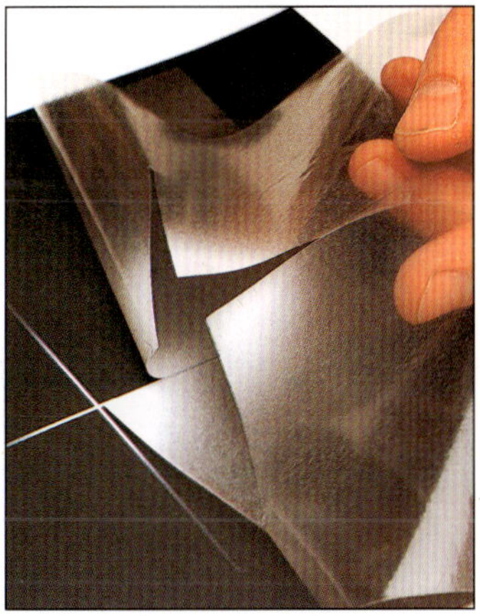

2 The mask is shown being removed, revealing the greater density of white at the center of the starburst, fading out toward the ends of the arms.

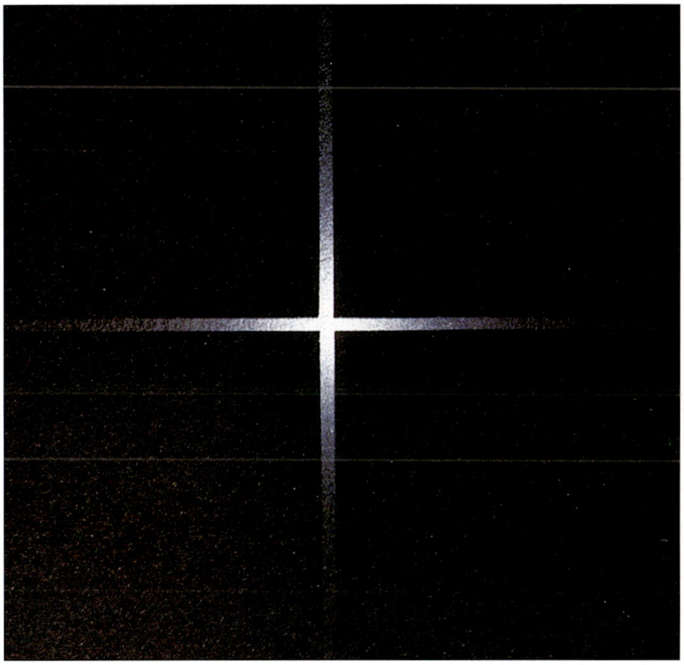

3 The finished example. If required, the number of arms may be increased in any proportion using the same mask, or new masks could be cut depending on the desired effect.

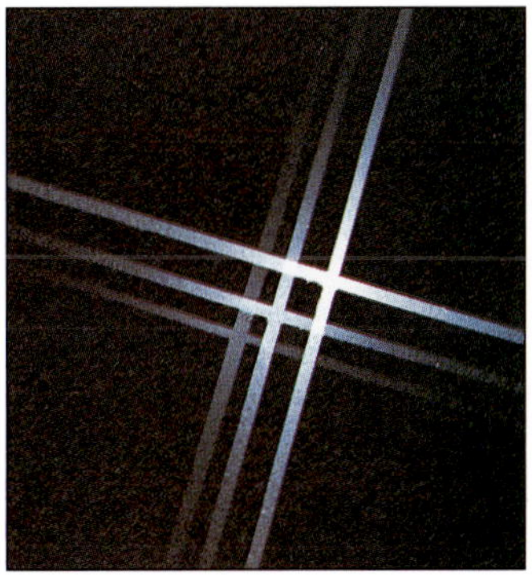

4 In this example, the same mask has been used twice, but in different positions and with different degrees of intensity at both the center and in the lengths of the arms, making the larger of the two appear brighter and nearer to the observer. Note, too, that they are both angled in relation to the artwork.

STENCILS

When it is necessary to produce repeat pattern artwork, the stencil becomes a useful aid, although excessive use of a paper stencil will soon give distorted images because of the effect the paint will have in wrinkling the paper. Thick cardboard is a more stable material for stencils, but it can be difficult to cut intricate shapes. The thickness of the cardboard may also cause a narrow, unsprayed edge around a shape, if the airbrush is held at an angle while spraying. Natural or man-made objects can also be used as stencils, giving an infinite number of patterns.

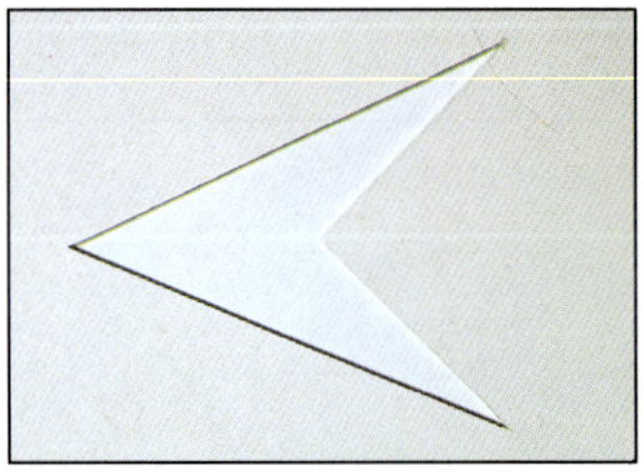

1 A simple shape has been cut into stiff cardboard for use as a stencil.

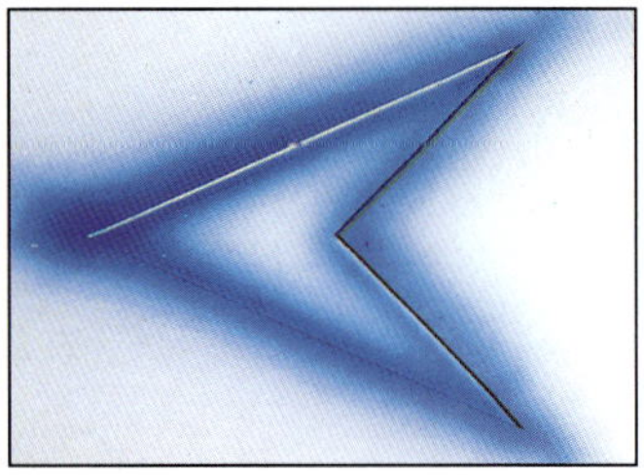

2 Here the spraying is restricted to the edges of the stencil, with no color being applied to the center.

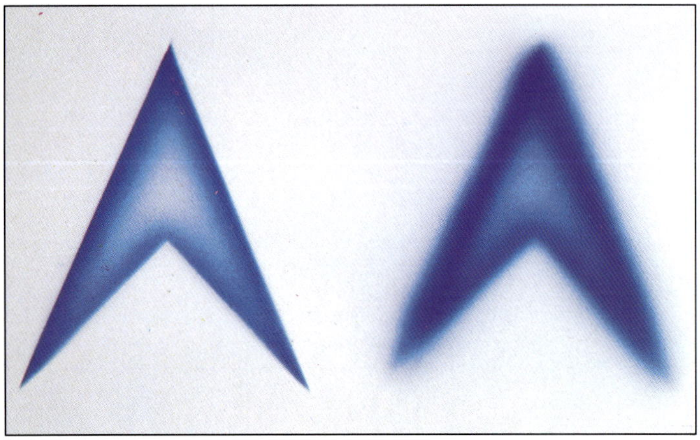

3 The finished result shows, on the left, the effect when the stencil is held flat on the surface, while that on the right shows the effect when the stencil is held above the artwork. Notice that when it is held away from the artwork, the residual color encroaches over a wider area, both outside and inside the stenciled shape.

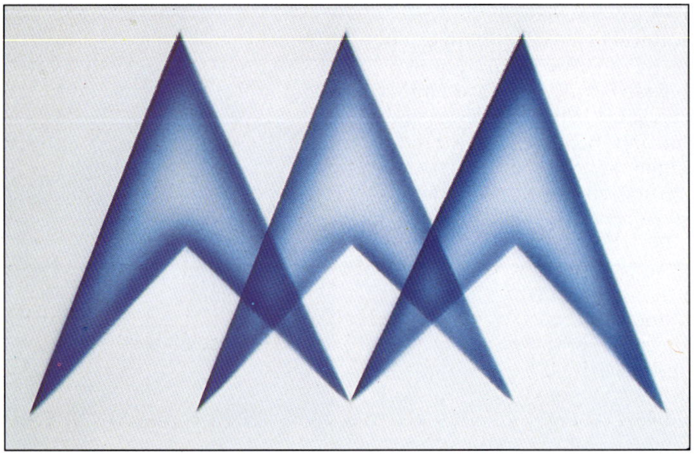

4 A simple symmetrical pattern obtained by overlaying the same stencil.

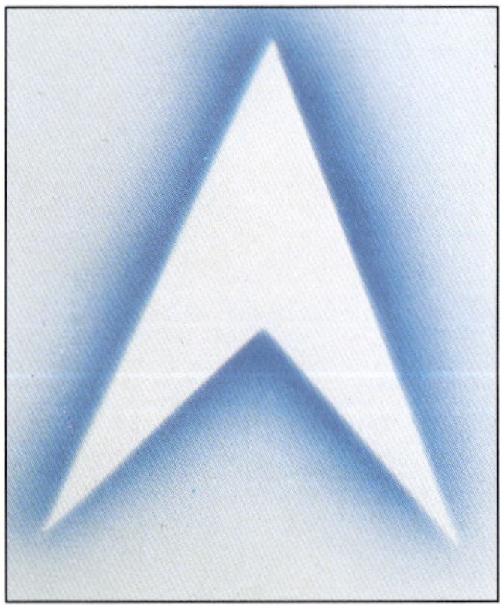

5 This example is the reverse, in that the stencil now consists of the shape originally cut from the cardboard. This has been laid on the board and the color sprayed around it. When using a flimsy stencil, such as paper, it is possible to hold it in place, but care is required to prevent the spray from producing a distorted silhouette shape of whatever is holding the stencil down.

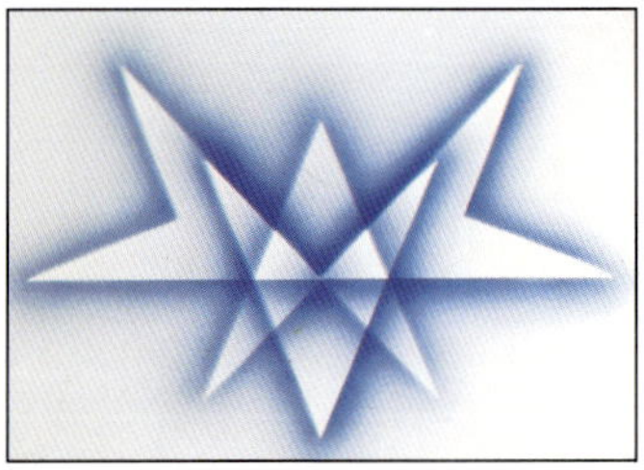

6 Using the same stencil as in step 5, a multiple overlapping pattern has been achieved.

TAPE MASKING

People who do drafting work use a transparent, self-adhesive masking tape, called invisible masking tape, which is matte-finished. It is suitable for drawing or inking on, and therefore ideal for repairing drawings, especially when these are prepared on drafting film. This tape is also useful in airbrushing when, as in the example illustrated here, small areas have been exposed out of sequence. It may be cut and used in the same way as masking film and similarly has a low-tack adhesive which does no damage to the artwork.

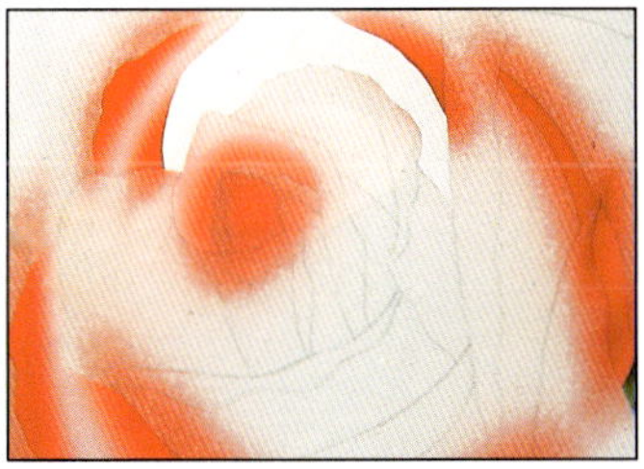

1 Referring to the example described and illustrated under the heading FILM MASKING, three stages in the use of tape masking are shown here. In the process of cutting and removing film for different areas of the rose, a piece of film was taken off prematurely. Matte transparent tape was used to re-cover the exposed petal, which was then cut to shape.

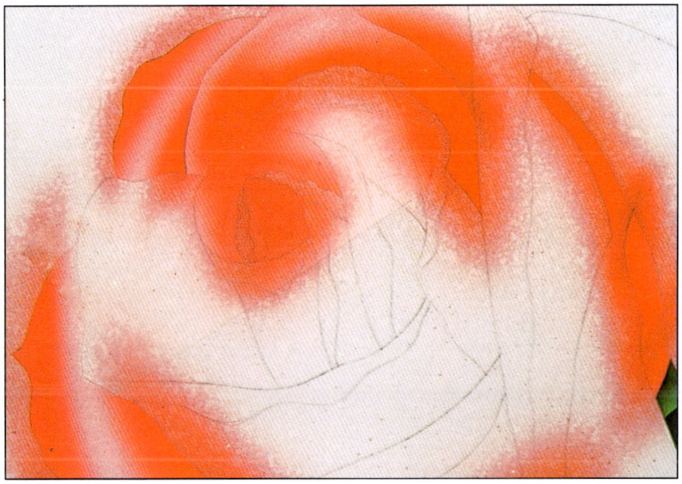

2 With the tape in place, the petal was sprayed corresponding to the correct order in the sequence.

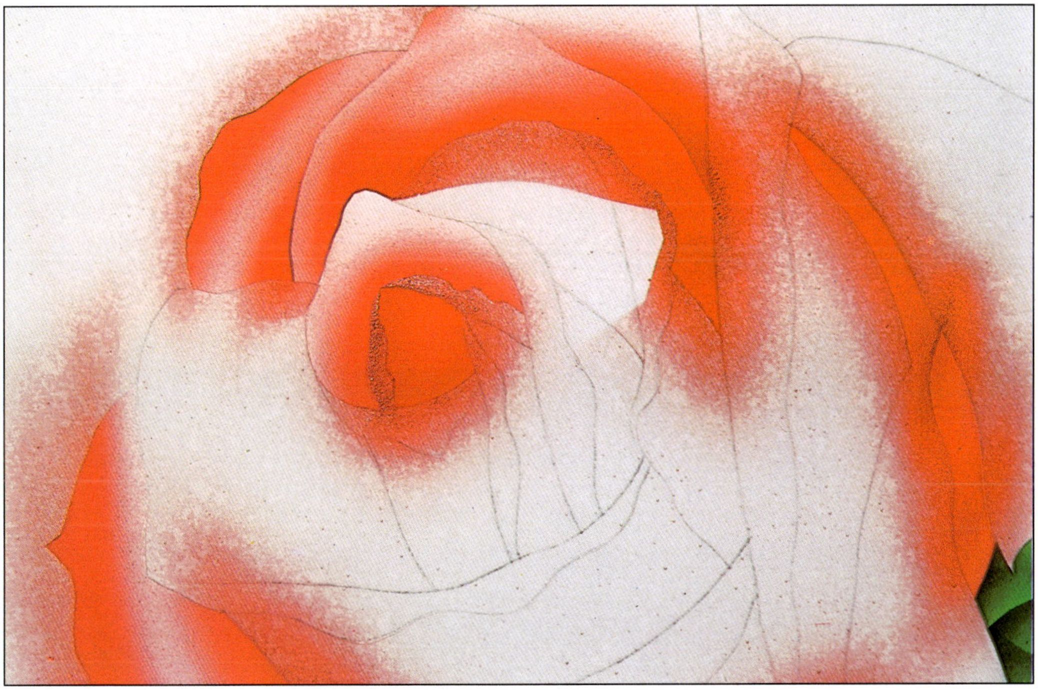

3 When complete, the transparent tape was lifted off and the spraying sequence continued.

TEMPLATES

Useful aids in airbrushing are the many and various die-cut templates used in drawing illustrations. These are used in much the same ways as hand-cut stencils. The examples which follow show simple applications for ellipse, circle and French curve templates.

There are two things which need particular attention if you are using plastic templates in airbrushing. One is that the sprayed color dries slowly on the plastic, so you should make sure the underside of the template is clean and all excess color has been wiped away if you are using it more than once. Also, if the template consists of multiple shapes, use tape to mask off the ones surrounding those being sprayed; otherwise, residual color may fall through and create shadowy silhouettes where color is not wanted.

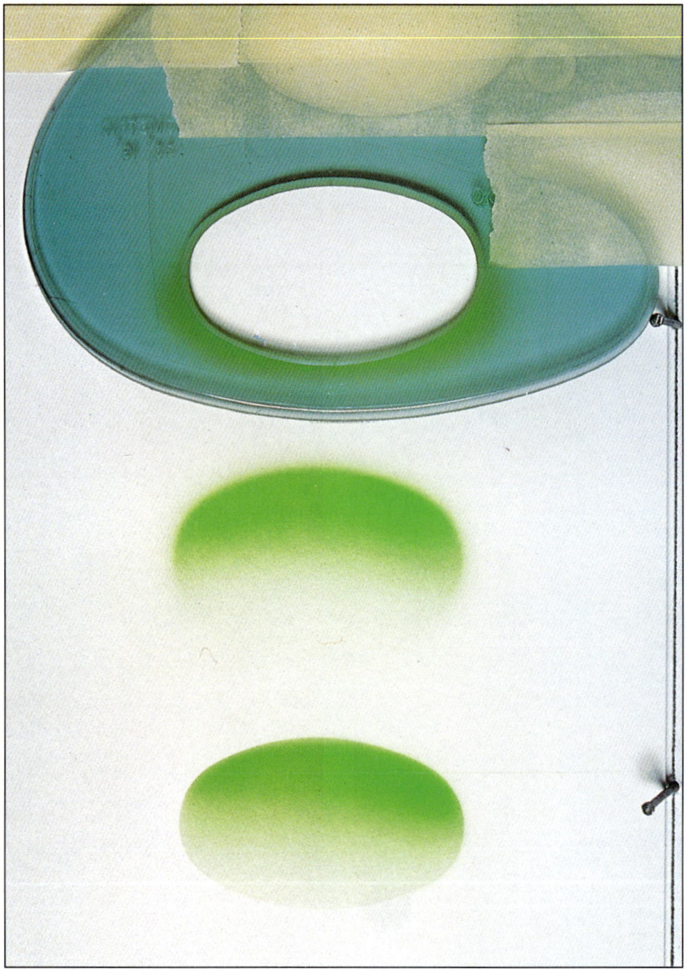

1 This example demonstrates the use of a typical ellipse template. The spraying is directed through the required size and angle of the ellipse, either as flat color or, as here, gradated color. The uppermost ellipse has been sprayed holding the template at a distance away from the artwork, while on the lower one the template has been laid on the surface of the artwork.

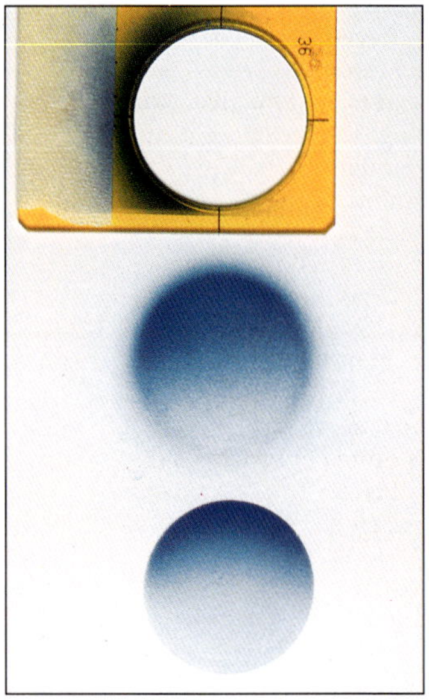

2 A circle guide template has been used here, both holding it away from and laying it on the artwork, as in the previous example.

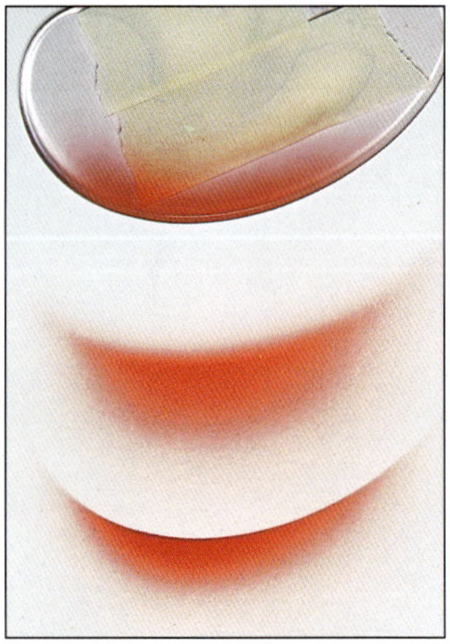

3 This shows a French curve being used in the same two ways. The use of French curves, as with any template, needs special care to prevent residual color from being sprayed around those parts of the curve not required.

TORN PAPER MASKING

If the exterior silhouette being sprayed is not confined by predetermined dimensions, torn paper can be an effective form of masking. To illustrate one application, it might be required to create an impression of the sea, and torn paper prepared in a variety of wave shapes could be used to define the waves over a presprayed base color. By slightly moving the torn paper horizontally to the left or right after the first spray, the waves will take on a quite convincing appearance, albeit in a stylized manner. Reference should also be made to ANGLED SPRAYING, CARDBOARD MASKING and LOOSE MASKING.

Special Effects

1 In this example of special effects, a simple illustration of receding mountains is shown, and in the first stage, a torn paper or thin cardboard mask is prepared. The border of the illustration is protected with masking film which will remain in place until the final stage. Note that what has been removed from the paper mask is the shape of the mountain, and not the surrounding area. Because this first shape will be in the foreground, the mask is positioned on the lower part of the artwork.

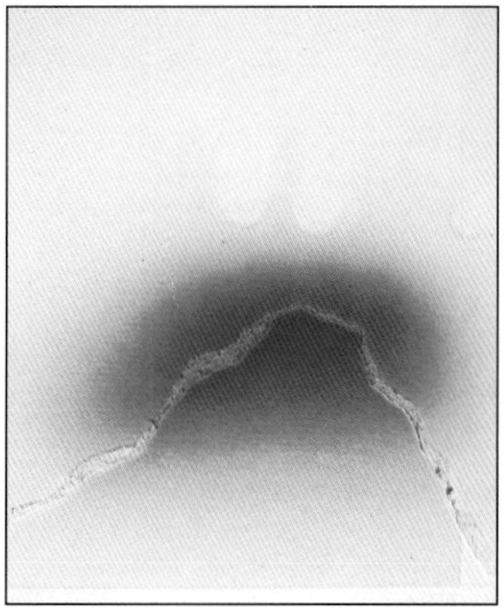

2 The first application of color is sprayed in transparent watercolor, gradating from the top to the bottom of the mountain. As this mountain is nearest the observer, the strength of color and shading is the most intense – the subsequent stages will show a gradual softening of tonal values as they appear to recede from the observer.

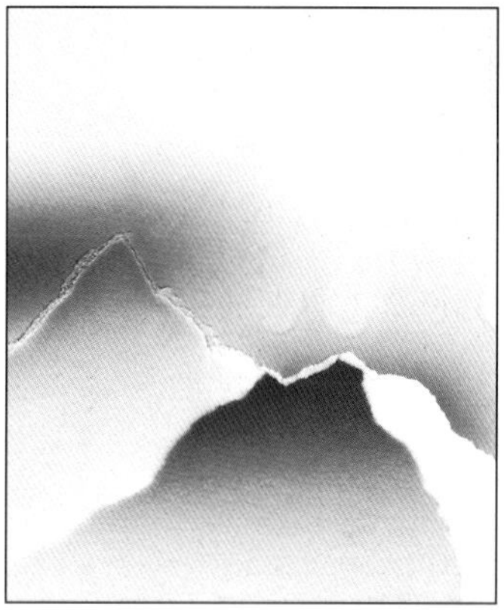

3 A new shape is torn into the paper, positioned on the artwork and sprayed in a slightly less intense color.

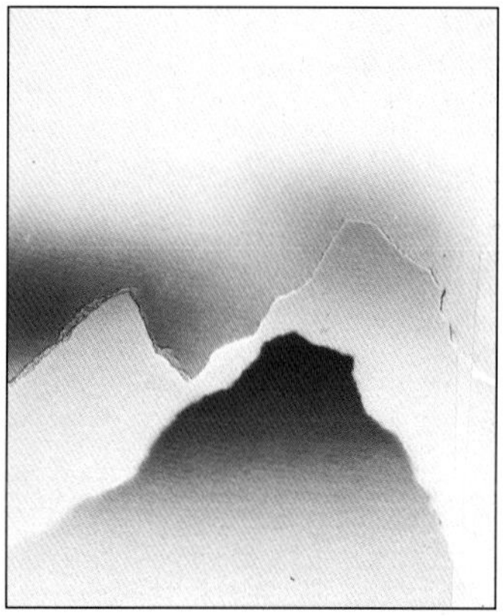

4 The process is continued as the impression of depth is increased. It will be noted that shapes already sprayed are not protected by a mask. This ensures that the tonal value of those shapes representing mountains in front of the one currently being sprayed retain their strength.

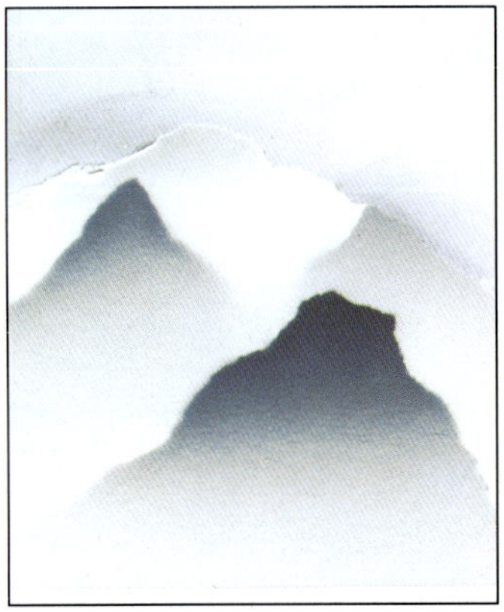

5 Again the shape is changed, sprayed more lightly. It covering less area than before.

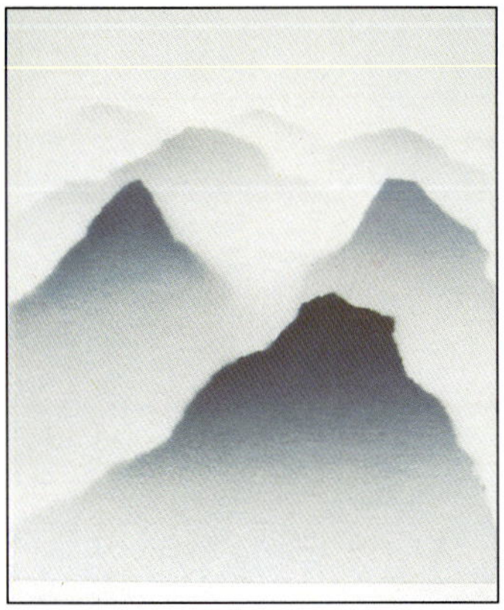

7 When the very pale shapes in the far distance have been completed, the torn paper masks are discarded and the sky is sprayed. This is a lightly gradated shade of color running from the top of the artwork to a level just above the mountain tops.

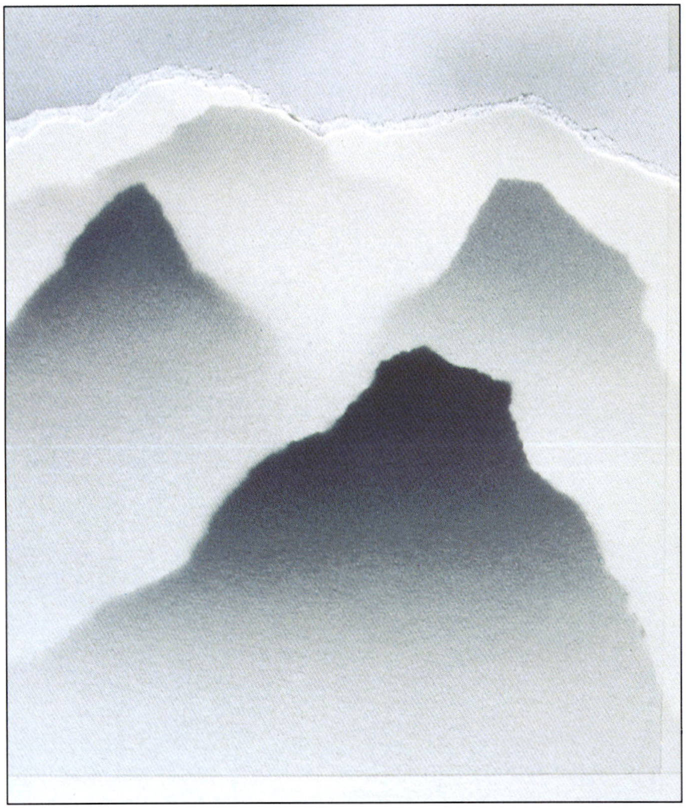

6 Another background shape is sprayed, maintaining the lighter shades established previously.

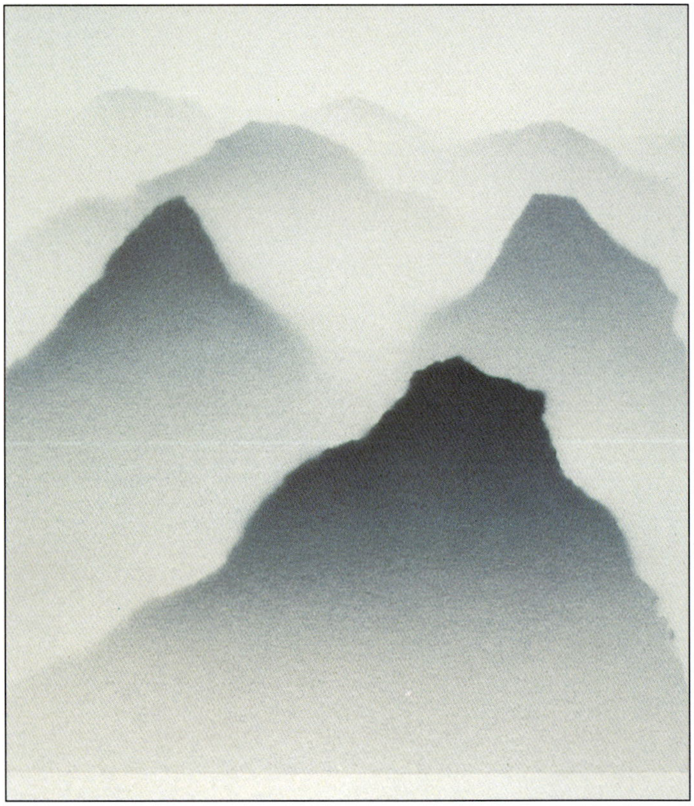

8 The masking film delineating the outer borders of the illustration is now removed and the final result gives an illusion of depth, distance and space.

TRANSPARENCY

This technique refers to objects which are transparent to a greater or lesser extent. It requires a far greater control in the application of sprayed color than does the representation of solid objects, because it is easy to overspray and in so doing to knock back the transparent effect, in which case the process has to start again. The example used here to illustrate transparency is a simple cube, and no allowances are made to include reflected colors or highlights which might be apparent from surrounding objects.

In advertising illustration, there are many examples of objects airbrushed in this way which would not, in reality, be transparent. Many of these illustrations come from the imagination of the illustrator and are done to achieve a particular effect and often for impact. To reach this standard requires skill, practice and an understanding of the changes in light and reflections as seen through a transparent object. GHOSTING is very much related to this technique, and the two may be used together in order to gain a better understanding of the application of transparent effects.

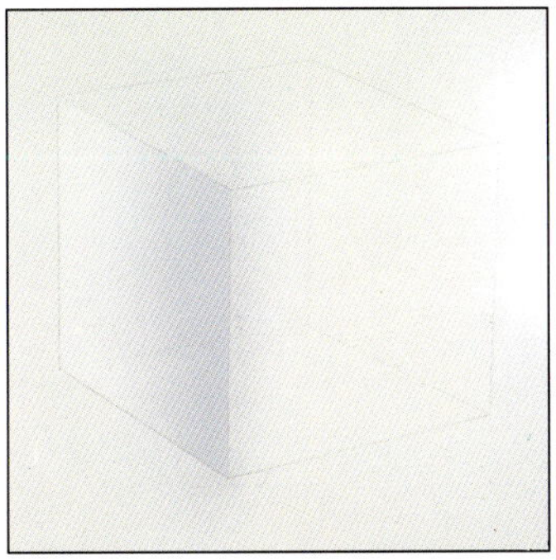

1 The drawing of a cube showing all six faces has been prepared and covered with masking film. The naturally visible left-hand face in the foreground is exposed and sprayed with a gradated shade of color running from the leading edge to that furthest away from the observer.

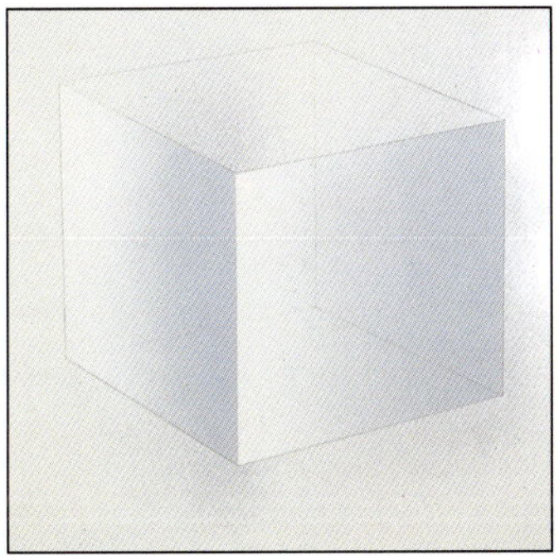

2 The right-hand face is now cut and sprayed, again with a gradated shade, but from the extreme right-hand edge toward the leading edge.

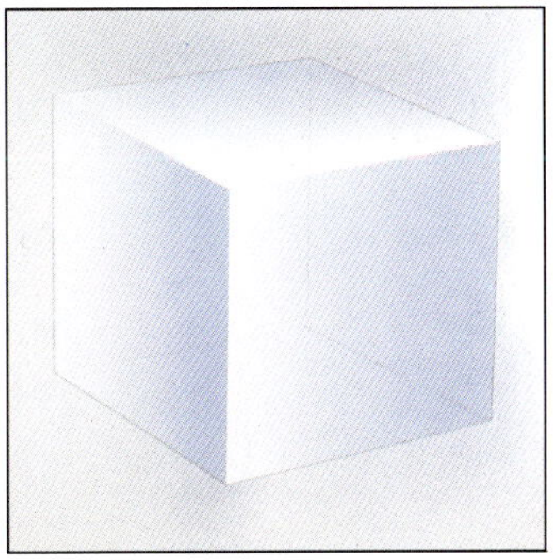

3 The top, horizontal plane is sprayed next, the shading running from top to bottom.

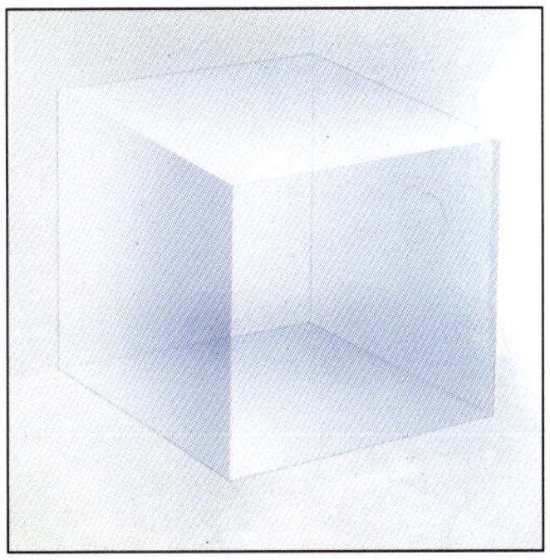

4 The inner face of the cube lying on the ground plane is sprayed next, with the depth of shading gradating from the furthest corner away from the observer toward the leading edge corner.

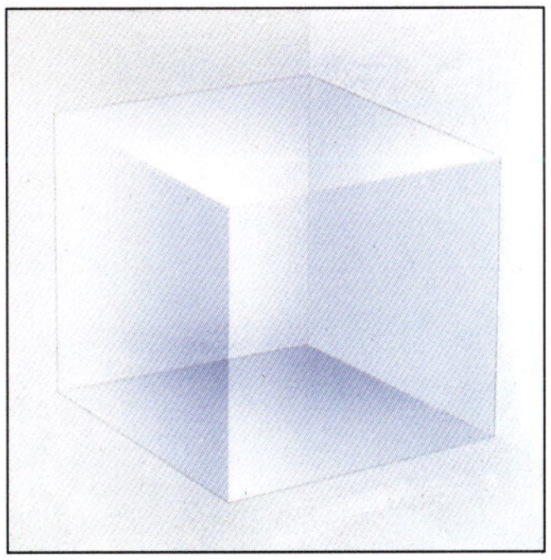

5 The vertical edge representing the corner of the cube furthest away from the observer is masked and sprayed with a gradated shade running from left to right.

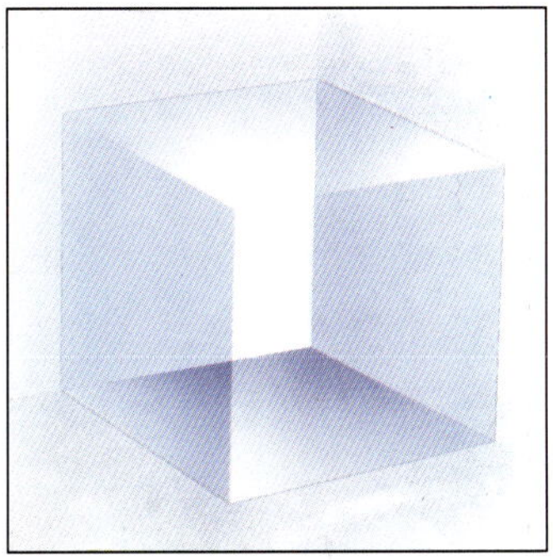

6 The left-hand inner face at the back of the cube is sprayed with a gradated shade.

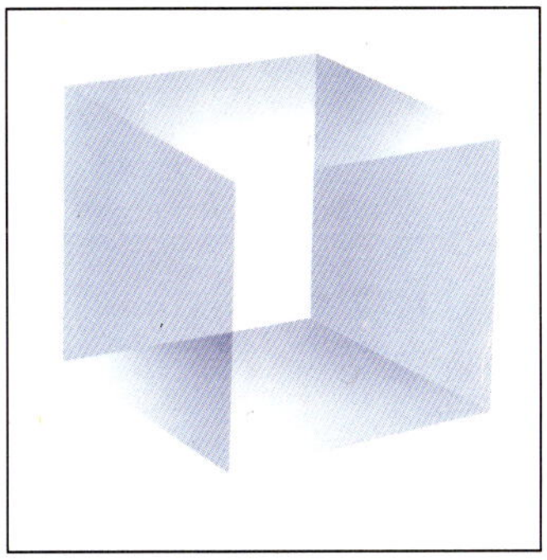

7 Finally, all masking film is removed.

Finger Style
Brian Robson

Some consider the airbrush to be a tool only for technical illustration, which has no place in any other type of graphic imagery. Such viewpoints misunderstand the reason for using any aid in the production of an illustration. If a desired effect or finish is best obtained with an airbrush, or any other tool, then would it not be appropriate and sensible to use it? The illustration reproduced here is a case in point, for it might at first appear that spraying would not be the best means of arriving at the finished result. Nevertheless, an airbrush has been used, showing the illustrator to have complete control over the airbrush and the density of color applied to each part of the illustration. It relies very much on the technique of rendering transparency, with FABRIC MASKING at the top left and bottom right contrasting well with the FLAT TONES of the two circle segments.

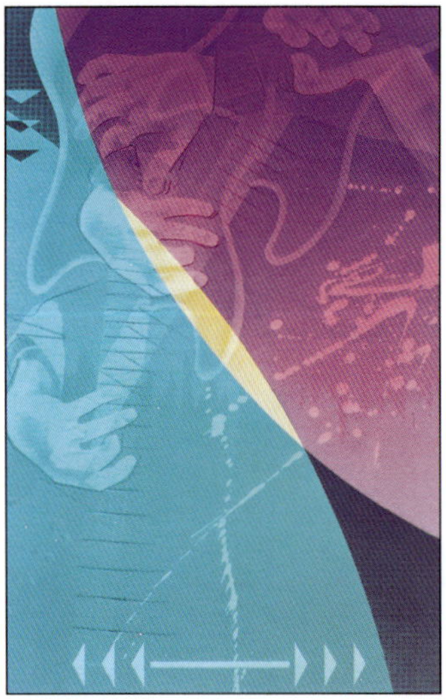

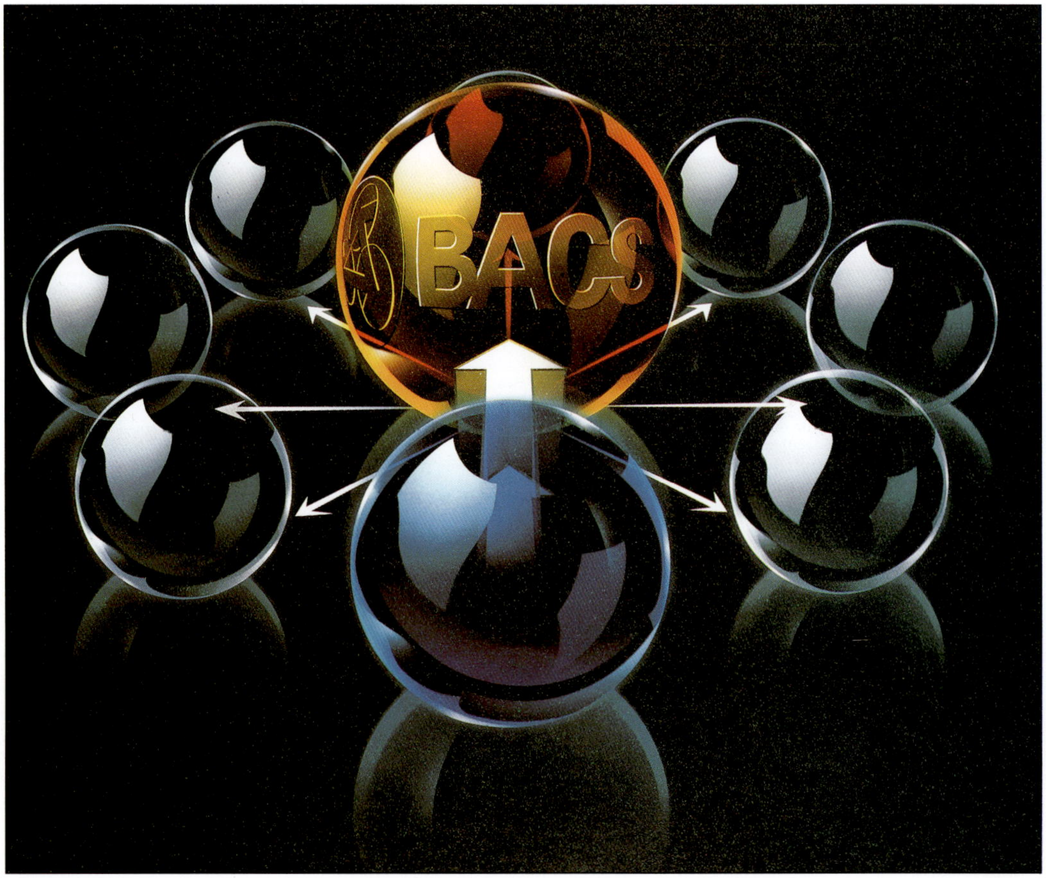

BACS
John Brettoner

As mentioned in the introduction to this technique, far greater control is required in the spraying of transparent objects than solid ones, especially if other objects are to be shown behind. Control is required both of the amount of color applied and the density of the shades, each being dependent on the degree of transparency of the object. Careful planning is also required to ensure that any oversprayed color is applied in the correct sequence, so that there is no doubt as to which surfaces or objects are transparent, and which are in front or behind. The technique applied to spraying transparent objects cannot be identified from a single example of a finished illustration. Because of this, preparatory color notes should be made before starting on a piece of finished artwork and the sequence of spraying worked out beforehand.

The example reproduced here shows a very simple, but highly effective, rendering of eight glass balls centered around a larger one carrying the BACS logo, all set against an opaque background with a subtle reflection of part of the grouping. The quality of transparency has been achieved by OVERSPRAYING the ball immediately behind the one in front with a soft shade of the latter's base color. This is particularly obvious with the black-and-white ball lying behind the gold-colored BACS ball. It will be noted that the ball at the back has a HIGHLIGHT which has been sprayed with a lower-key shade of the gold, rather than the white applied to its neighbors.

VIGNETTING

A vignette is a drawing which is not contained by any clearly defined borders or edges, but either fades into the background or stands on its own. In airbrush illustration work, vignetting is used to achieve the same result by gradating the colors that make up the background. Sometimes it can be used to fade out the object itself, especially if one side or area is considered unimportant to the central theme of the illustration.

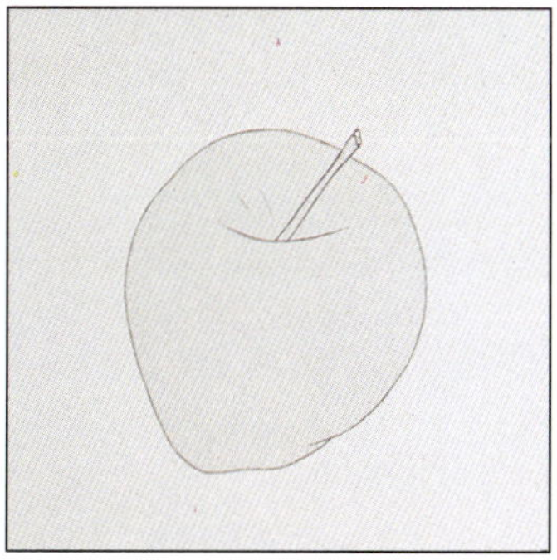

Fading In a Background

1 An illustration of an apple has been drawn and, to protect it from the background spraying, has been covered with masking film. The edges of the square which will contain the apple and its background have also been masked.

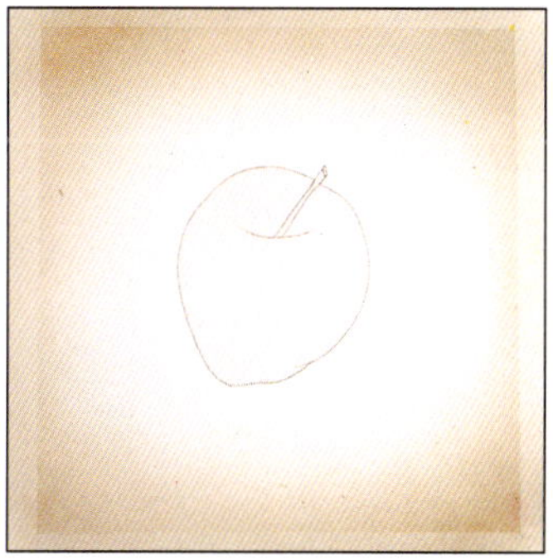

2 The spraying begins with a gradual build-up of a gradated shade, from the outside edges of the box inward.

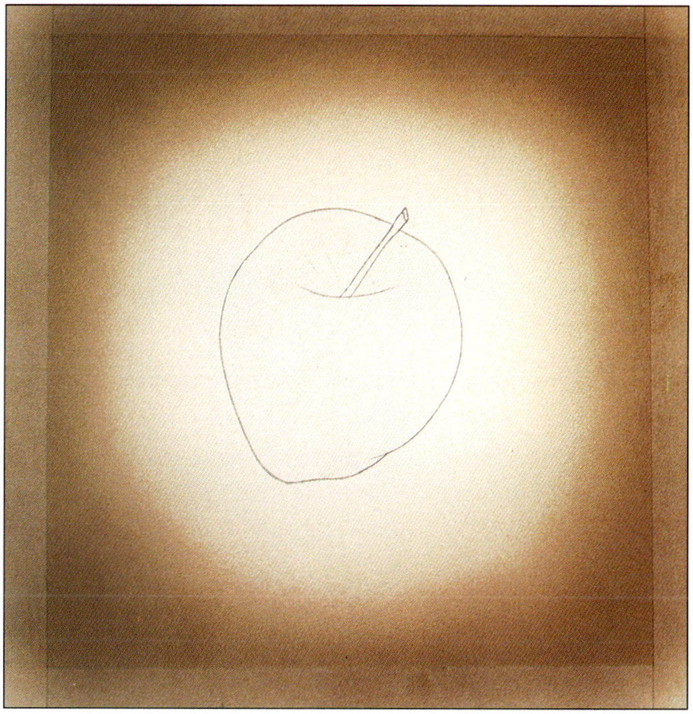

3 The shade is increased until the required depth is reached.

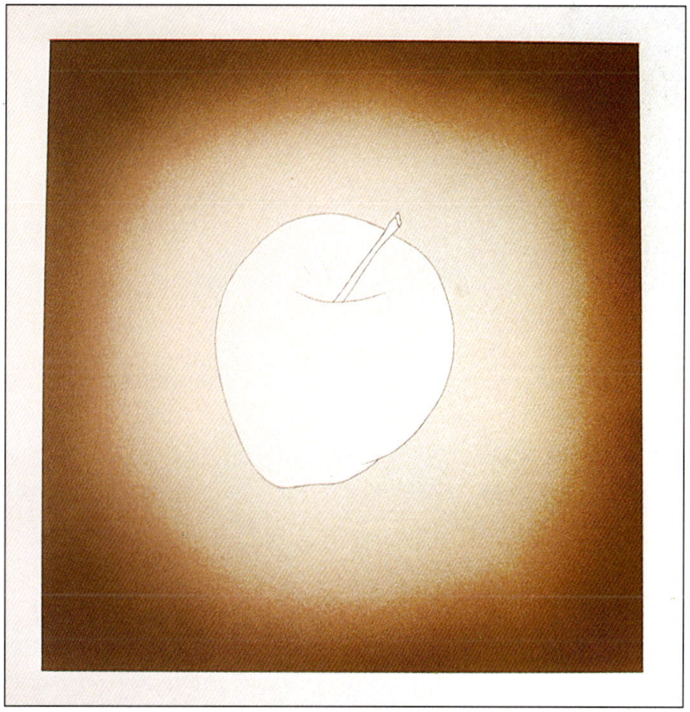

4 When the vignette is completed, the mask protecting the edges of the box is removed.

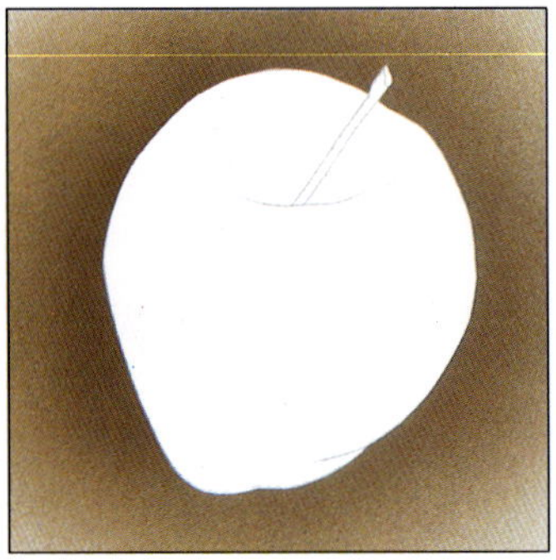

Fading Out a Background

1 In this demonstration a faded background is required, but gradated from the object outward. Here the apple has been protected with masking film.

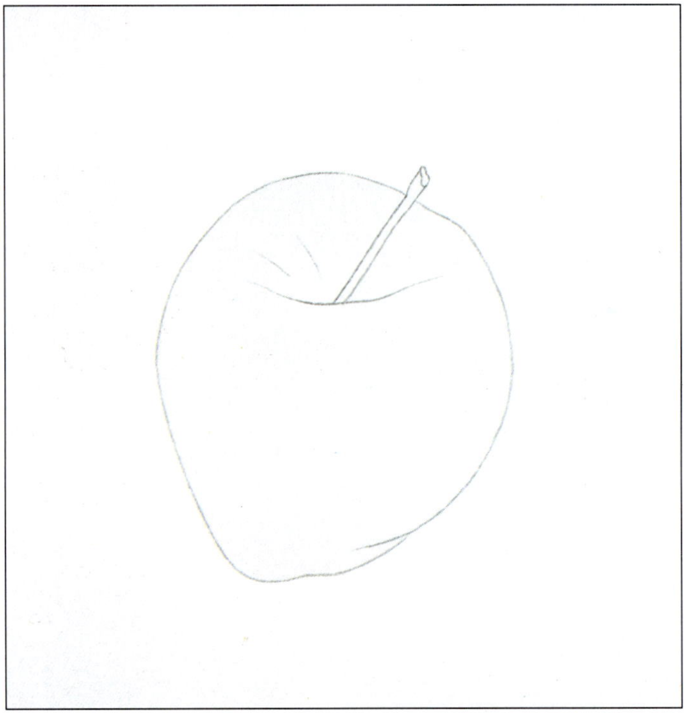

2 Spraying has started from just within the edges of the mask and an even shade is built up all around the apple.

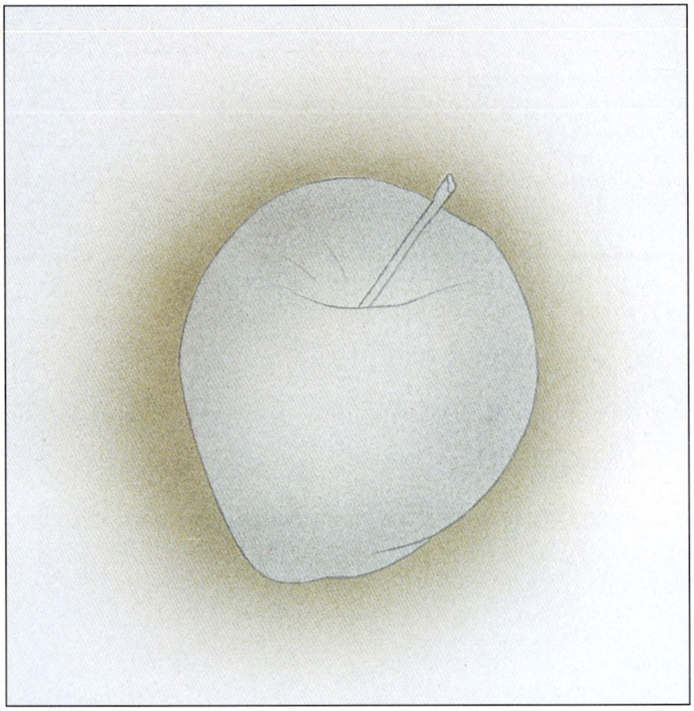

3 The depth of color is increased to harden the contour of the form.

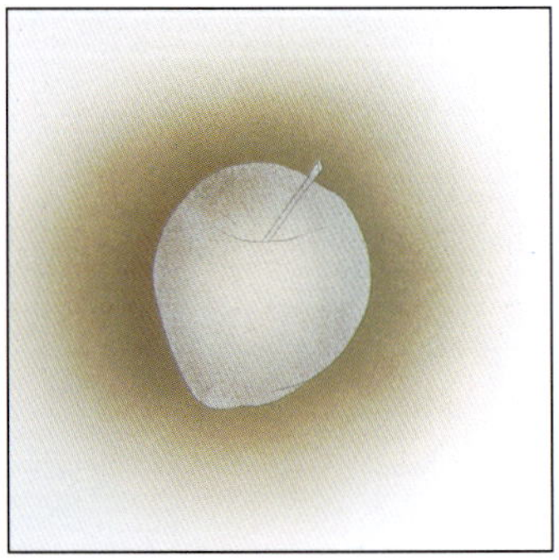

4 When enough color has been sprayed, the mask on the apple is removed, showing the vignetted background outlining the shape and fading gradually outward.

WINDOW HIGHLIGHTS

By its very name, this technique refers to the reflection, usually on a curved surface, of a window. It is visible under a range of light conditions, but as a highlight is more pronounced when the light source coming through the window is particularly strong. As a technique, this is useful for enhancing the appearance of a highly polished, but opaque object in a stylized manner, especially when no other reference source is available. It is an extremely popular device and can be seen in airbrushed illustrations from any period. When taken further by the inclusion of surrounding detail, both on and near the window, the effect can be one of super-realism, a style developed with great expertise by many of the Japanese exponents of the airbrush.

Though effective, window highlights should be used with caution, and they are not applicable to all surfaces or subjects. For example, it would be inappropriate to use a window highlight on the hubcaps of a modern 18-wheeler, regardless of how polished and glossy the metal: the chances of such a vehicle being housed indoors so that it would accurately reflect patches of light passing through a window would be very slim.

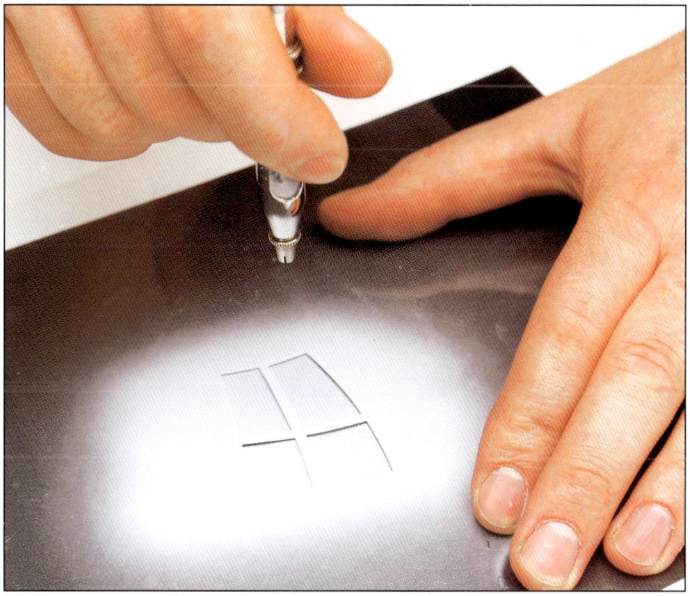

1 In this demonstration the window shape has been carefully cut out of acetate sheet and placed in the required position over a pre-sprayed base color. Opaque white is then sprayed through the mask.

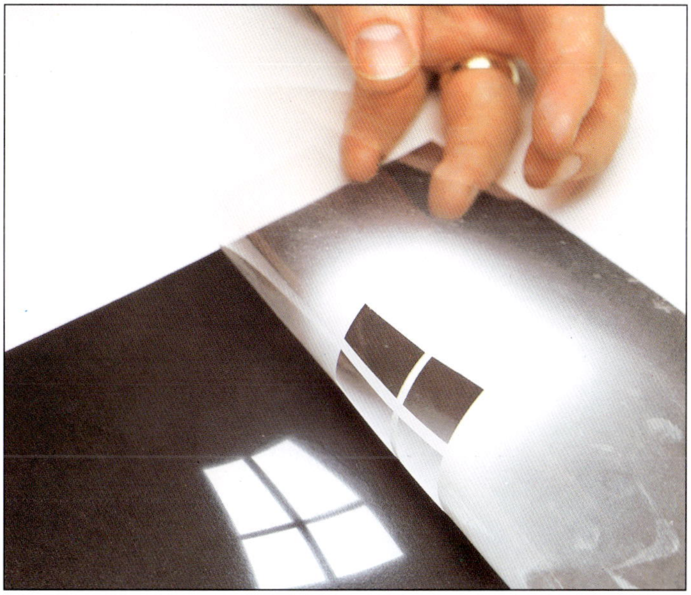

2 This photograph demonstrates the effect with the mask pulled back. Notice that the shape of the stylized window is curved. When used on a curved object, the curves of the window should conform to those of the object. It is, of course, acceptable to cut the mask with allowances for the distortion which sometimes becomes apparent through perspective, but this will require close observation of a real example. By using an acetate mask, the resulting effect will be to give a soft edge to the highlight. The degree of softness will be determined by the distance the mask is held away from the artwork. Of course, a hard edge could be obtained by using self-adhesive masking film.

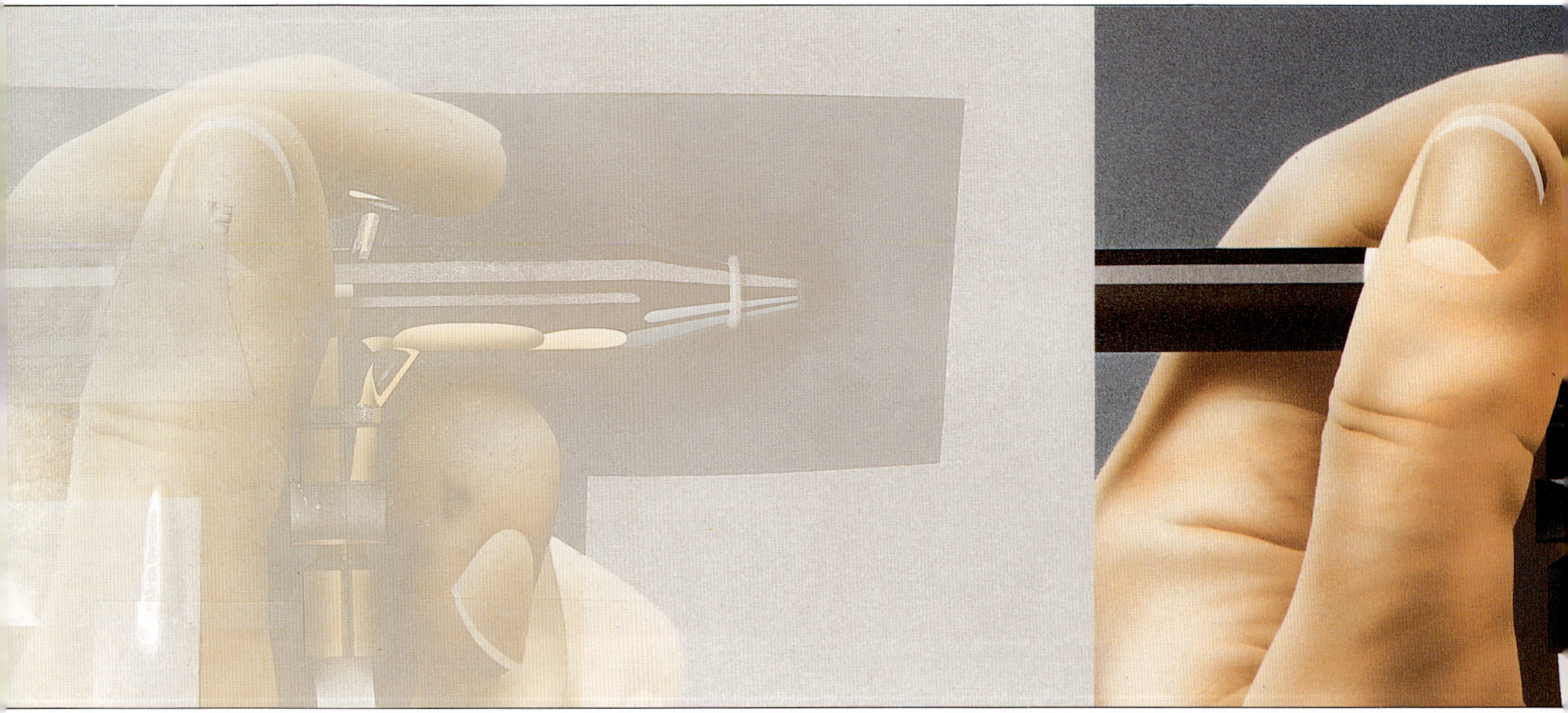

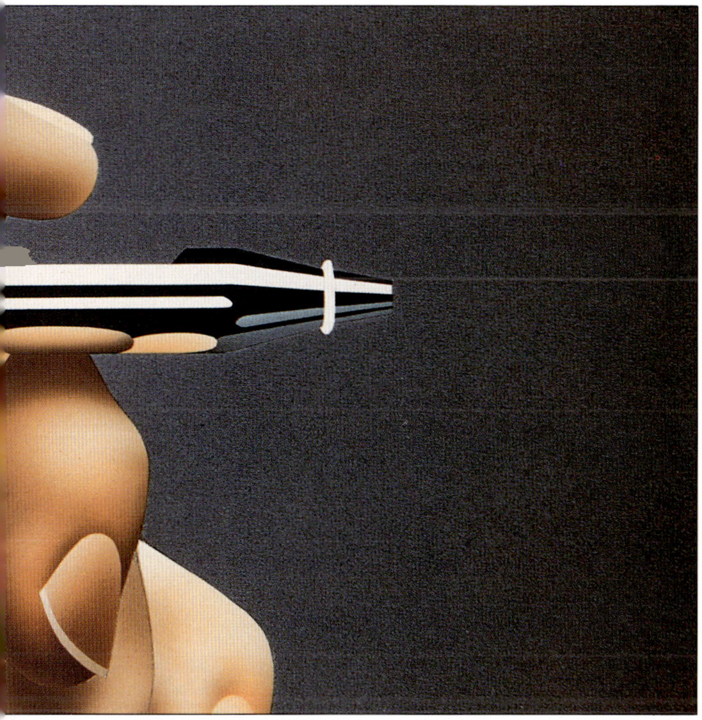

PART TWO
THEMES

THE FOLLOWING SECTION OF THIS BOOK includes finished examples of artwork produced with the aid of an airbrush, either in whole or in part. All of the work has been produced by practicing illustrators, and, as stated in the introduction to the techniques section, has been selected because of the quality of technical skill apparent in the work as applicable to the airbrush. This is not to mean that the selection is completely representative of the standards being achieved today; a combination of space restrictions and a lack of access to some illustrators' work has meant that many examples which *should* be included have unfortunately had to be omitted. The Themes have been loosely divided under seven section headings; cursory examination of some examples will show that they could equally be placed under other headings and therefore any aspiring illustrators should not restrict their study to those headings in which they have an interest, but should study *all* examples. By doing this a greater understanding of how best to use an airbrush for a specific effect will be gained.

TRANSPORT

Transport and industrial themes are traditionally the two principal subject areas, which have provided more airbrush-rendered illustrations than any other. The subject of transport is naturally vast and, although most forms are represented here, these examples merely signal the broad spectrum of diverse approaches. However, the aspiring airbrush illustrator can find much to learn in developing his or her own techniques.

Since the widespread introduction of the airbrush as an aid in the preparation and production of visual communication, illustrators have quickly appreciated the value of this tool in rendering the many facets of transportation subjects. In commercial use, the theme can be seen in advertising, posters, manuals, textbooks – especially for children – and in general and specialist magazines.

Three sets of illustrations are included which deal specifically with the subject of ships. This is unusual in that ships are rarely rendered in airbrushing, or indeed in any other medium, possibly because they are inherently more complex than other forms of transport. This is reflected in the fact that few commissions for illustrators are offered by the industry, with the possible exception of yacht-building, but even then, the majority of illustrations tend to be flat, orthographic images. The examples reproduced here are all three-dimensional in presentation and show three quite different approaches to the subject.

Vehicles and aircraft seem to be equally popular with illustrators and commissioning clients. Both are well represented here and, as diverse as these subjects are, so too are the approaches adopted by the illustrators in airbrushing them. In some cases it is a very personal approach, while in others the viewpoint and rendering is dictated by the needs of the client.

Reference material for transportation subjects is abundant, if you have the patience to look, especially for historical subjects which may require visits to specialist libraries or professional institutions. Often photography is used as a foundation for an illustration. This is perfectly acceptable, but may create visual distortions if not used with care. Because these subjects are technical, heavily three-dimensional and often large scale, careful preparatory drawing is essential.

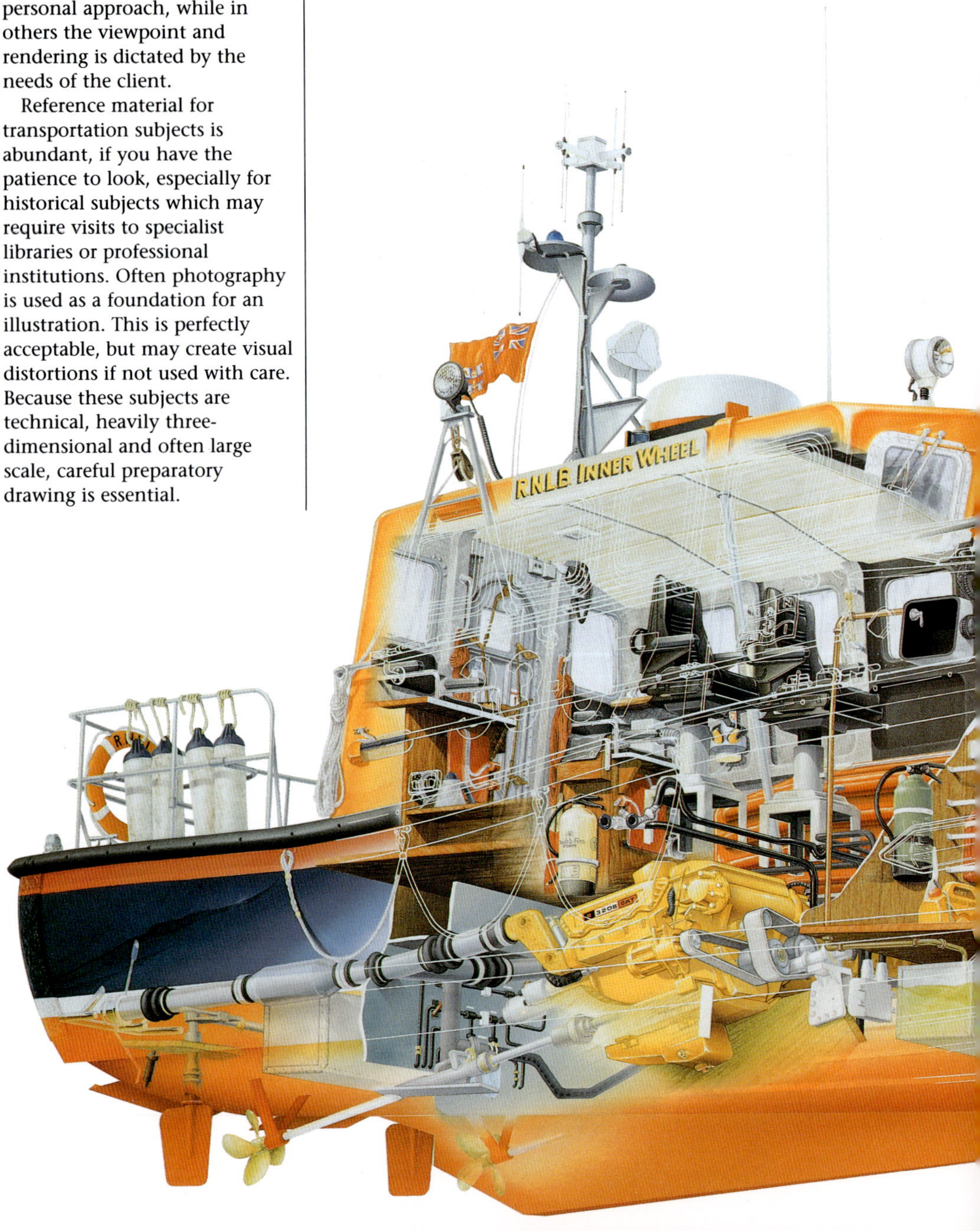

▶ **4-Wheel Drive Quad Runner •** ***Hide Nakajima***

STYLE

Typifying the high quality of Japanese airbrush art, this image is made solid by combined airbrushing and hand painting. The qualities of the medium and the tonal values are sensitively controlled; for example, in the difference between mat and polished surfaces. Each is balanced and in sympathy with its neighbor, without excessive gloss on reflective materials.

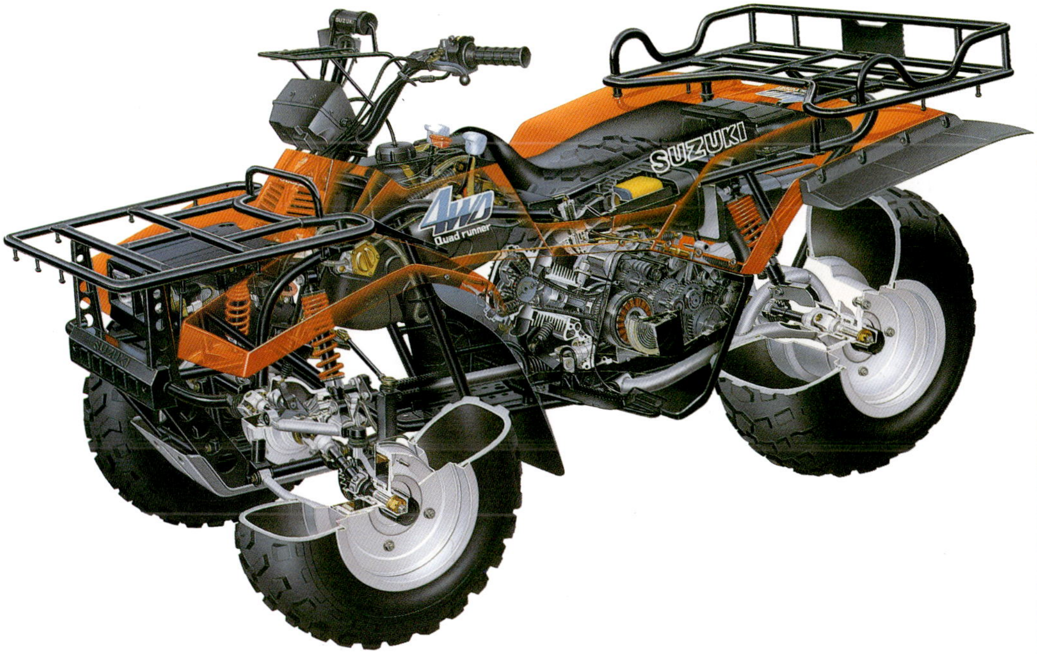

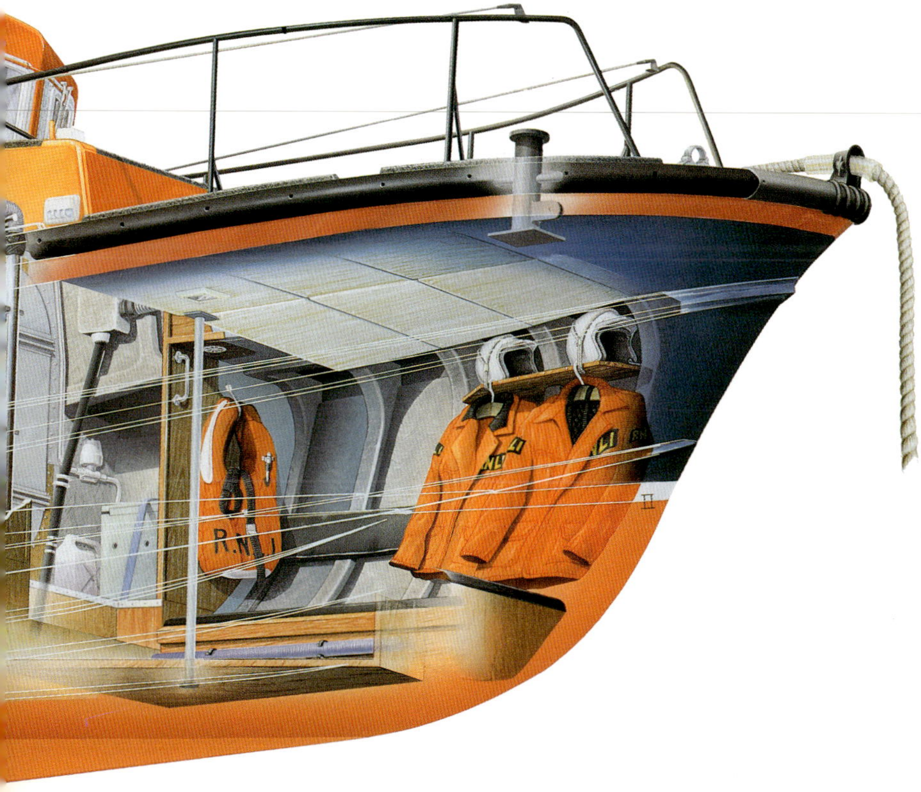

Brede class lifeboat ***Inner Wheel*** **•** ***Martin Woodward***

CONCEPT

A deliberately unusual yet effective viewpoint – as possibly seen by a person being rescued, albeit from an extreme angle – allows a clearer insight into the layout of this modern, single deck lifeboat.

TECHNIQUE

Drawn using the builder's plans as a primary reference source, extensive use has been made of GHOSTING and LINING-IN in order to maintain the overall shape of hull and superstructure, with internal details shown as solid items. Careful control of tonal balance is required when airbrushing areas in relatively weak colors, as on the superstructure and the lower part of the hull, especially when seen against the white of the artboard.

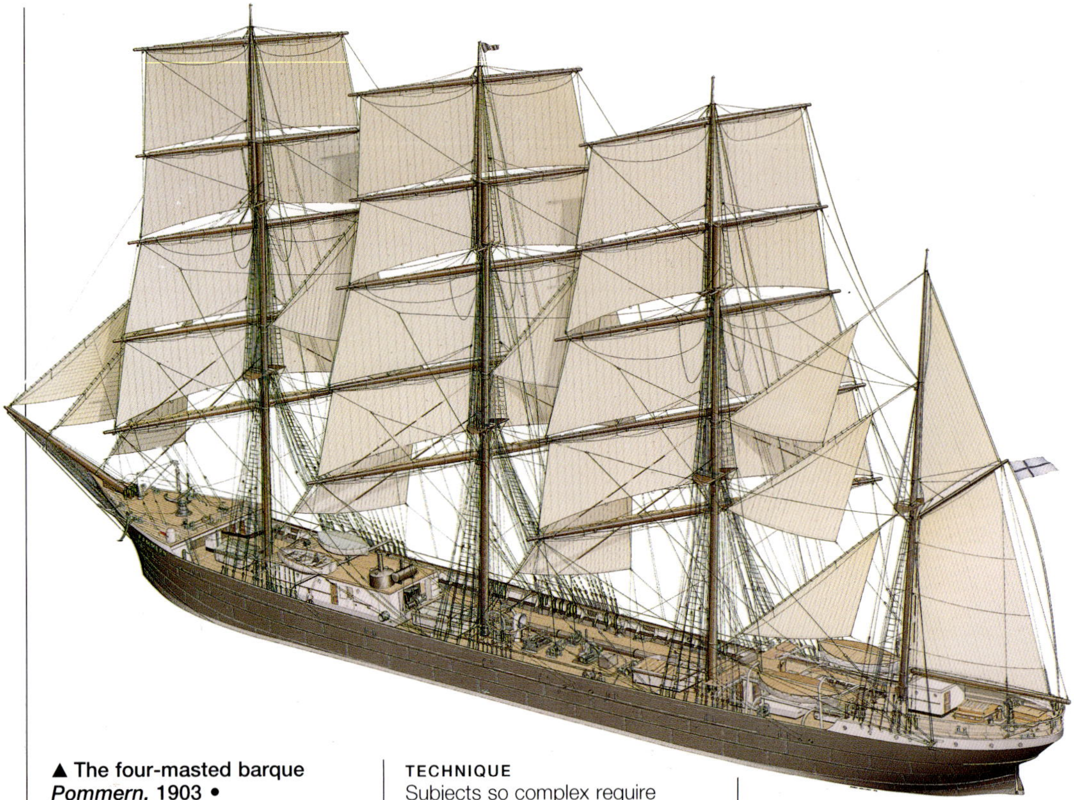

▲ The four-masted barque *Pommern*, 1903 • *Simon Williams*
▼ The deck and accommodation of the *Pommern*, 1903 • *Malcolm Tween*

APPROACH
These illustrations are from a series about the *Pommern*, one of the last ocean-going, cargo-carrying, square-rigged sailing ships, now preserved in Finland as a museum piece. All images were to be large enough for display on board, and suitable for poster reproduction.

TECHNIQUE
Subjects so complex require careful planning, with perhaps more time spent on the drawing stage than on the color artwork. Mixed media and mixed techniques were employed for accuracy and visual effect. Transparent watercolor was the base throughout, with gouache to highlight details and define different surfaces. Airbrushing was specially effective for large areas of GRADATED TONE and CAST SHADOW, such as on the sails and hull.

The cable-laying ship *CS Alert* • *Ross Watton*

SUBJECT
Detailed and accurate informational illustrations of ships are rare, and rarer as subjects for airbrush rendering. The sheer size and complexity create potentially insurmountable problems in combining exterior shape with interior layout and/or construction. This image, commissioned for the launch of the ship, was required to show only those interiors directly associated with cable laying and recovery. This was achieved through extensive use of GHOSTING, with minimal cuts, but it was still necessary to add a "scrap" view of the stern to illustrate recovery equipment.

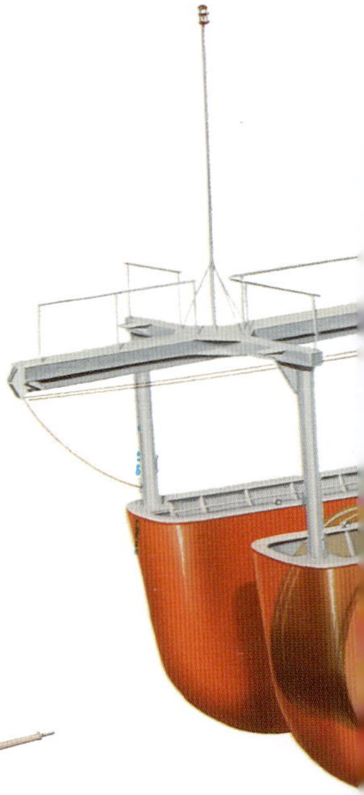

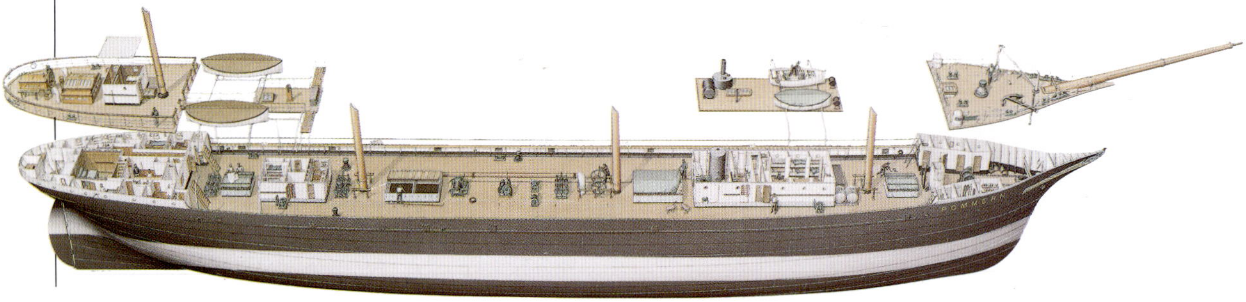

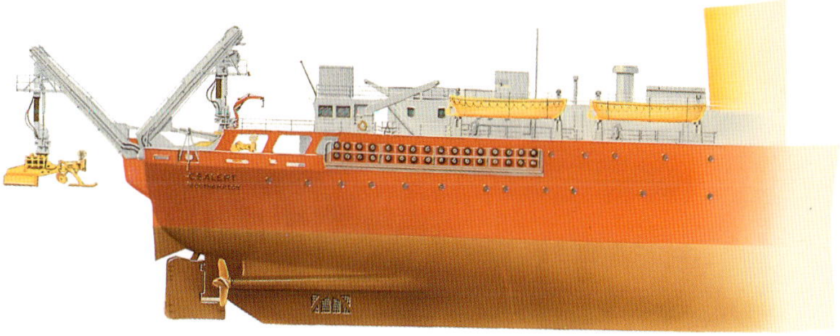
C.S. ALERT

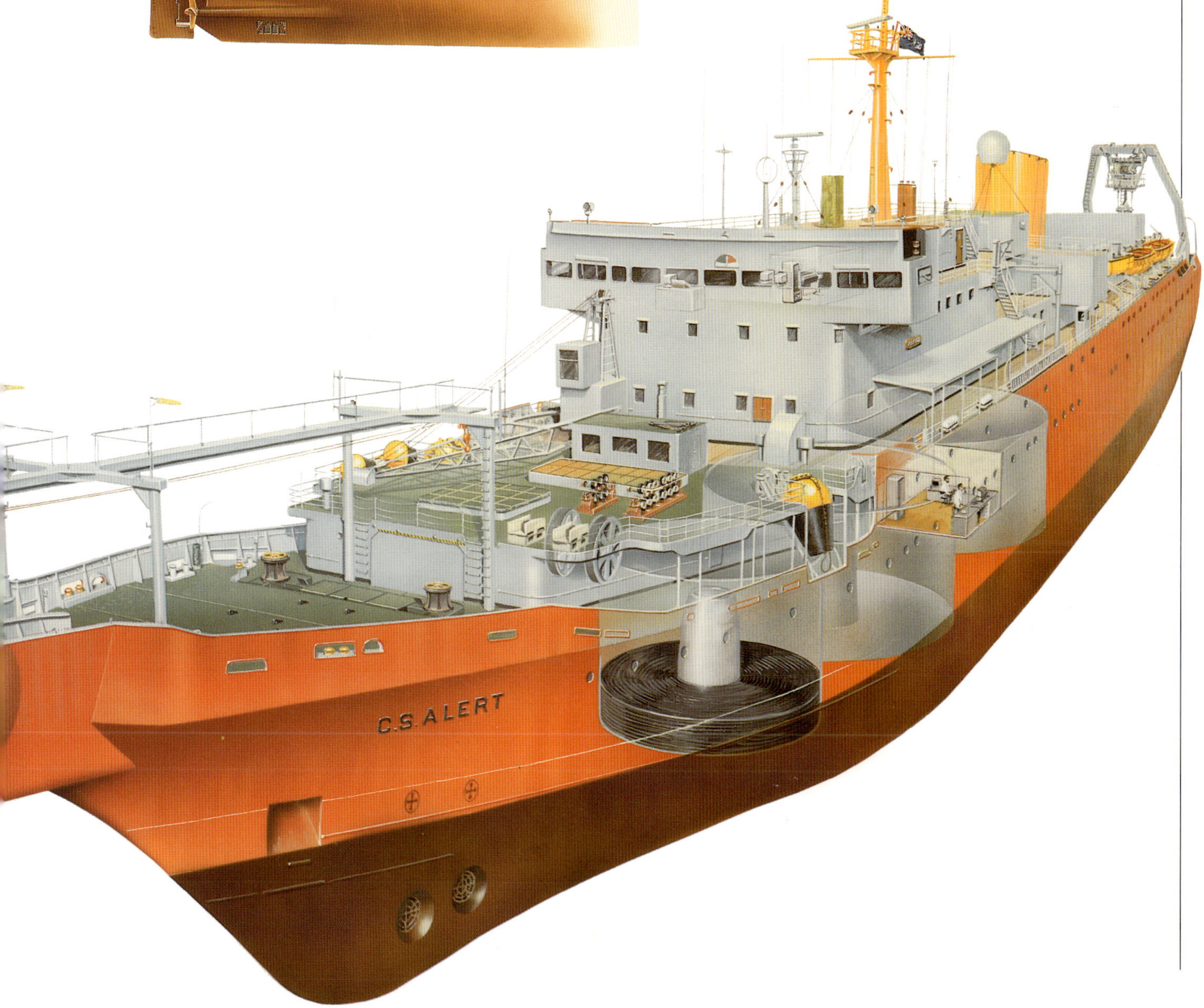
C.S. ALERT

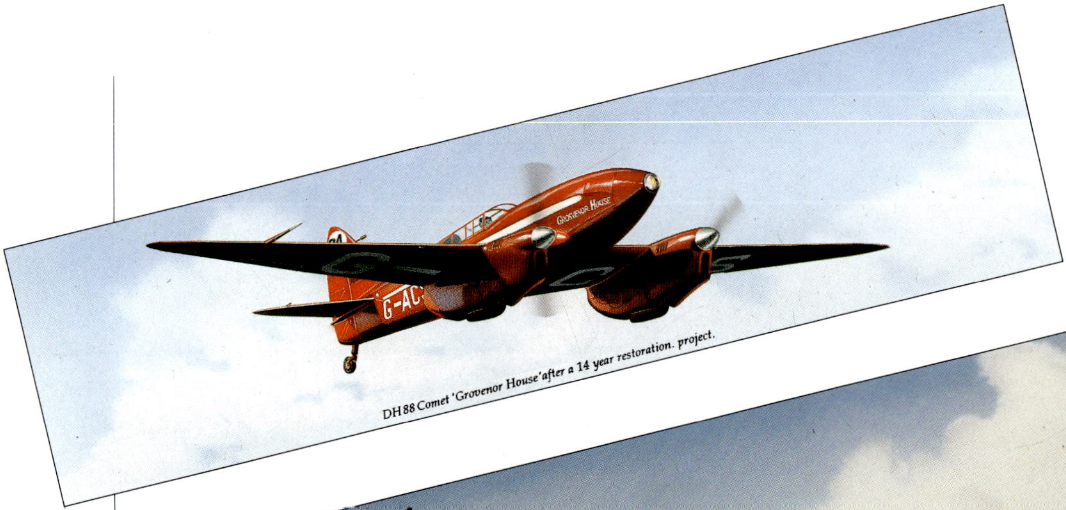

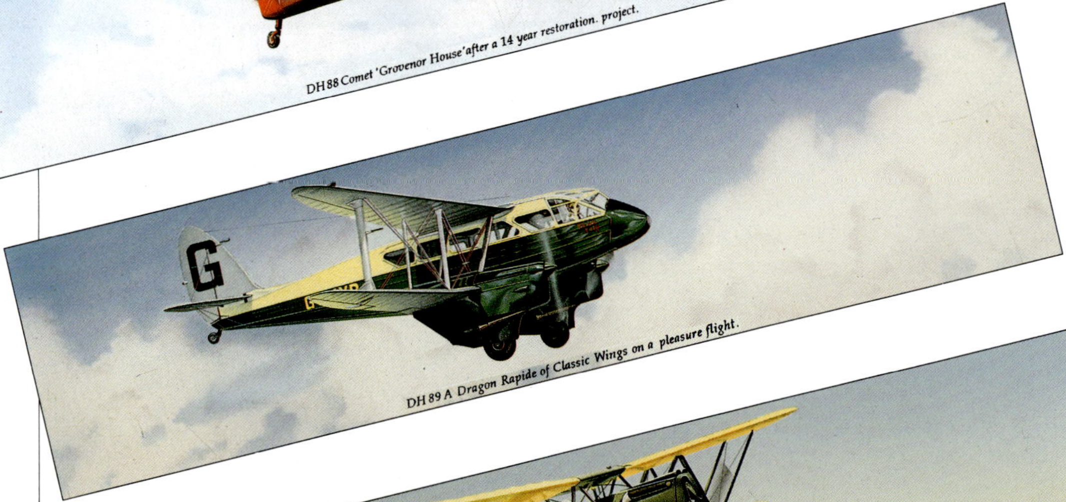

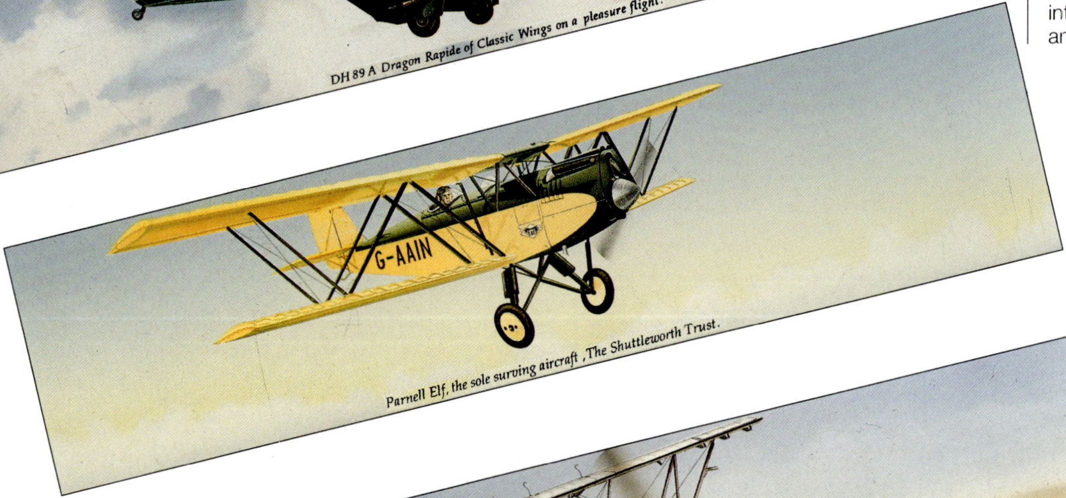

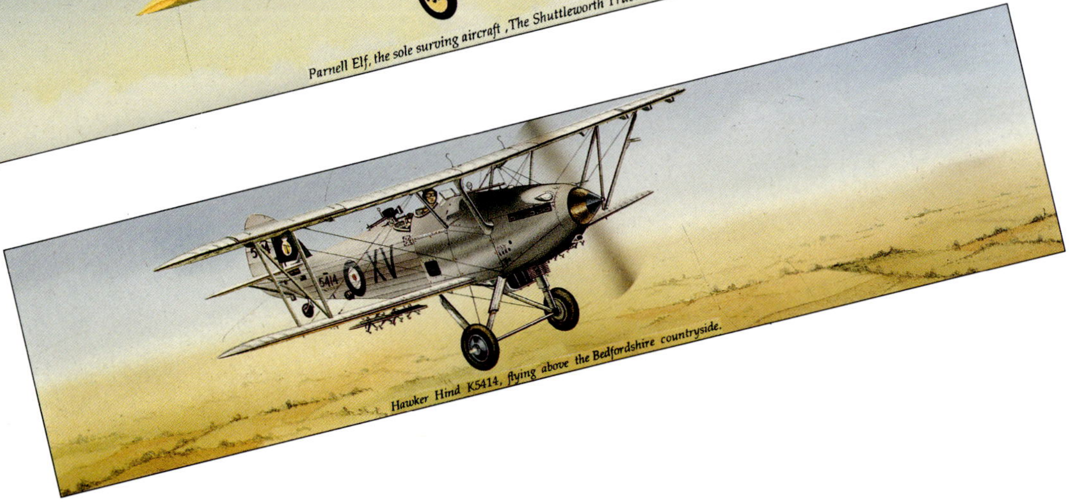

DH 188 *Comet*, Hawker *Hind*, Parnell *Elf* and DH 89A *Dragon Rapide* • *Anthony Lawrence*

STYLE

These relatively small illustrations, from a book on restoration of aircraft, demonstrate the depth of detail and accuracy attainable with the airbrush, though confined by the fixed frame of an extremely narrow landscape format.

TECHNIQUE

The aircraft were sprayed in transparent watercolor using FILM MASKING, with LOOSE MASKING to add shadows and reflections. The small scale prevented use of complicated masks. Minor adjustments of tone and contrast were hand-painted after spraying. Torn, soft tissue was used to mask the cloud effects. Notice how secondary reflected colors give the subject a sense of belonging to the image as a whole, integrating the treatments of aircraft and sky.

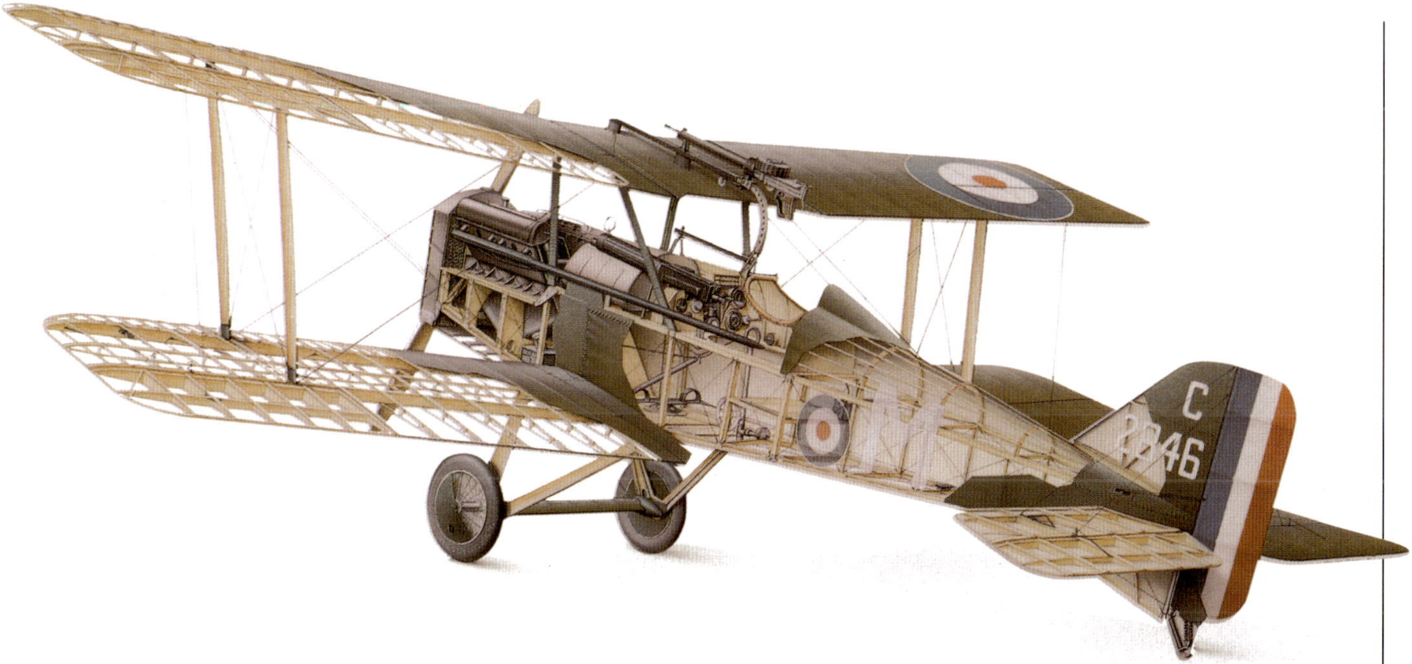

SE5a, and detail •
Malcolm Tween
COMPOSITION
Unusually, the illustrator has shown the aircraft from the rear and resting in its correct attitude on the ground. This realistic angle in no way confuses the extensive interior information shown through the cut areas, and allows structural detail to be seen on both upper and lower wing surfaces. Loose-masked CAST SHADOW sets the aircraft firmly on the ground.
STYLE
Combining watercolor and gouache on watercolor board, the artist has achieved well-balanced color and tonal values. Minimal white gouache OVERSPRAYING to add HIGHLIGHTING softens the image without destroying the subject's solidity. Close study reveals FREEHAND SPRAYING, LINING-IN, and RULING.

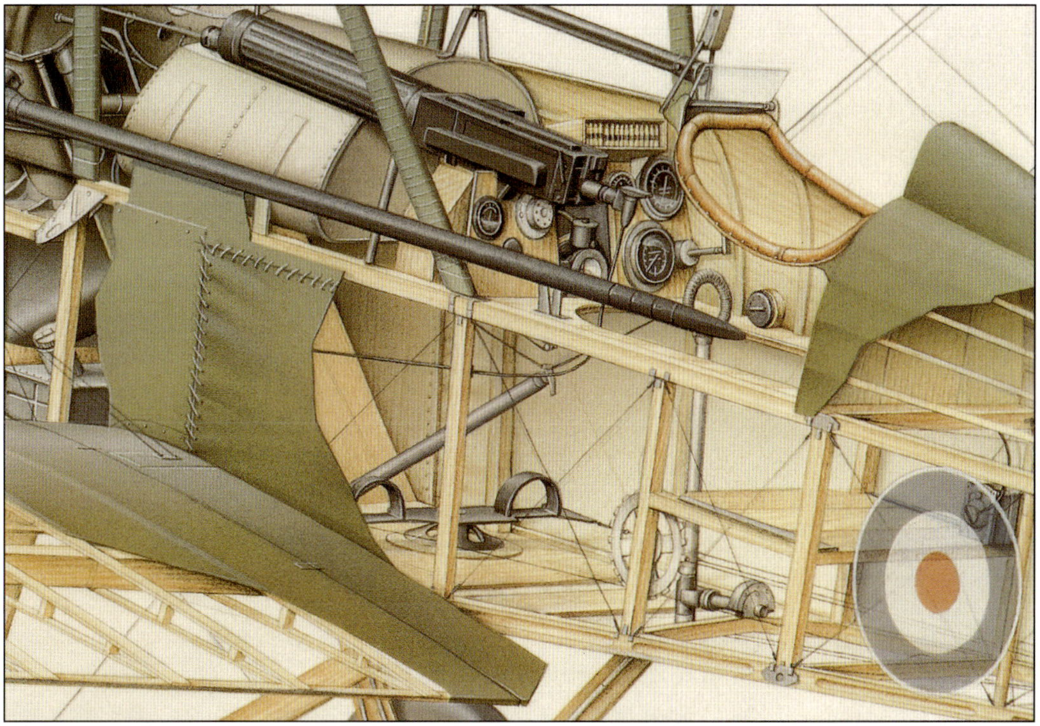

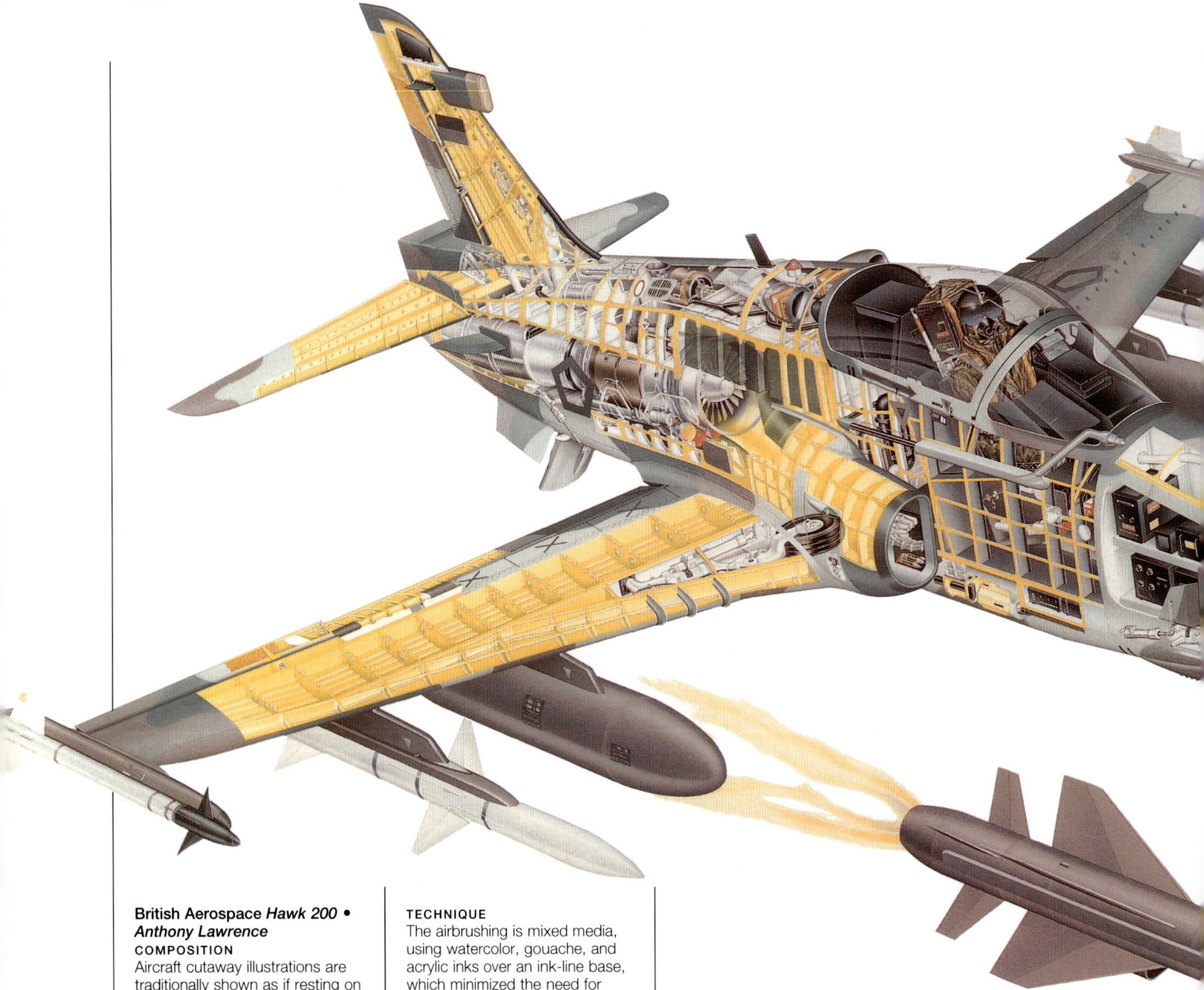

British Aerospace *Hawk 200* • *Anthony Lawrence*

COMPOSITION

Aircraft cutaway illustrations are traditionally shown as if resting on the ground, but here the illustrator decided to depict the airplane in flight, with the undercarriage retracted and about to release a missile, using representational colors for interior and exterior detail.

TECHNIQUE

The airbrushing is mixed media, using watercolor, gouache, and acrylic inks over an ink-line base, which minimized the need for LINING-IN after spraying. LOOSE MASKING with acetate sheets created soft edges between the camouflage tones and colors, the colors being sprayed flat to develop form and contrast before OVERSPRAYING with watercolor and white acrylic.

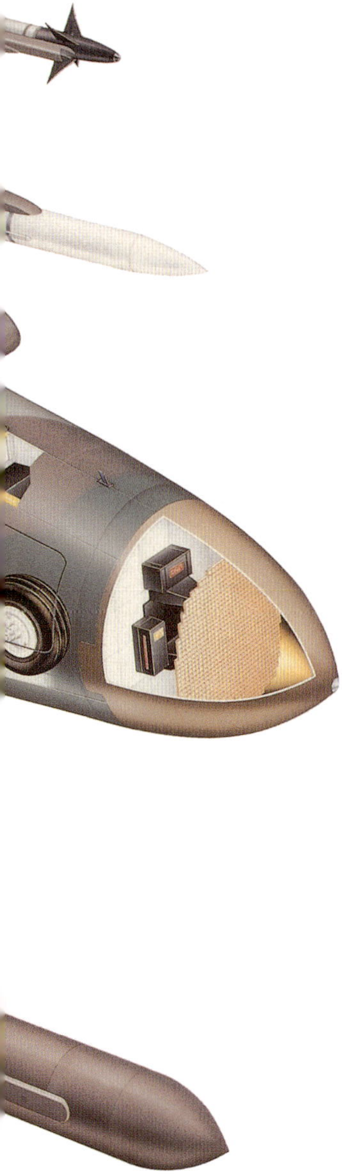

USAF General Dynamics F-16A *Fighting Falcon* Forward Instrument Panel • *Kevin Cowlard*

APPROACH
To show the application of hi-tech systems in modern aircraft, detailed illustrations of cockpit interiors are commonplace. This example even attempts accurate detail of readings for altitude, fuel consumption, and speed.

TECHNIQUE
A subject drawn close to full size requires great care with hand painting and LINING-IN. Losing patience in the completion stages can seriously undermine the quality and finish of the final image. The close detail of the instruments contrasts with loose FREEHAND SPRAYING of sky and clouds.

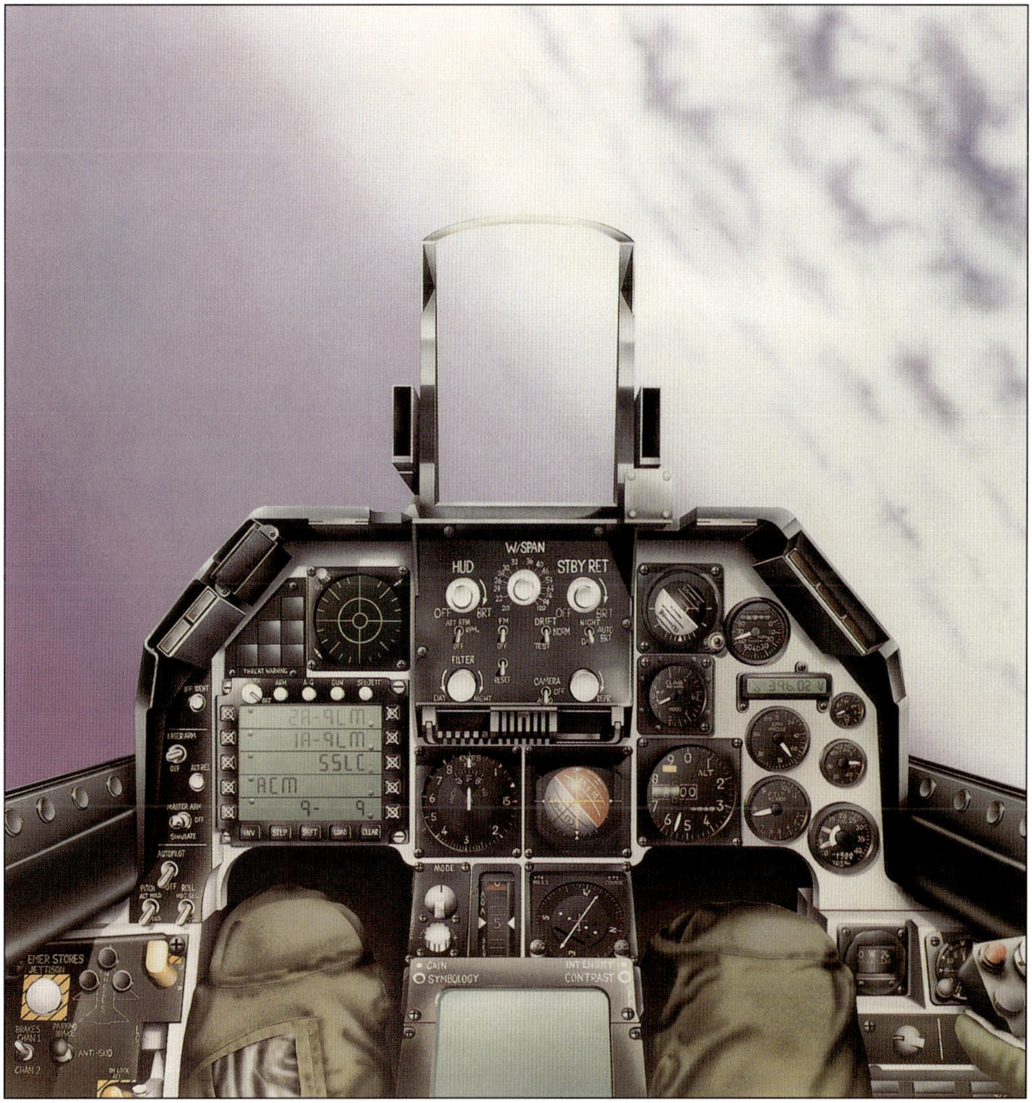

Recovery Vehicle Wheeled (General Service) 6x6 Foden • ***Malcolm Tween***

COMPOSITION

The brief required the illustration to draw attention to the character of the vehicle and include specified internal details. The less oblique view met these objectives and achieved maximum image size for reproduction on a landscape format poster.

TECHNIQUE

The airbrushing was applied to a mat gray-line bromide print taken from a perspective drawing. Body color was sprayed with a single film mask, adding HIGHLIGHTING and shadows with LOOSE MASKING. Note the careful tonal balance of areas shown by GHOSTING. LINING-IN and hand painting were kept to a minimum, because of problems with the paint adhering to the bromide.

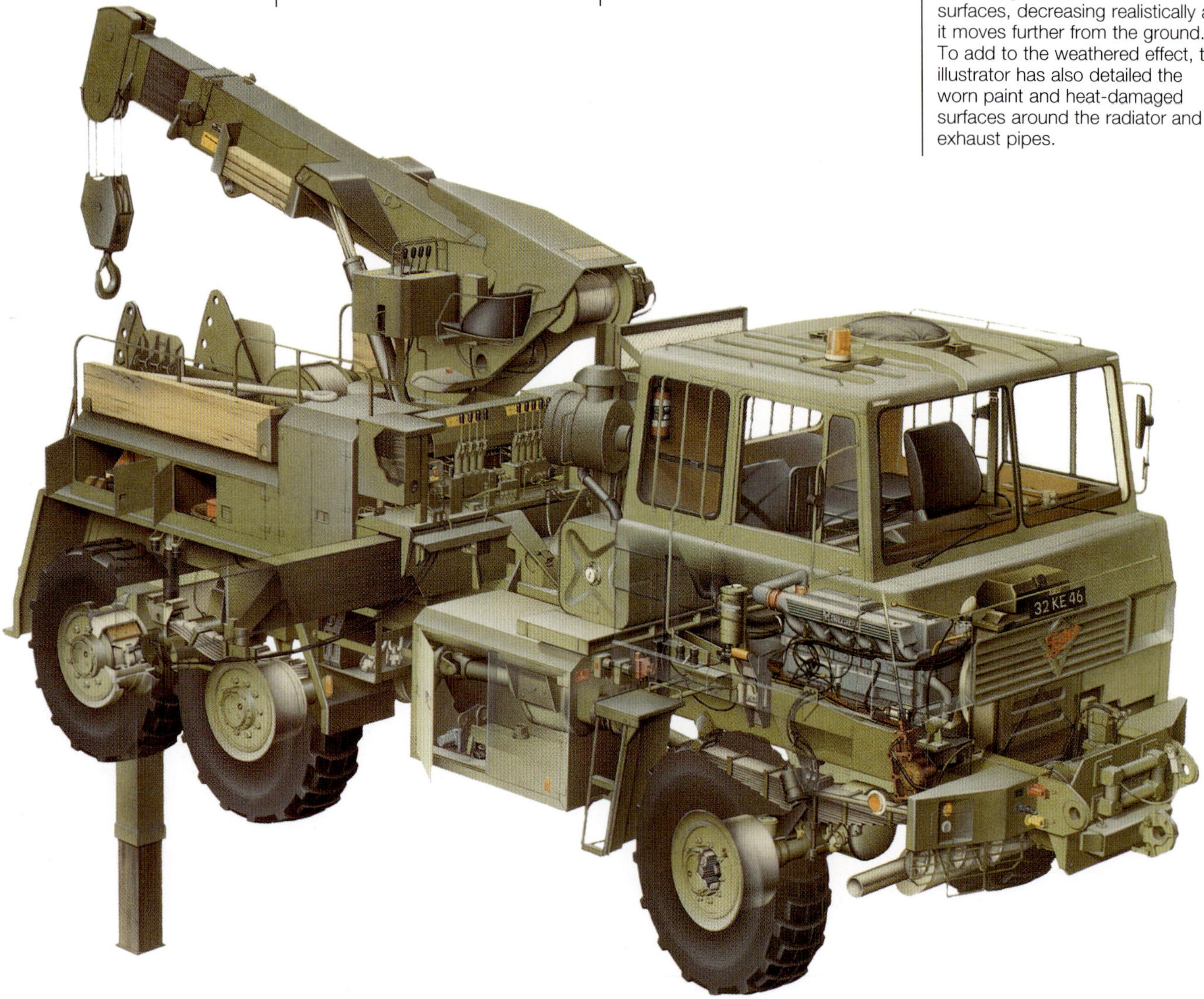

▶ Caterpillar Wide Gauge Tractor • ***Anthony Lawrence***

TECHNIQUE

This illustration demonstrates the use of the airbrush to achieve a weathered look. Through extensive but controlled use of SPATTERING, combined with restricted tonal variation, the surface texture shows the tractor as a genuine working vehicle rather than in the artificial environment of a showroom. The spattering is predominant on lower surfaces, decreasing realistically as it moves further from the ground. To add to the weathered effect, the illustrator has also detailed the worn paint and heat-damaged surfaces around the radiator and exhaust pipes.

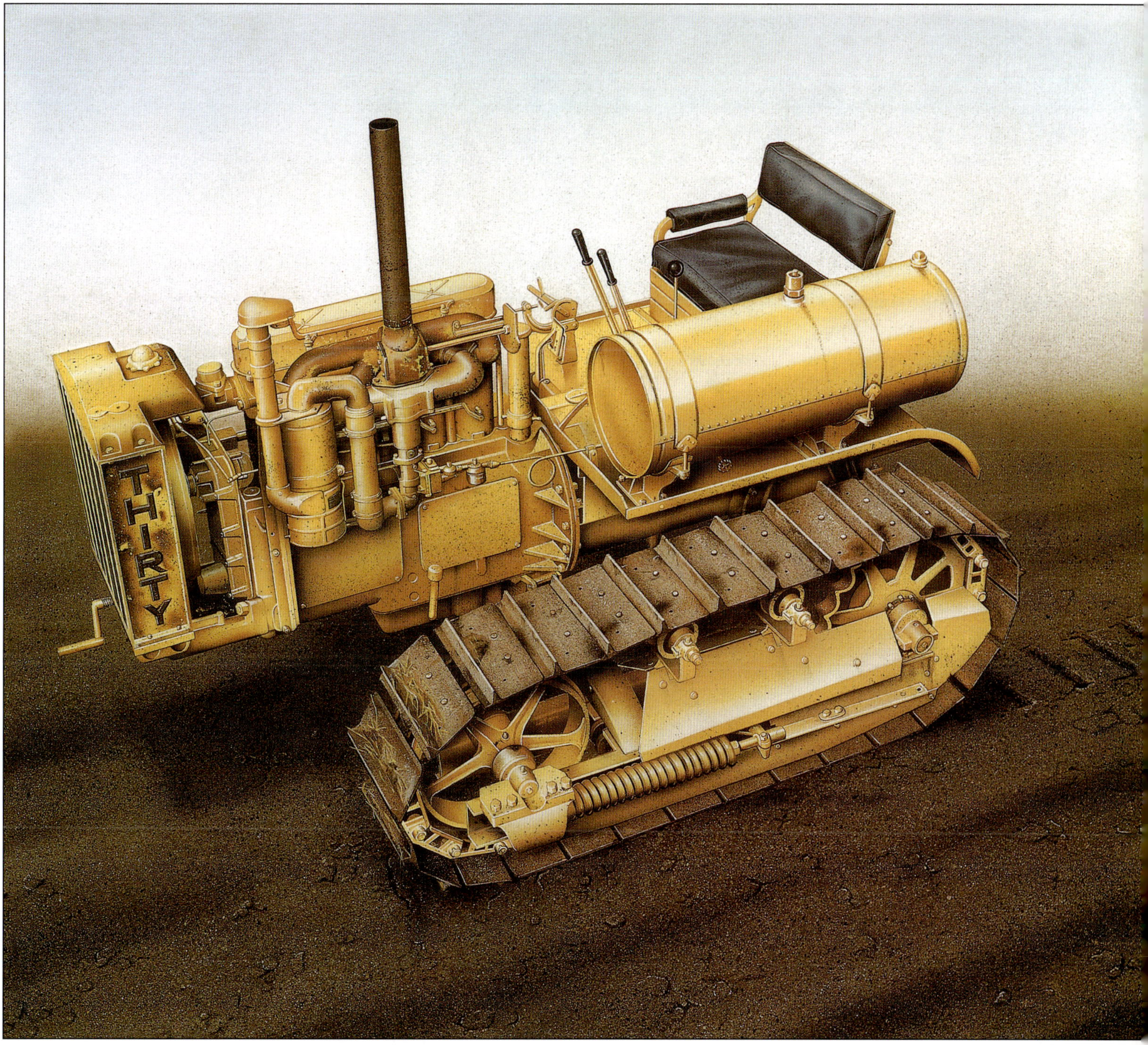
THIRTY

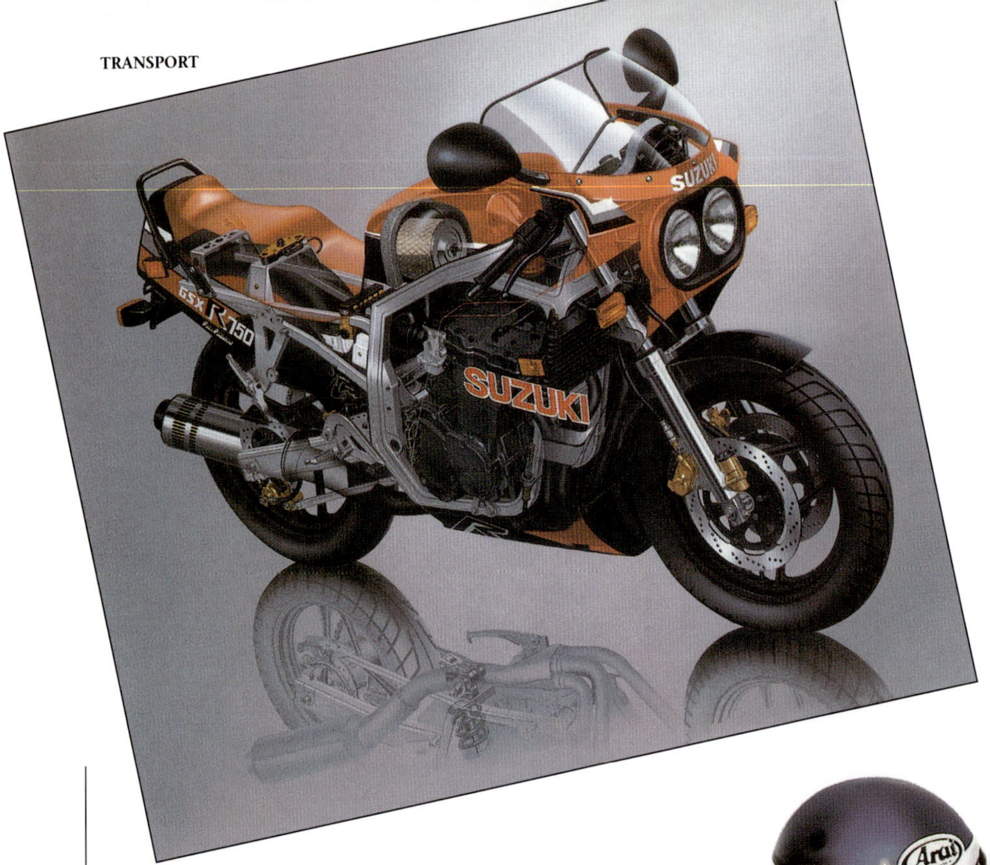

Suzuki 750 Motorcycle • ***Hide Nakajima***

COMPOSITION

Using almost the same angle as in the previous example, but from the other side, this illustrator has drawn everything in line with the center. To give the subject a base, he has chosen to put a part-reflected mirror-image underneath. This provides an opportunity to show details, such as the rear suspension spring, that would otherwise be invisible without a cutaway.

TECHNIQUE

Only selected areas have been revealed by GHOSTING; the engine, for example. Detail was built up with opaque color. The background was sprayed with GRADATED TONE, varied to give the impression of a slight glow behind and beneath the motorcycle, projecting its silhouette.

▼ Harris-Kawaski • ***Andy Burton***

TECHNIQUE

The powerful image relies in part on the technical skills deployed and subconscious awareness of the subject to convey the full impact. For example, a simple technique has been used to describe the texture and finish of the driver's leather suit: overlaid on top of the airbrushed HIGHLIGHTING, and very carefully applied, are small hand-painted dots of almost pure white. Other highlights use LOOSE MASKING and GRADATED TONES, and still others are no more than small scratches (see SCRATCHING BACK). The motorcycle's headlamp is extremely effective, but looked at closely, it can be seen that the rendering method is incredibly simple. The background shows the same technique as in previous images including spectators.

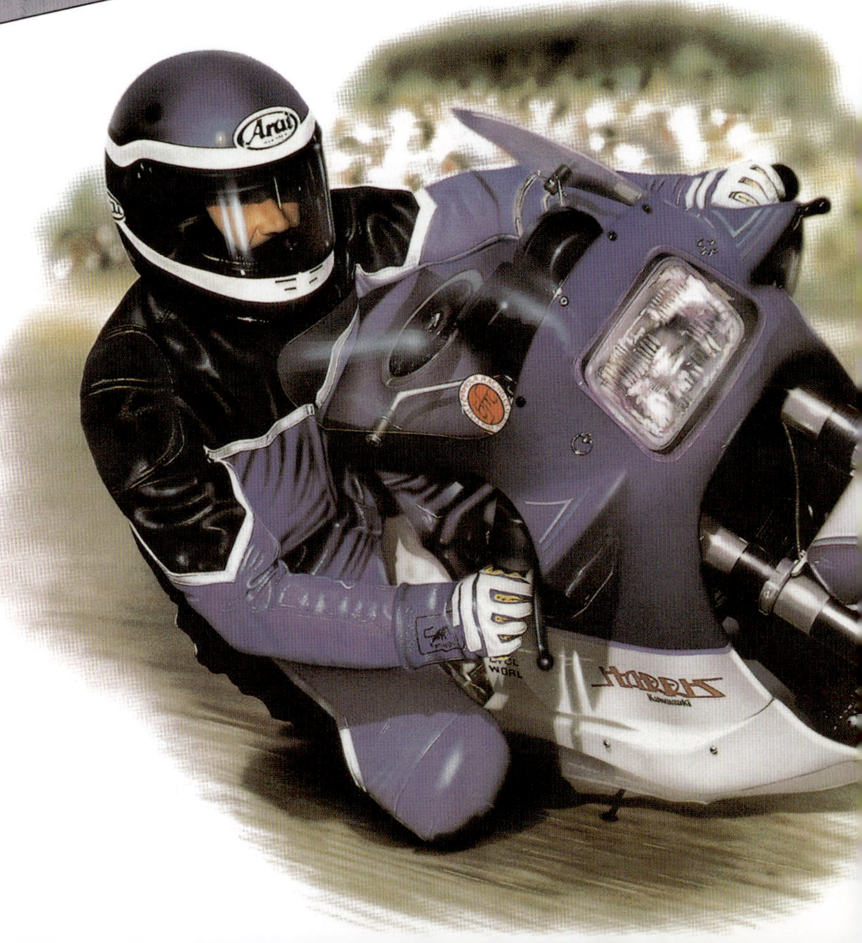

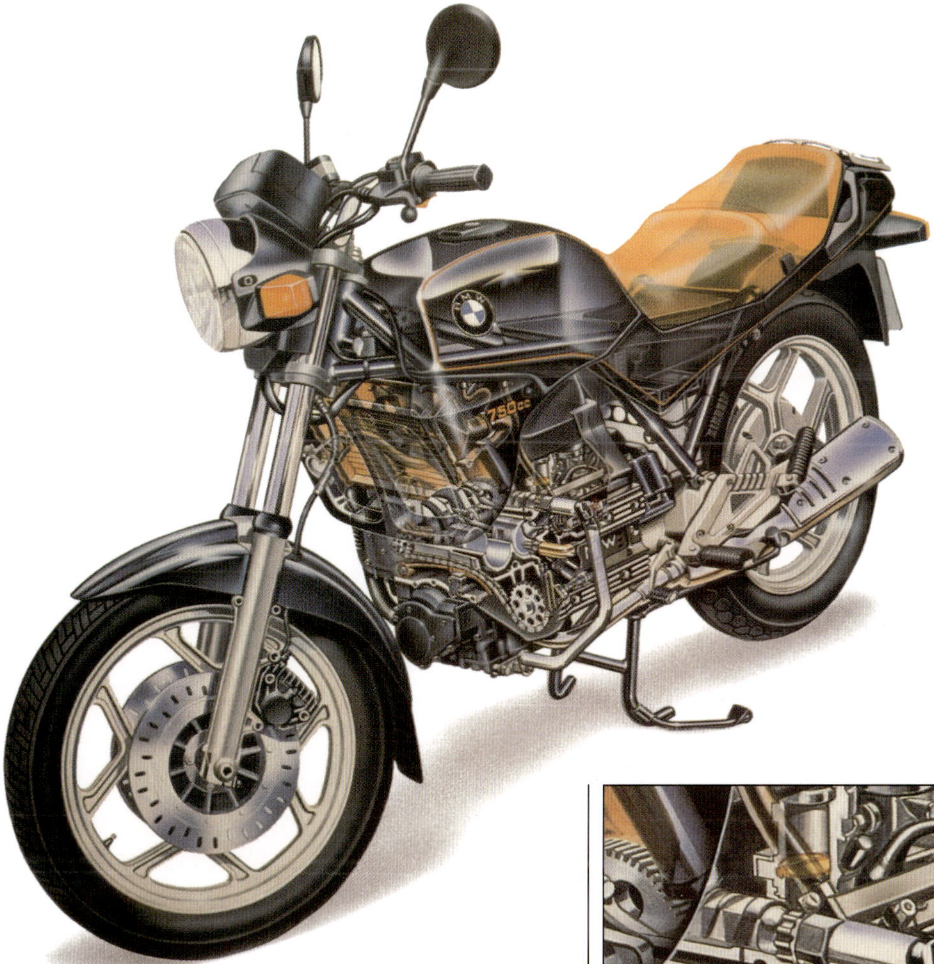

BMW Motorcycle Cutaway •
Arthur Phillips

COMPOSITION

Little variation can be introduced to such a subject, especially when the brief demands technical and visual accuracy. The illustrator has broken the narrowness of the image by showing the motorcycle at rest with the front wheel turned, and therefore out of alignment with the center line.

TECHNIQUE

TRANSPARENCY is the keynote, with the white artboard allowed to show through the color. Extensive use has been made of GHOSTING, LOOSE MASKING, HIGHLIGHTING, and LINING-IN. Effective and subtle FREEHAND SPRAYING of the ground shadow ensures the image does not appear to be floating in space.

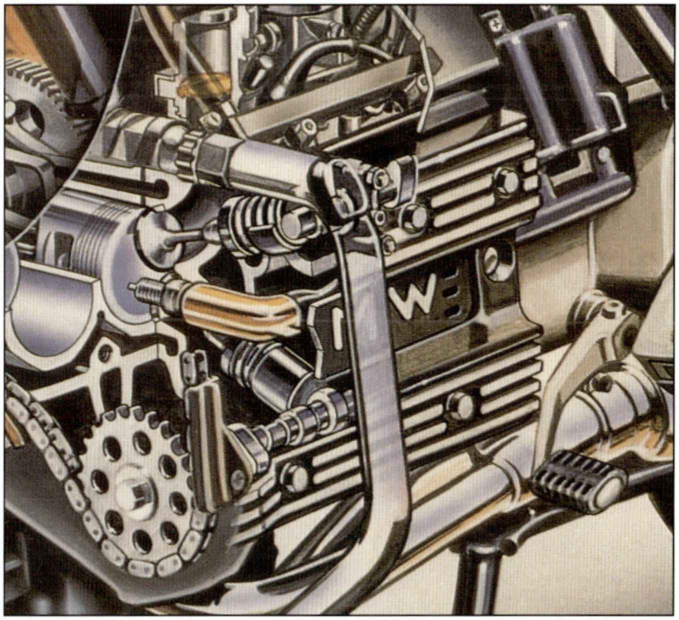

BMW 750cc motorcycle (detail)
• Arthur Phillips

TECHNIQUE

This detail view shows the apparent simplicity of technique employed to render this complex subject. The majority of the illustration relies very much on a black holding line, within which the colors of the various components have been airbrushed. And because of the complexity of detail, the application of color has been kept relatively uncomplicated with minimal use of secondary or tertiary tones.

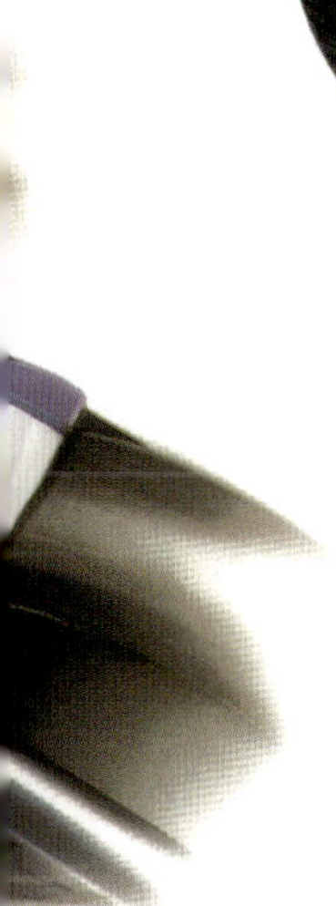

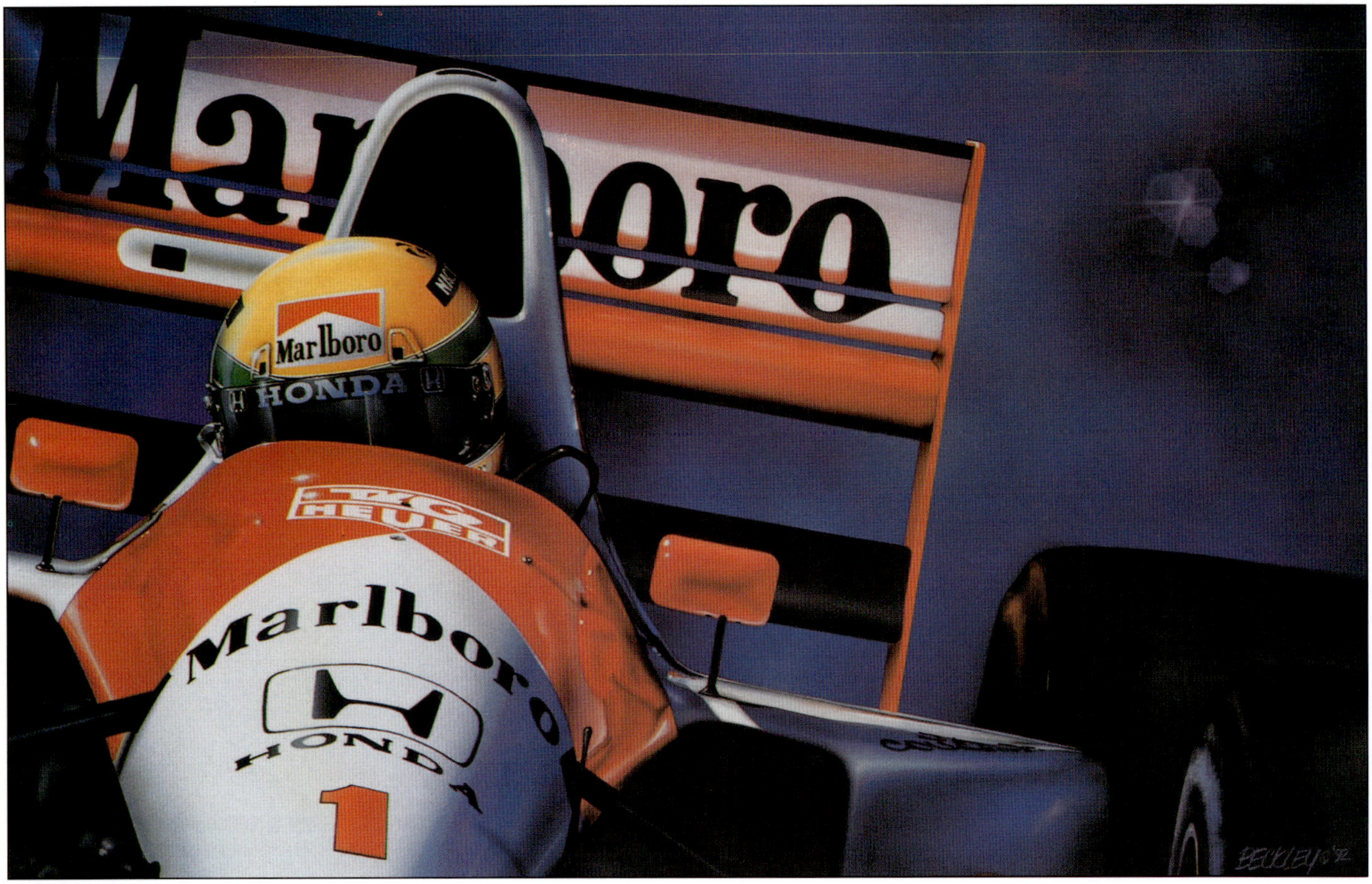

Untitled • *Scott Beckley*

APPROACH

While the car and its advertising are clearly identifiable, the composition and background color give the subject an almost surreal or abstract quality. Both this and the illustration, right could be said to fulfill the requirements of the same brief, but with very different interpretations of the subject. The two images stand objective comparison. The first was an attempt to portray part of the car in its natural environment, possibly as seen through a television camera, while in this case there is a more dramatic composition, and the highly polished surface texture of the car body is shown as if new, adding to the surreal effect.

▶ Goodyear • *Malcolm Tween*

TECHNIQUE

A traditional use of airbrushing in watercolor with some gouache. While having a soft, almost delicate touch to the way the colors have been sprayed, the subject retains a strong sense of solidity, movement and speed, in light conditions which are reflected in the color changes and tonal balances in the car. ACETATE MASKING, CAST SHADOWS, DOT CONTROL, and DOT HIGHLIGHTS, FILM MASKING, FREEHAND SPRAYING, GRADATED TONES, KNOCKING BACK, LINE CONTROL, LINING-IN, LOOSE MASKING, and TRANSPARENCY have all been used to good effect.

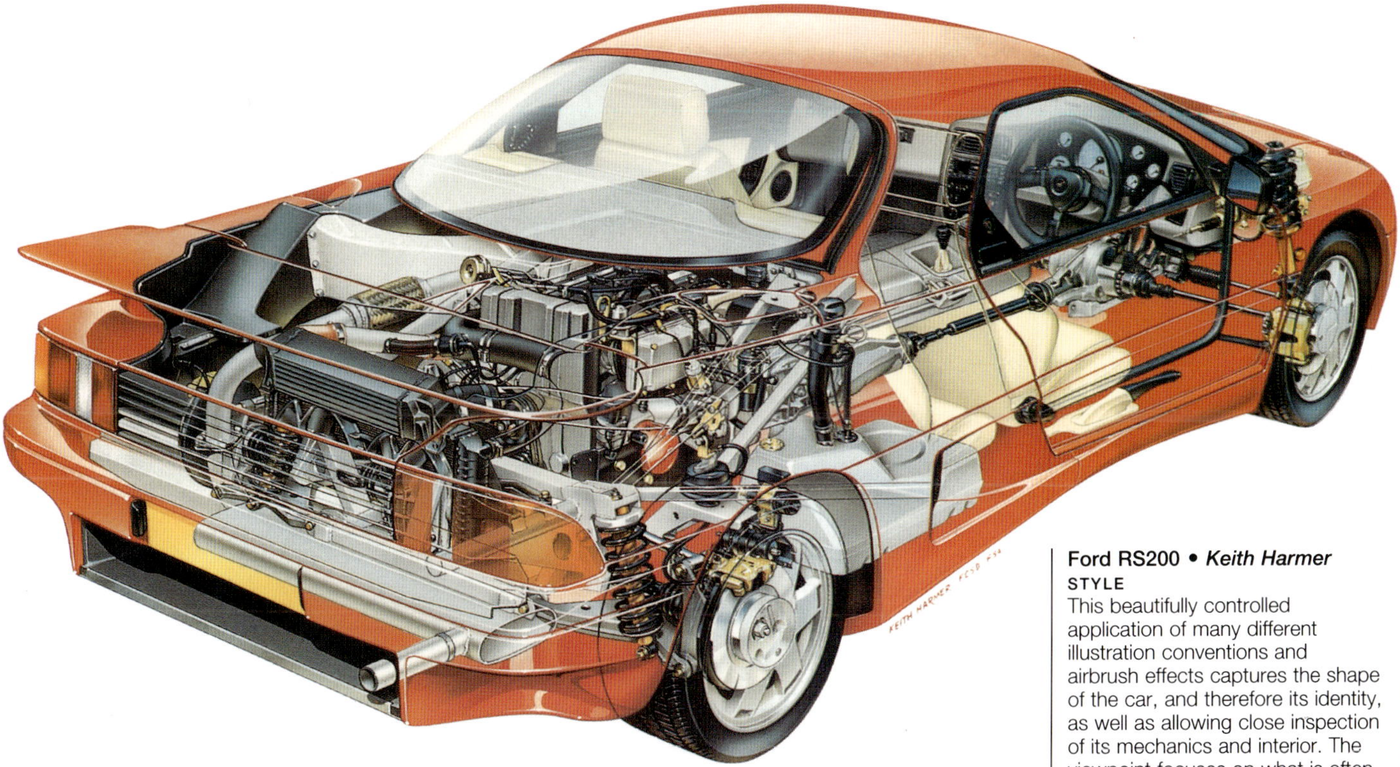

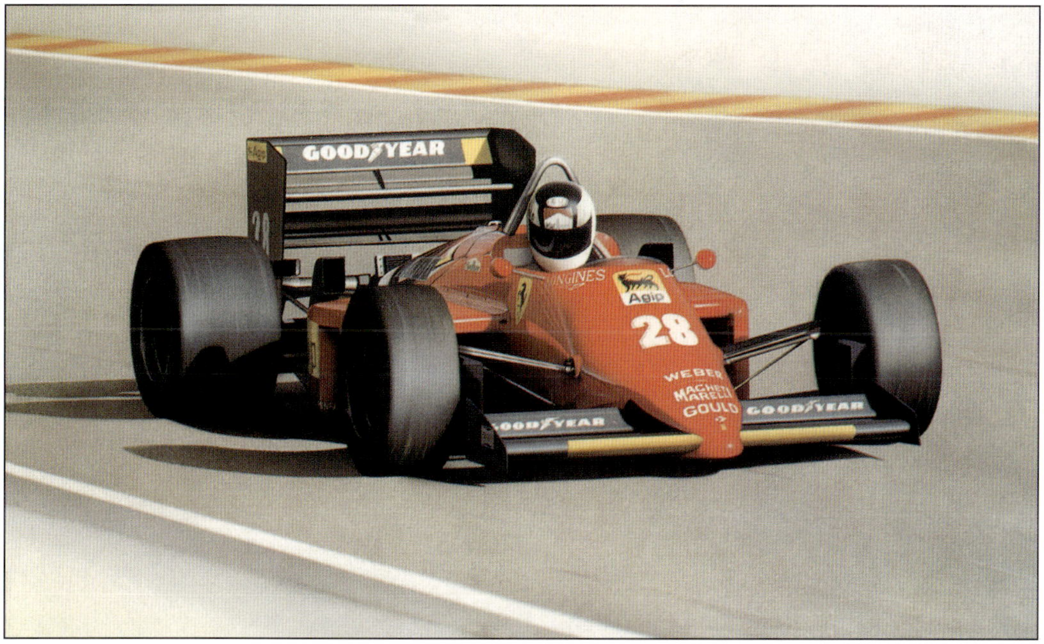

Ford RS200 • *Keith Harmer*

STYLE

This beautifully controlled application of many different illustration conventions and airbrush effects captures the shape of the car, and therefore its identity, as well as allowing close inspection of its mechanics and interior. The viewpoint focuses on what is often considered the most important element after styling – the engine; yet much else is seen.

TECHNIQUE

A full repertoire of techniques includes CARD MASKING, CHROME EFFECTS, FILM MASKING, FLAT TONE, FREEHAND SPRAYING, GHOSTING, GRADATED TONE, HIGHLIGHTING, LINE CONTROL, LINING-IN, LOOSE MASKING, OVERSPRAYING, RULING, and TRANSPARENCY.

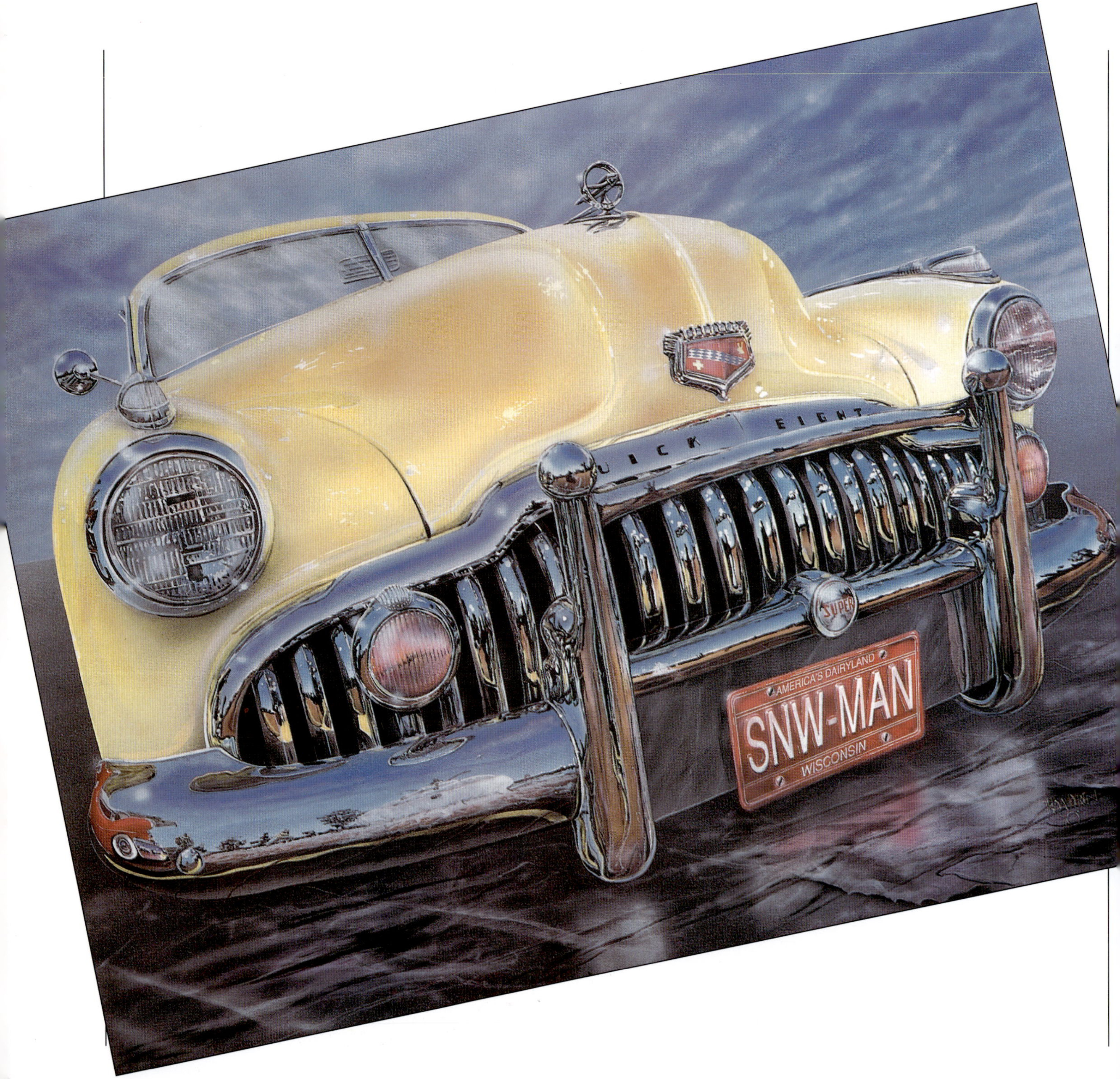
EIGHT
SUPER
AMERICA'S DAIRYLAND
SNW-MAN
WISCONSIN

Snowman • *Thom Petersen*

CONCEPT

The inspiration behind this exaggeratedly and dramatically drawn car came from the illustrator's childhood memories, which is partly evidenced by the reflections in the bumper and the number plate.

TECHNIQUE

The extensive use of bright, contrasting colors with equally strong contrasting highlights contributes to the overall image of a highly polished and excessively chromed car from the 1950s. Within the boundaries of FILM MASKING, much use has been made of FREEHAND SPRAYING, in particular on the body, in the sky and on the ground.

▶ Sports car • *Keith Harmer*

TECHNIQUE

The limited palette and apparent simplicity of technique in this rendering are remarkably successful. Of particular note is the subtle and carefully controlled GRADATED TONE applied to the hood of the car, with the introduction of reflected colors from the "sky," enhancing the smoothness and finish of the surface texture. DOT HIGHLIGHTS combined with STARBURSTS have been selectively applied to add further to the reflective effect. The broken surface on which the car stands adds contrast and helps project the car towards the viewer.

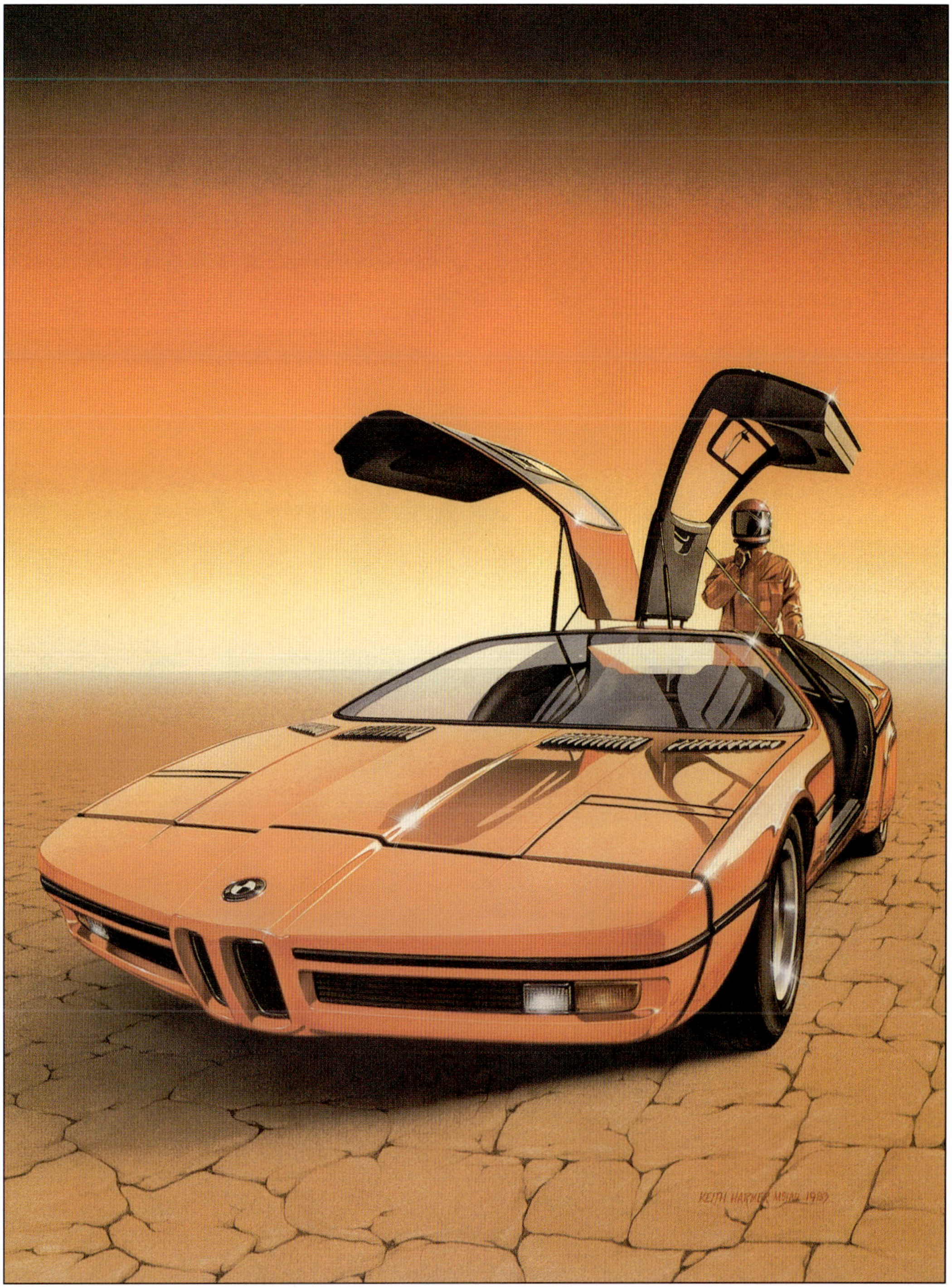

INDUSTRIAL DESIGN AND ENGINEERING

About thirty years ago, the airbrush was primarily seen as something which technical illustrators, working in the publications departments of manufacturing companies, used in the rendering of highly technical and mechanical subjects for a limited and specialized audience. Such renderings often took the form of a highly finished and prestigious illustration, depicting the subject in a pristine condition that the user would hardly recognize. However, such illustrations served, and in a limited way continue to serve, the potential customer in giving a clear idea of what the product would look like, in ways which a photograph could not.

Because of this, and due to their obvious similarities, industrial, technical, scientific and engineering subjects have much in common with transportation, and undoubtedly lend themselves to rendering with an airbrush.

Standards of airbrushed illustration today have been influenced by the incredible quality of work coming out of Japan, especially on transport and industrial-based subjects. This is not to suggest that the western world has not produced its illustrators of repute or comparable standard. In the USA, for example, airbrushing has developed beyond the mere accurate rendering of a subject into the realms of a more conceptualized approach. In the UK, however, there remains a healthy tradition of applying the airbrush as a tool for rendering a subject as it is, without the emphasis on super-realism apparent in much of the work from Japan.

There is much to be said in favour of the airbrush being used on industrial and engineering subjects. Although it is demanding of both patience and skill, it is in fact often easier to render the complexities of modern technical subjects in this way than by hand-painting, especially if the subject is shown in three-dimensional perspective. What must never be apparent on the finished artwork is obvious evidence of mask cutting or badly applied lining-in and ruling. To qualify these observations, it must be stressed that a certain level of skill in hand-painting is a prerequisite to developing skills with the airbrush, for the two are inseparable and are often combined in a single illustration.

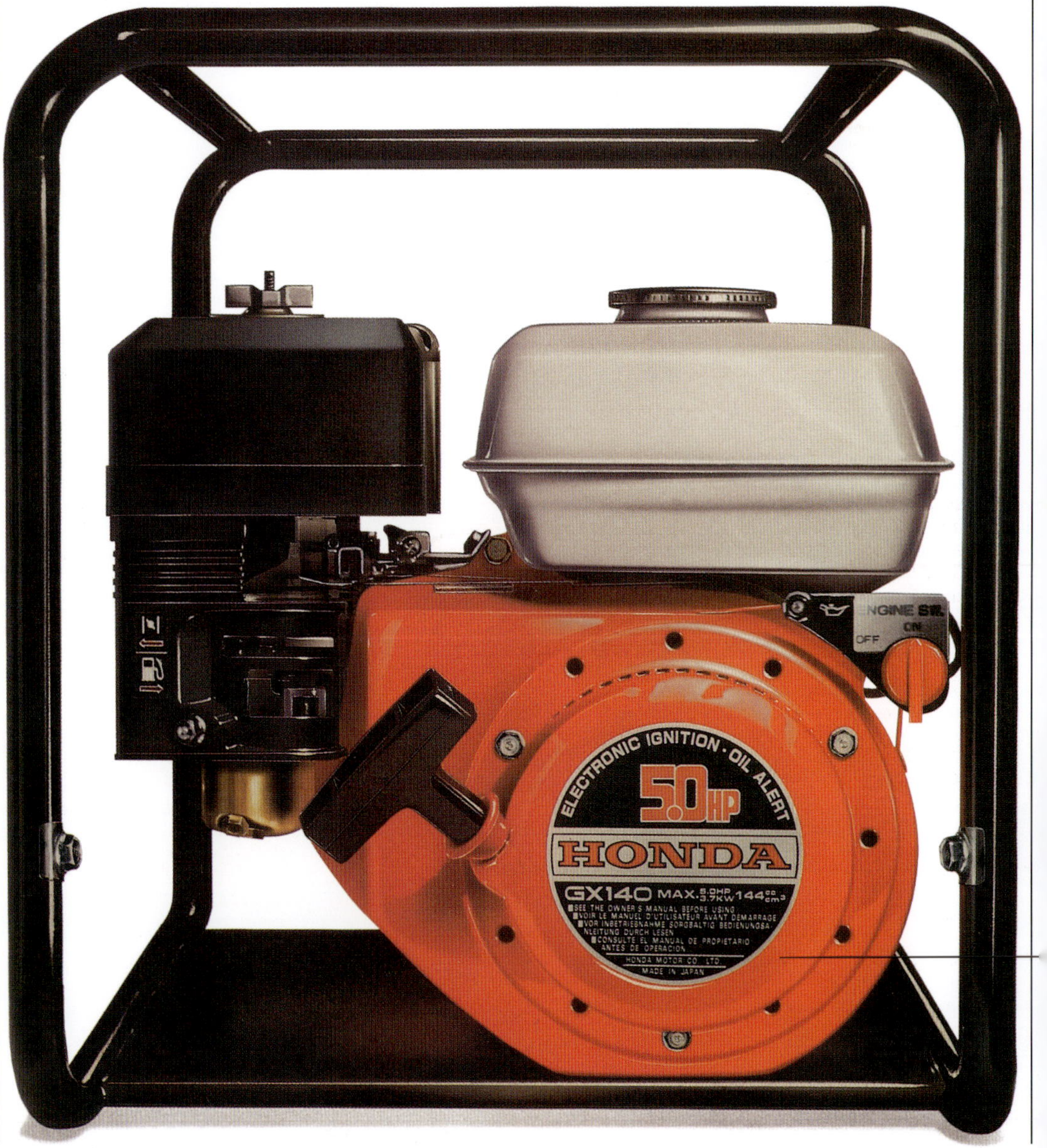

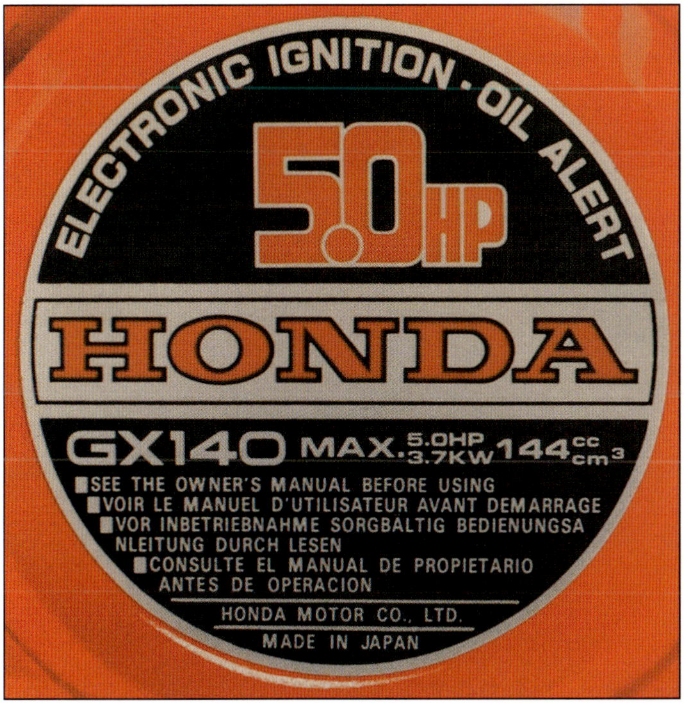

▼ Single Seat Submersible • *Nick Hawken*

STYLE

The variety of surface textures ranges from the naturally highly polished yellow casing and transparent dome to the semi-mat, black-and-white "arms" and black base. The contrast between these materials allowed a distinctive style to be developed.

TECHNIQUE

Careful GHOSTING, OVERSPRAYING, and LOOSE MASKING helped to achieve the contrast on the dome and casing. On the dome, the illustrator has successfully introduced secondary colors which, besides delineating its shape, accurately reflect colors from other parts of the submersible. The same approach to other areas has given the image a cohesive completeness.

◀▲ Honda 5 HP Portable Engine • *John Brettoner*

APPROACH

It is easy to over-emphasize HIGHLIGHTING and reflected colors in CHROME EFFECTS. This shows how simplicity, carefully planned and applied, can achieve the best result. The restricted palette, based on actual colors, also contributes to its success.

TECHNIQUE

LOOSE MASKING has created subtle reflected color, and the simple highlights on the black enamelled bars convey shape and surface texture without unnecessary special effects. Inability to reproduce printed text often spoils technical illustrations: in this image, the manufacturer's label dominating the engine casing is almost beyond fault.

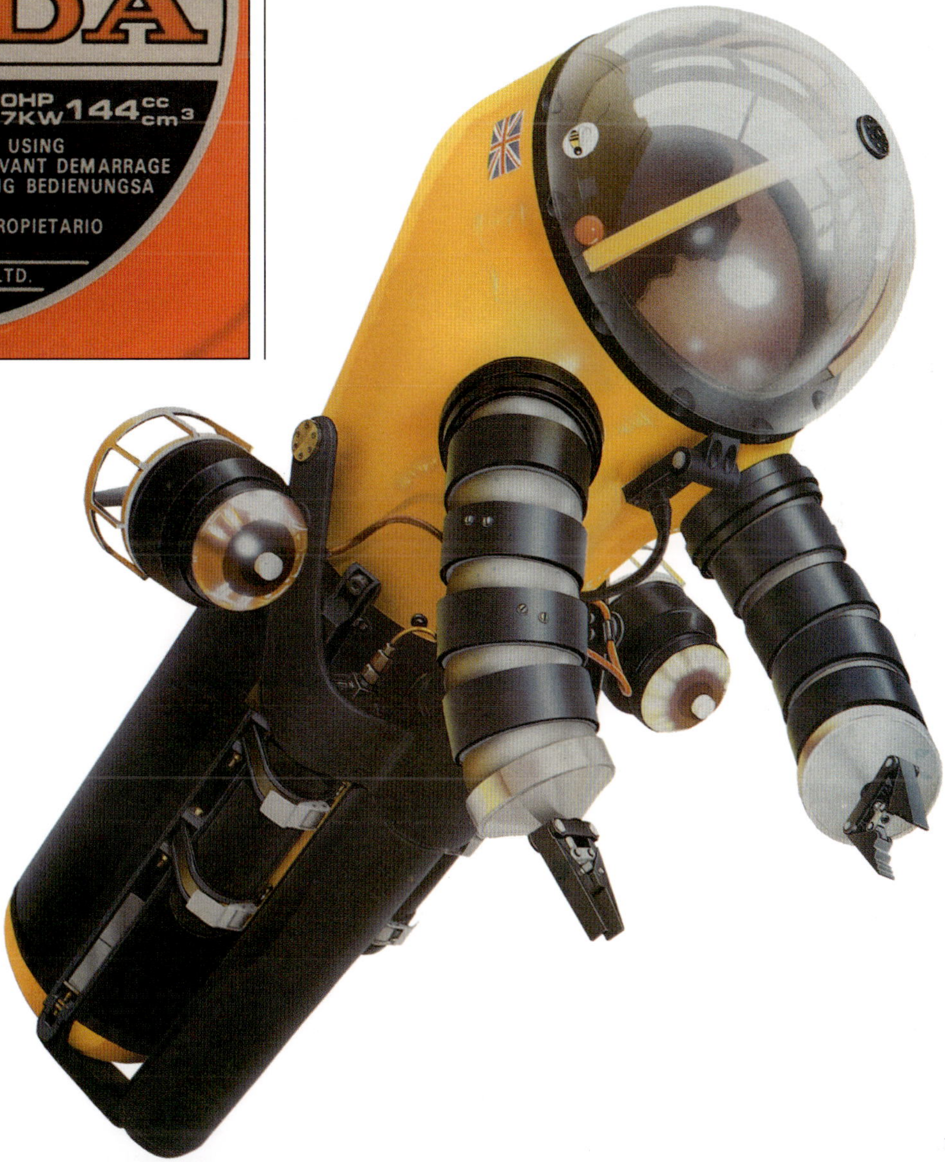

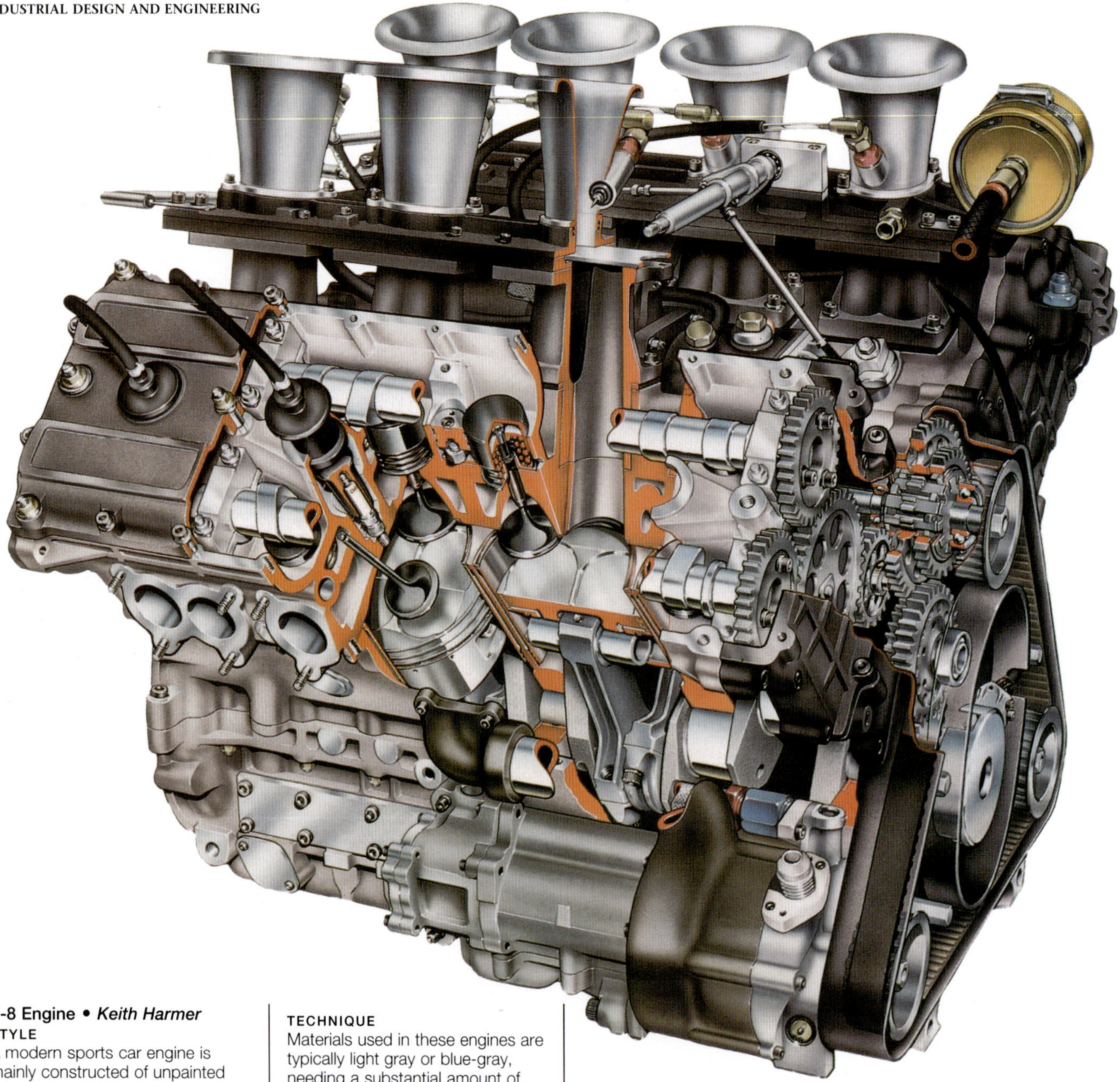

V-8 Engine • *Keith Harmer*

STYLE

A modern sports car engine is mainly constructed of unpainted light alloys, which are glossy or semi-glossy. If airbrushed too excessively, these can appear as a confusing array of abstract patterns, detracting from the overall image. Here the illustrator has found a good balance of subtle color changes and contrasting values.

TECHNIQUE

Materials used in these engines are typically light gray or blue-gray, needing a substantial amount of HIGHLIGHTING to complete the image. A simple rendering method resembling CHROME EFFECTS has been very effectively applied to technical detail.

Landrover TDI Engine •
Andy Burton

APPROACH

The aim was to capture the rugged, functional image of this manufacturer's engines and vehicles, yet depict it in a modern style to emphasize that it is also hi-tech engineering.

TECHNIQUE

The original line illustration was redrawn in white over a flat black tone, and selected areas treated with gouache OVERSPRAYING, using FILM MASKING and LOOSE MASKING. With only part of the image rendered completely, the overall effect creates an impression of intense light pulling out the airbrushed details.

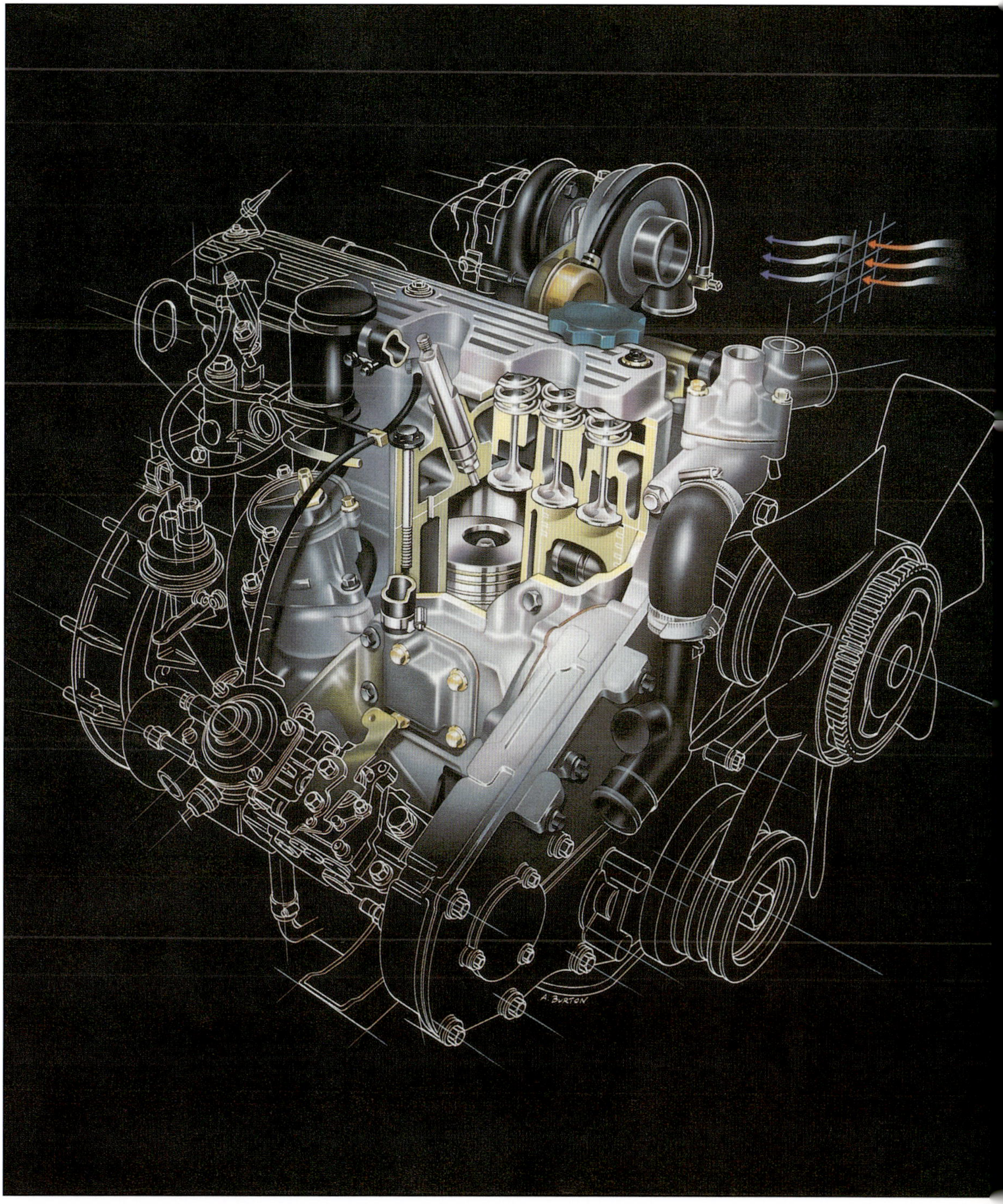

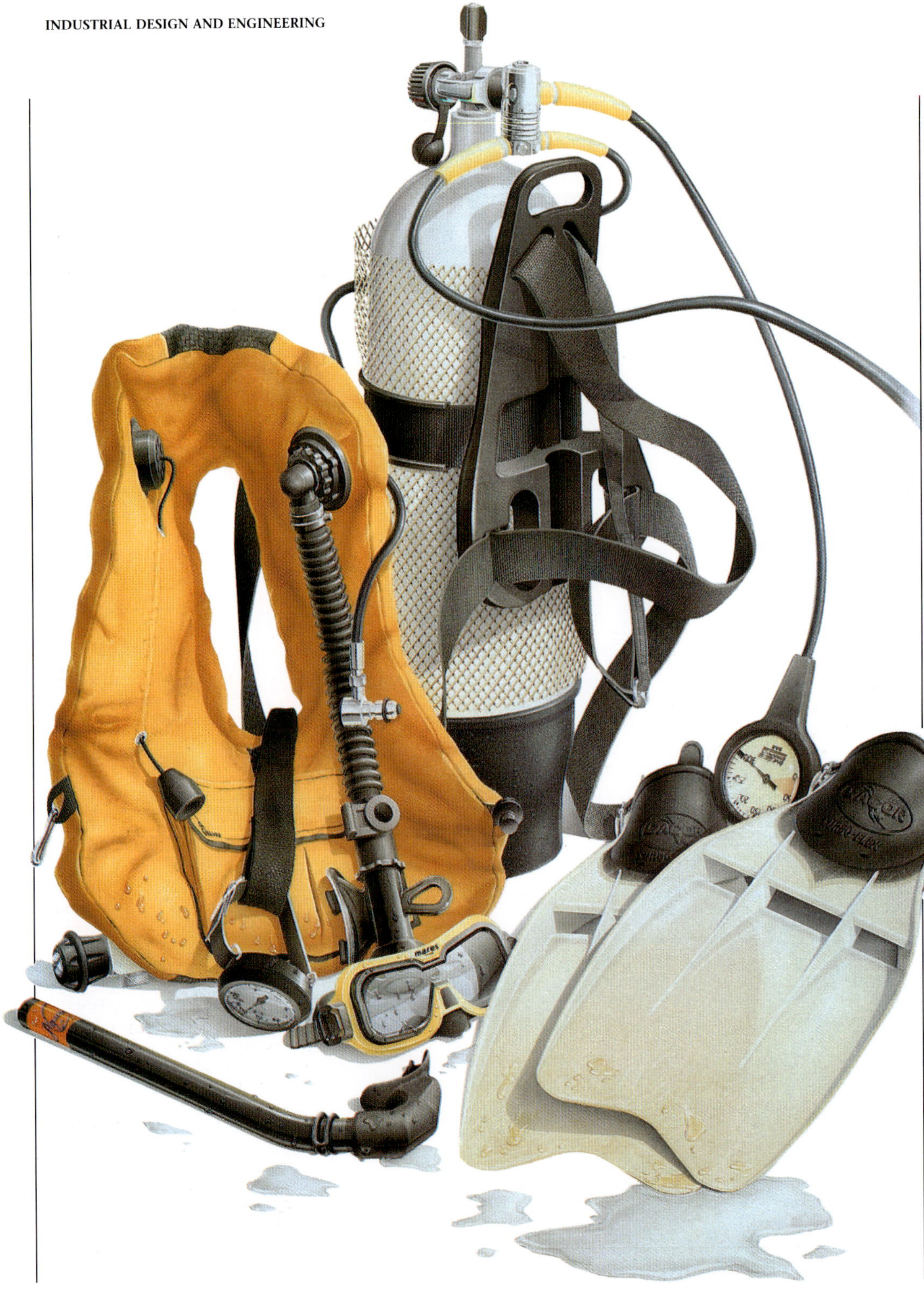

◀ **Aqualung still life** •
Martin Woodward

INSPIRATION

The related items which make up this composition were used as a vehicle to render different surface textures in as realistic a manner as possible, through the primary application of an airbrush.

TECHNIQUE

A wide variety of techniques have been employed, both in the airbrushing and through the necessary application of LINING-IN and hand-painted details. The surface textures have been well captured, especially those items which are composed of repetitive patterns, making for a realistic and effective illustration.

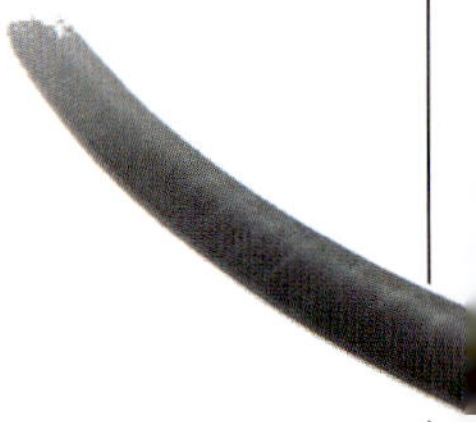

▶ **Aqualung mouthpiece** •
Martin Woodward

TECHNIQUE

Rendered in watercolors with hand-finished LINING-IN, this competent and professional illustration demonstrates the care and control required when airbrushing a subject that has a limited color range and is made of comparatively dull or mat surface finishes.

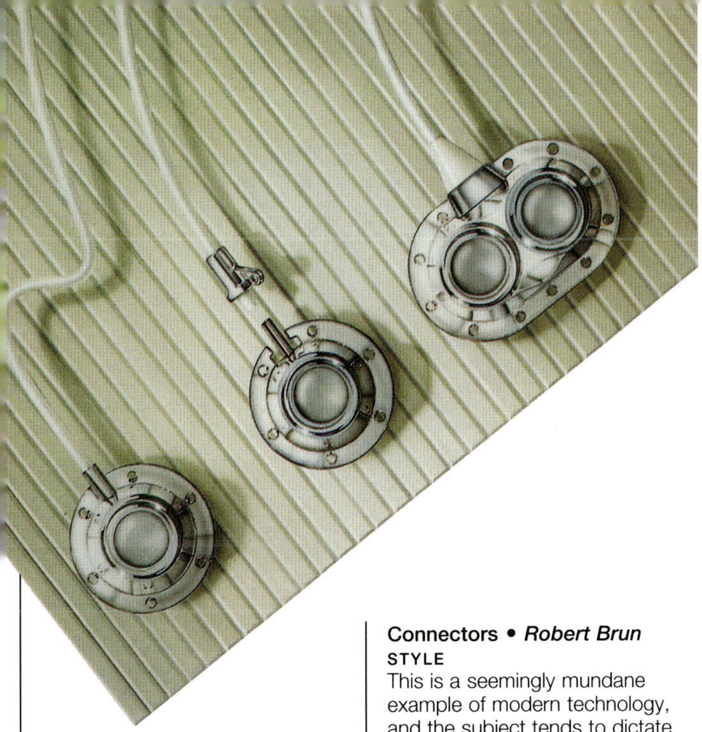

Connectors • ***Robert Brun***

STYLE

This is a seemingly mundane example of modern technology, and the subject tends to dictate the style. But the accuracy and control of the airbrushing captures subtle colors and surface finishes.

TECHNIQUE

FREEHAND SPRAYING, LINING-IN, and LINE CONTROL are all evident in this image. Form depends on GRADATED TONES and CAST SHADOWS, the latter applied with LOOSE MASKING.

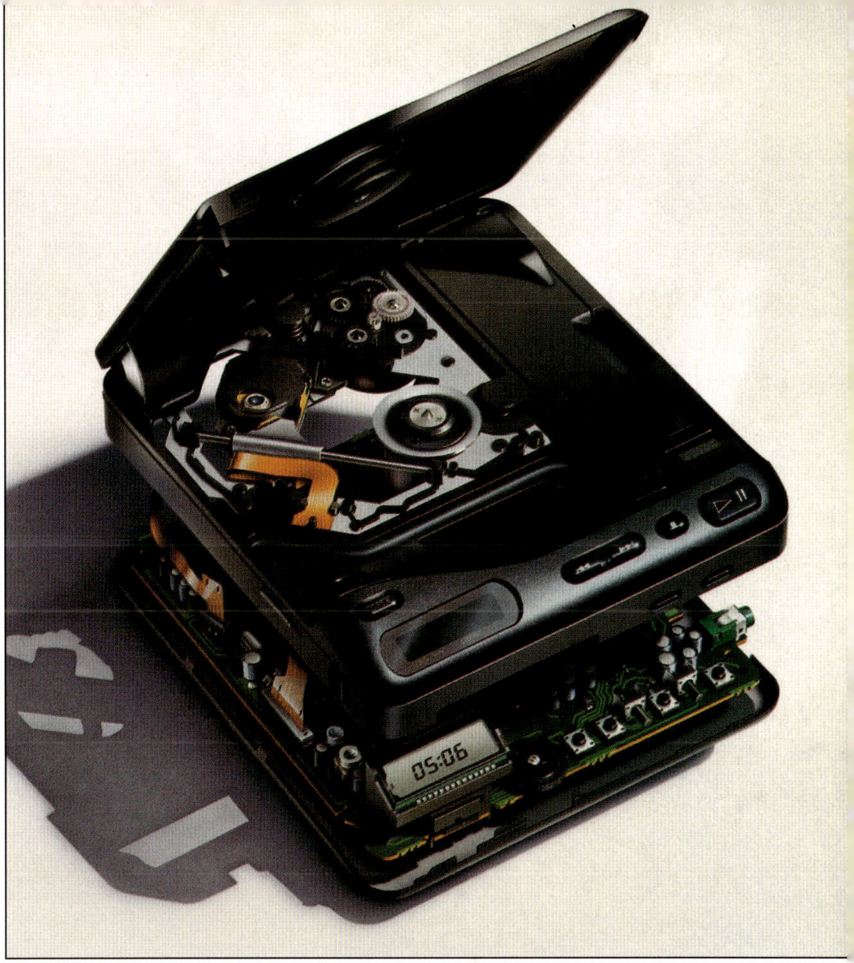

Portable CD Player • ***Matthew White***

COMPOSITION

Negotiating limitations imposed by the subject itself, the illustrator has produced a fine piece of work. The composition draws the eye directly to salient features, clearly and without confusion.

TECHNIQUE

The image displays a diverse range of airbrush techniques. SPATTERING indicates exterior surface texture, in comparison to the smoother interior finish. Modern technological equipment often has minimal surface variation in color or texture, which means a full understanding of monochrome rendering is essential, often difficult to control in airbrushing because so much of the image has to be masked, preventing a continuous overview.

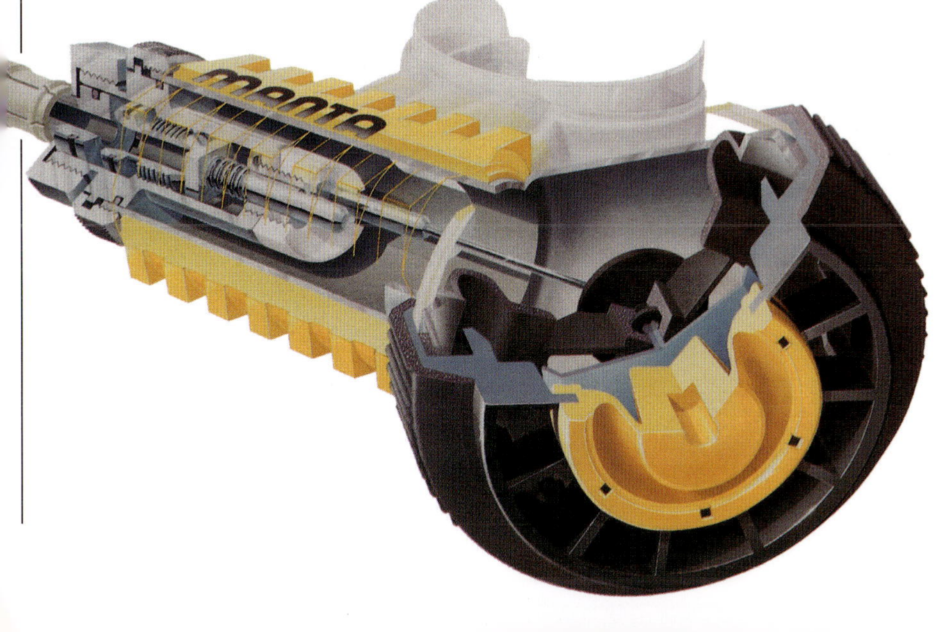

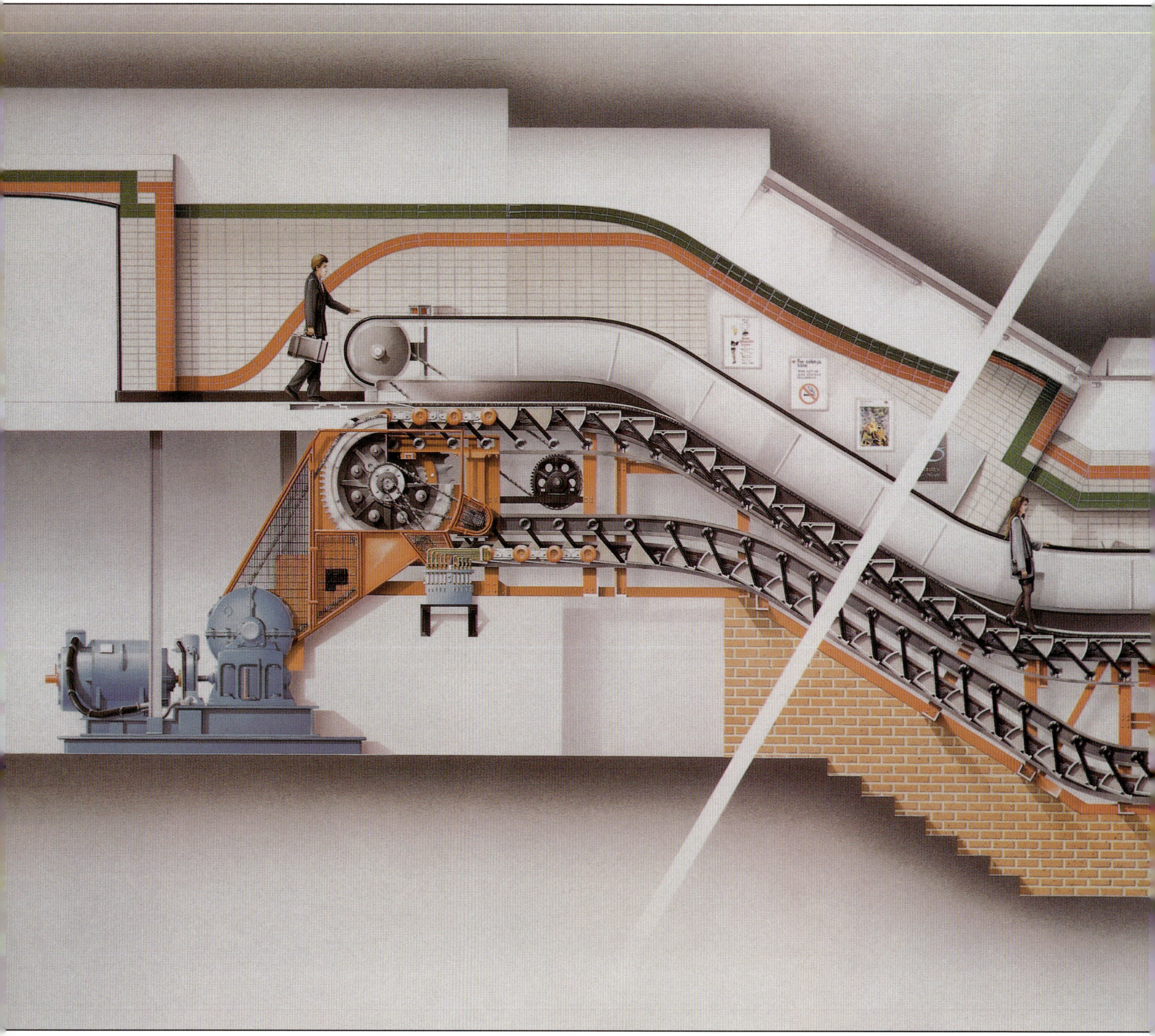

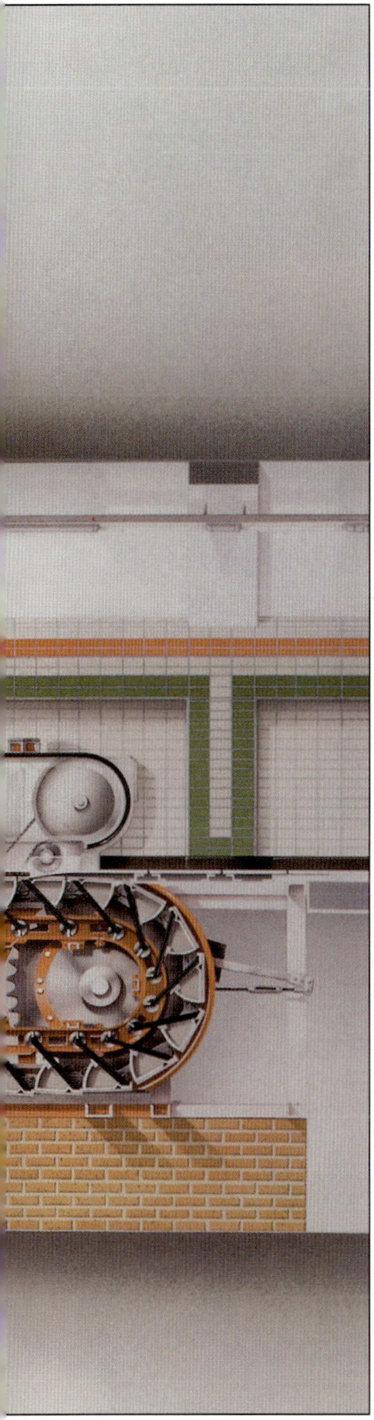

◀ Escalator poster •
Martin Woodward

CONCEPT

This orthographic illustration was commissioned by the London Underground to demonstrate to the public how little they actually see of an escalator in normal use and how complex one really is. It is used as a poster when maintenance is in progress.

TECHNIQUE

Drawn from plans and an actual escalator, the image is airbrushed in watercolors with hand-painted LINING-IN to add detail. The break in the illustration is intentional, because the detail between the top half and lower half is merely repetitive and therefore offers no additional information. The illustrator has attempted to create depth by the use of CAST SHADOWS and GRADATED TONES. These techniques have also been used to highlight the structure and mechanics of the escalator itself. This approach requires a full understanding and appreciation of the subject in order to convey the impression of variable depths, which would be far easier if the subject were drawn in perspective rather than orthographically.

Xerox 8840 Photocopier •
Colin Brown

TECHNIQUE

The illustrator has concentrated on achieving the maximum visual effect from the internal components of the copier. Each is treated as a separate item and, except for the red casing covering the rollers, where GHOSTING has been employed, no further detail is shown within them. The blend of colors between the red casing and black rollers has been carefully sprayed, avoiding a large overlap which would have produced a muddy brown mixture. The repetitive shapes and seemingly simple airbrushing of the paper trays are well handled, as is the consistency of the base color and shadows made by LOOSE MASKING.

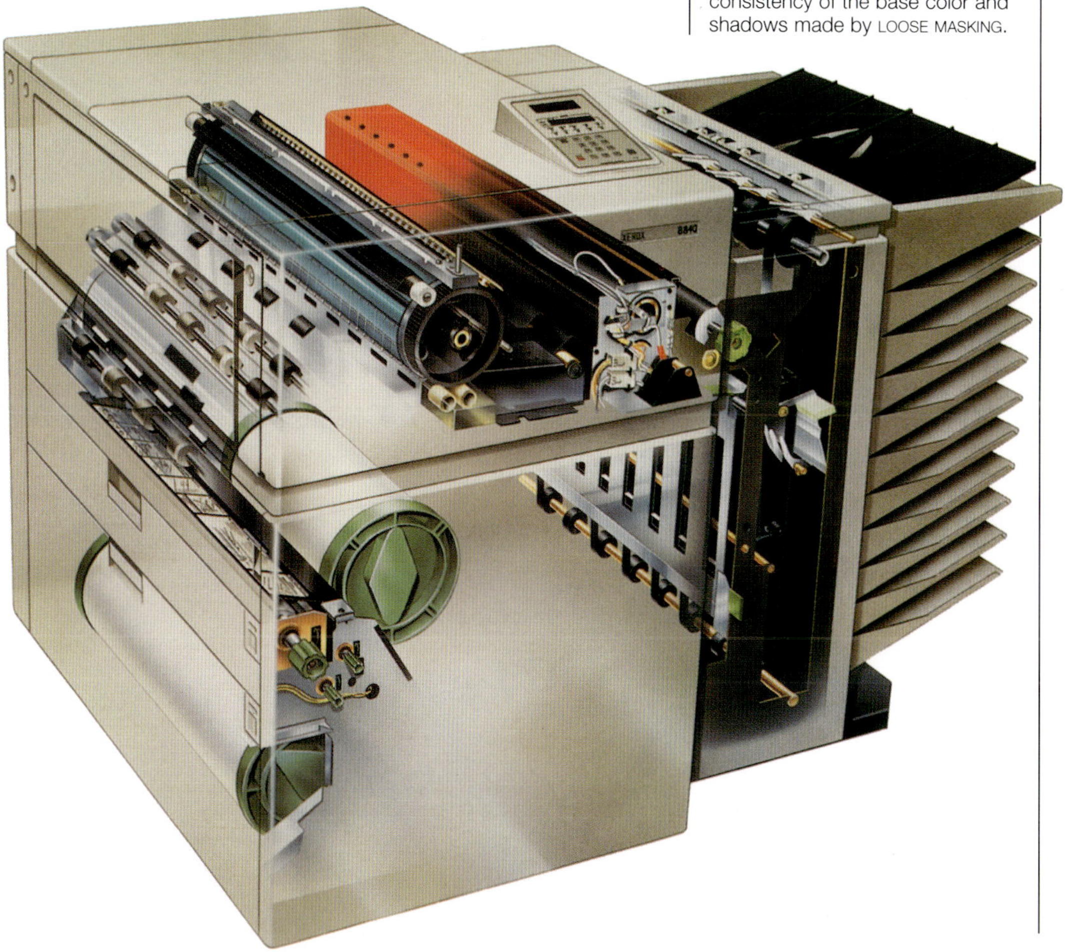

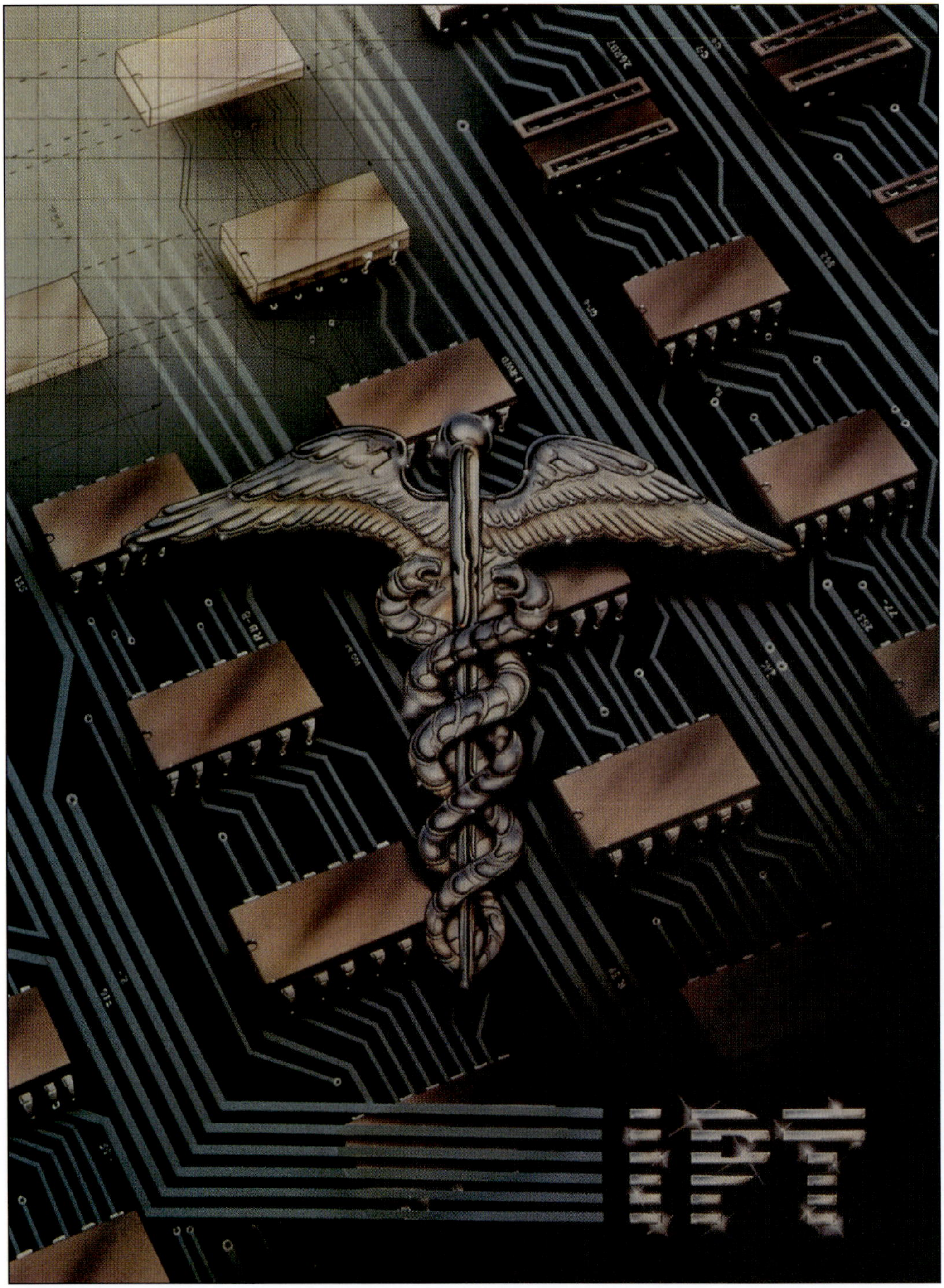

IPT • *Rodino Bautista*

APPROACH

The way in which the microchips fade into a designer's working drawing is an effective device commonly employed to avoid the visual dullness that is a potential problem when rendering a series of repetitive items.

TECHNIQUE

The airbrushing used a mixture of transparent and opaque colors, achieving consistency in color control and tonal balance. LINING-IN was restricted to the small lettering and winged badge in the foreground. FREEHAND SPRAYING was employed to render HIGHLIGHTING on the upper surfaces of the microchips.

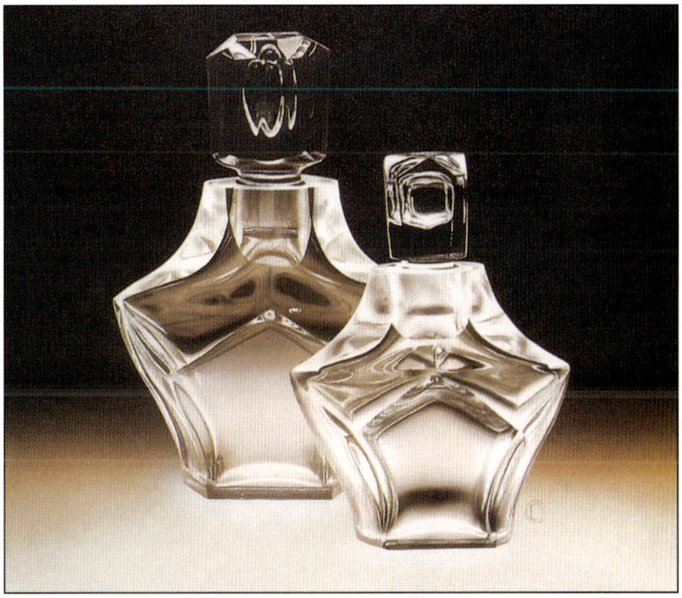

Perfume Bottles • ***Catherine Dittmer***

APPROACH

Clear glass is never easy to airbrush, having no apparent color of its own. Color and definition usually come from surrounding objects. Careful planning and control of color application are needed to avoid excessively bright, unrealistic highlights.

TECHNIQUE

Keen observation has produced an image of almost photographic intensity. The limited monochromatic background provides the only color to be reflected as abstract shapes in the glass, an effect which is particularly pleasing in the solid bottle tops. FILM MASKING, FREEHAND SPRAYING, and LOOSE MASKING have been used to good effect.

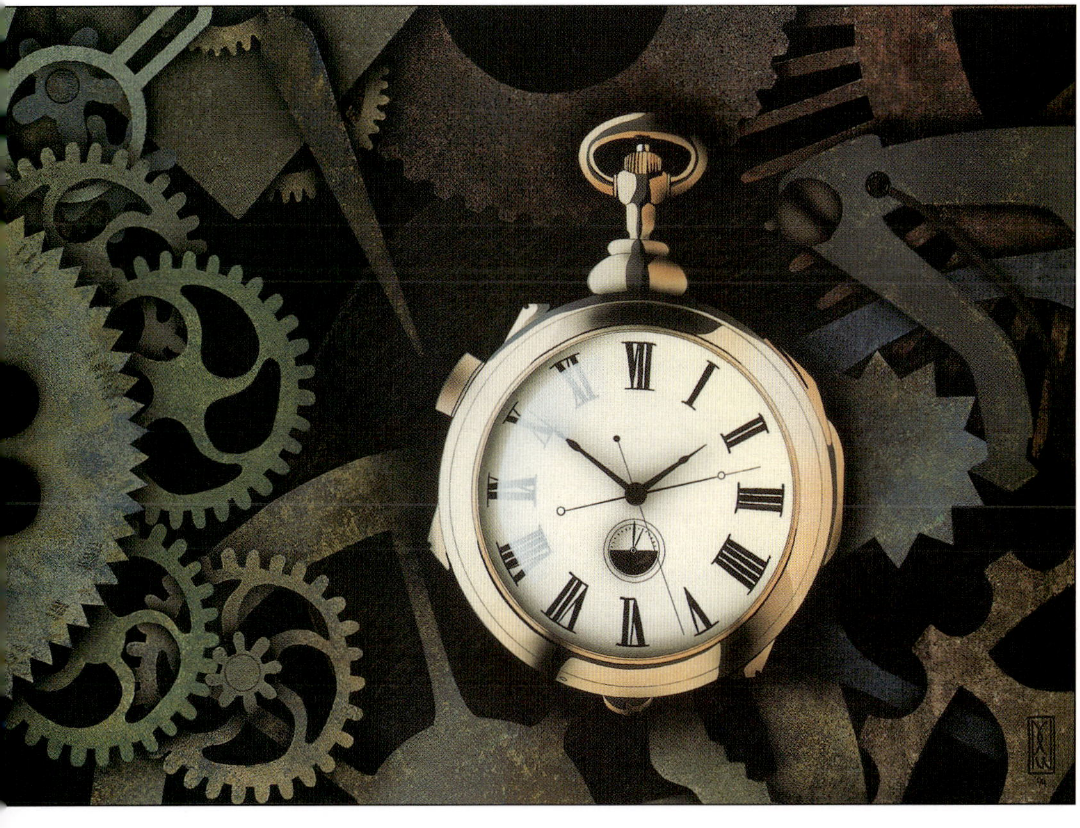

Stopwatch • ***Patrick C. Wanebo***

COMPOSITION

The placing of the highly finished stopwatch against a backdrop of dull, aged cogs and other components of watch and clock movements makes for a strongly contrasting image which enhances and exaggerates the polished surface texture of the central piece. The simplicity of color choice on the stopwatch itself adds to the overall effect.

TECHNIQUE

SPATTERING has been used to give the weathered look to the background pieces, while FILM MASKING combined with GRADATED TONES contribute to the HIGHLIGHTING of the stopwatch. GHOSTING and OVERSPRAYING have been used on the watch face, with the hand-drawn Roman numerals painted in beforehand.

FOOD AND DRINK

This is probably the fastest growing subject area that airbrush illustrators have turned their attention to in the past few years. The wide range and diverse nature of subjects that come under this theme, and their exciting textures and colors, give illustrators the ideal opportunity to demonstrate their skills. This is because, unlike most other subjects, everyone is familiar with food and drink, and therefore everyone can readily identify with them. The complexity of the packaging which often accompanies the products gives further scope to the expression of the airbrush artist's talents.

A particular difficulty in the airbrushing of foods and drinks is in the nature of their composition and texture. A variety of textures is often apparent in one single item, such as in some fruits. And although applicable to all subjects or themes, and regardless of technique, the ability to draw accurately is particularly important when illustrating food. There are many aids and systems which have been developed over the years for preparing drawings of technical subjects. They can be and are used on food subjects, but generally speaking this practice is unnecessarily time-consuming and tends to make the finished illustration rather mechanical and lifeless. Strong freehand drawing by observation is recommended, supplemented, if required, by photographic reference.

Many of the illustrators commissioned to produce images of food and drink are primarily technical illustrators, or at least started their professional careers as such. It would seem that the need to observe and understand the shape and form of things, which is one of the prerequisites of a good technical illustrator, comes into its own when rendering food and drink.

The ability to observe is not restricted to the drawing stage, but is equally important when spraying with the airbrush. It extends to the colors, tones, reflections and surface textures. The airbrushing techniques previously described are all usable, but the intrinsic qualities of the subject must never be forgotten. It is too easy to spray an apple, for example, with such a high degree of surface polish that it looks as if it were made of enameled steel – all very well if that is the intended effect, but is it really like that? Here again, close study of how professional illustrators approach such a problem is a worthwhile exercise in itself.

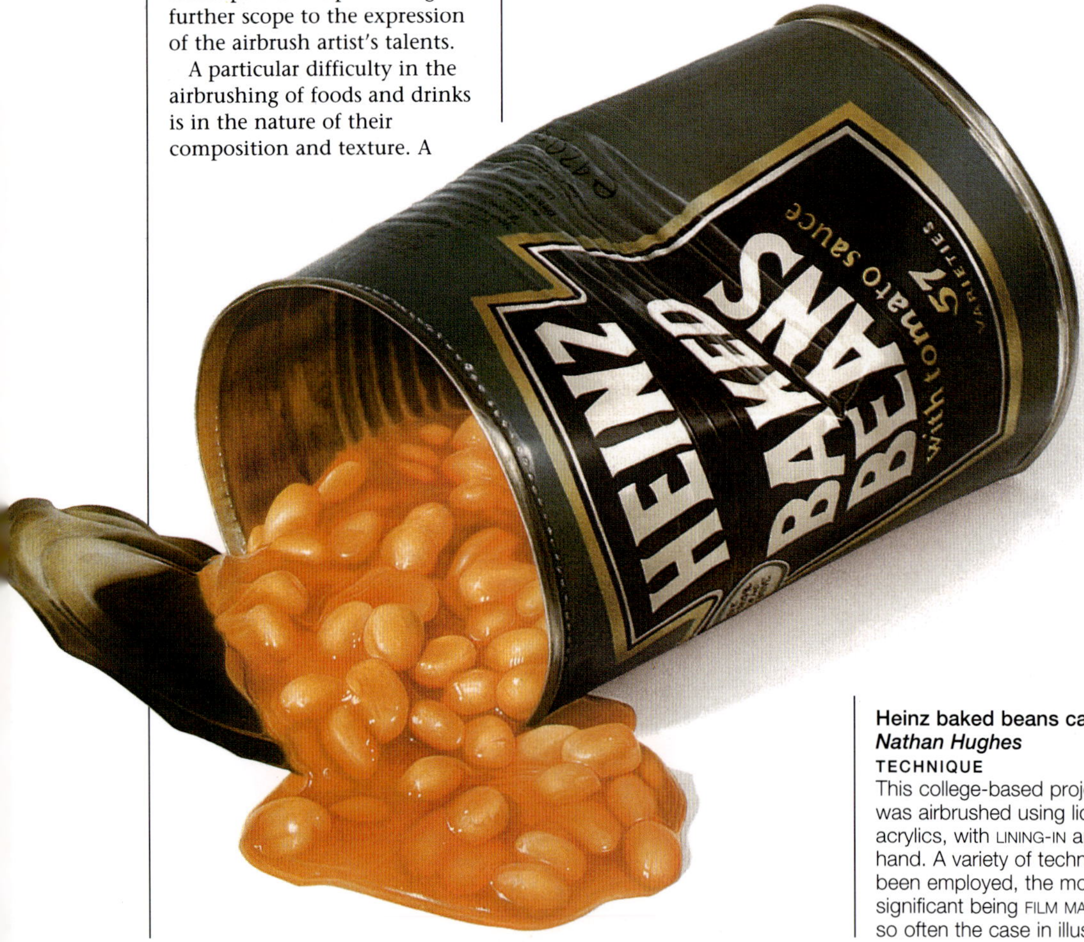

Heinz baked beans can •
Nathan Hughes
TECHNIQUE
This college-based project on food was airbrushed using liquid acrylics, with LINING-IN applied by hand. A variety of techniques have been employed, the most significant being FILM MASKING. As is so often the case in illustrations which include a brand name as part of the composition, great care is required to ensure that the quality of the lettering is comparable to the quality of the airbrushing. This needs special skill when cutting acetate or film masks, to avoid unsightly white edges which often cannot be satisfactorily hidden by hand painting.

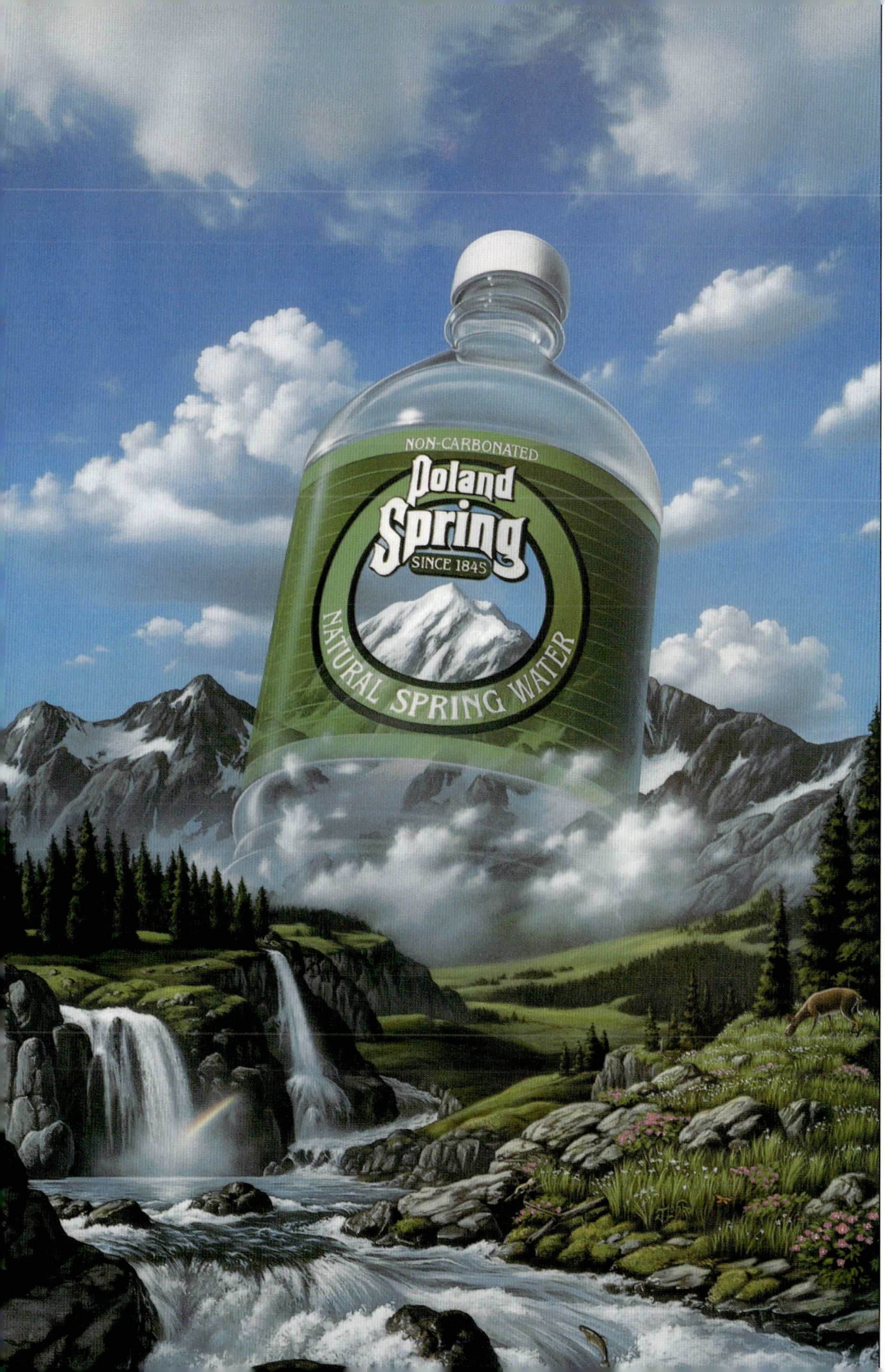

Poland Spring • ***Jerry LoFaro***

CONCEPT

This self-promotional piece demonstrates how specific subjects may be placed in a directly related context. The approach is often used to promote an environmentally friendly or healthy product, using nature and landscape to convince the consumer of the product's merits. The composition and color balance are extremely well done, making the bottle a cohesive part of the image as a whole.

TECHNIQUE

An exaggerated perspective gives the impression of a vast canvas, though the original is only 13 x 20in. It was rendered in acrylics, both airbrushed and hand painted, with variations of CARD MASKING, DOT CONTROL, FILM MASKING, FREEHAND SPRAYING, GHOSTING, GRADATED TONES, and LINING-IN.

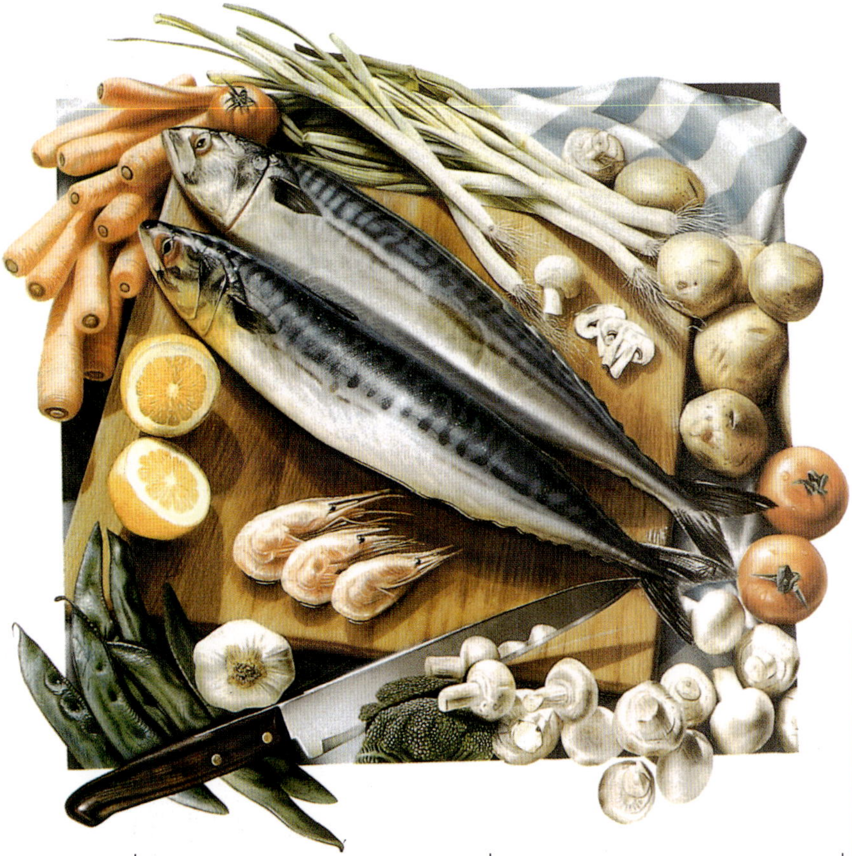

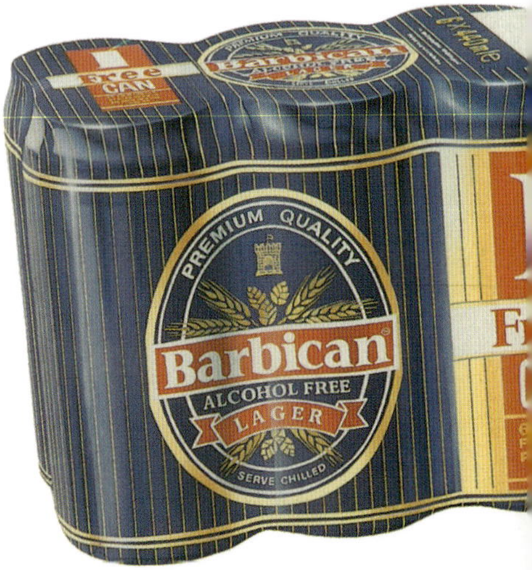

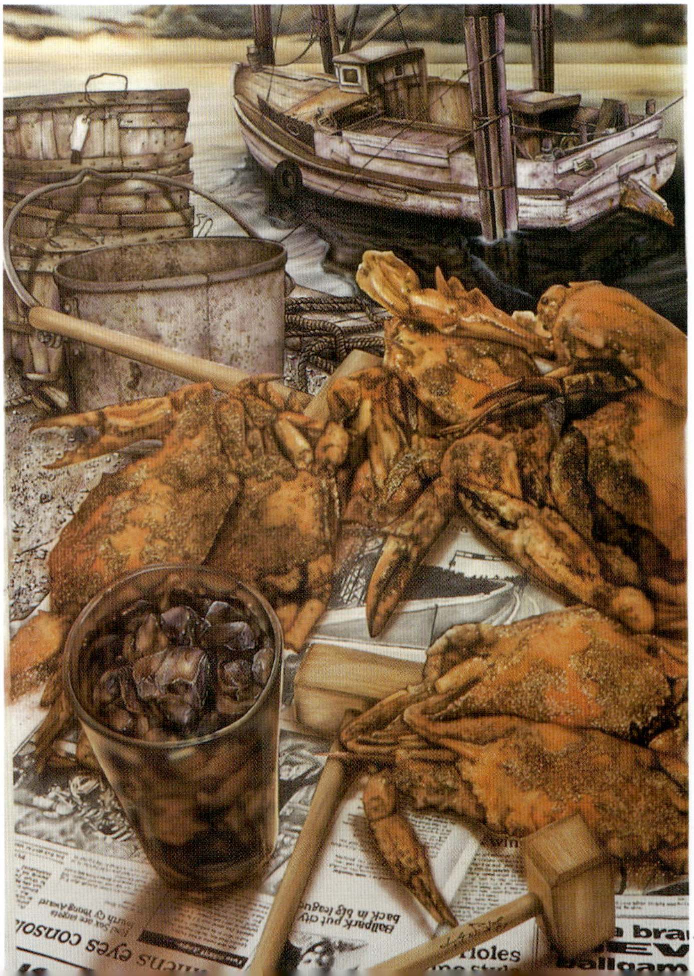

Fish on wooden board • *Nathan Hughes*

COMPOSITION

This almost plan-view image of two mackerel surrounded by various vegetables, shellfish and fruit has been carefully composed to create a pleasing illustration which works in any direction, as you can see by rotating the page. The exactitude of the shadows and light source suggests that photographic references were used to supplement the "live" arrangement. Although there is a wide color range, the overall illustration does not appear gaudy; each component is balanced by its neighbors. The use of accurate and equally sharp images reflected in the surface of the knife blade immediately identifies the blade as being highly machined and polished – almost to the point of giving the impression of being chromed.

▶ Untitled • *Kurt W. Bittle*

CONCEPT

One of a planned series on Maryland harvests to be marketed as limited edition prints, this artwork demonstrates an impressive use of mixed media. The perspective is somewhat exaggerated, the composition being conceived more as a fine art painting than as an illustration.

TECHNIQUE

The artist used many different types of masking, as well as FREEHAND SPRAYING, to achieve the effect, applying particular techniques to depicting the varied textures, such as the weathered bucket and wooden containers, the out-of-focus effect suggesting condensation on the sides of the glass, and subtle contrasts between the crabs, the drink, the mallets, and the loose newspaper sheets. Surface detail was built up with graphite and colored pencils over airbrushed opaque color.

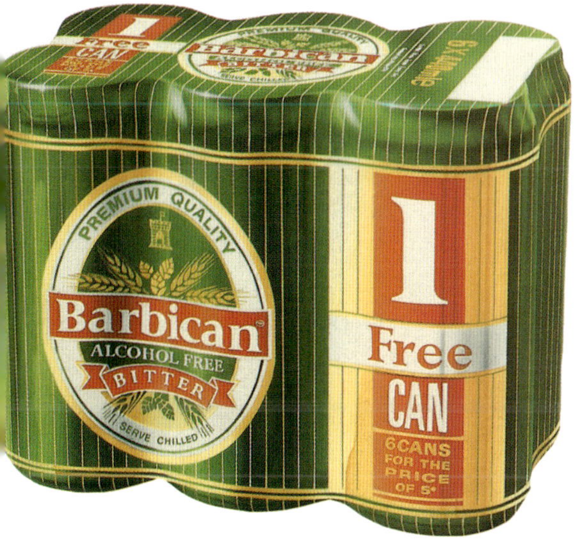

▲ **Barbican Beer Cans •**
Chris Mitchell
CONCEPT
The commission to illustrate a new package design for beer and lager cans was straightforward enough, except that the illustrator had no three-dimensional packaging to work from. The image therefore represents the artist's impression.
TECHNIQUE
Well-executed lettering was essential, as this is such a prominent part of the image. The foreshortened letters at the top of the packages and concave curvature on the front have been perfectly captured. Note particularly how HIGHLIGHTING has been oversprayed using LOOSE MASKING to achieve a soft edge. LINING-IN to render the numerous vertical lines – as important as the lettering here – shows great accuracy and consistency.

Clearly Canadian •
John Brettoner
TECHNIQUE
An excellent example of color control and balance, especially when the image is almost monochrome, and with blue as the primary base color. The extreme contrast between the base color and the pieces of fruit scattered among the ice adds an intensity of color which does not detract from the obvious subject of the illustration. The details are highly accurate and realistic, particularly the bottle tops, the neatly executed hand-drawn lettering, the water droplets, and the overprinted images of fruit on the necks of each bottle, which have individual highlights created by the thickness of the printing inks. The ice cubes have been sprayed using a combination of LOOSE MASKING and FREEHAND SPRAYING, which allows each cube to be clearly identified without making the shapes too dominant and gives an even, abstract quality that contrasts well with the harder edges of the bottles.

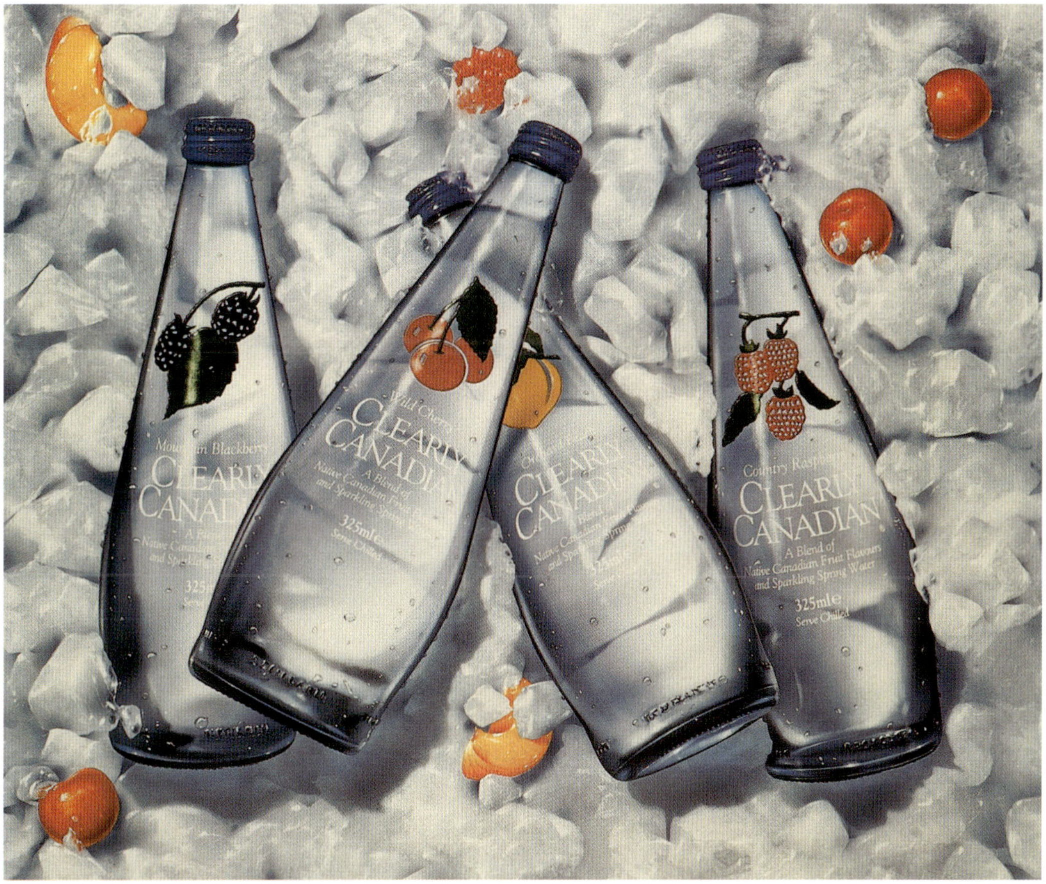

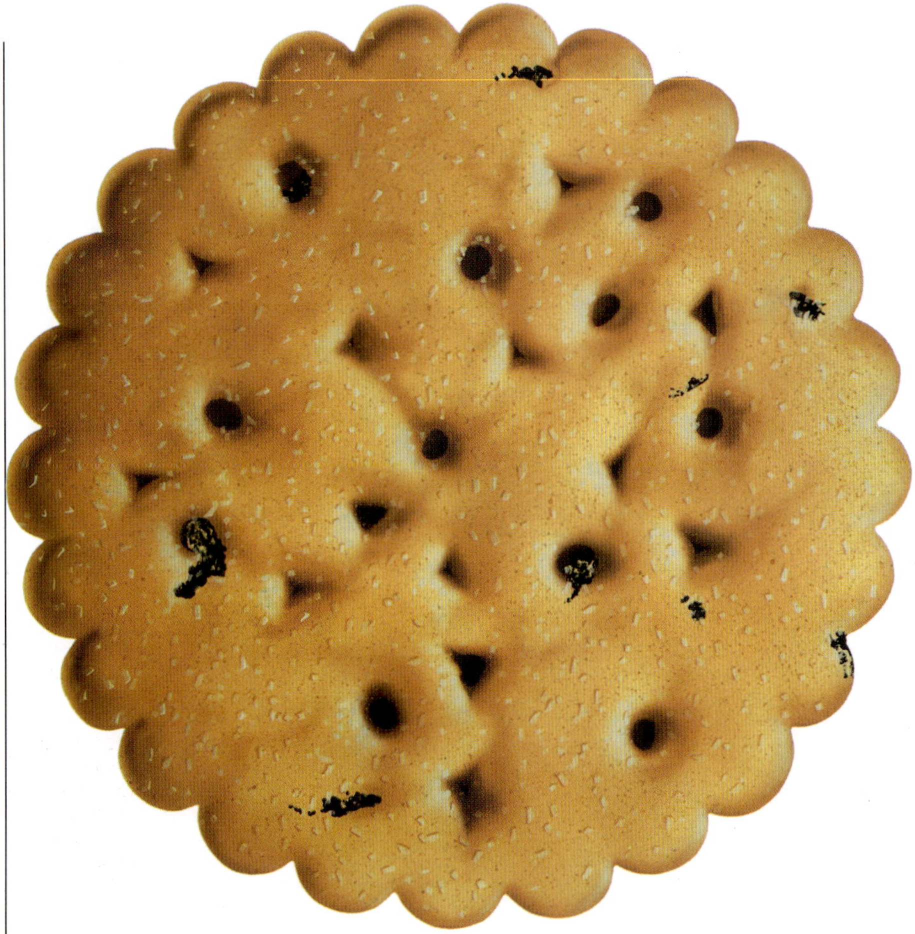

▼ **Jaffa Cake** • ***Chris Mitchell***

BRIEF

The illustration was required in support of a packaging display, but in this case for the retailer, not for the product packaging itself. It would have been difficult to photograph the Jaffa cake for reproduction: the chocolate would have been melted by studio lights; also, the perfect example of a Jaffa cake does not really exist, but the airbrusher can produce one of ideal color, shape, and texture.

TECHNIQUE

The overall dramatic effect of the finished image is achieved through subtle use of light and shade, enhancing the textures to create the impression of a "live" product. The dimpled, irregular chocolate surface was created by FREEHAND SPRAYING, with LOOSE MASKING used to add HIGHLIGHTING. Grainy outer texture contrasts with smooth airbrushing of the orange filling.

Shortcake and Currant Cookie • ***Colin Brown***

TECHNIQUE

To achieve an effective, realistic image of the top surface of the cookie, it was drawn hugely over life-size, at 14in square. Within FILM MASKING, a FLAT TONE was applied as a base, over which FREEHAND SPRAYING was used to show shape, form, and shadows. Deeper shadows in the dimples, and the currants, have clearly defined, harder edges. The sugar crystals scattered over the surface are represented as small polygons, each with its own CAST SHADOW, some also with individual HIGHLIGHTING. To keep a correct tonal balance, they have been painted with slightly transparent off-white.

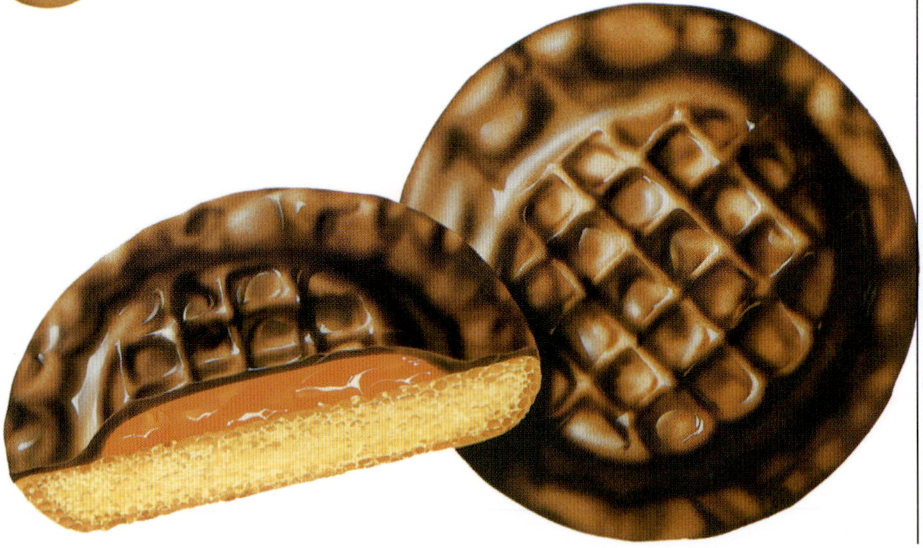

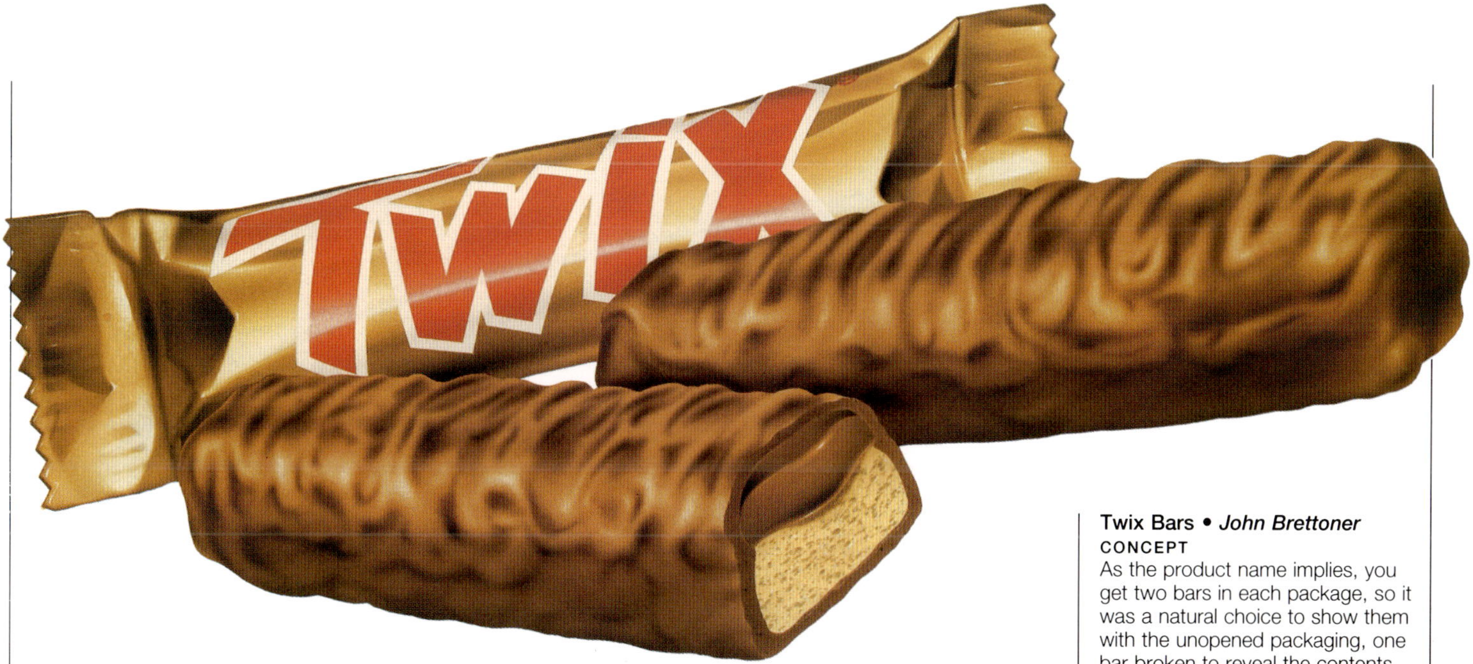

Twix Bars • *John Brettoner*

CONCEPT

As the product name implies, you get two bars in each package, so it was a natural choice to show them with the unopened packaging, one bar broken to reveal the contents. This also provided maximum visual interest from the surface textures and contrasts.

TECHNIQUE

The packaging was sprayed using LOOSE MASKING to establish the creases, and HIGHLIGHTING to catch the glossy effect. The corners of the creases each have their own tiny, carefully placed highlights, sometimes no more than a scratched dot. The chocolate surface was airbrushed either with CARD MASKING or by FREEHAND SPRAYING.

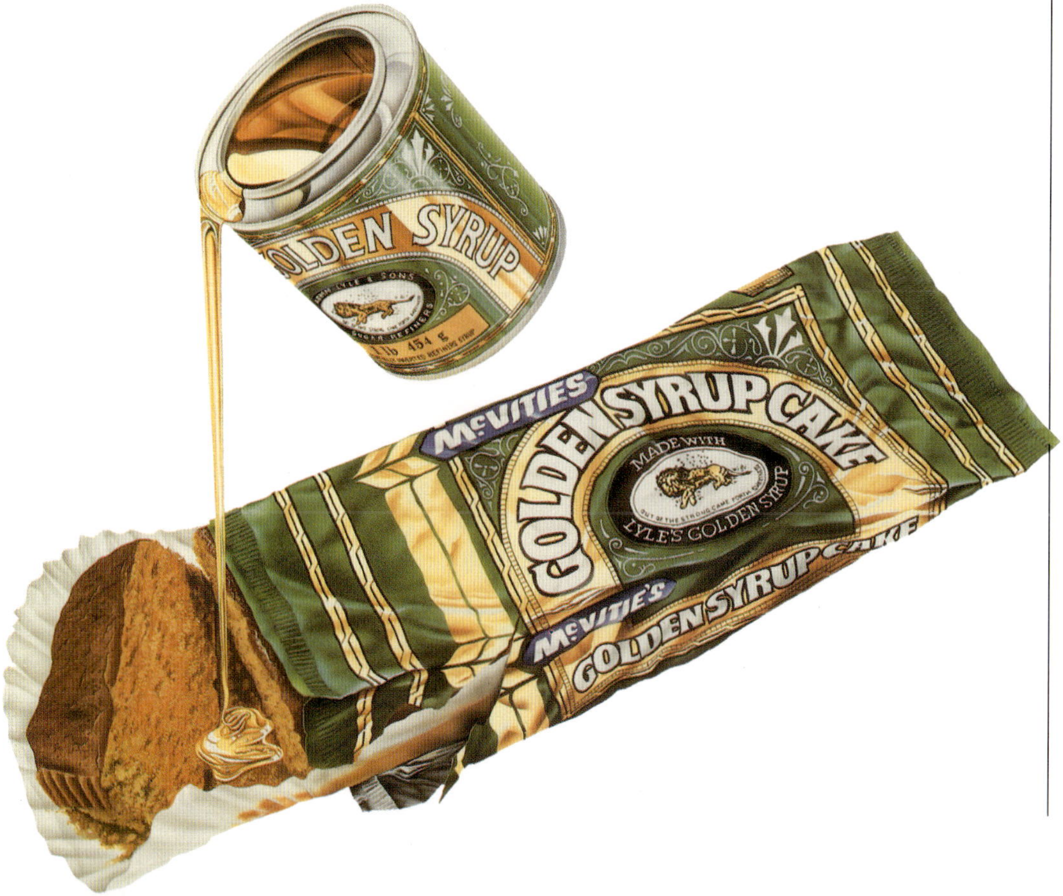

Golden Syrup Cake • *Colin Brown*

TECHNIQUE

The contrast between the highly reflective surfaces on the can of syrup and the crinkled packaging of the cake wrapper is well controlled and beautifully handled. Using off-white LINING-IN for the scroll-work decoration has enabled this part of the image to "sit" on the same level as its green base: a purer white would have appeared proud and separate.

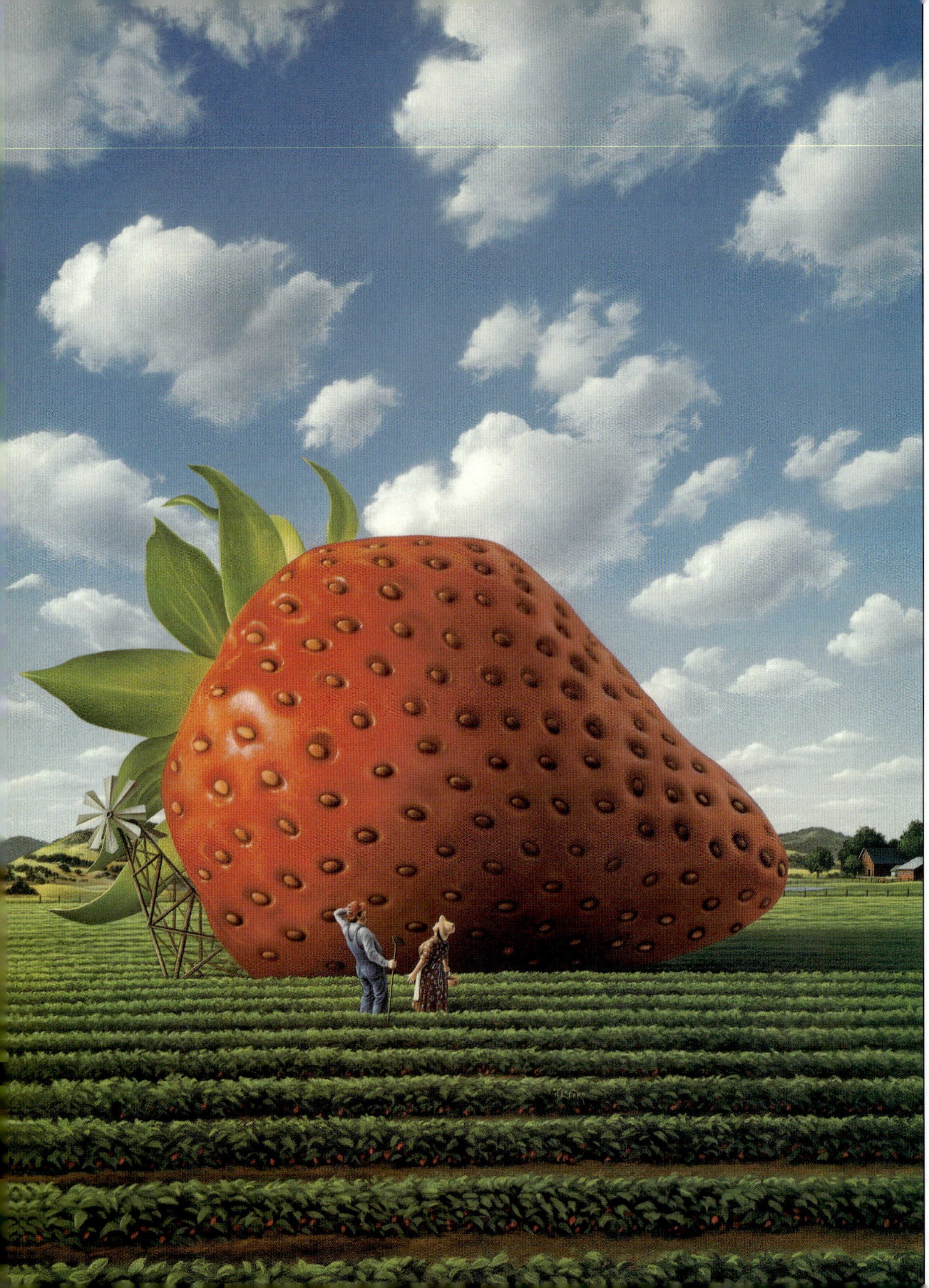

Coping with Unexpected Growth
• *Jerry LoFaro*

CONCEPT

Surprisingly, this illustration has nothing directly to do with food and drink. It was part of an advertising campaign for a photocopying company. The large scale implied by composition and technique accurately reflects the actual size; the piece measures 24 x 23in.

TECHNIQUE

Acrylics were used throughout, in airbrushing and hand painting. The clouds, for example, combine both techniques to achieve the desired effect. The strawberry is almost surreal; not so much because of its size in relation to the figures, but in the way the texture makes it appear as if made of inflatable rubber, or similar flexible material with an inherent sheen. The GRADATED TONES and HIGHLIGHTING are particularly well executed.

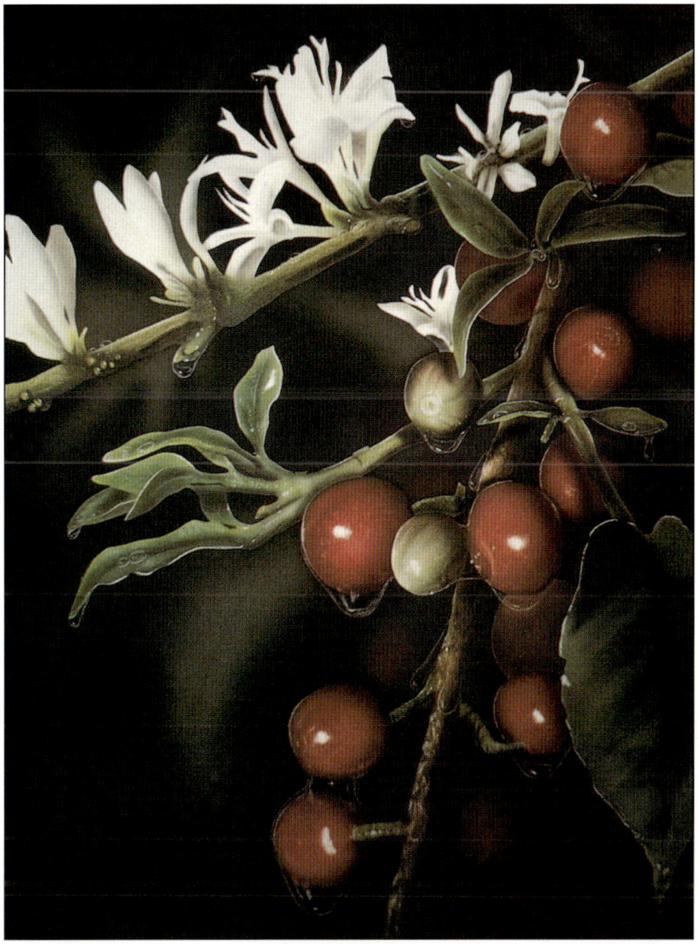

◀ Coffee plant • *Gregory M. Hurley*

TECHNIQUE

The rendering in this acrylic-based airbrush illustration is a combination of impression and realism. Interestingly, it relies very much on SCRATCHING BACK to achieve the effect of water drops on the fruit and leaves.The effect is further enhanced by the intense and very localized highlights on each fruit, against an overall background of deep and dark tones which appear to have been applied using FREEHAND SPRAYING techniques.

▼ Apples • *John Brettoner*

TECHNIQUE

These exquisitely airbrushed apples demonstrate the color control and contrast required when illustrating so many similar objects. There is a perfect balance between each apple and the rest. Note the simplistic but effective treatment of the water drops, each with its own highlight and shadow composed only of base-color variations and a small touch of white.

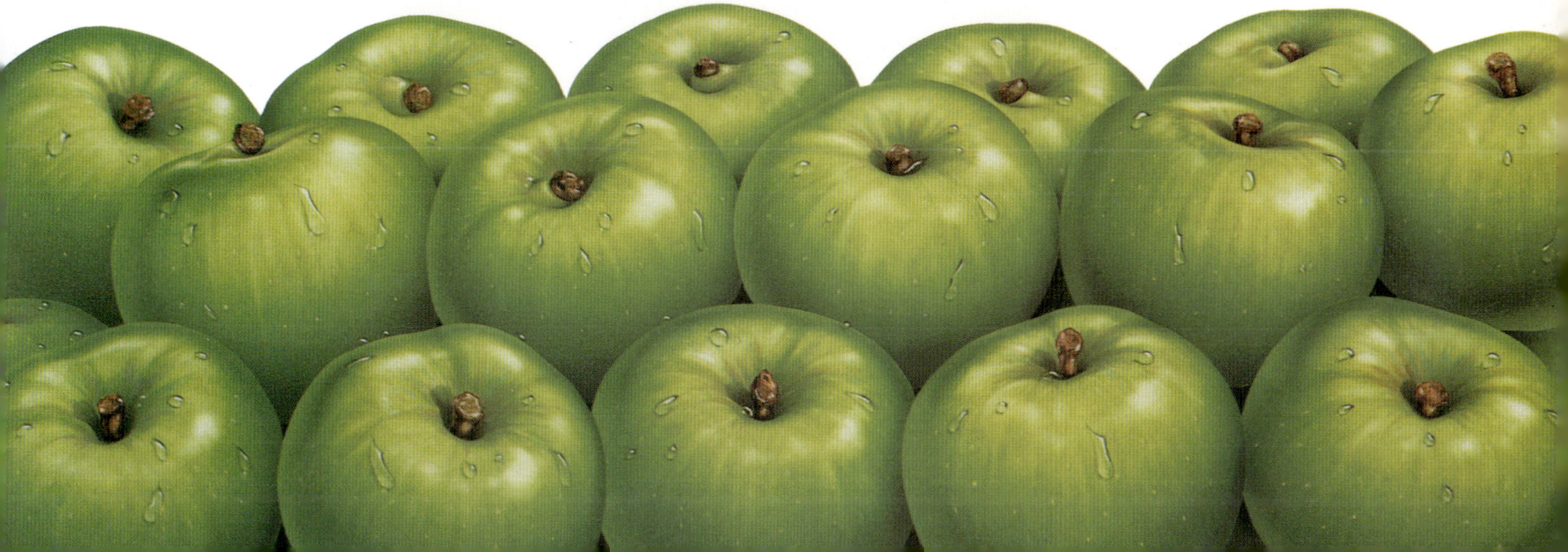

ARCHITECTURE

Architectural illustration is a comparatively new field which has seen an increasing use of the airbrush as a primary tool in rendering, especially when architectural subjects are central in an advertising campaign. The traditional method of rendering buildings was to use pure, transparent watercolors, applied by hand on a base which was invariably a handmade watercolor paper. Partly through a desire on the part of clients to have more glamorous images of proposed or existing buildings, illustrators have extended their techniques to include airbrush applications.

Because the majority of new buildings rely very much on surface texture as part of the overall design concept, and because of their size, the illustrator must be very careful not to use the airbrush in such a way as to make the finished illustration look more akin to an industrial or engineering subject. The examples reproduced in this section range from hypothetical buildings, through illustrations of proposed developments, to existing buildings – and interiors – which have been restored. They demonstrate the use of the airbrush as the central technique, and also as a means of applying very specific and localized textures, to complement hand rendering. There are also examples which are more schematic in approach, giving sufficient variety to enable a student of airbrushing to select a technique and style appropriate to the purpose.

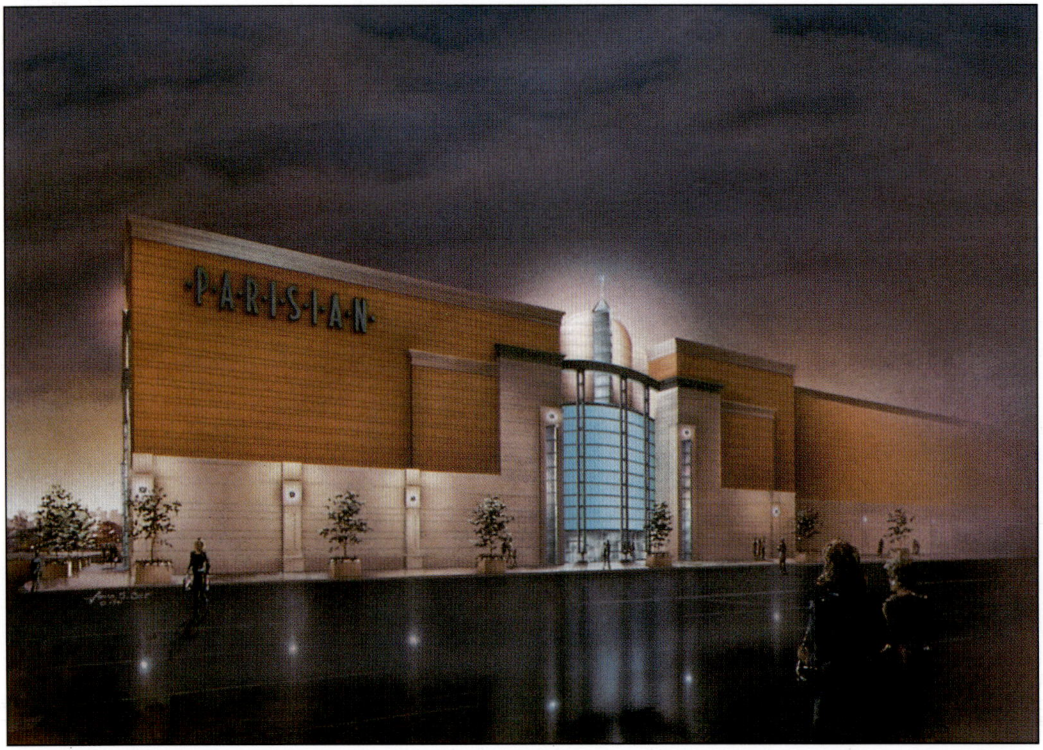

Proposed Parisian retail store •
Anita S. Bice

TECHNIQUE

Although the perspective drawing follows the traditional method for architectural illustrations, this image departs from convention in that the proposed building has been rendered with an airbrush rather than in watercolors applied by hand. Using FILM MASKING as a base, OVERSPRAYING has been applied to achieve GRADATED TONES, the latter employed in particular to the right where the building fades into the night sky. LOOSE MASKING has been used to create the soft-edged reflections on the ground, which also gives the effect of a rain shower having just passed over. The intensity of color and light in the area of the entrance draws the eye, ensuring that the building is clearly identified.

Hong Kong Cityscape •
Colin Brown

COMPOSITION

In this dramatic and impressive illustration, the downward viewpoint creates a severe but effective sense of height. The oblique perspective is broken by the angle of the helicopter, which draws the eye. Both composition and style exemplify the hectic, fast-moving lifestyle generated by a modern metropolis.

TECHNIQUE

The nighttime effect is conveyed by strong use of CAST SHADOWS, DOT CONTROL, GRADATED TONES, FREEHAND SPRAYING, HIGHLIGHTING, and reflected colors, rendered in gouache and acrylics. The photographic technique of using time exposures to indicate moving traffic has been realistically copied by spraying soft-edged lines onto the freeways.

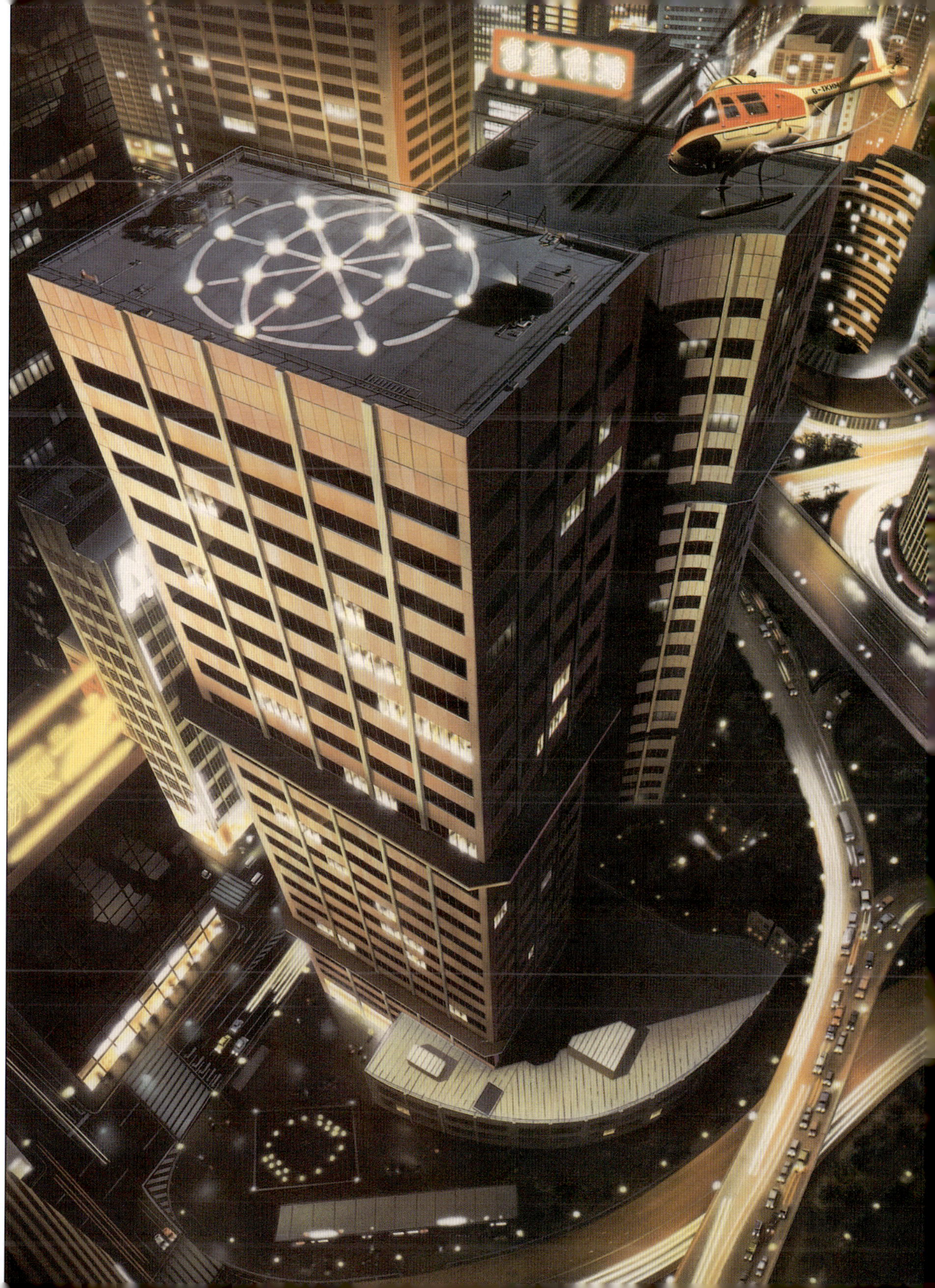

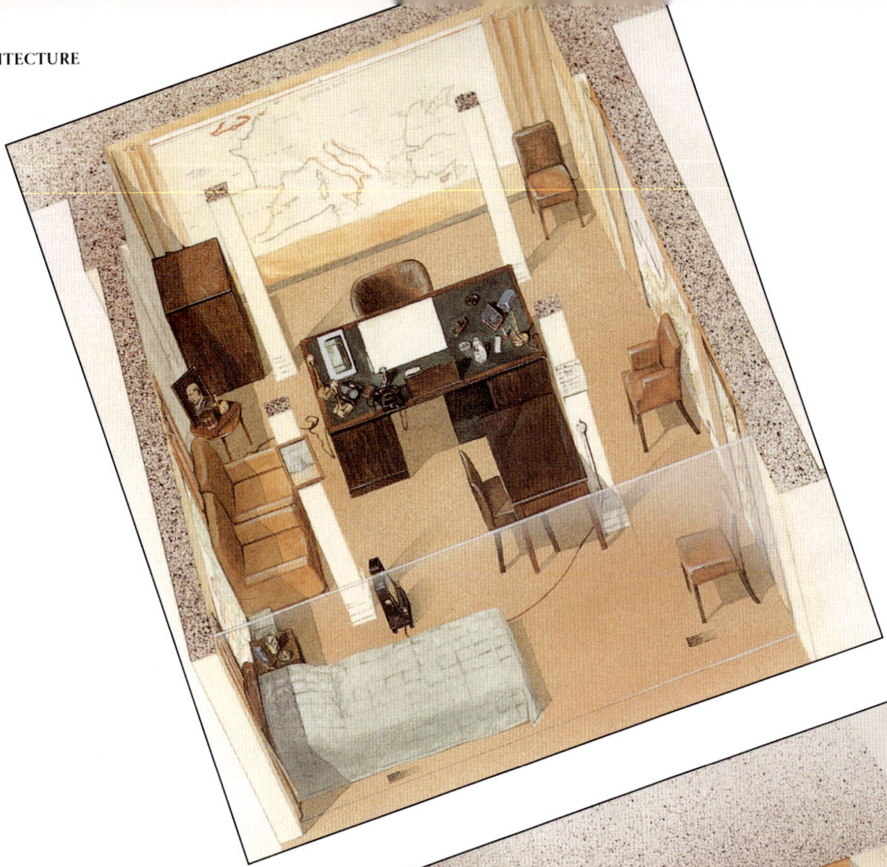

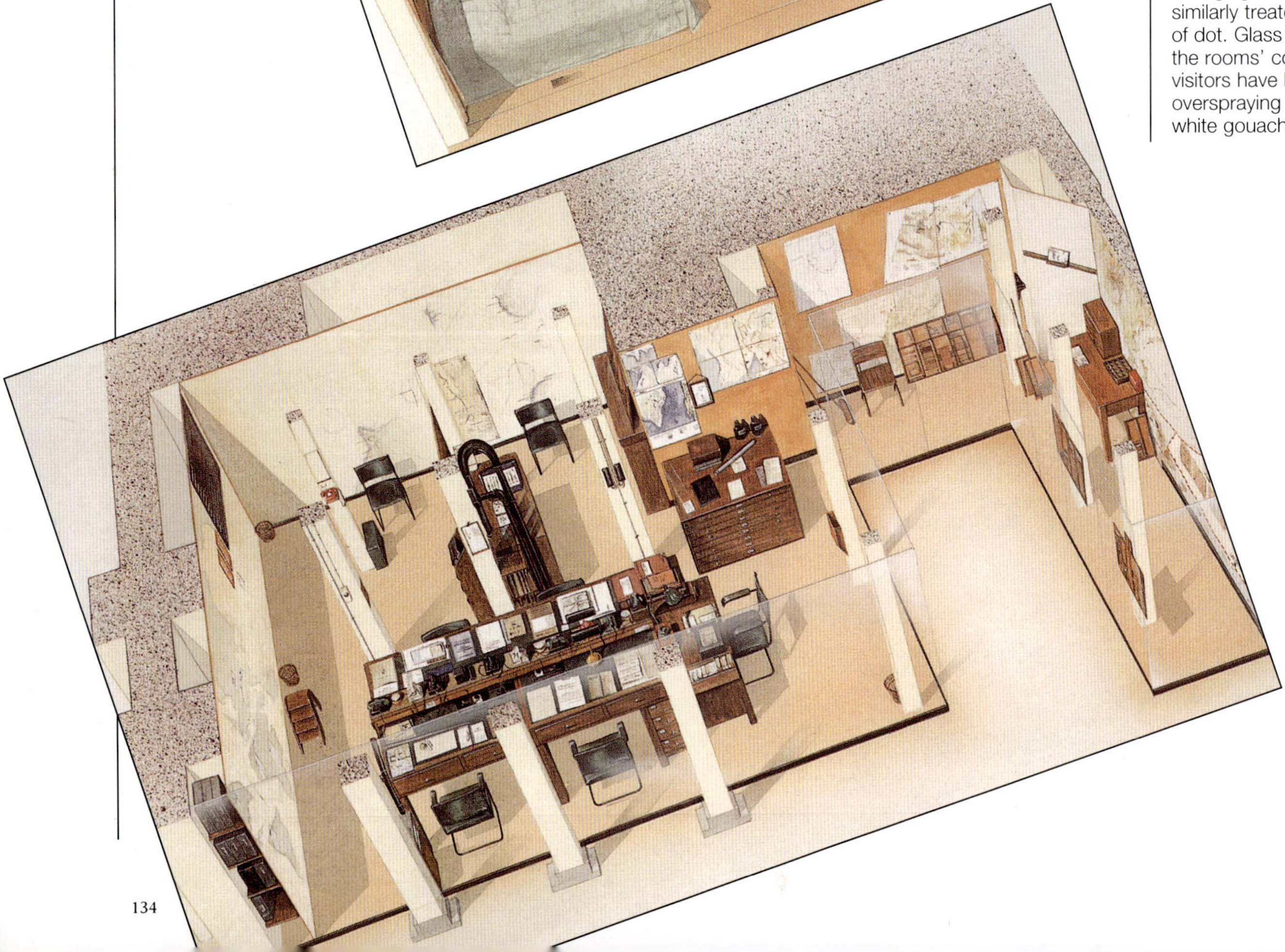

The Cabinet War Rooms: Churchill's Bedroom; The Cabinet War Rooms: The Map Room • *Clifton Hepburn*
The underground center of Britain's wartime government has been preserved for public viewing. The complexity of the layout prevented visitors from acquiring an overview, so these illustrations were commissioned for both on-site display and reproduction.

TECHNIQUE
The two images are part of a series in which the same mixed-media techniques were applied to all to maintain continuity. To distinguish clearly between the smooth surface textures inside the rooms and the sectioned walls, heavy SPATTERING was applied, with OVERSPRAYING to create layers of changing colors. The carpets were similarly treated, with a finer grade of dot. Glass partitions separating the rooms' contents from the visitors have been defined by overspraying the upper edges with white gouache.

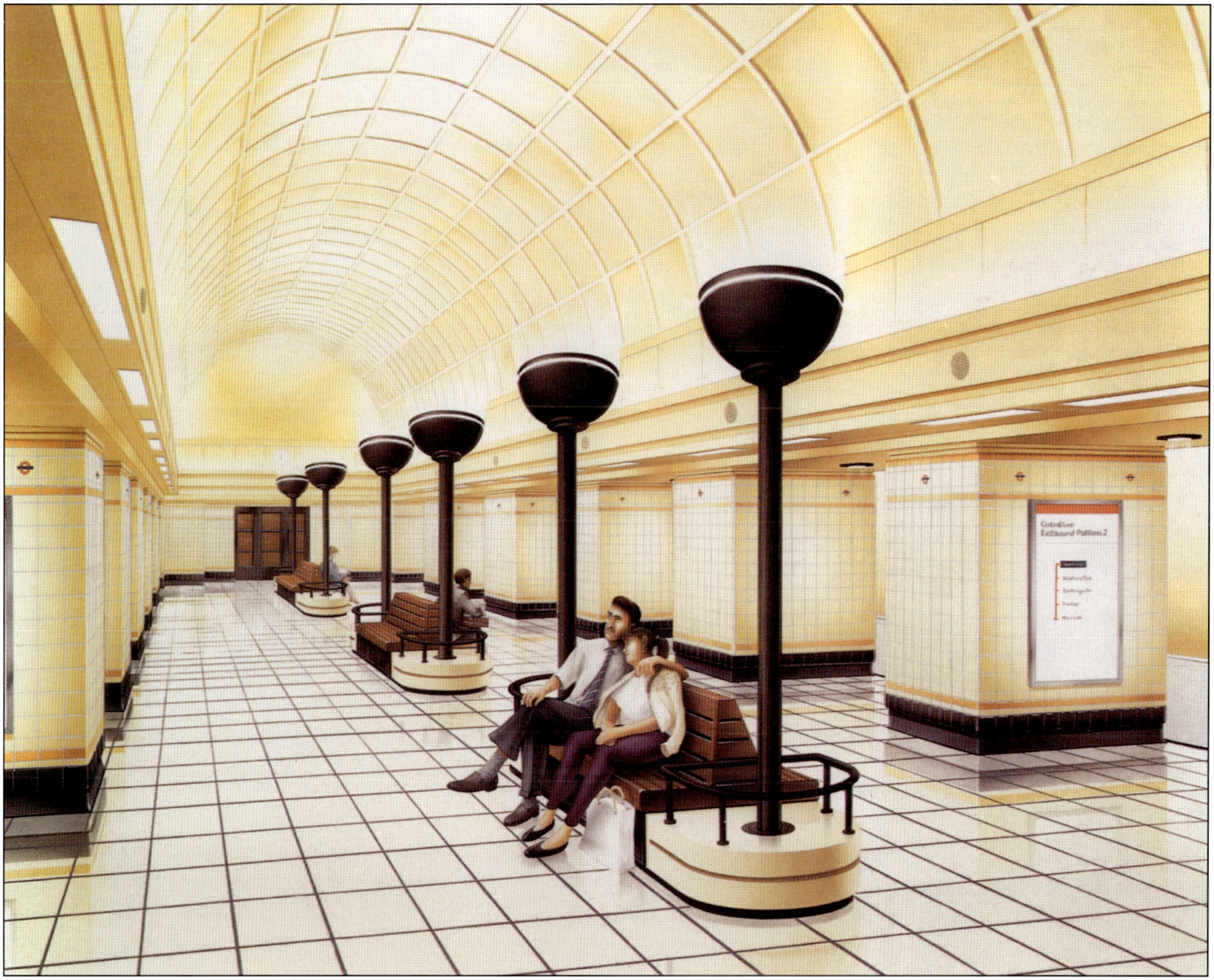

Gants Hill underground station • ***Martin Woodward***

TECHNIQUE

The two-point perspective by its nature gives a certain distortion to the subject, because it exceeds the natural cone of vision.But the drawing system and the airbrushed finish give an added sense of scale, creating the impression of a wide, airy and bright interior. The perspective and depth are further enhanced by the dramatic use of the lines delineating the floor tiling and the semi-circular curve of the high ceiling. Extensive use has been made of FILM MASKING with GRADATED TONES overlaid to show the bright and reflective surfaces on all levels, especially on the floor. Note the simple application of thin white lines to add highlights to the lower band of black tiles.

The Royal Engineers Museum •
Martin Woodward

TECHNIQUE

The past few years have seen increasing use of this form of presentation and rendering to explain the shape and layout of historic buildings. In this example the illustrator has combined traditional and transparent airbrush techniques over a single line base. The combination of the line base with the GRADATED TONES of vertical surfaces that stand opposite the light source adds to the three-dimensional effect of the image, while the flat plan – shown in perspective and lying immediately below the perspective rendering – allows the ground floor layout to be clearly followed. The first-floor plan is superimposed in the main perspective, again using transparent and gradated tones, but in a sufficiently different color to maintain clarity. A simple but effective approach which works well, especially as intended on the center pages of a booklet promoting the museum.

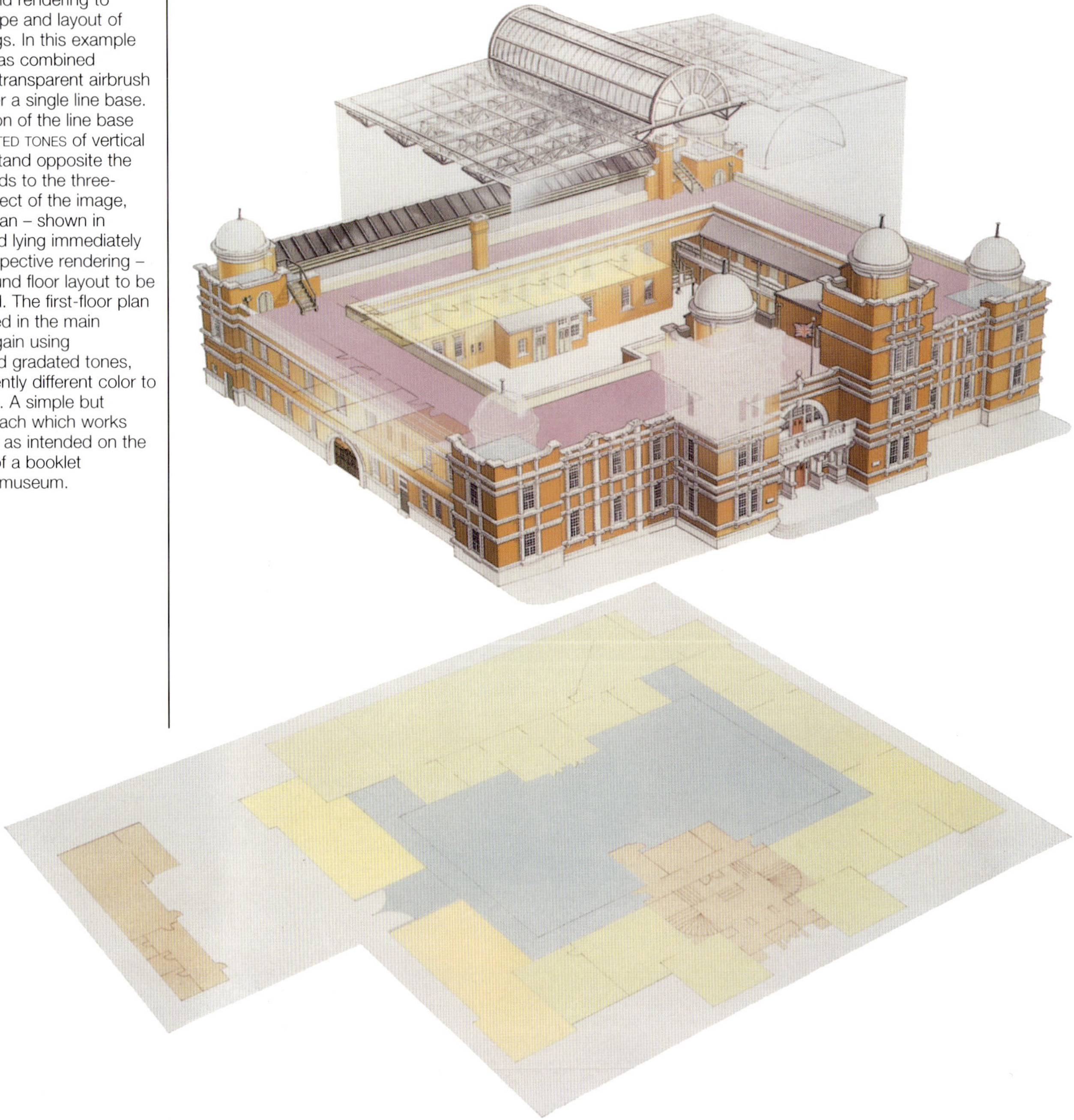

In Perfect Control • ***Jorgen Larsson***

STYLE

This image combines architectural and topographical illustration. The high viewpoint reveals the complete network under control of a computer known as SPIDER. This style is popular with large corporations to convey the socially beneficial aspects of such a system.

TECHNIQUE

The combination of gouache, watercolor, and pencil relies on airbrushing as a base. FREEHAND SPRAYING was used throughout, over which the detail was added, including a substantial amount of LINING-IN.

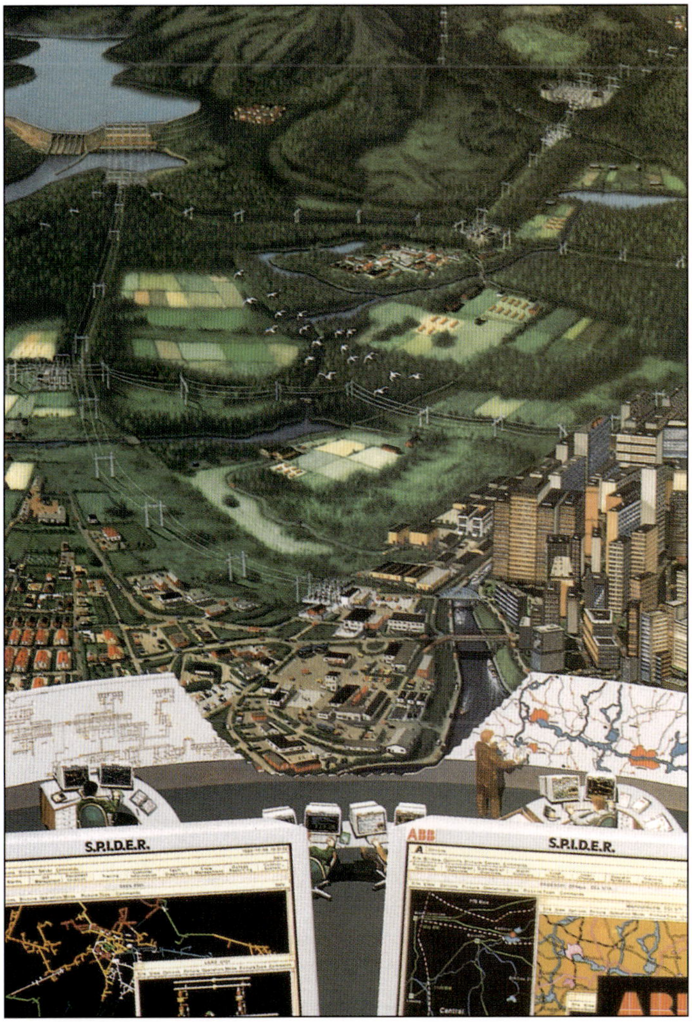

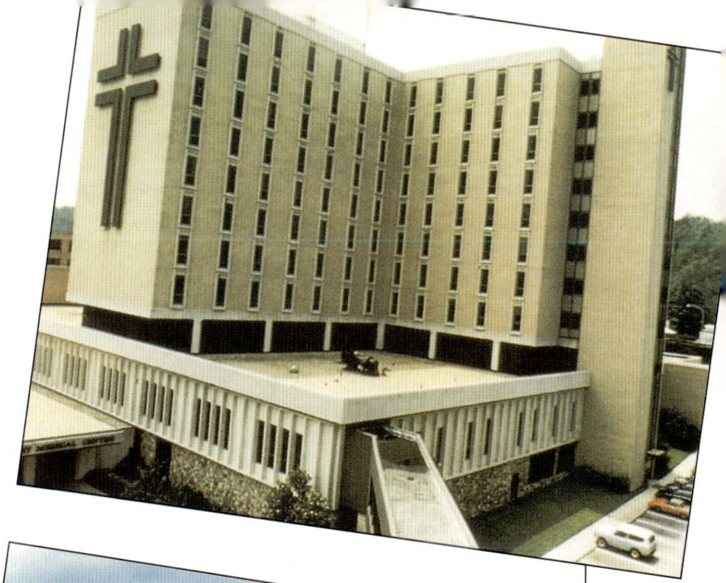

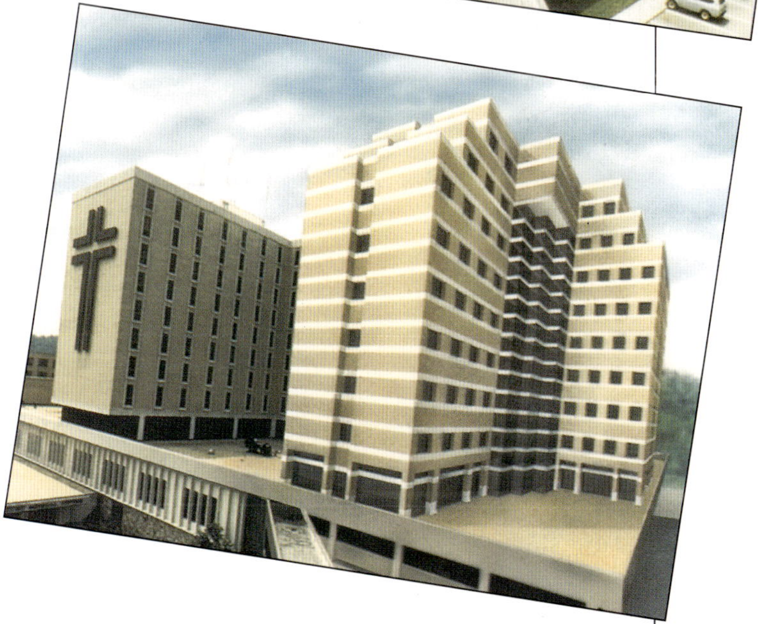

Proposed Medical Facility Addition and Photograph of Existing Facility • ***Anita S. Bice***

CONCEPT

The photograph was used as the base for illustration of the proposed extension. This method ensures that the perspectives are compatible and saves time on the preparatory drawing. It also enables the illustrator to create a balance of color, tone, and texture, since the new building would be constructed in the same materials as the old.

TECHNIQUE

The extension was drawn onto an enlarged print and airbrushed in acrylics, which are sufficiently opaque to cover the photographic detail as required. Unlike photo-retouching, the airbrushing does not enhance the existing image, but is a new and separate piece of artwork superimposed.

HUMAN AND ANIMAL

It is recognized that the human form is one of the most difficult to draw and render in any medium accurately and with total conviction. The problems are further enhanced with airbrush rendering, for the very mechanical nature of the tool can easily make the subjects appear lifeless and lacking movement; both essential ingredients for a successful illustration of a human or animal model. These subjects are also the ones for which photographic-based reference material is often the only source, so a sympathetic or lively rendering is all the more important.

Examples are also included here of the highly specialized field of medical illustration, which naturally fits in well with the subject of the human form. However, in some respects this area is also closely related to industrial imagery and food and drink. The relationship with industrial subjects is because of the need for absolute accuracy with no room for even the slightest error or artistic licence, unless the purpose of the illustration is purely visual rather than instructive, as in a design for the cover of a medical magazine, for example. With food and drink, the connection is through the many variable surface textures and abstract shapes which make up anatomy.

In order to acquire a fuller understanding of the techniques employed in the examples reproduced here, the detail contained within each illustration should be studied at some length. Follow this with an equally detailed examination of illustrations within other themes, for it will become apparent that many technical aspects are identical; it is the process which is often different.

On some illustrations it is necessary to apply as much hand-painted work as spraying. When this is required, it is essential that the two techniques appear seamless as far as the finished illustration is concerned. It looks very amateurish when the brushwork is not integrated with the spraying.

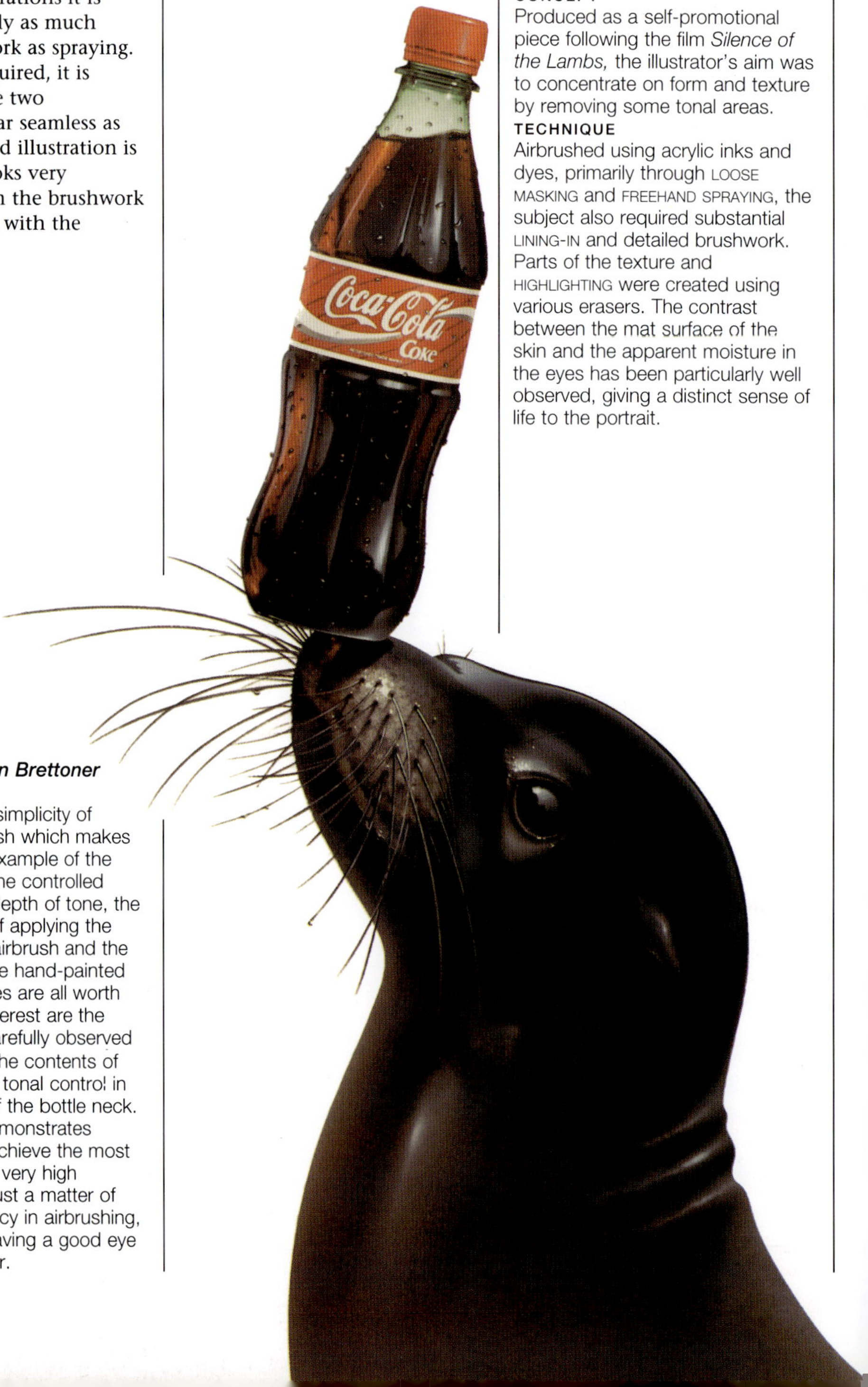

Coca Cola • *John Brettoner*
TECHNIQUE
It is the apparent simplicity of technique and finish which makes this an excellent example of the airbrusher's art. The controlled palette, the right depth of tone, the overall accuracy of applying the color through an airbrush and the quality of line in the hand-painted finishing techniques are all worth close study. Of interest are the subtle and very carefully observed color changes in the contents of the bottle and the tonal control in the clear plastic of the bottle neck. This illustration demonstrates precisely that to achieve the most effective image to very high standards is not just a matter of technical proficiency in airbrushing, but of the artist having a good eye for detail and color.

▶ Anthony Hopkins • *Duncan Gutteridge*
CONCEPT
Produced as a self-promotional piece following the film *Silence of the Lambs*, the illustrator's aim was to concentrate on form and texture by removing some tonal areas.
TECHNIQUE
Airbrushed using acrylic inks and dyes, primarily through LOOSE MASKING and FREEHAND SPRAYING, the subject also required substantial LINING-IN and detailed brushwork. Parts of the texture and HIGHLIGHTING were created using various erasers. The contrast between the mat surface of the skin and the apparent moisture in the eyes has been particularly well observed, giving a distinct sense of life to the portrait.

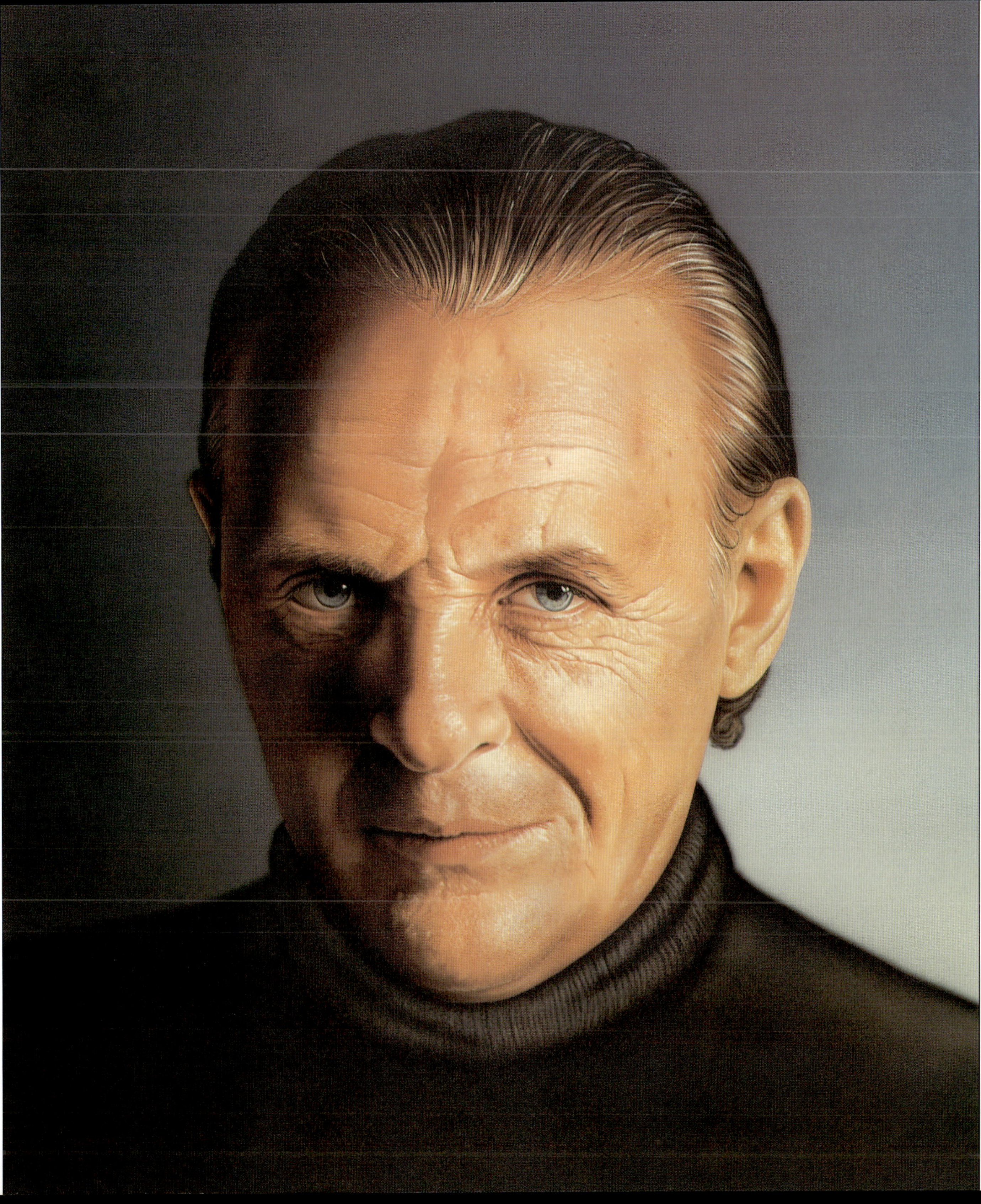

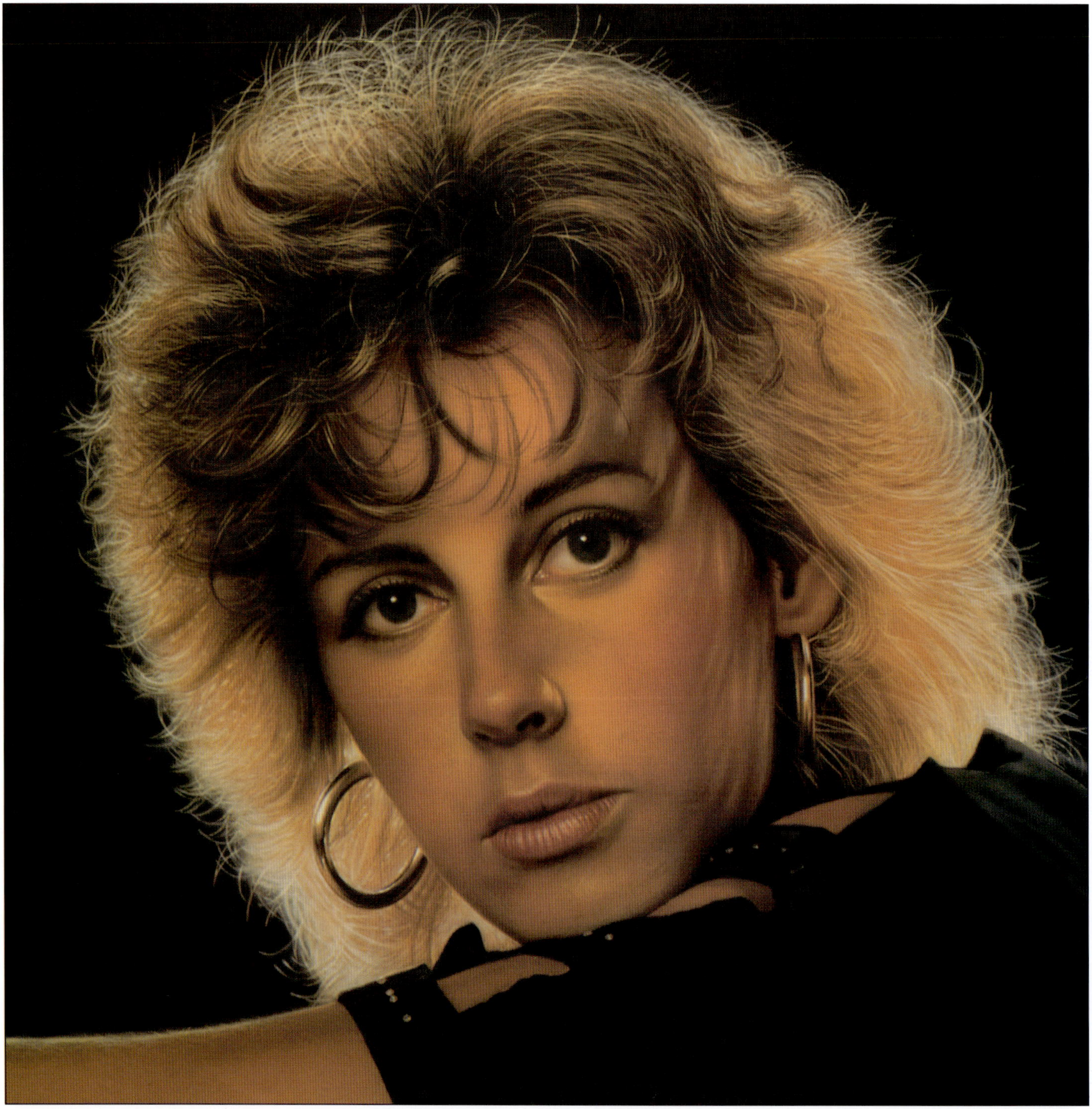

◀ **Female** • ***Simon Dewey***
CONCEPT
By way of contrast, this portrait aims to enhance the inherent beauty of the subject, rather than highlight the natural imperfections that can be found in anybody's face. This is a frequent application of airbrushing, to which it is admirably suited.
TECHNIQUE
The outstanding quality of the image can be found by examining the small details, which are more realistic than the kind of "plastic" interpretations of the female face often seen in airbrush art. The image brings together contrasts of surface texture, light, and shade, with color balance and contrast, which all complement each other to produce a convincing and sensual portrait. Note the primary light source, located behind and above the subject.

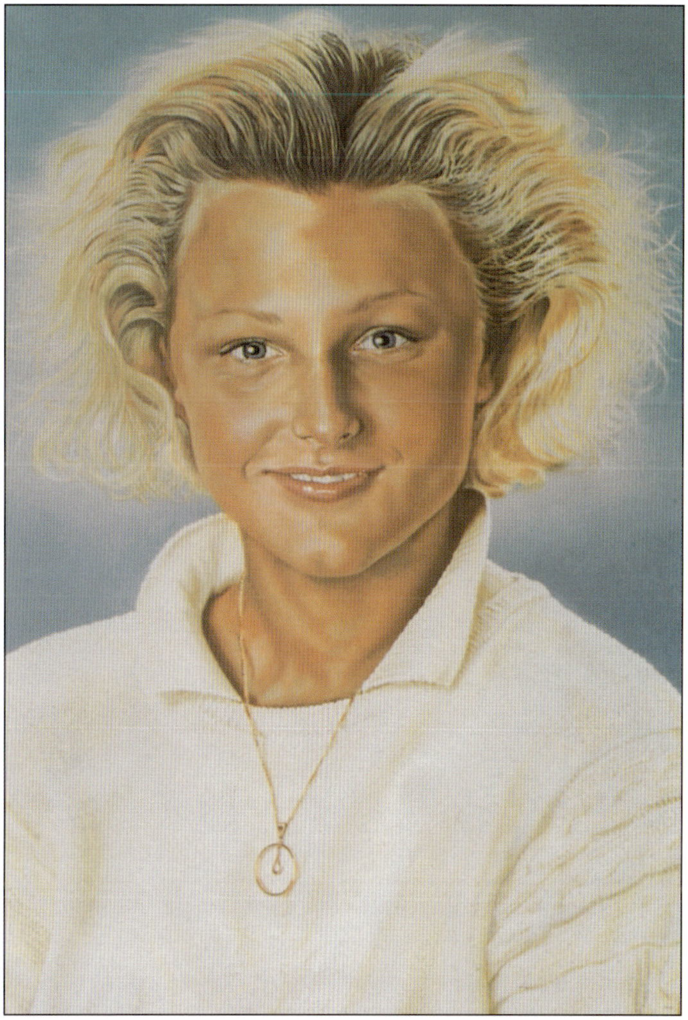

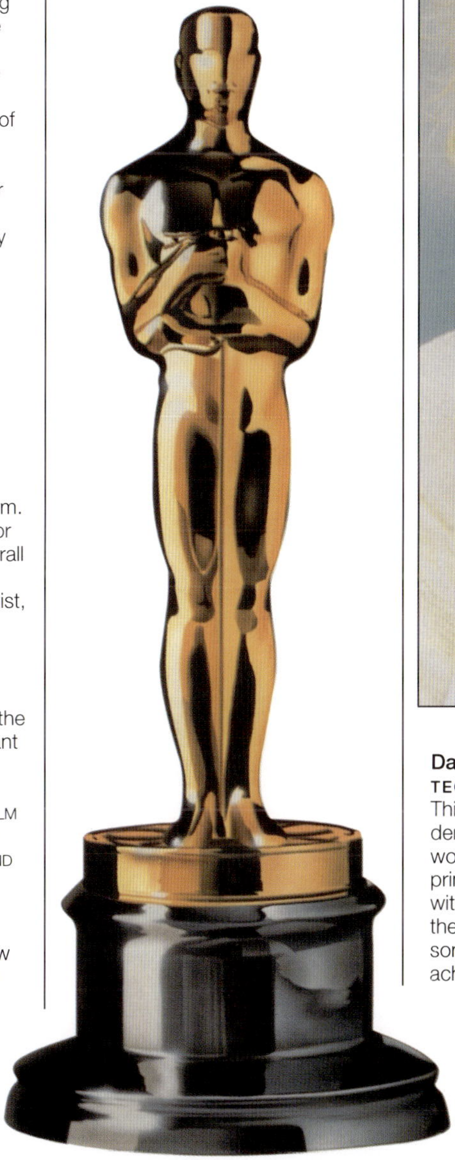

Oscar • ***Colin Brown***
CONCEPT
Though not actually human, Oscar's basic proportions obviously relate to the human form. This image was commissioned for the cover of a TV guide. The overall shape does not allow for much imagination on the part of the artist, but the subject gives scope for interpretation.
TECHNIQUE
The lack of hard edges to the original molding, combined with the intensely reflective surfaces, meant breaking down the form into a series of abstract shapes. These have been simply defined with FILM MASKING and LOOSE MASKING, over underlying base areas of FREEHAND SPRAYING, using gouache throughout. HIGHLIGHTING was applied using DOT CONTROL and GRADATED TONES. A strong shadow line to the right brings base and figure together.

Daddy's Girl • ***Jörgen Larsson***
TECHNIQUE
This is a self-promotional piece demonstrating the artist's ability to work extensively with an airbrush, primarily using FREEHAND SPRAYING, with brushwork limited to details of the girl's pullover and hair. There is some interesting modeling to achieve the shallow depths typical of young people's faces, and the irregularities common to all. A natural puffiness about the face has been effected by many variations in tonal values and selective reflected HIGHLIGHTING. No attempt has been made to accentuate the girl's attractive features, or give her an artificially enhanced "plastic" look.

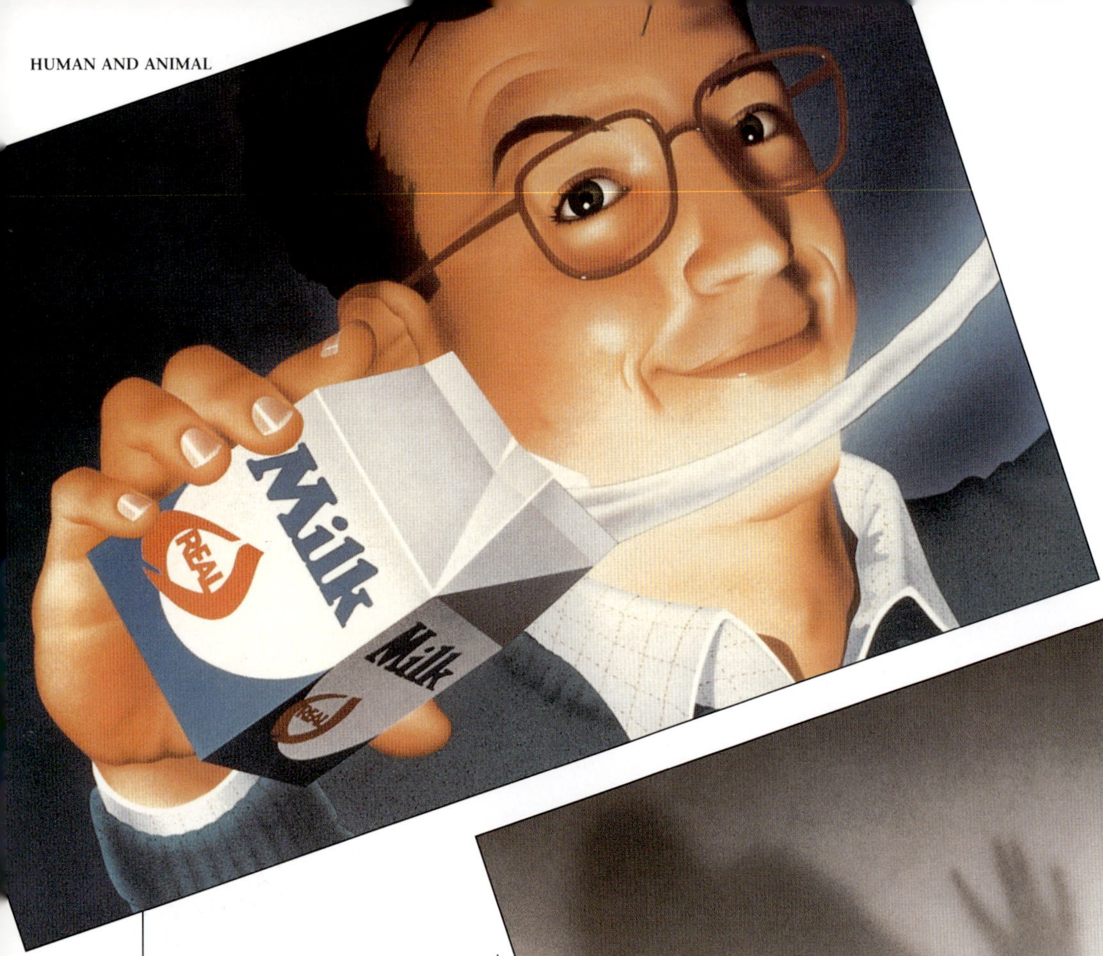

◀ **Greg Smallidge • *Stephen Peringer***
TECHNIQUE
The subtle conversion of the human face and form into semi-caricature is a popular technique used by illustrators when producing work for the advertising industry, and this clean, simple and effective example is typical. Its apparent simplicity belies a level of airbrushing skill as competent as the most photographically realistic illustration. The face in particular utilizes a mixture of FILM MASKING with GRADATED TONES and FREEHAND SPRAYING, with LOOSE MASKING being used to bring out facial undulations which do not have hard edges. It was sprayed using inks specially manufactured for airbrushing.

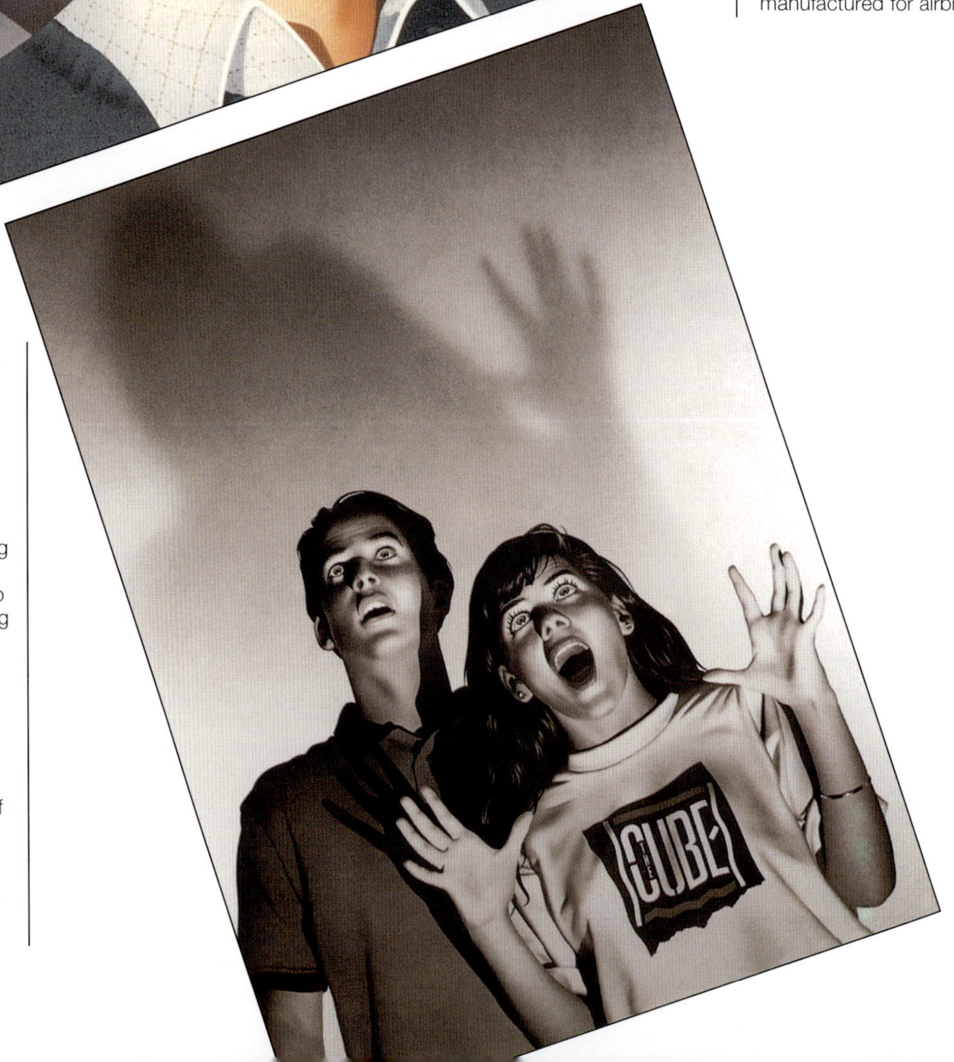

Killer Store Invades Walla Walla • *Stephen Peringer*
CONCEPT
To re-create the mood and atmosphere of a 1950's horror movie, the artist has rendered the image in monochrome. A comparatively simple but effective approach has been adopted, using a composition which directs the viewer's eye from the couple up to the shadow of "something" coming toward them.
TECHNIQUE
The composition is enhanced by the strong, crisp outlines of the couple against the loose-masked shadow freely projected onto the wall behind them. The figures' clothes and faces use a mixture of LOOSE MASKING and FREEHAND SPRAYING, with deep contrasts which add to the overall effect of the event taking place in a semi-lit room. Acrylics were used throughout.

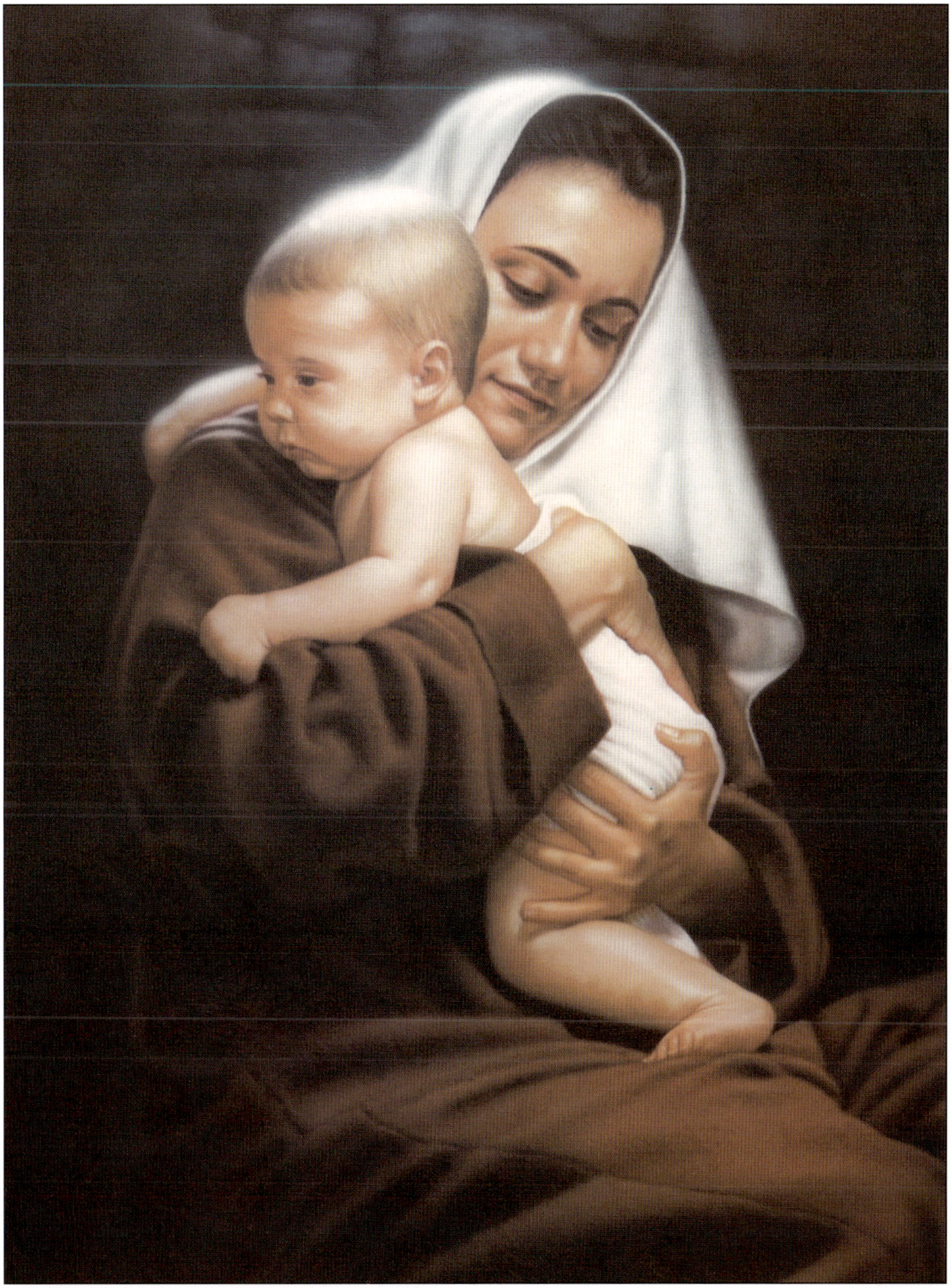

Mother and Child• ***Simon Dewey***

CONCEPT

Obviously a strong religious influence underlies this image, though the theme has been treated in a very contemporary manner and with a remarkable sense of realism. Both mother and child have features typical of our time, yet the implication is clear: note, for example, the freehand highlight on top of both heads.

TECHNIQUE

Extensive FREEHAND SPRAYING has achieved the natural undulations in skin and flesh. The mother's heavy brown gown relies very much on freehand work to produce the numerous folds and creases, in particular the carefully observed changes where the material lies close to a seam. The fibers do not lie in the same direction because of the cut of the cloth, and this seemingly insignificant point makes an important contribution.

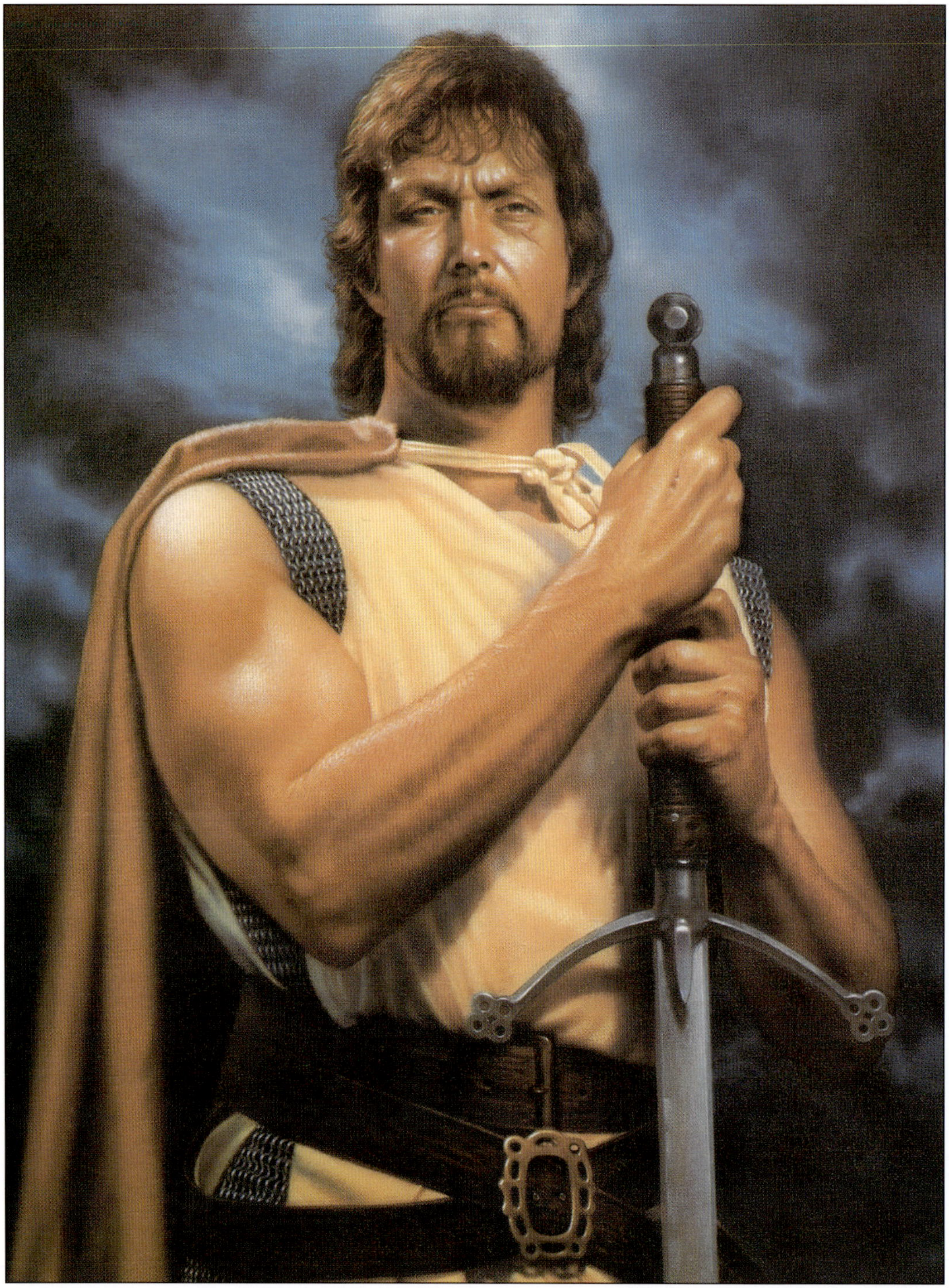

Warrior • ***Simon Dewey***

CONCEPT

This dramatic image uses the film industry's mix of 20th-century realism and period costume, rather than adjusting the human features to suit the period implied. This is an approach very common in fantasy art. The viewpoint is subtle, but sufficient to convey that the man is above average height.

TECHNIQUE

The application of stronger HIGHLIGHTING to the face and other exposed areas of skin suggests that the subject has been engaged in intense physical action, which adds to the narrative impression. The clothes and accessories have been carefully observed, using FREEHAND SPRAYING and LOOSE MASKING to show folds and movement in the various materials. LINING-IN has been applied to fine detail, such as the hairs on the man's arms and face, and small scratches on his sword.

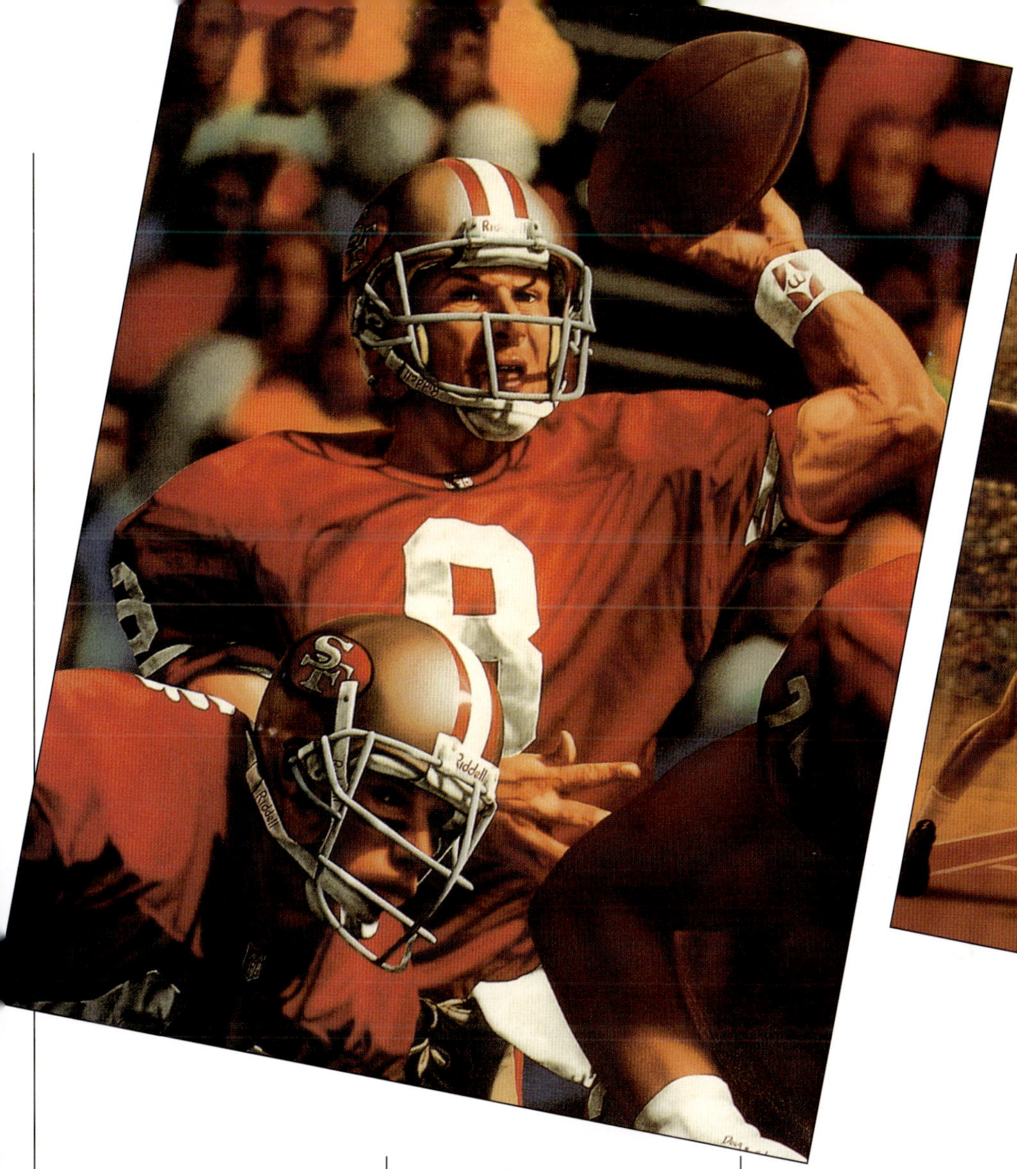

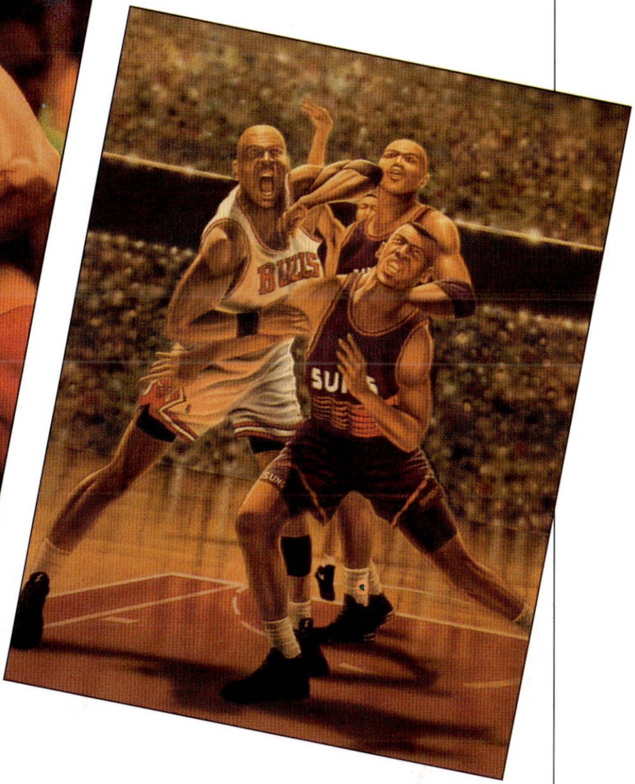

MVP Steve Young •
Doug Meythaler

CONCEPT

This is a dramatic and powerfully composed image, concentrating on the single named player; but note the nearness of the spectators, and therefore the greater implied detail than in the previous examples. It is a large-scale acrylic painting, 35 x 44in.

TECHNIQUE

The realistic three-dimensional effect has been achieved without resorting to the artificial finish of photo-realism. At first glance, the image could be a still from a film sequence. There are no hidden or unusual airbrush techniques that achieve the level of quality, just careful observation and application of the airbrushing and supporting hand-painted areas. The closeness of the central character means that everything about him must be complete: the shadows, all appearing to come genuinely from the same light source; the tones and contrasts; the detail of fabrics and materials. Every element must be considered as important as the next, however insignificant to the image overall.

Untitled • ***Mark Villarta***

APPROACH

In this stylized yet realistic interpretation of a particular moment in a basketball game, the composition revolves around the three central players. The ground and upper and lower stands of spectators provide a horizontally divided background. The spectators are represented with an out-of-focus technique, using DOT CONTROL and FREEHAND SPRAYING. This provides a scene-setting, non-conflicting backdrop against which the sharply contrasting players immediately attract the eye. To accentuate the HIGHLIGHTING on the players, an eraser was used to lift out even more color.

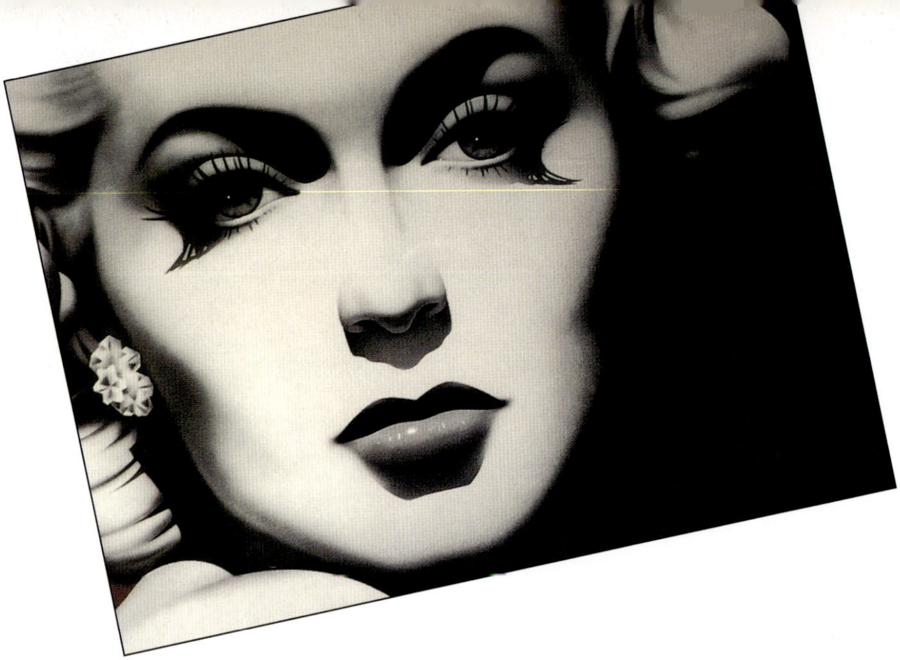

9th Seattle International Film Festival • *Stephen Peringer*

COMPOSITION

This illustration was produced for inclusion on a poster advertising the film festival. It is rendered in monochrome using airbrushing inks. As a subject it is fairly typical, yet underlying the clichéd Hollywood face is an interesting concept in that the artist has combined the facial features of four different actresses: Gene Tierney's eyes, Marlene Dietrich's nose, Hedy Lamarr's lips and Lana Turner's hair! The use of an above-center light source gives an equal balance of shadow to left and right, allowing the cheeks to be left almost white, thereby highlighting the facial features.

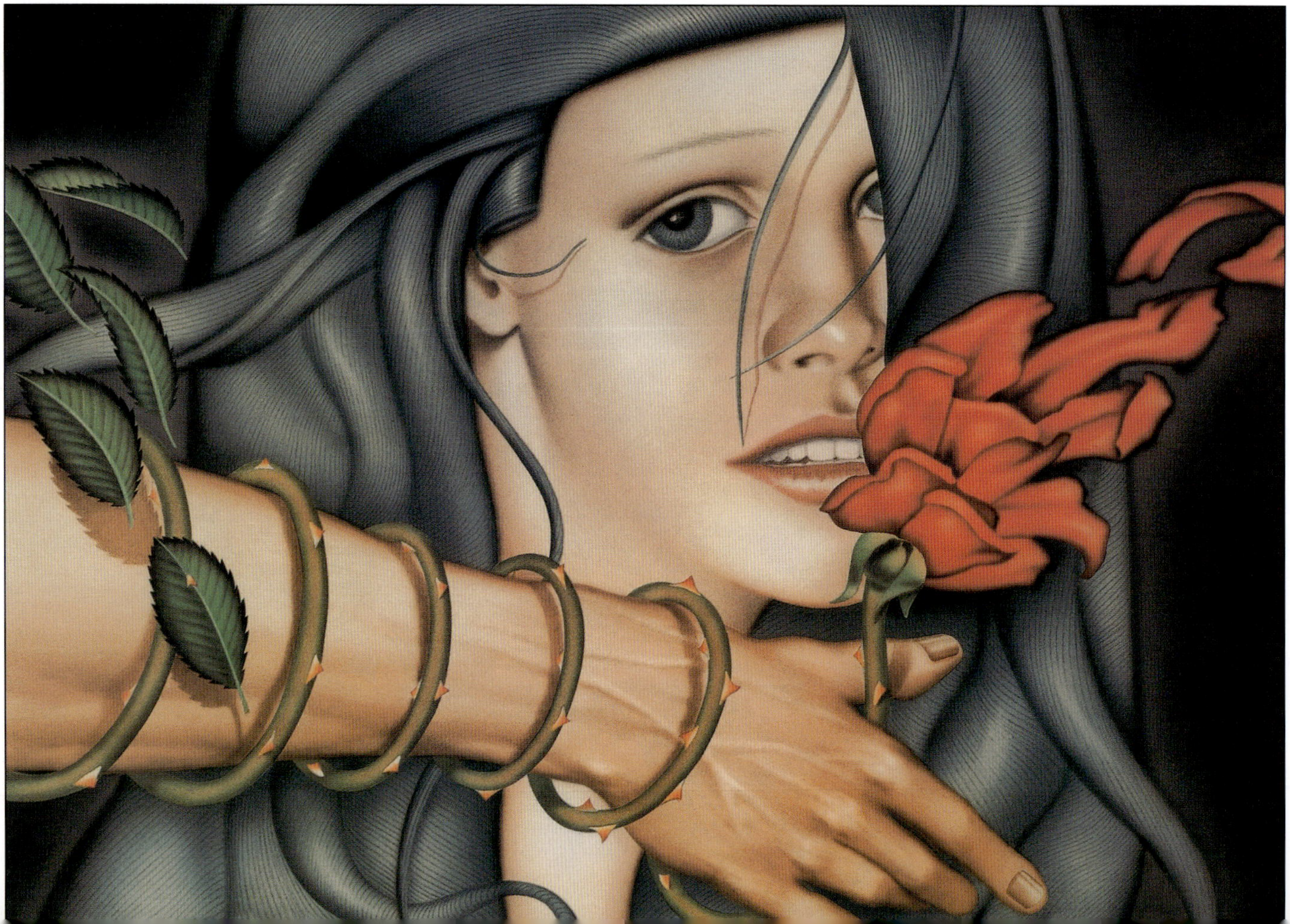

Mark Devours Himself •
Travis A. Louie

CONCEPT

In this commission, for a nightclub specializing in alternative music, the clients specifically wanted an image that would complement their music and was intended to be shocking. Interestingly, though it is monochrome and does not include the blood and terrified expressions usually associated with such images, it does shock.

TECHNIQUE

Substantially, the technique is FREEHAND SPRAYING to bring out detail, shape, and form. The tonal values have been very well controlled, with no single area left unclear. The lack of strong, direct, or reflected HIGHLIGHTING does not diminish the very three-dimensional impression. Being unable to rely on color changes to help delineate different components, a relatively simple approach produces the best effect.

◀ In the beginning • *Bryan Ceney*

TECHNIQUE

This is a mixed-media illustration, drawn predominantly with colored pencil, with airbrushing restricted to the almost mechanical and somewhat disturbing rendering of the rose, thorn and the leaves, creating an image of strong contrasts. To add to the contrast between the two techniques, in the colored pencil rendering the illustrator has built up very fine detail, in terms of both surface texture and a generally realistic image, while the airbrushing has been applied in an almost simplistic manner.

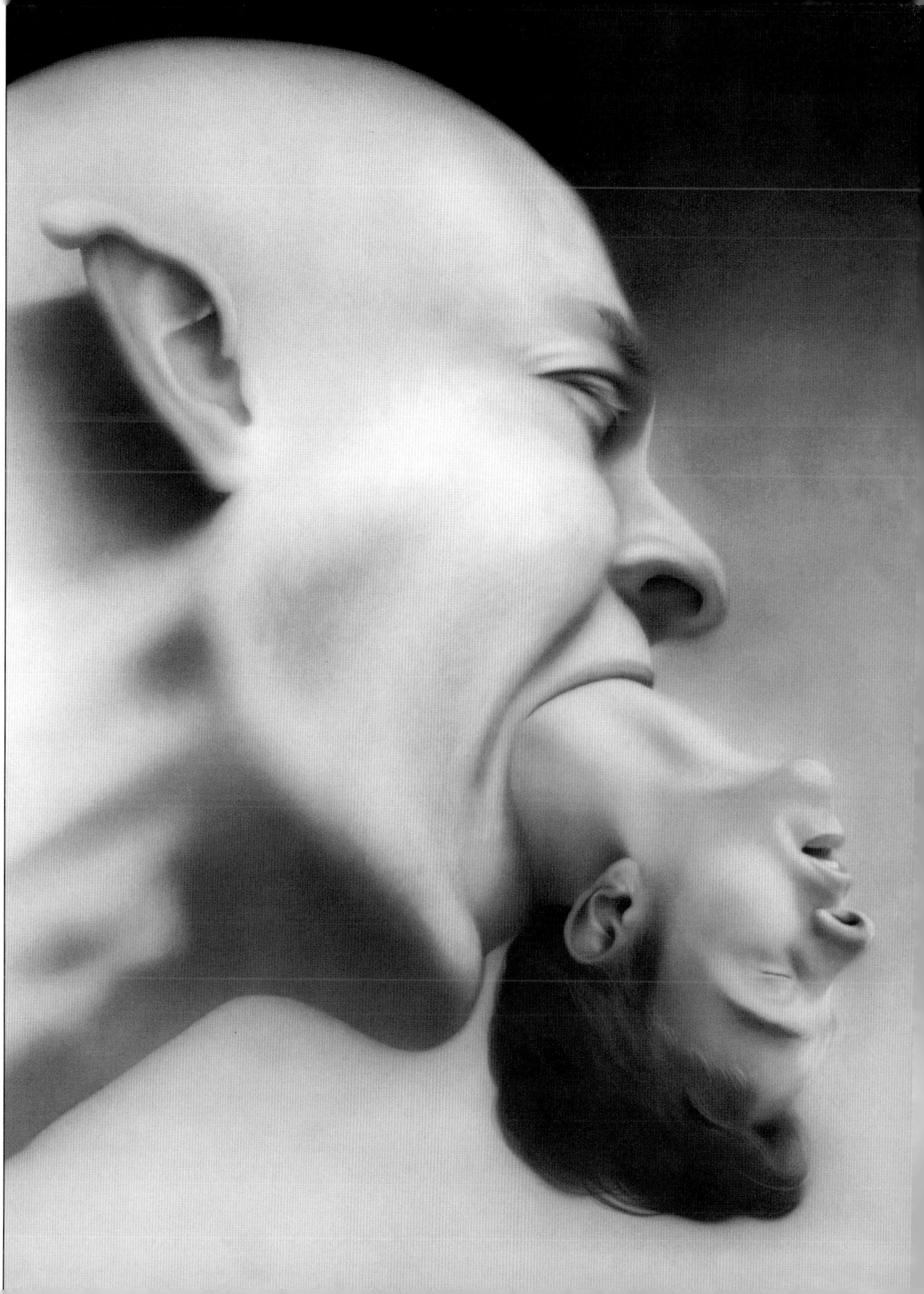

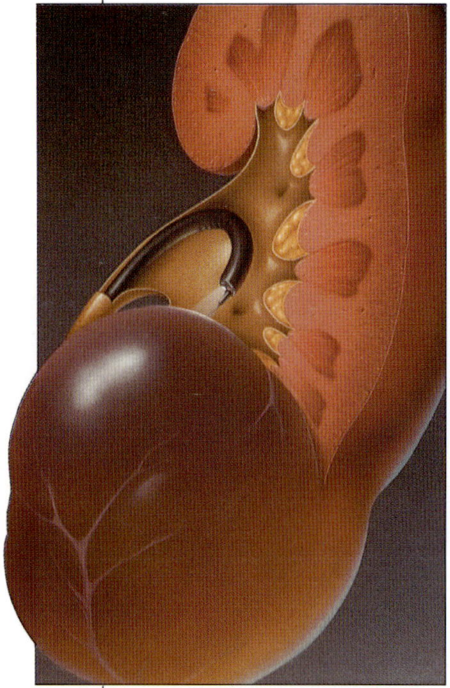

▲ **Renal Cyst Treatment** • *Brian Evans*

TECHNIQUE

This acrylic illustration was commissioned for the cover of a medical journal. The use of reflected light, the luminous GRADATED TONES created through TRANSPARENCY, and the carefully selected locations and application of HIGHLIGHTING, combine to make an image which is exceptional in its own right and as an example of a beautifully controlled airbrushing.

Duodenal Anatomy • *Brian Evans*

CONCEPT

Medical illustration is a highly specialized field which requires a clear, thorough understanding of the subject so that any image is unquestionably accurate, especially if used as a teaching aid or guide to treatment. There is no room for error or artistic license.

TECHNIQUE

This self-promotional piece in acrylics uses the convention of "cutting" areas to show internal shape, texture, and parts which would not otherwise be visible. The use of CAST SHADOWS with LOOSE MASKING adds substantially to the three-dimensional effect. Localized HIGHLIGHTING gives moisture to the surface textures. Both the central image and the sectioned detail have been placed in an overall design context, creating a cohesive whole and explaining the direct correlation of one part to another.

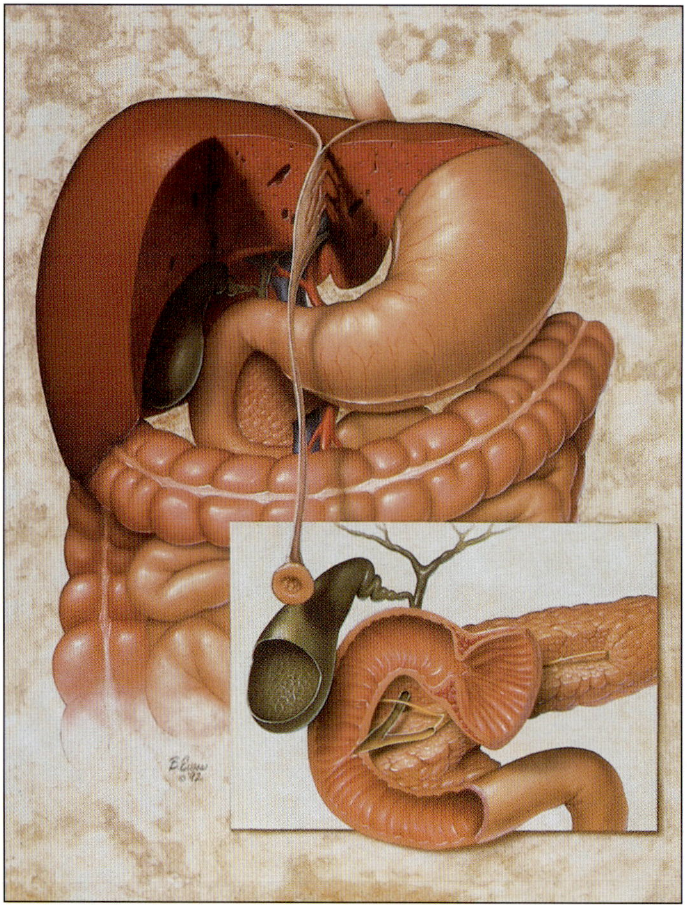

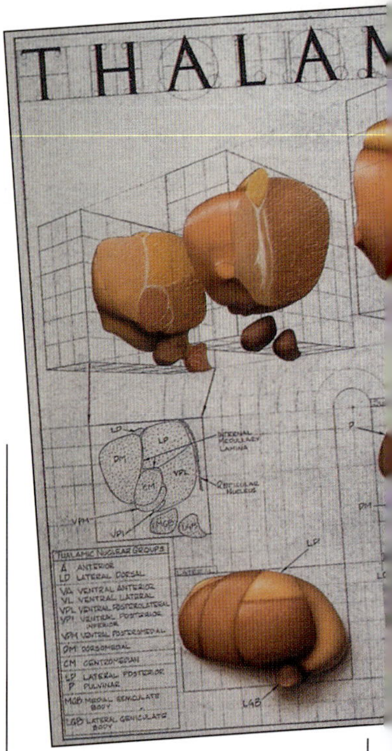

▲ **Thalamus** • *Brian Evans*

TECHNIQUE

An interesting and successful combination of full-color images against a monochrome backdrop, all contained within a carefully designed composition. The apparent simplicity of the airbrushing hides a broad range of skillfully applied techniques, including CAST SHADOWS, DROP SHADOWS, FILM MASKING, GRADATED TONES, HIGHLIGHTING, LINING-IN, LOOSE MASKING, OVERSPRAYING, and SPATTERING.

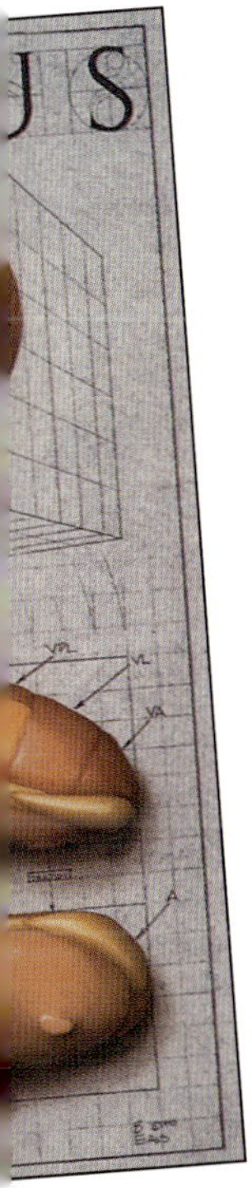

▶ **Chronic abdominal pain •**
Todd Buck
TECHNIQUE
This acrylic-based illustration utilizes two distinct and separate techniques to very good effect. The specific subject is airbrushed as one illustration, combining a schematic outline of the human body with detailed rendering of the abdomen. To put this in the context of the body as a whole, the illustrator has drawn a Renaissance-style figure in sepia pencil on tinted paper. In producing the work in this way, the illustrator has allowed it to be used either as one complete image or as two separate ones. The airbrushing is extremely competently handled, giving a very strong three-dimensional image, which although almost monochrome is very sharp and clear.

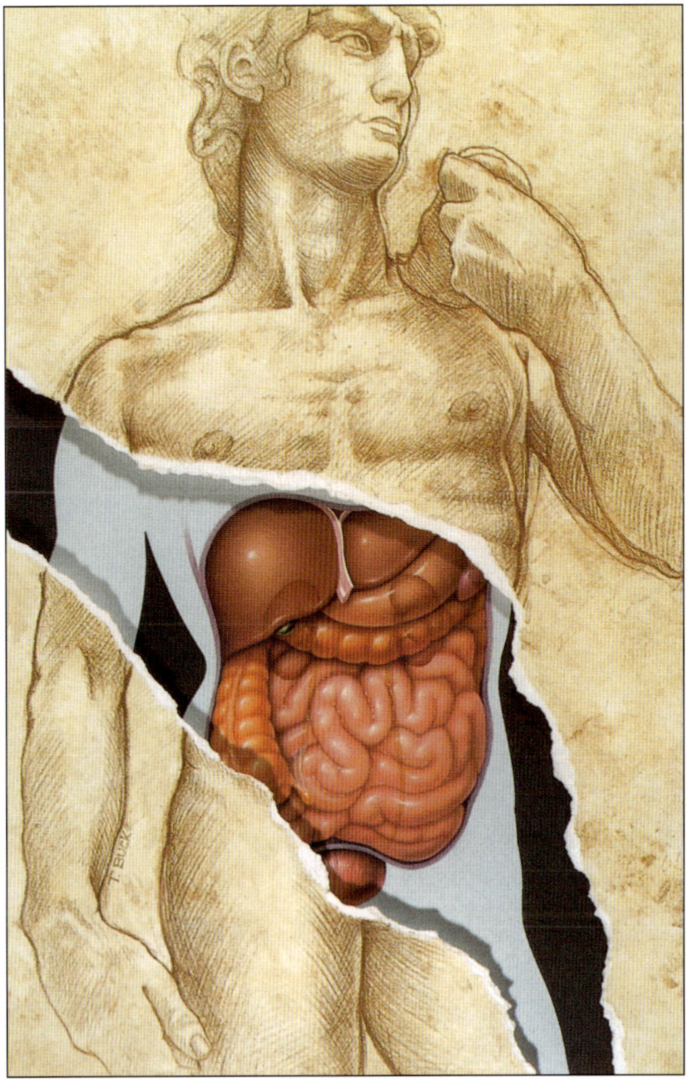

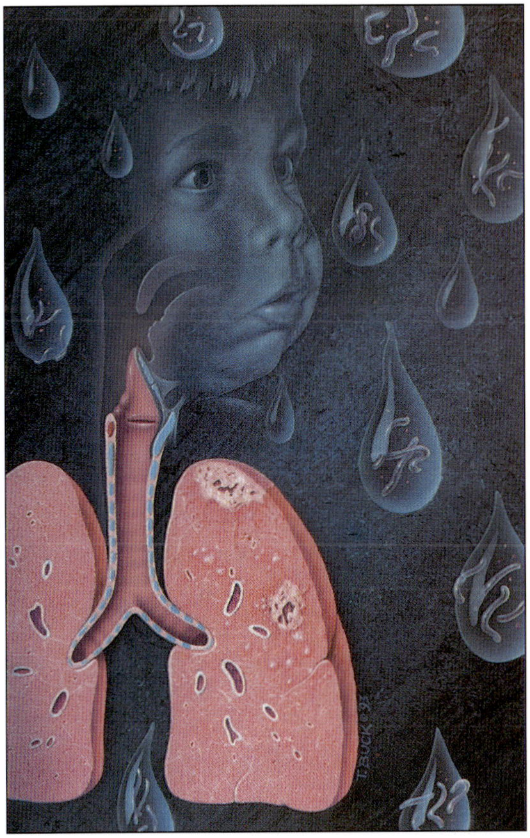

◀ **Tuberculosis in children •**
Todd Buck
COMPOSITION
This illustration was produced for the front cover of a medical journal dealing with children's medicine. The combination of schematic-style illustrations with a more realistic style requires careful preparation and a strong sense of abstract design skills; even though the illustration itself may not be abstract, the overall shapes which make up any image will always be abstract if seen in the context of their silhouettes. In this example, airbrushed in acrylics, the illustrator has combined the two approaches successfully, and has further combined two different schematic techniques for the lungs and the tuberculosis virus.

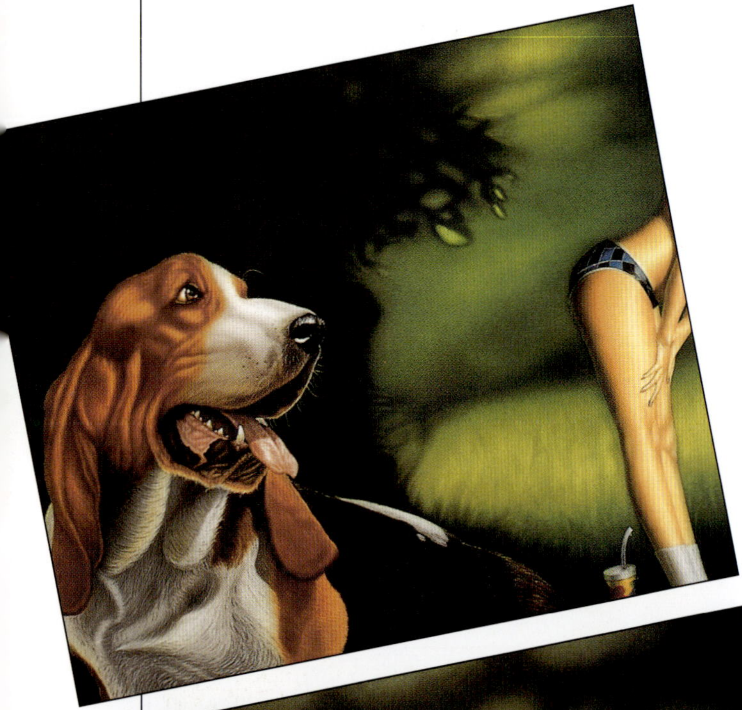

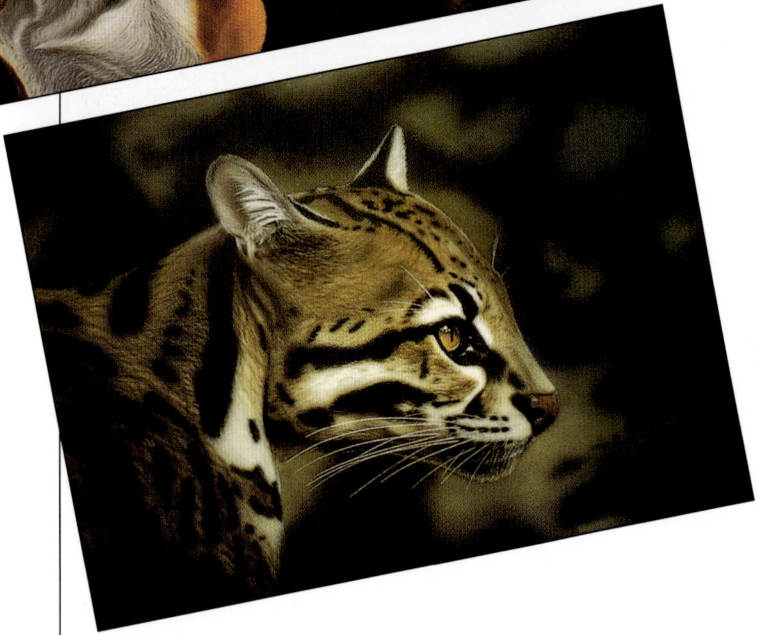

◀ A day in the park • *Samuel Salfino III*

TECHNIQUE

Airbrushed using liquid acrylics, this illustration combines a wide variety of airbrush techniques. The foreground and middle distance have been rendered in sharp focus. The background to the left has an almost flat and very deep tone that changes to FREEHAND SPRAYING and LOOSE MASKING on the right to achieve the out-of-focus effect of the grass and outline of the tree.

Ocelot • *Gregory M. Hurley*

TECHNIQUE

This competent, photographic-based acrylic image also uses the technique of a sharp foreground with an out-of-focus background. To achieve the sharply delineated lines of the cat's whiskers and parts of its fur, SCRATCHING BACK was applied once the base colors had been airbrushed. The use of softly GRADATED TONES and DOT HIGHLIGHTS to render the eye is very effective, giving life and depth to the subject.

▶ Carousel Ponies • *Thomas Cain*

CONCEPT

Drawn from an actual antique carousel, this image makes a good combination of accuracy and impression, effectively achieved with the airbrush. The accuracy of the ponies, their finish and the materials from which they are made, almost qualifies as technical illustration. With the addition of bright, reflective lights and gaudy fairground colors, the whole remains balanced and in control.

TECHNIQUE

The airbrushing was in acrylics on linen board, a texture that can be used selectively to good effect. After FILM MASKING to separate individual shapes, LOOSE MASKING with acetate was applied to form and shadows. Extensive HIGHLIGHTING was required, some applied by brush and LINING-IN. FREEHAND SPRAYING of shadows has added to the depth, though the many different light sources diminish cast shadow.

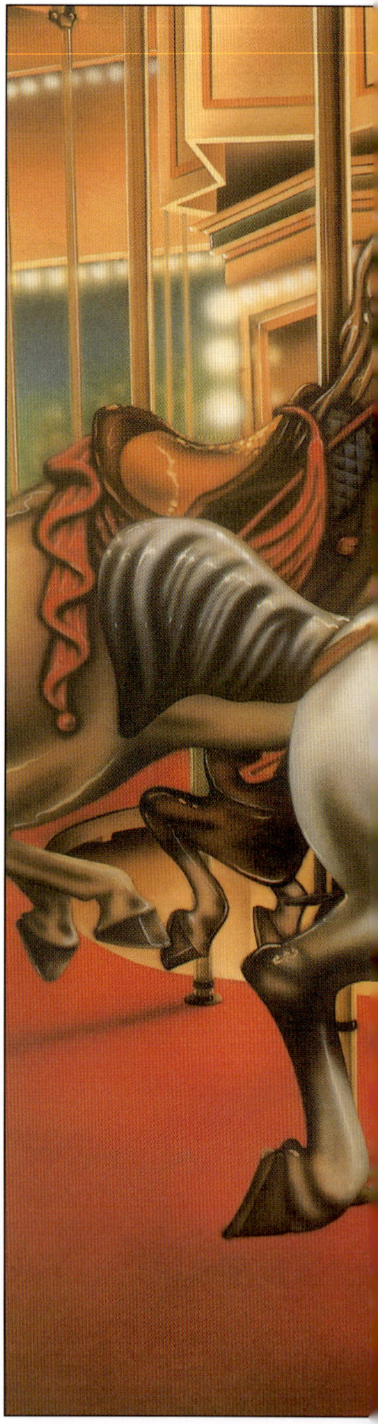

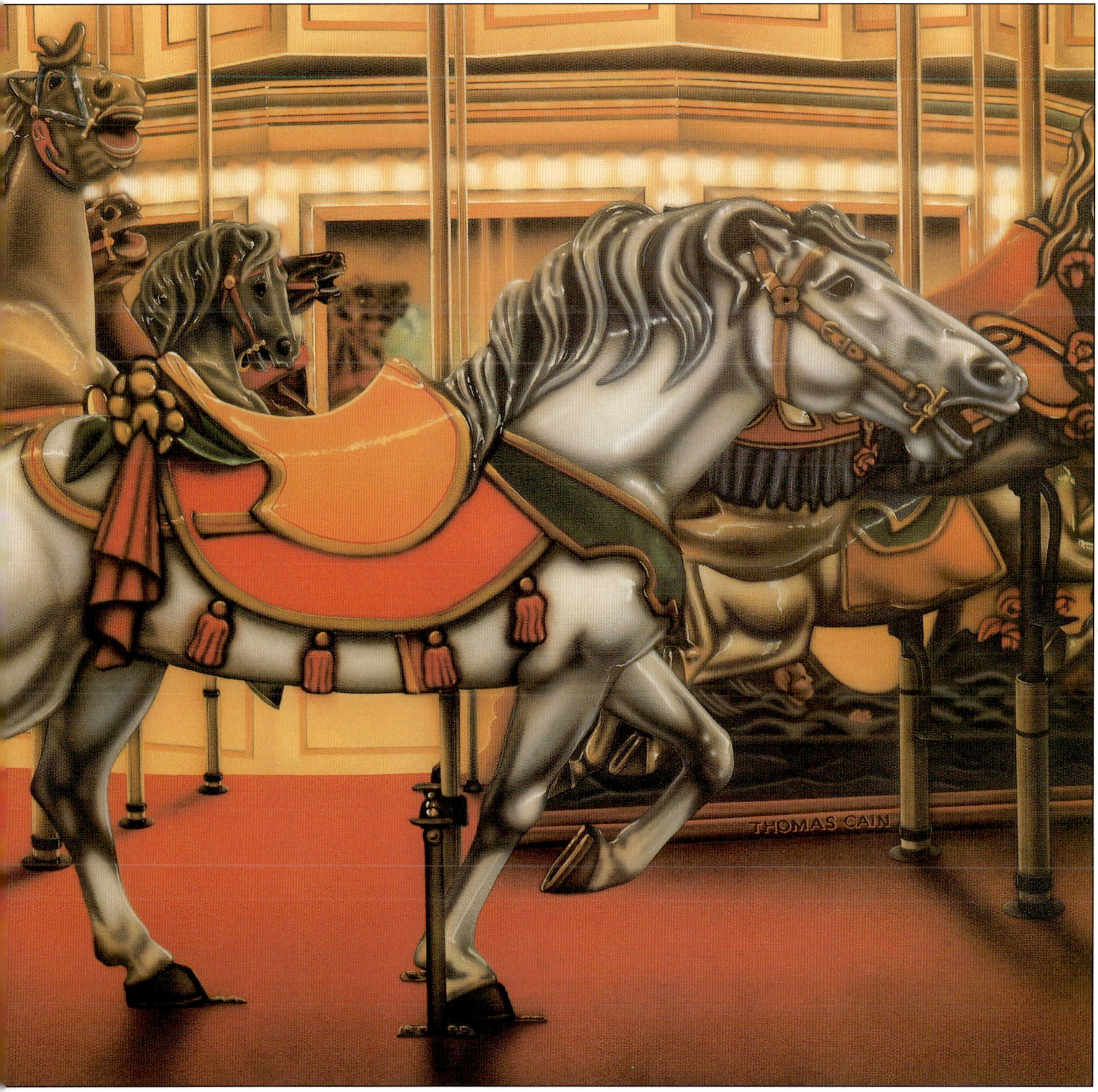
THOMAS CAIN

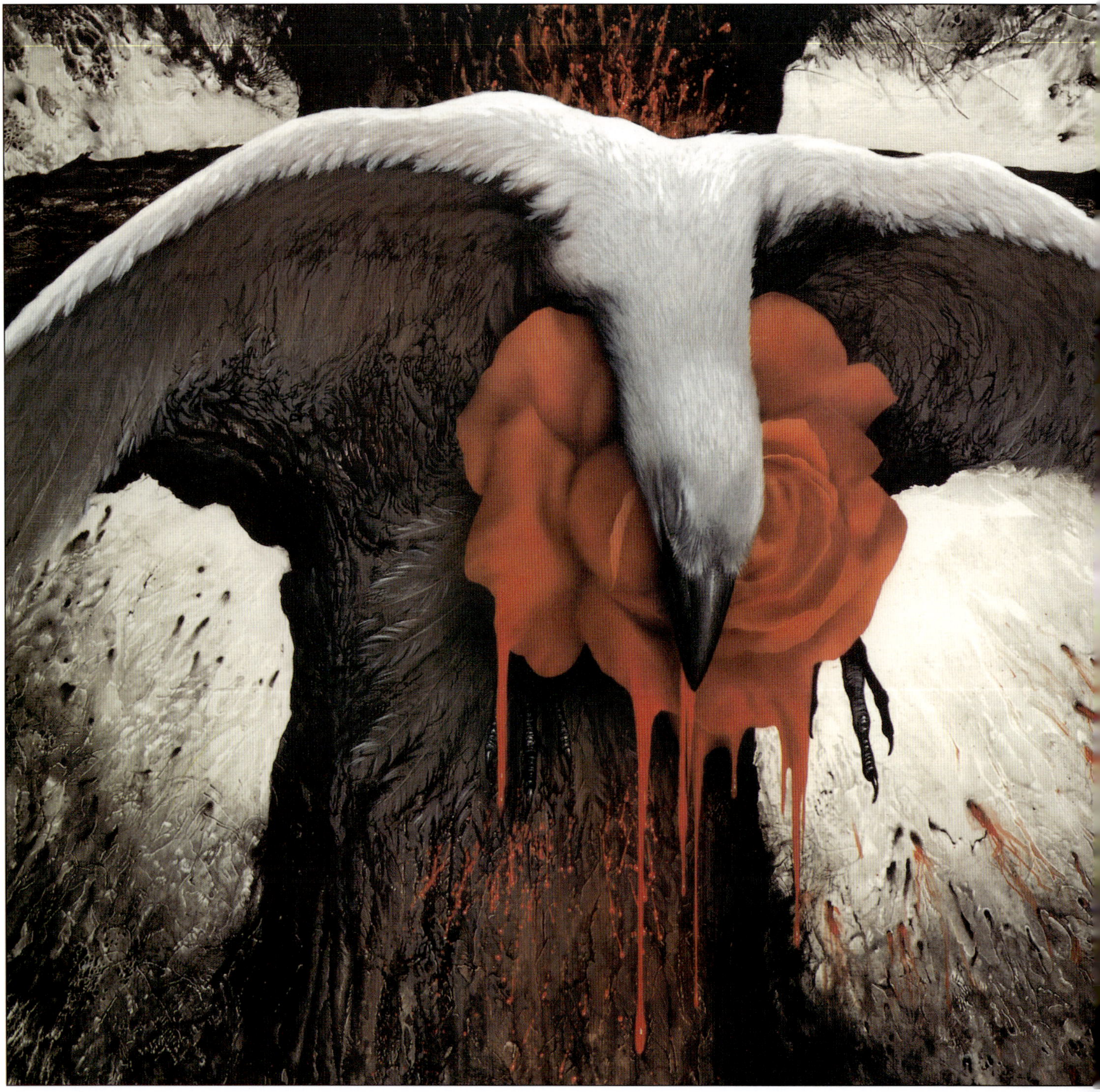

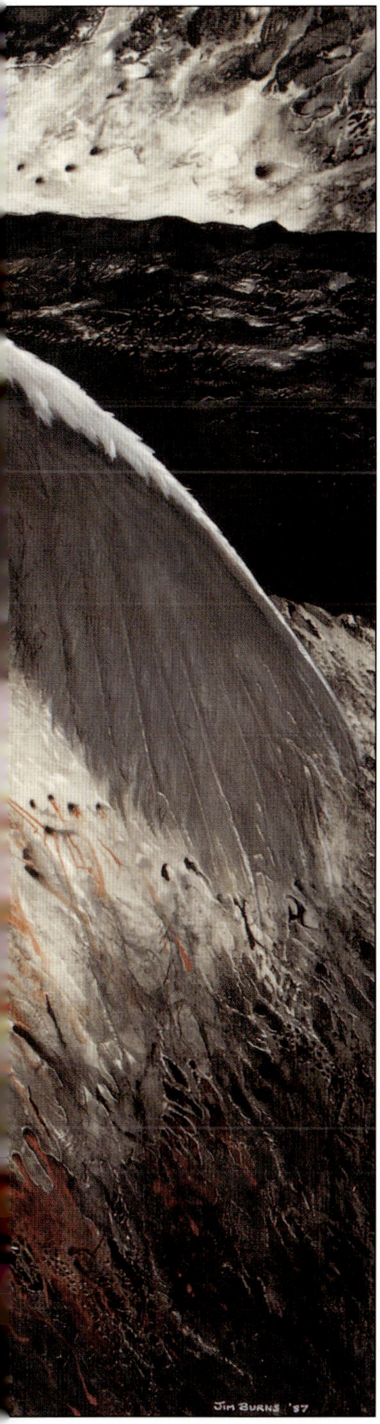

Songbirds of Pain • *Jim Burns*

CONCEPT

The origin of this illustration was a book of short stories of the same title. It is an inspirational piece interpreting comments by the book's author. This type of painting allows maximum freedom of expression, subject only to the depth of the artist's imagination.

TECHNIQUE

Acrylics have been used throughout, on a base of gesso-primed hardboard. In a mixture of airbrushing and hand painting, the airbrushing is concentrated primarily on the rose, with a combination of FILM MASKING, LOOSE MASKING and FREEHAND SPRAYING to achieve the shape and definition of each petal.

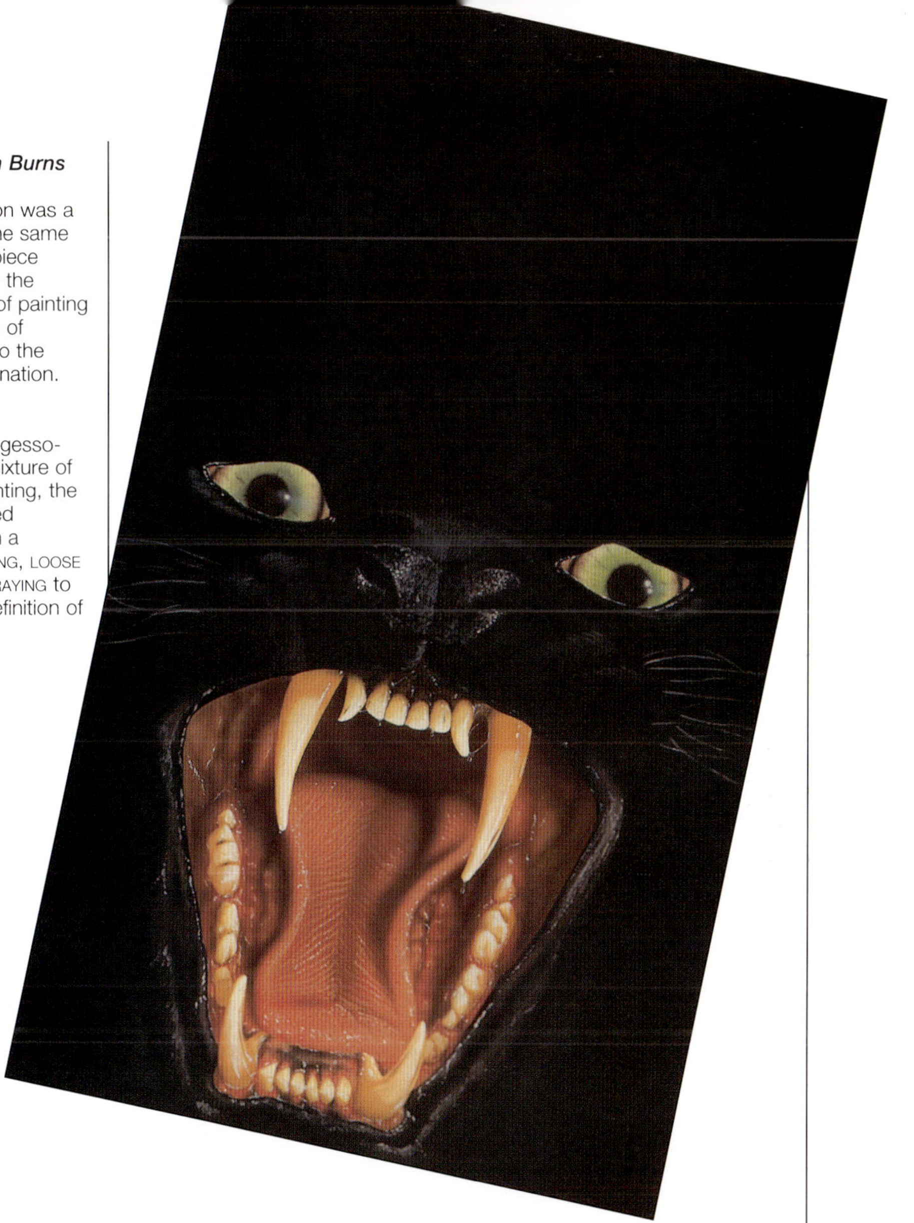

Panther • *Paul Campion*

CONCEPT

A commission for use on a standard-format paperback book required a composition that would accommodate the title and other overlaid type matter. This has resulted in the panther being positioned principally in the lower half of the illustration's total surface area. The use of the panther's base color as the background color means that only the mouth, eyes and very front of the face are sharply delineated. In relation to the contrasting colors, this is very effective.

TECHNIQUE

The textures of the teeth and tongue are specially notable, each precisely defined. The tongue, for example, has been airbrushed using FILM MASKING, LOOSE MASKING, and FREEHAND SPRAYING, with hand-painted highlights added.

ADVERTISING

This is a generic term to cover a wide and incredibly diverse range of outlets for the airbrush illustrator. Examples here include designs for products and services from paperback books to fast food outlets. Many of the illustrations reproduced within the other themes sections were created specifically for advertising purposes, yet their very clearly identifiable subjects and the techniques employed to render them made them more suitable for inclusion elsewhere. However, the context in which the illustrations may have been intended is often an important consideration, in terms of the way in which the illustrator has tackled the task, which is more clearly recognized in the examples shown under this heading.

Within the context of the client's brief, sometimes within very clear parameters and in other cases granting the illustrator a free hand, a wide range of techniques is apparent and an equally wide range of concepts. In many of these examples the preparatory design, layout and interpretation of the illustration is of equal importance as the way the finished artwork is rendered. The titles of most pieces give a clear indication of the process between original brief and finished illustration.

Sword •*David Scutt*

CONCEPT

This illustration was commissioned for use on a paperback book cover. Although the complete sword was not visible as eventually printed, it is shown here in its entirety.

TECHNIQUE

The use of textured or colored paper adds to the overall effect, allowing a strong, contrasting image which, although having only minimal depth in reality, retains three-dimensional properties. The base colors were applied by airbrushing, with a substantial amount of hand painting added to give detail and highlights, although DOT HIGHLIGHTS have also been used. The flame and smoke coming out of the top of the scabbard were created by FREEHAND SPRAYING and LOOSE MASKING, with touches of hand painting to add smaller and more intense flames. The CAST SHADOW of the sword on the background ensures an integrated effect.

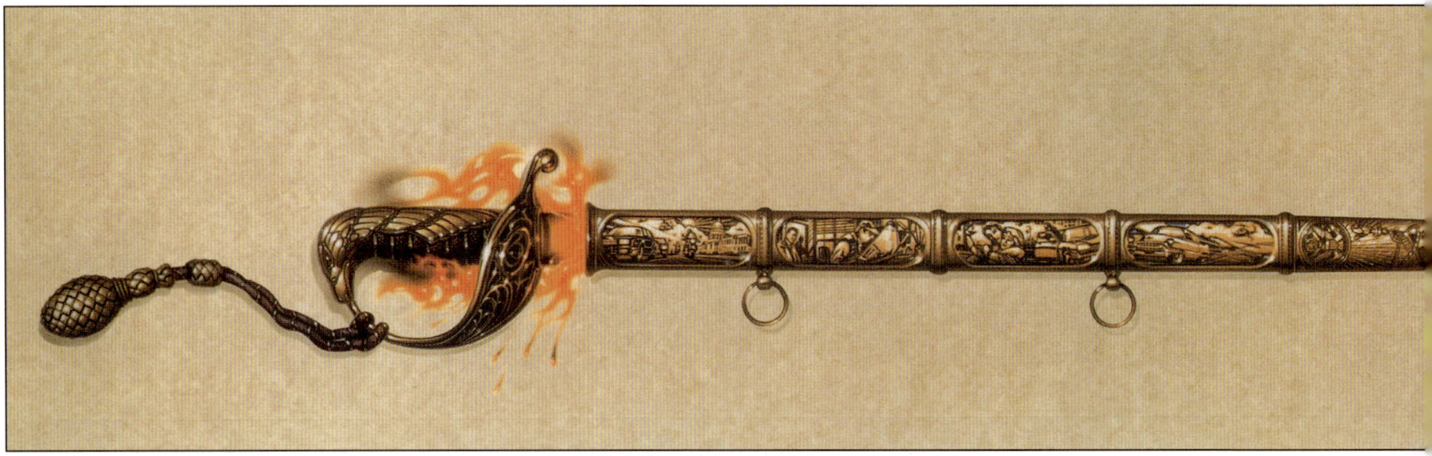

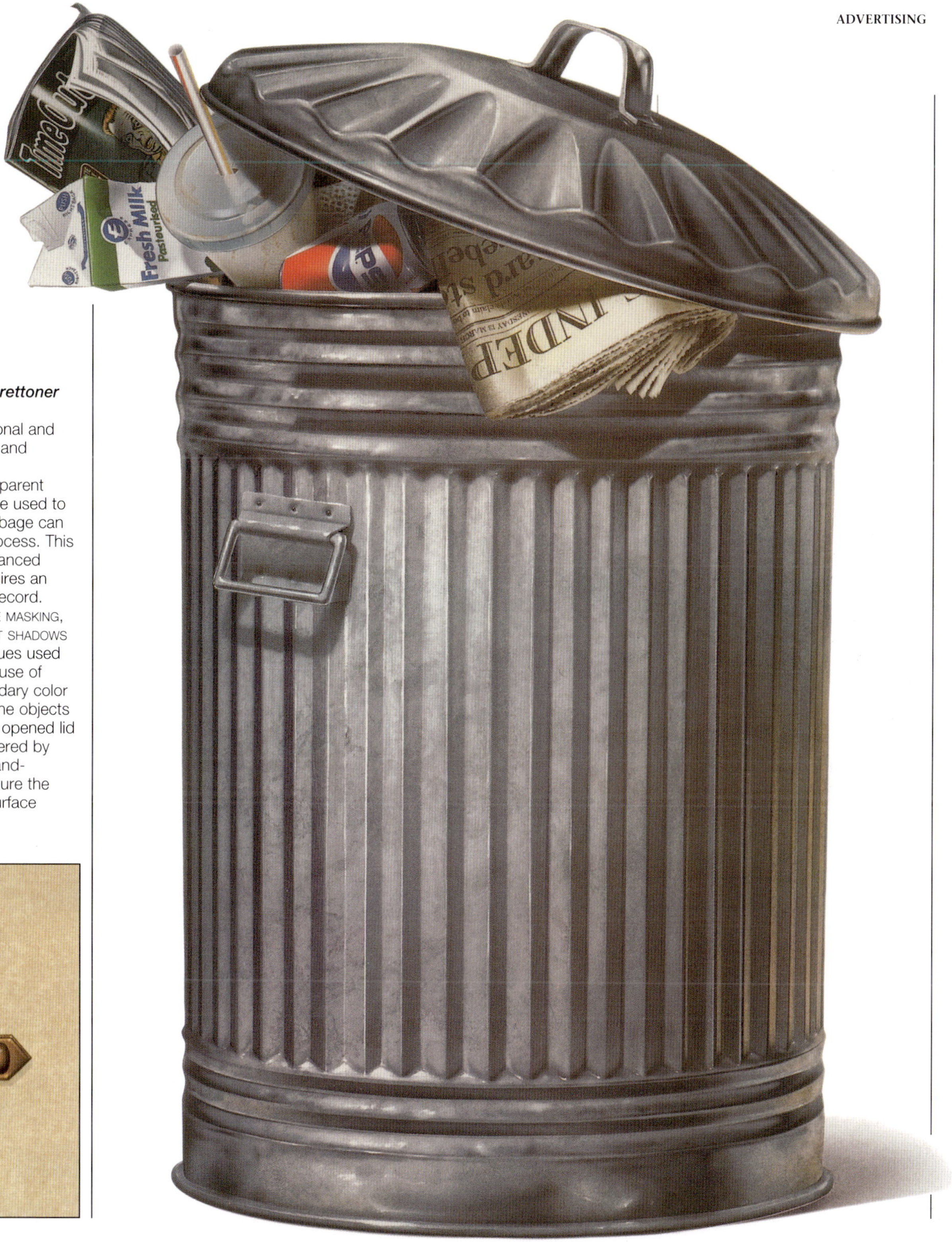

Garbage Can • *John Brettoner*

TECHNIQUE

To maintain consistent tonal and color balance on a large and dominant area requires considerable skill; the apparent simplicity of the technique used to render the aluminum garbage can underlines a complex process. This relates only partly to advanced airbrushing ability; it requires an ability to look, see, and record. FREEHAND SPRAYING, LOOSE MASKING, SCRATCHING OUT, and CAST SHADOWS were among the techniques used to airbrush the can. The use of reflected light and secondary color is particularly effective. The objects visible through the partly opened lid have been carefully rendered by airbrushing, each with hand-painted additions to capture the different materials and surface textures.

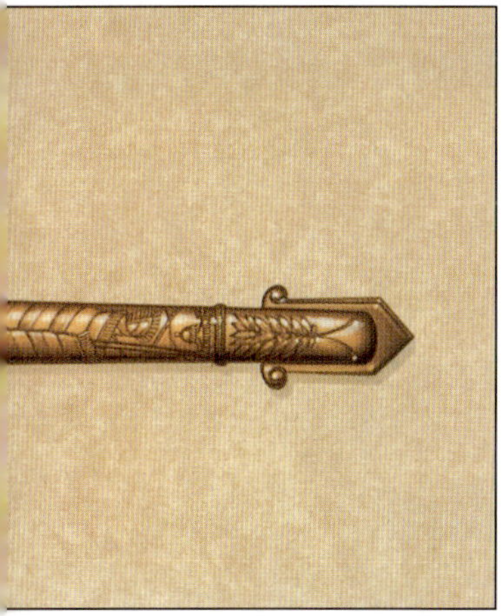

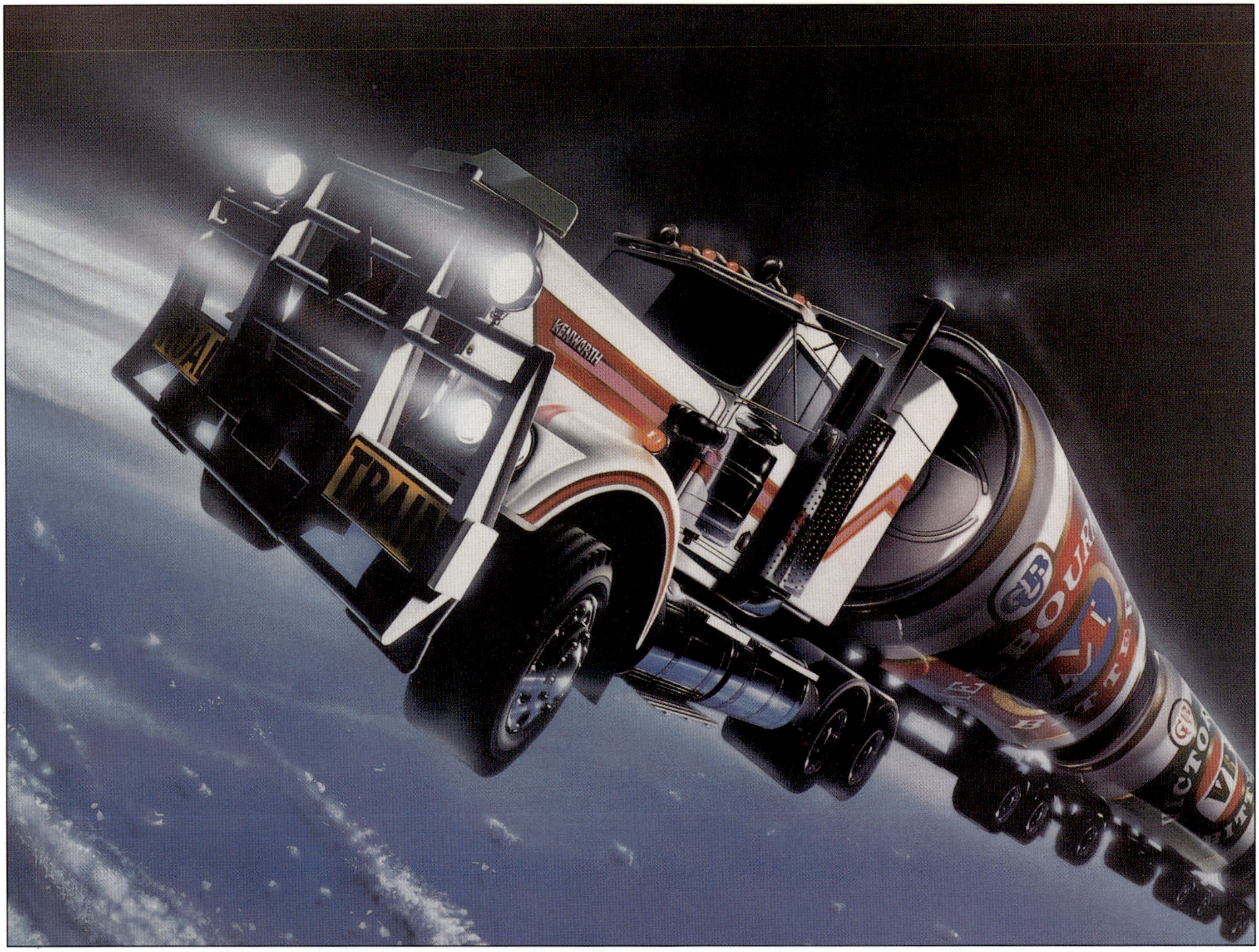

Melbourne and Victory Bitter • ***John Brettoner***

CONCEPT

Advertising agencies like to promote the impression that a product is so good, it must come from out of this world. This approach offers illustrators the opportunity to experiment with composition and technique, and to develop their own imaginative ideas.

TECHNIQUE

While there are no unusual techniques employed, it is worth studying specific qualities of the airbrushing. The glow and beams of light coming from the headlamps are very well controlled, capturing the impression of light seeming to dissipate the further it gets from its source. The soft edges to the cans of beer and their trailers give an almost mystical feel, as if the truck and its cargo approach from the depths of outer space.

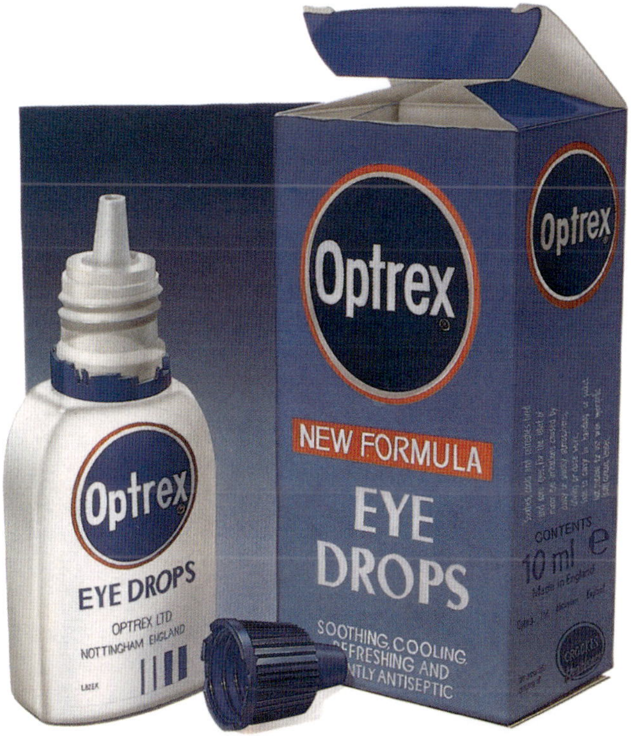

Optrex • *Keith Hume*

CONCEPT

This self-promotional work was designed primarily to demonstrate a cohesive balance between objects made of different materials, in such a way as to make them work together as a single illustration.

TECHNIQUE

The base airbrushing was completed in gouache, with some watercolor, applied through FILM MASKING with GRADATED TONES. FREEHAND SPRAYING and LOOSE MASKING were used to bring out soft edges. The lettering on the bottle was applied before the gradated tone representing slight shadow was added, exploiting the TRANSPARENCY of the airbrushed medium.

Pepsodent Family • *Colin Brown*

CONCEPT

The concept was to show not only the complete range of dental products under the identified brand name, but to animate them with a strong sense of humour.

TECHNIQUE

Airbrushed in acrylics and gouache, the image required careful color control because of the white base color of each product. Extensive use was naturally made of LETTERING TECHNIQUES, with careful attention to secondary and tertiary lettering. The background employs LOOSE MASKING, FREEHAND SPRAYING, and GRADATED TONES to achieve the effect of the stage setting, and to provide contrasting but appropriate ground color.

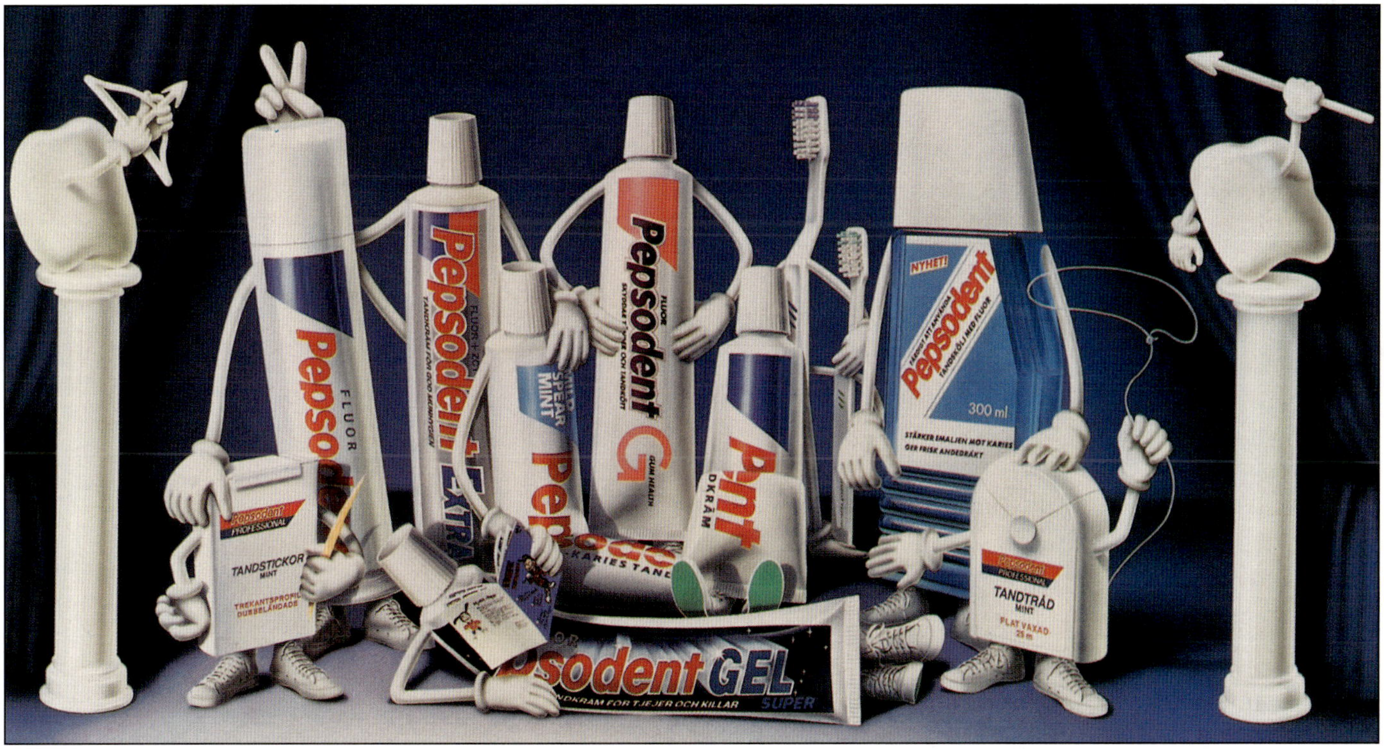

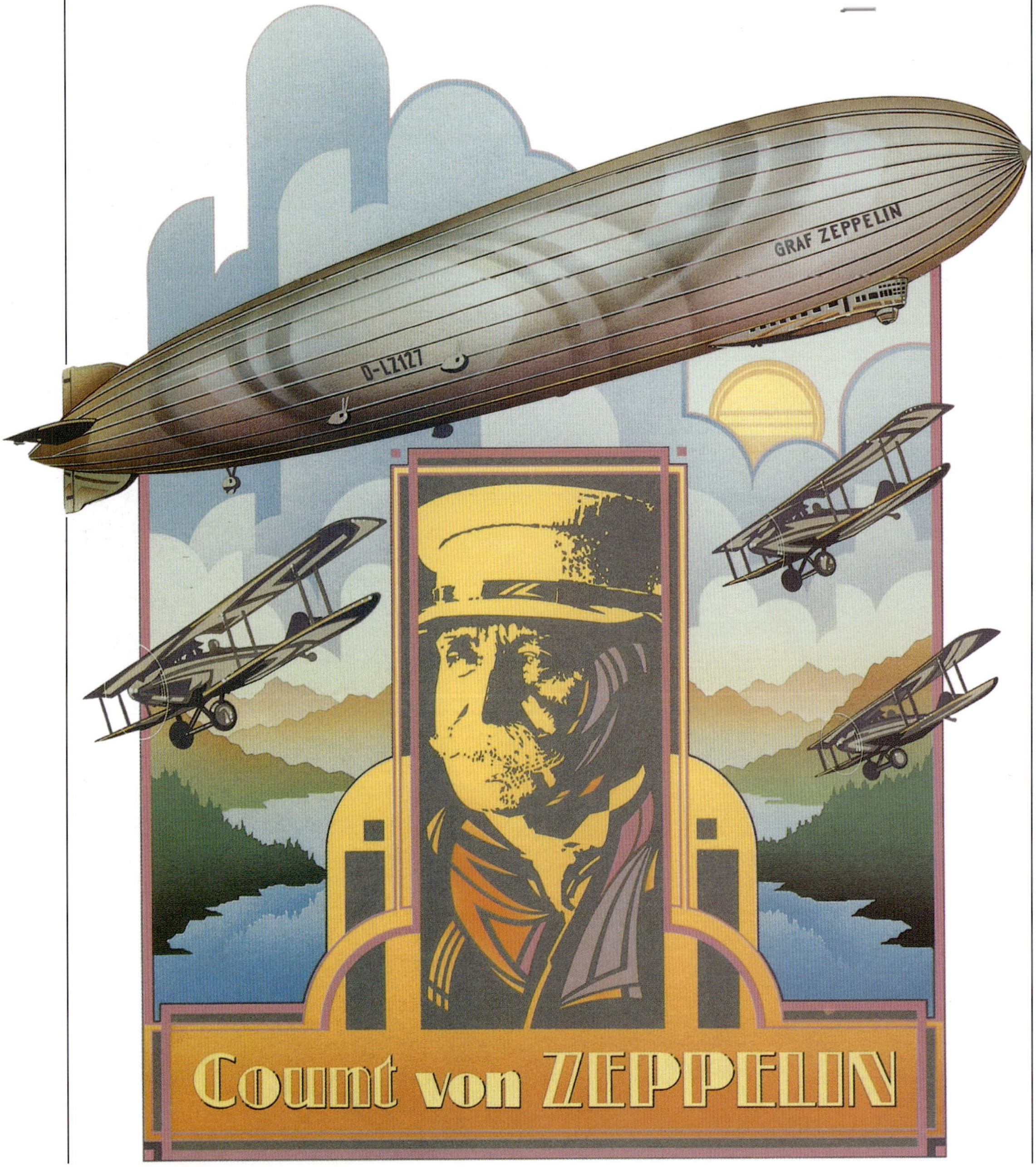

▶ **Black Dahlia**
• ***Stephen Peringer***

INSPIRATION
The idea for this poster stems from an unsolved and notorious murder case, involving a beautiful and seemingly mysterious Hollywood actress.

TECHNIQUE
Airbrushed in inks, the rendering is effectively monochromatic. The balance and composition rely very much on the juxtaposition between face and lettering, which gain added depth from the strength of the predominant color. The complete image's impact is enhanced by the simplicity of technique and detail. FILM MASKING, LOOSE MASKING, FREEHAND SPRAYING, and GRADATED TONES are the principal techniques.

Count von Zeppelin •
Stephen Hunter

CONCEPT
Travel posters of the 1920s and 1930s have stood the test of time, in that they remain excellent examples of both the advertisers' sense of design and the artists' ability to produce dramatic and beautifully composed images, often with a limited palette. The majority clearly show the empathy necessary between a large two-dimensional image and the text or headlines that support it. The influence of such early posters is obvious here, and the excellent airbrush work demonstrates that even a subject comprising relatively simple, mainly flat shapes requires as much skill in application as, for example, the most complex cutaway.

TECHNIQUE
To reproduce the period feel with the airbrush required extensive use of FILM MASKING and GRADATED TONES. It was essential that the masks were cleanly cut, as any slight imperfections would be immediately visible and impossible to correct.

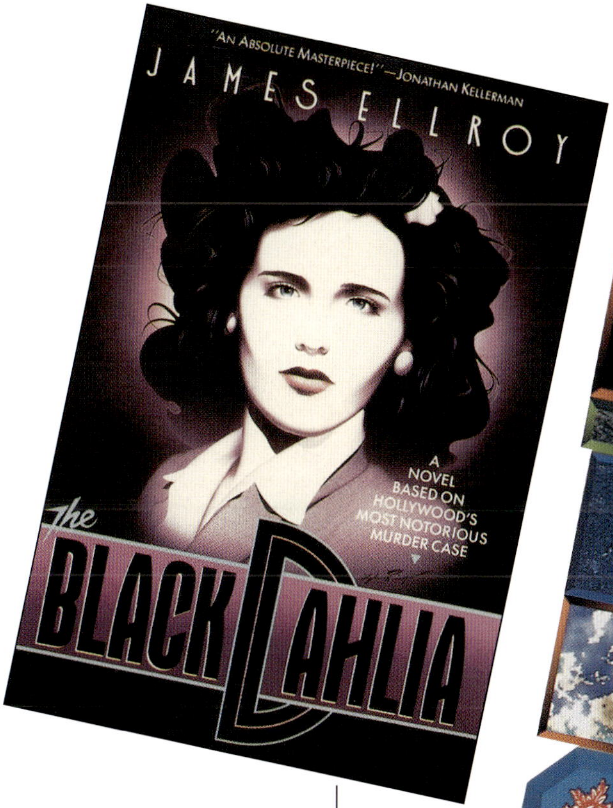

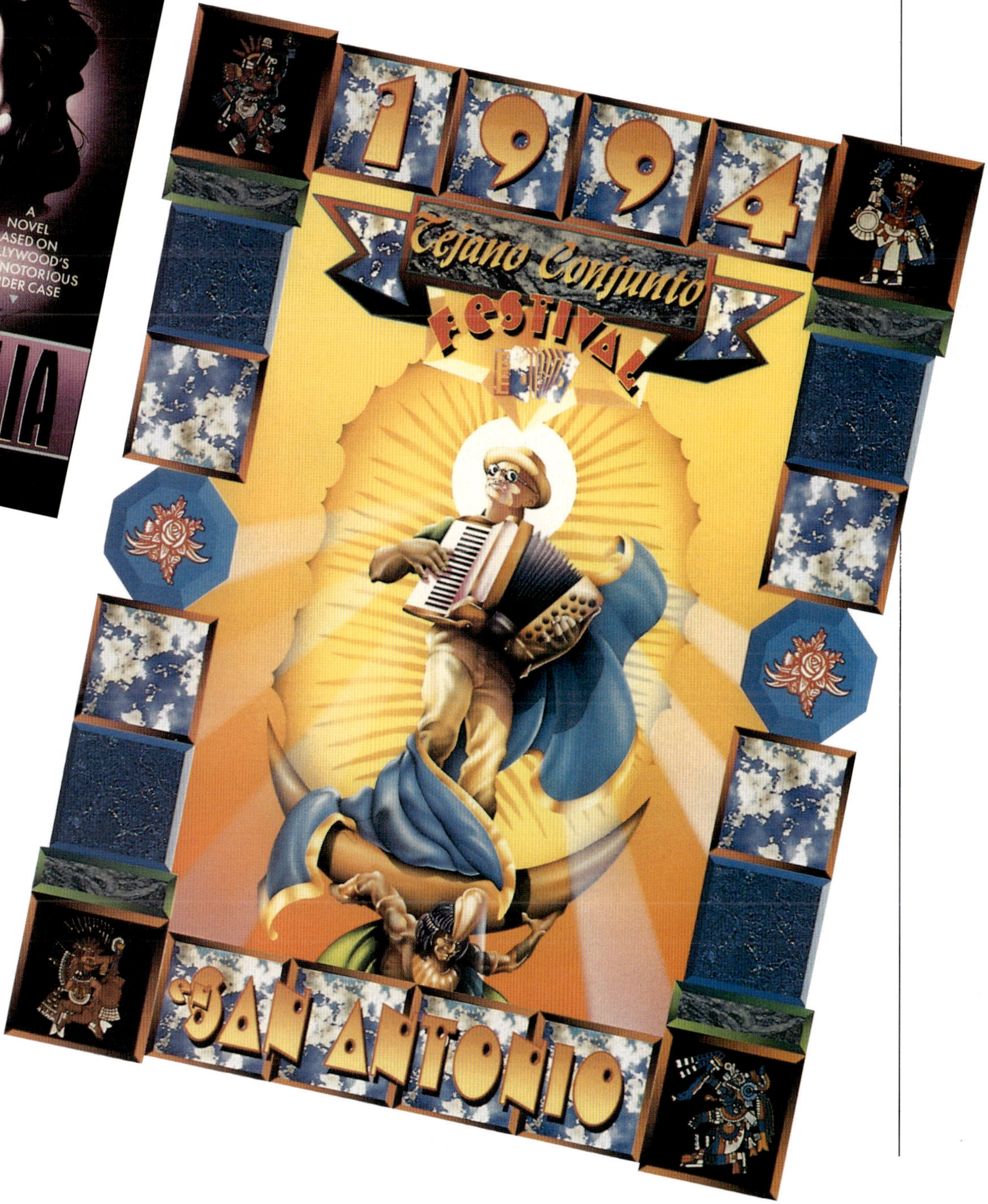

1994 Tejano Conjunto Festival • *Richard O. Menchaca*

TECHNIQUE

Designed and executed for the annual Tejano Conjunto Music Festival poster competition, this image represents the various cultures which have contributed to the development of conjunto music in the USA. A variety of techniques and applications have been employed, mixing the traditional airbrushing techniques with computer-generated imagery. This combination is becoming increasingly commonplace and allows an experienced illustrator almost infinite flexibility in arriving at compositions which would not have been possible previously. In terms of airbrushing techniques, and in relation to those described elsewhere in this book, the methods should be readily identifiable because of the clarity of the illustration.

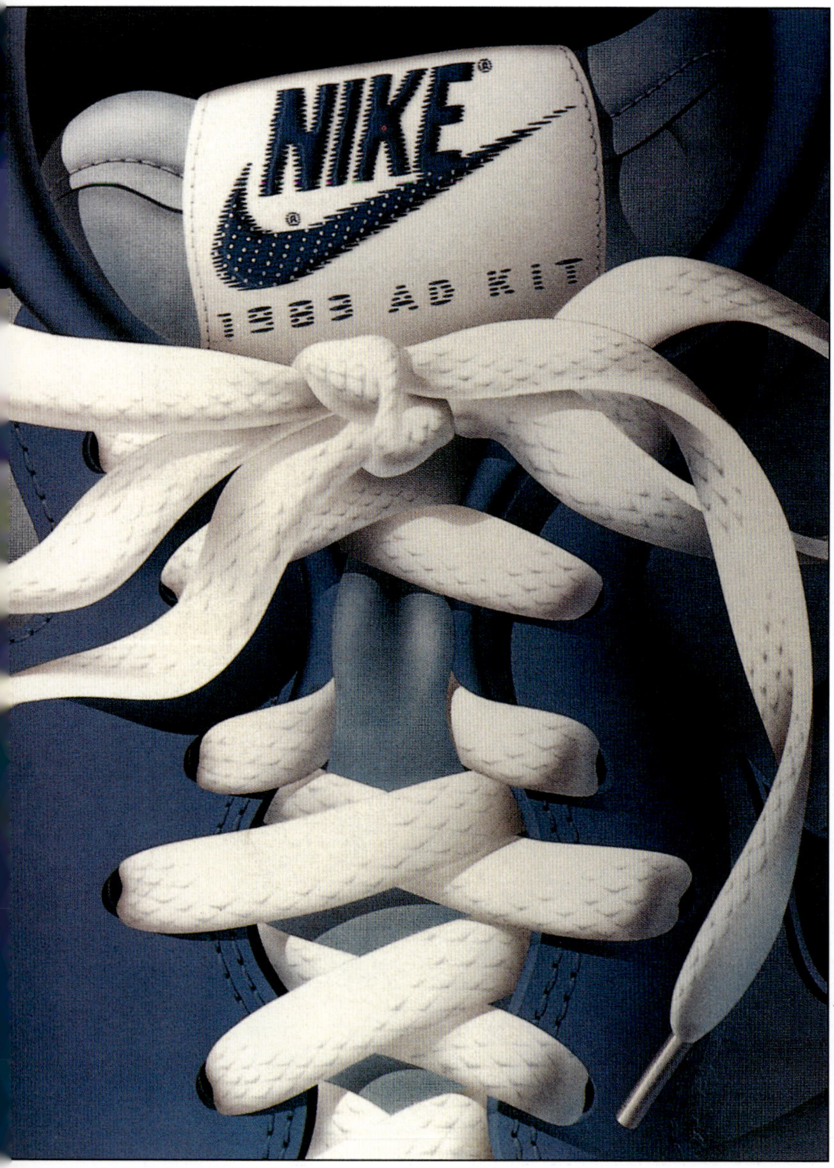

◀ **Nike Shoe** • ***Stephen Peringer***

CONCEPT

The aim of this work was to portray a soft, Disney-like quality in the character of the running shoe. It is a highly commendable example of technique and design, in which individual shapes have been somewhat simplified.

TECHNIQUE

The airbrushing is conventional, using inks through FILM MASKING and LOOSE MASKING, with GRADATED TONES as appropriate. Of special note is the textured effect on the light blue areas, achieved by airbrushing through a piece of flexible window-screen, of the kind used for mosquito protection (see FOUND OBJECT MASKING). It is particularly effective within the scale of this illustration.

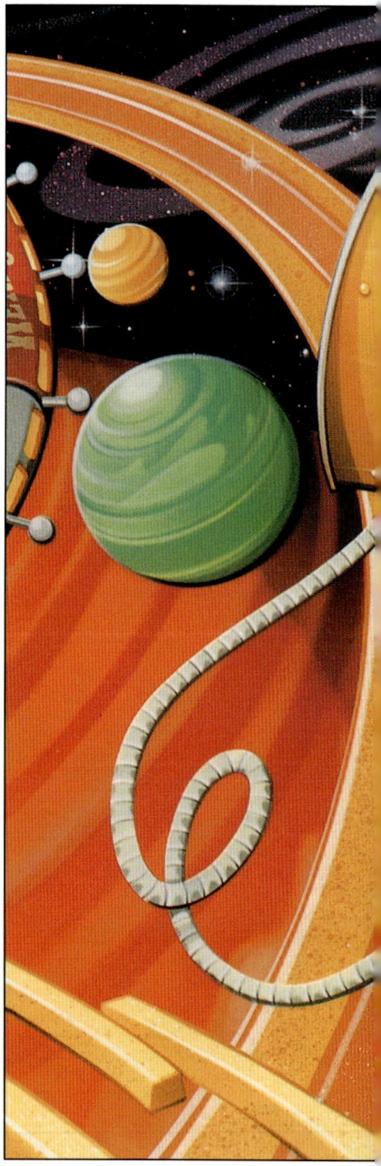

Burgers in space • *Mark Otnes*

COMPOSITION

A very stylized, effective and well-drawn image, inspired by the outlet's children's "fun meal" bags. The illustration has a distinctive cartoon feel about it, which requires careful drawing and a unified approach to achieve a balanced image. The use of distorted or exaggerated perspective and proportions – notably on the astronaut and shuttle – adds substantially to the effect, while the color range has obvious appeal to young children.

TECHNIQUES

The primary techniques around which others have been employed are FILM MASKING and LOOSE MASKING. The LINING-IN follows the same bold approach, with strong outlines being applied to areas in the foreground and immediate middle distance.

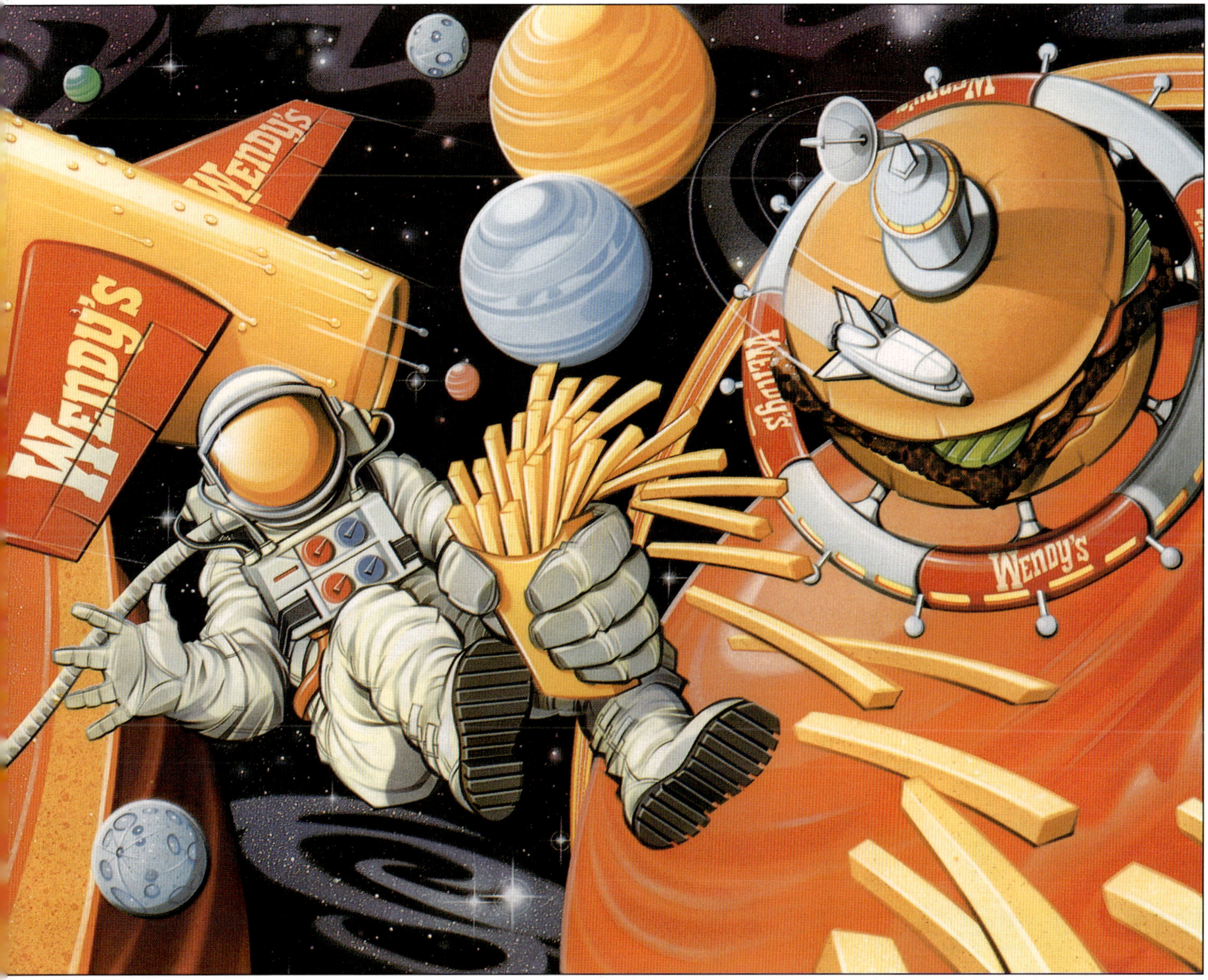

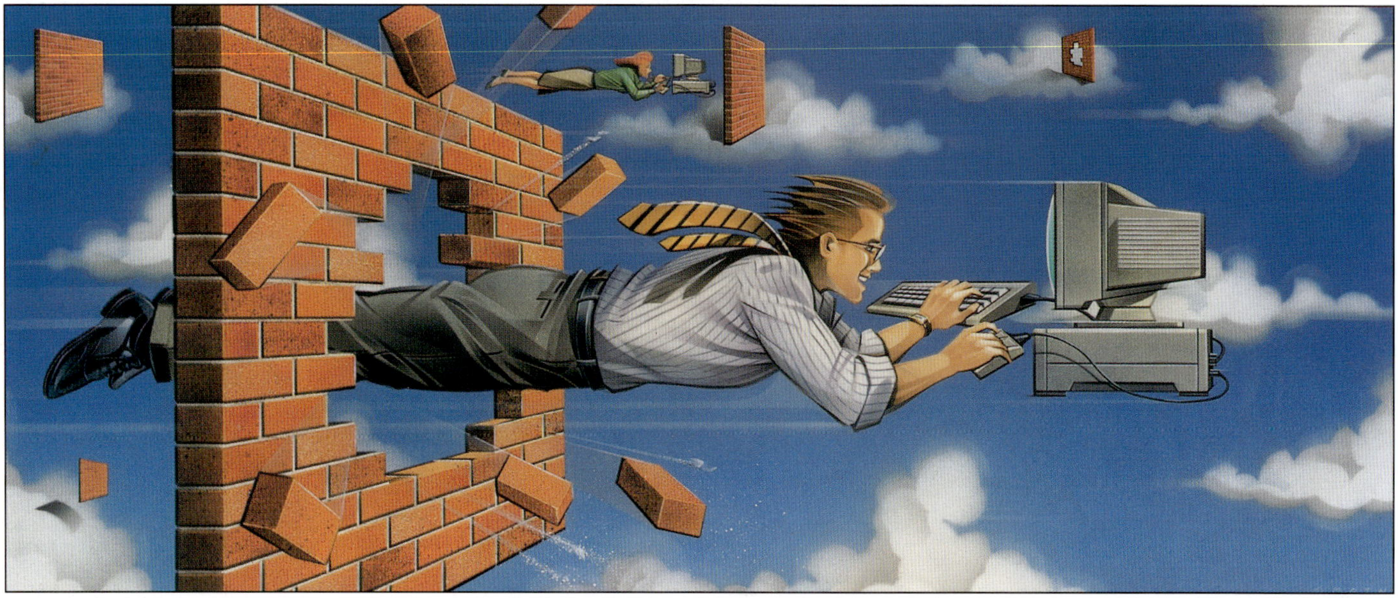

▲ **Flying computer guy** •
Mark Otnes

STYLE

A composition for a brochure designed to illustrate the success of breaking through computer output problems, the style and technique adopted are very reminiscent of advertising style in the 1940s.

TECHNIQUE

To achieve this distinctive, sharp style, extensive use is made of FILM MASKING and bold LINING-IN. ACETATE or LOOSE MASKING was used to give a slightly softer edge to areas such as the creases in the clothes, and in the outlines to the clouds. SPATTERING was oversprayed to give surface texture to the bricks, which also adds contrast to the gradated tones of the sky.

▼ **Beauty and the Beast** •
Osni Omena

TECHNIQUE

LETTERING TECHNIQUES construct the central and predominant image. The outline of the lettering uses FILM MASKING, with GRADATED TONES oversprayed, followed by SPATTERING to give a textured and weathered effect, as if the image were carved out of stone. Hand-painted touches have also been added to the lettering to show pitting of the surface. Soft-edged shadows added by FREEHAND SPRAYING offset the lettering against the white of the artboard. The image was designed for use as a logo, CD cover and embossing on jackets.

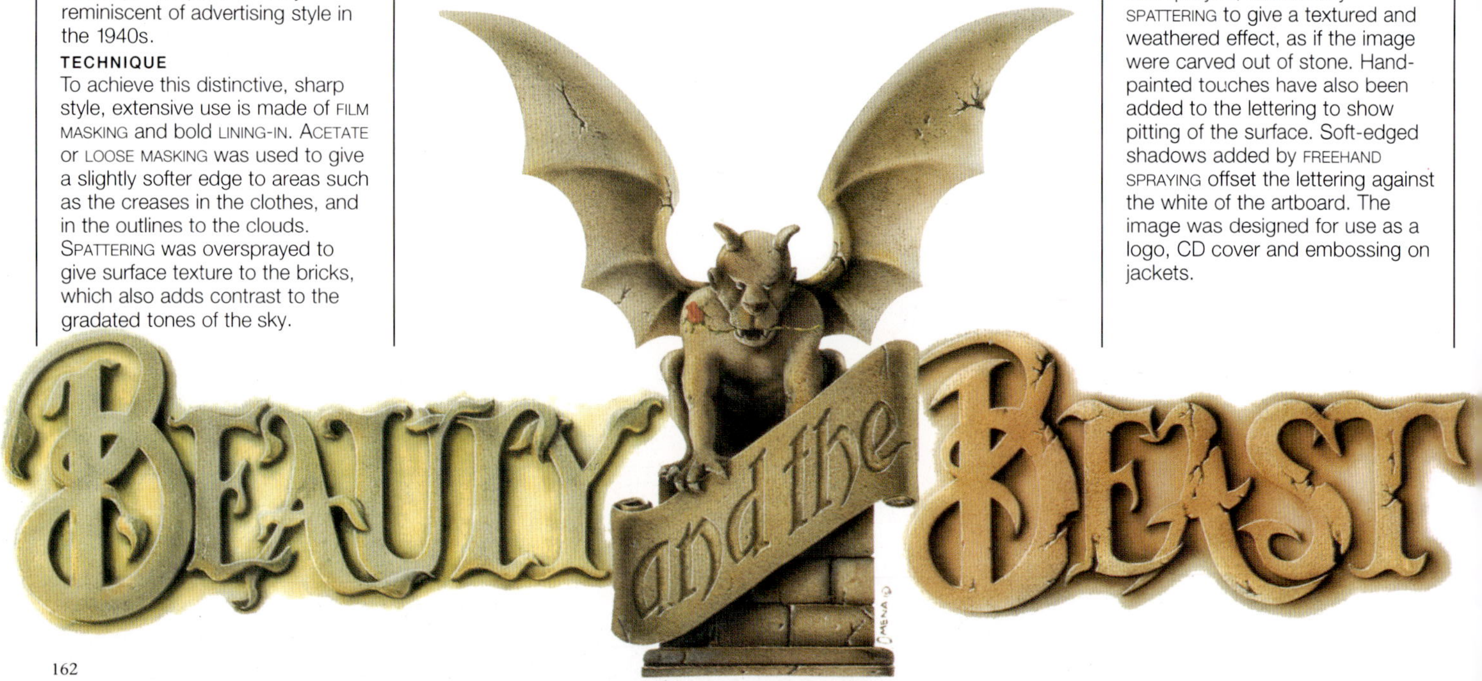

"Maybe the Best Way to Handle Risk is to Avoid it Altogether" • ***Jerry Lofaro***

COMPOSITION

Executed as part of a campaign for photocopiers, the message implied in the title is well defined in the composition of this strongly delineated illustration.

TECHNIQUE

Acrylics were used throughout, both through the airbrush and by hand-painting. The base color for the sky, for example, was airbrushed with a softly GRADATED TONE, over which very well executed hand-painted clouds were added, with touches of airbrushing being used in their shadows. Even though the setting is the forecourt of an Indian temple,with a very clearly defined light source, and the sky and clouds are almost secondary to the image, it is important that the direction of the light source is maintained in the shape and form of the clouds. The technique of using extremely tight detail in the foreground, with a simpler approach being adopted for the building and ground in the middle distance, accentuates the impact of the message. SPATTERING has been used on the ground and on the dome.

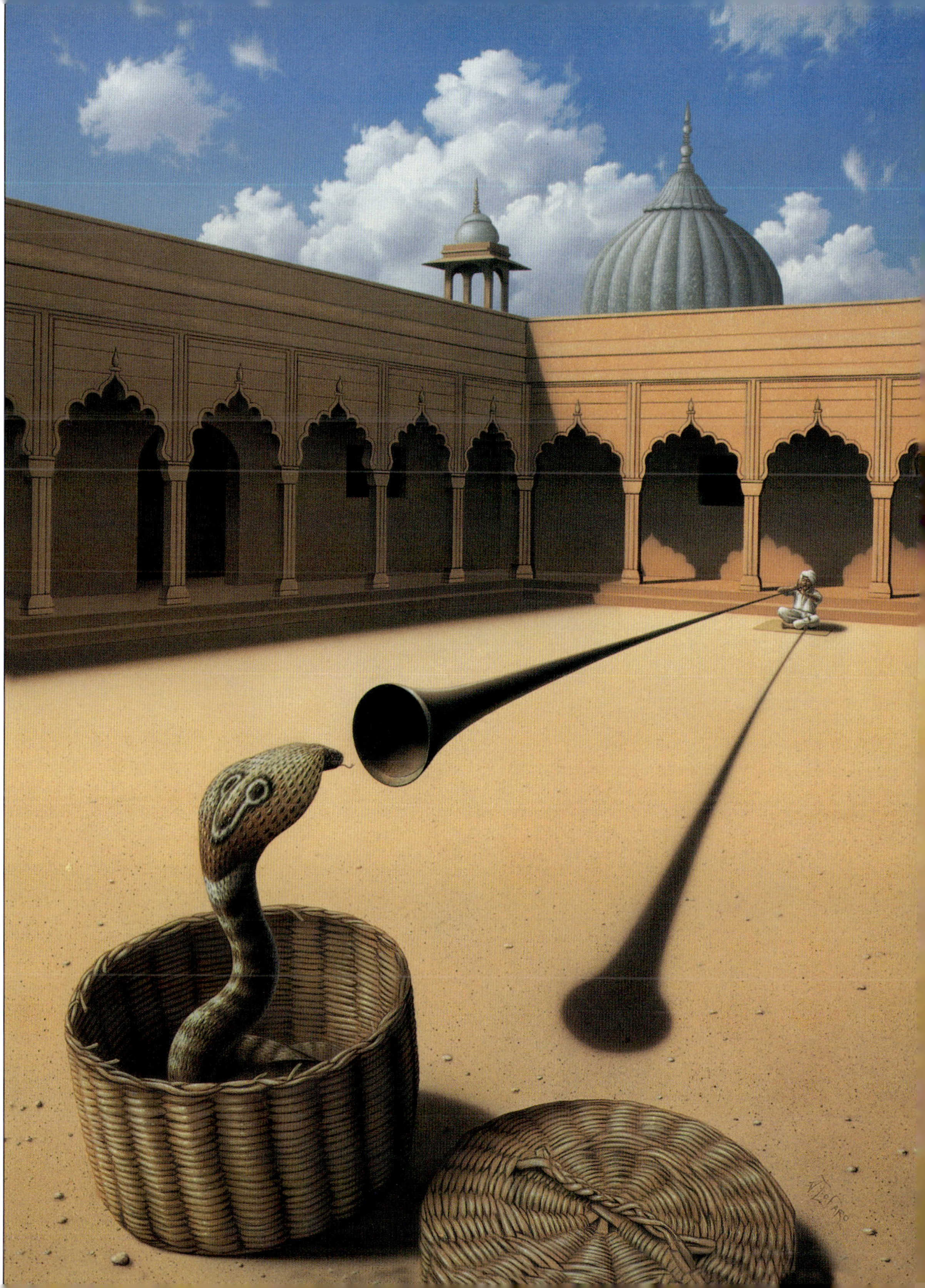

CONCEPTUAL

Airbrush artists such as the "realists," Michael English and Roy Castle, were among the first to utilize the airbrush in works which, for the sake of clarity, could be called "fine art." Here we have preferred the heading "conceptual" because it more readily fits the approach adopted by the majority of the artists whose work has been selected, even though in some cases the illustrations were produced for specific clients, most commonly one in the advertising industry. This aspect of airbrushed painting has now grown and many more artists across the world are employing the techniques available through the use of the airbrush. Sometimes it is applied in a very minor way to achieve a distinctive and localized finish, while in others the airbrushing is the primary means of applying color or tone to a painting; it very much depends on the objective and the message implied in the design.

Regardless of the inspiration or purpose of an illustration defined here as conceptual, the techniques do not differ very much from those employed elsewhere. However, for an artist to produce work initially through self-motivation, the conversion and transfer from imagination to paper opens up a wide range of possibilities. If the artist's knowledge and understanding of the limitations of the airbrush are good, the potential for interesting and unusual images is equally as good.

Clearly the airbrush has come a long way from being the traditional tool of technical illustration. One point which is apparent in all of the examples is that, regardless of subject or concept, there are few genuine shortcuts to producing good quality airbrushed illustrations. The very process of using an airbrush demands care and a high level of patience, which can only come about through extensive practice. As far as students of the technique are concerned, it is sometimes easier to concentrate on a small section of an illustration as a test piece, rather than try to copy some of the completed and often complex pieces shown here. Practice allows the techniques so learnt to develop toward producing works that other people may well wish to hang on their walls.

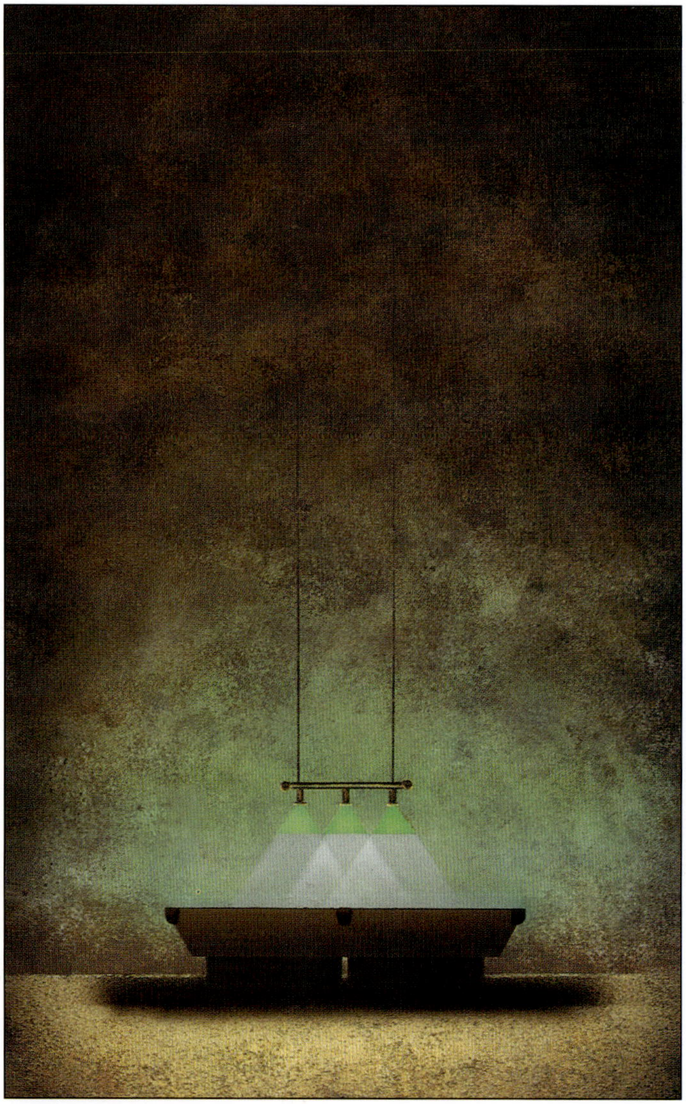

Pool Table • *Patrick C. Wanebo*

COMPOSITION

A powerful and dramatic representation of a pool table, with composition and palette helping to create an almost eerie atmosphere, in complete contrast to the usual settings in which pool tables are located. The simplicity of technique and lack of superfluous detail also add to the drama.

TECHNIQUE

Although the airbrush has been used in a limited capacity on this acrylic painting, it demonstrates the medium's versatility. It has been applied to rendering the suspended lights; the light itself; the table and its soft-edged shadow on the floor. It also supplied the GRADATED TONE of the green glow.

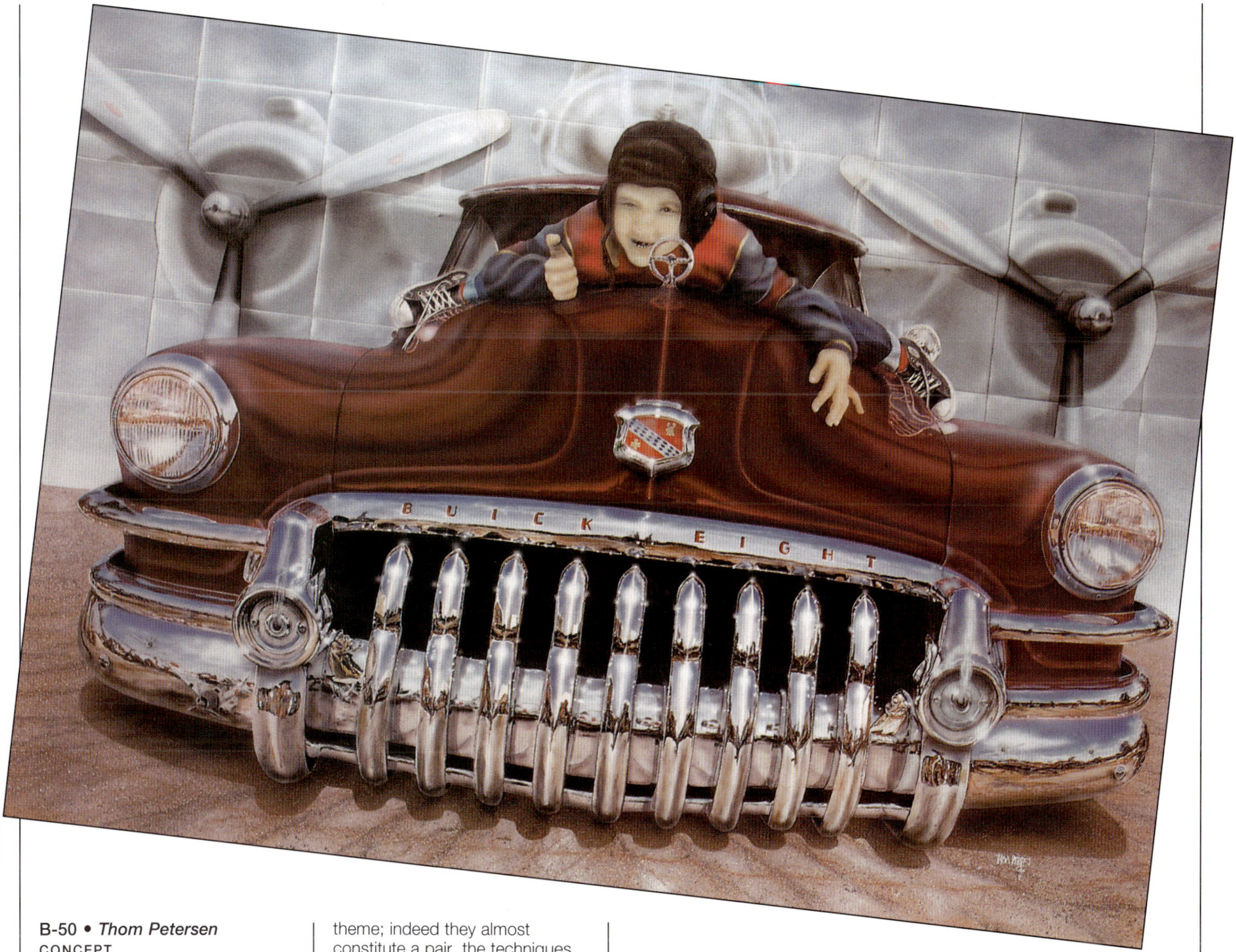

B-50 • *Thom Petersen*

CONCEPT

The artist uses his childhood memories as a foundation on which to produce an image with almost-hidden ones within; note the reflections in the bumper and the more overt ghosted image on the wall behind.

TECHNIQUE

Similar techniques have been used in this illustration as in that reproduced under the Transport theme; indeed they almost constitute a pair, the techniques and styles adopted being almost identical. Of particular note is the almost repetitive nature of the reflections in the chromed bumper. In such cases great care is necessary to avoid any difference in quality or style, which would destroy the balance and continuity required.

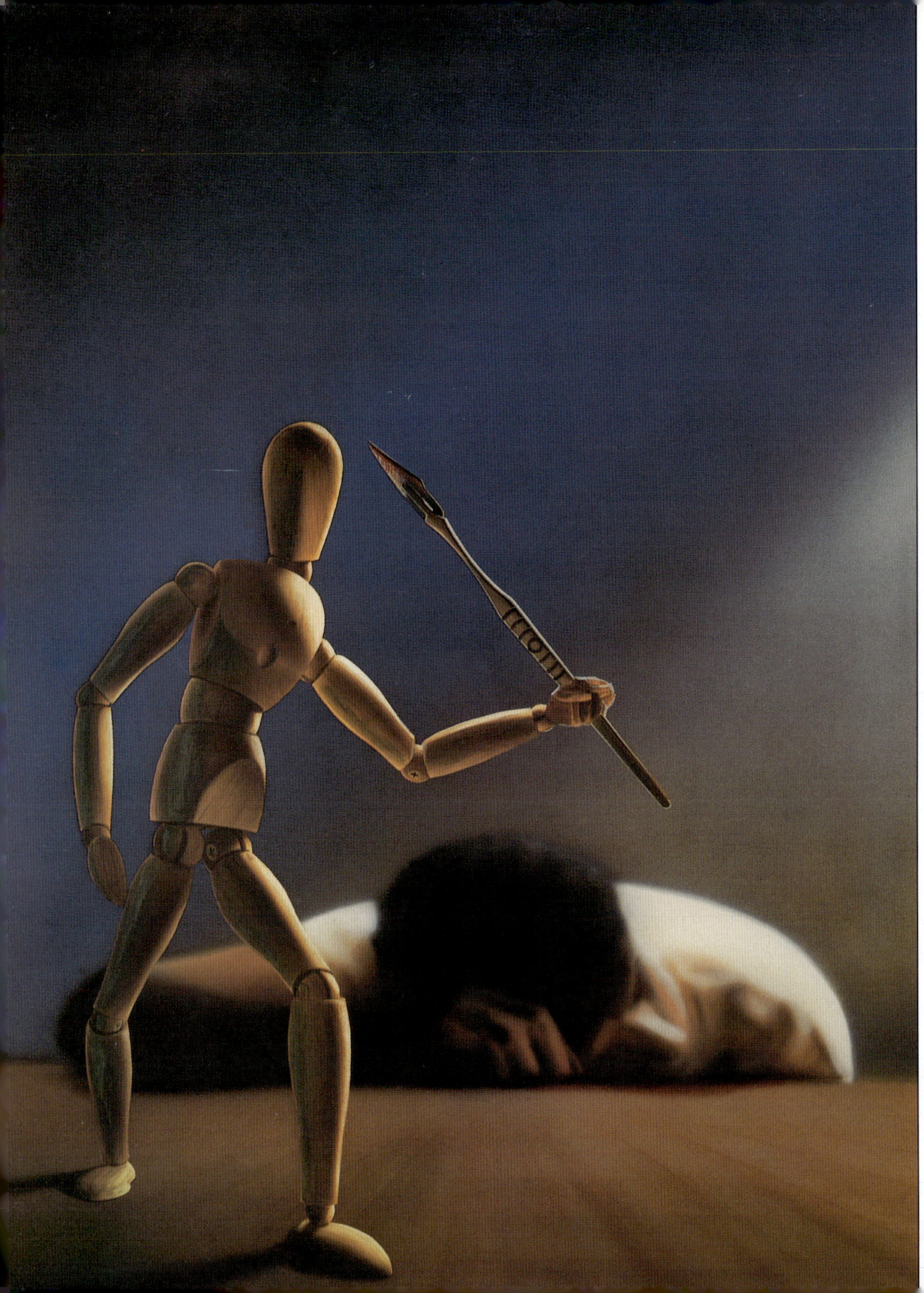

The Manikin • *Paul Campion*

CONCEPT

This is a version of the often-used science fiction concept of inanimate objects coming to life.

TECHNIQUE

A pure airbrush illustration, in that the image relies on hand painting only for small details of finish. The manikin, being in the foreground, has been rendered with contrasting effects, including a very good use of reflected light and color to enhance the three-dimensional impression. The prone victim has been sprayed entirely using LOOSE MASKING and CARD MASKING to give it an out-of-focus quality, thereby complementing the manikin. Strong and severe GRADATED TONES make up the background, and emphasize the hidden yet obvious light source.

▶ **Beneath an Opal Moon** • *David Scutt*

COMPOSITION

This is an unusual example of fantasy-style illustration, in that the composition is deliberately split between a highly finished area to the left and a flat, opaque color block to the right, possibly designed to incorporate text or caption. The central position of the distorted, masked face demands attention.

TECHNIQUE

FILM MASKING, LOOSE MASKING, GRADATED TONES, FREEHAND SPRAYING, DOT CONTROL, and HIGHLIGHTING techniques have all been well applied. The thin, wispy clouds are a good example of freehand spraying, demonstrating excellent control of air pressure and quantity of paint.

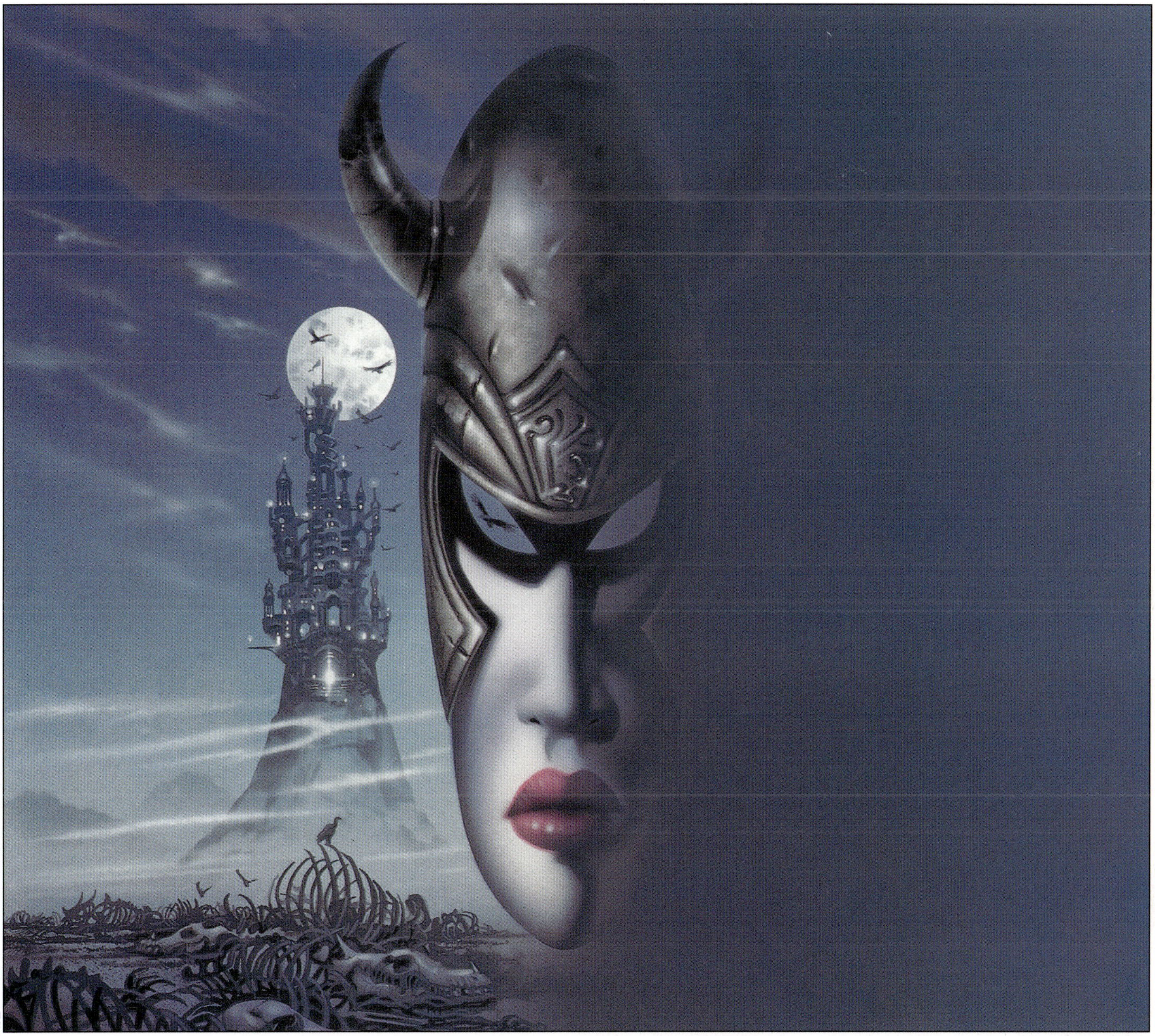

Under the gun •
Thomas J. Humpert
TECHNIQUE
An illustration which uses mixed-media techniques to combine heavy surface texture with the traditional smooth, neat finish obtainable from an airbrush. The drawing was made in pastel pencils and then fixed, followed by brush application of a gel medium. This gel was also applied to give a light surface texture to the barrel of the gun and on the globe, with a serrated-edged trowel used on the background. The form on the barrel and globe was airbrushed over this with liquid and transparent acrylic paints. A damp cloth was then scrubbed over the background to remove excess paint. This process was repeated a few times until the desired effect was achieved. Finally, colored pencils were used to pick out certain selected areas.

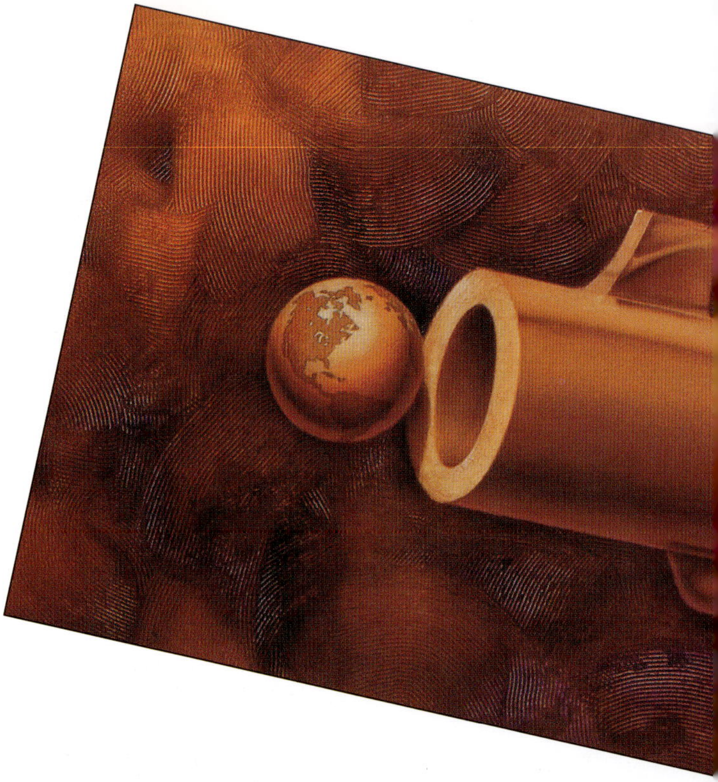

"There's Nothing Like a Nice Little Ride in the Park" •
Andy A. Zito
CONCEPT
The idea was to produce the effect of a never-ending rollercoaster. The limited but bright palette and total lack of any sign of human life take away the more usual impression of these rides being associated with fun and happiness. It shows how it is possible to achieve a sinister atmosphere by choice of colors, making some areas almost monochromatic enhances the effect.

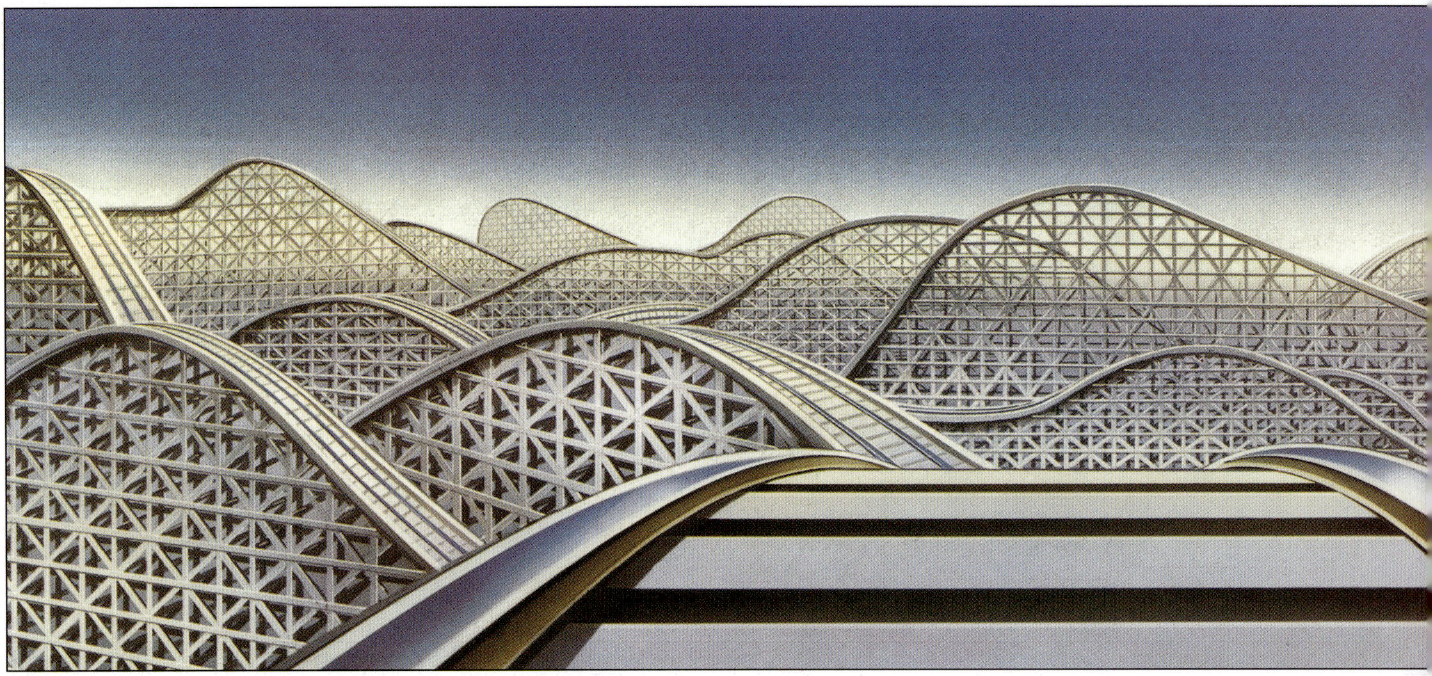

Fekarkana • *Malcolm Tween*

COMPOSITION

A very subtle and controlled piece of airbrushing, applied to an abstract composition including non-abstract images. It was commissioned more as a work of art than as a piece for reproduction and reflects, in part, the deeper interests or thought processes of both client and illustrator.

TECHNIQUE

FILM MASKING, ACETATE MASKING, LOOSE MASKING, SPATTERING, GRADATED TONES, HIGHLIGHTING, LINING-IN, and LETTERING TECHNIQUES are among various techniques employed. The dominant eye, looking directly at the viewer, uses simple but effective means to catch the impression of being moisture-filled and therefore naturally reflective. You can see within the iris and pupil the reflection of someone opposite, with a window offset to the left. This is sufficient to give the eye depth and realism, without the need for fussy techniques.

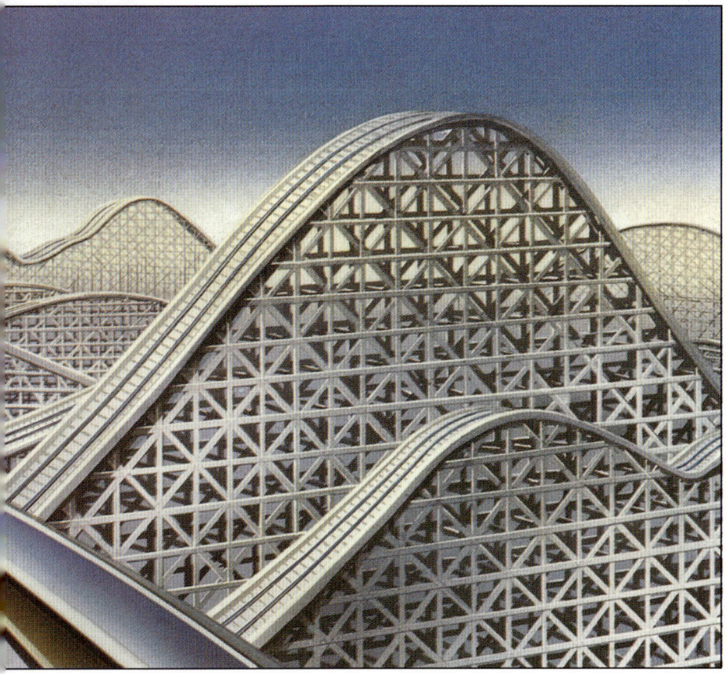

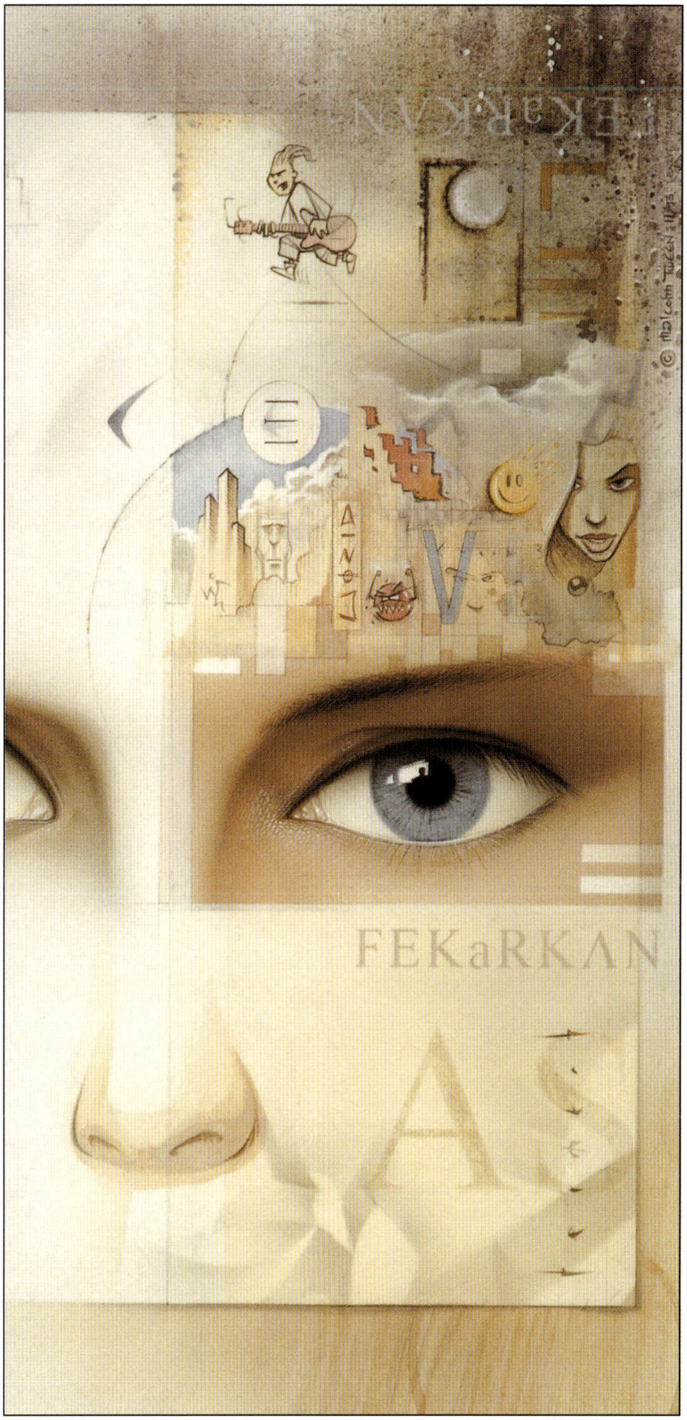

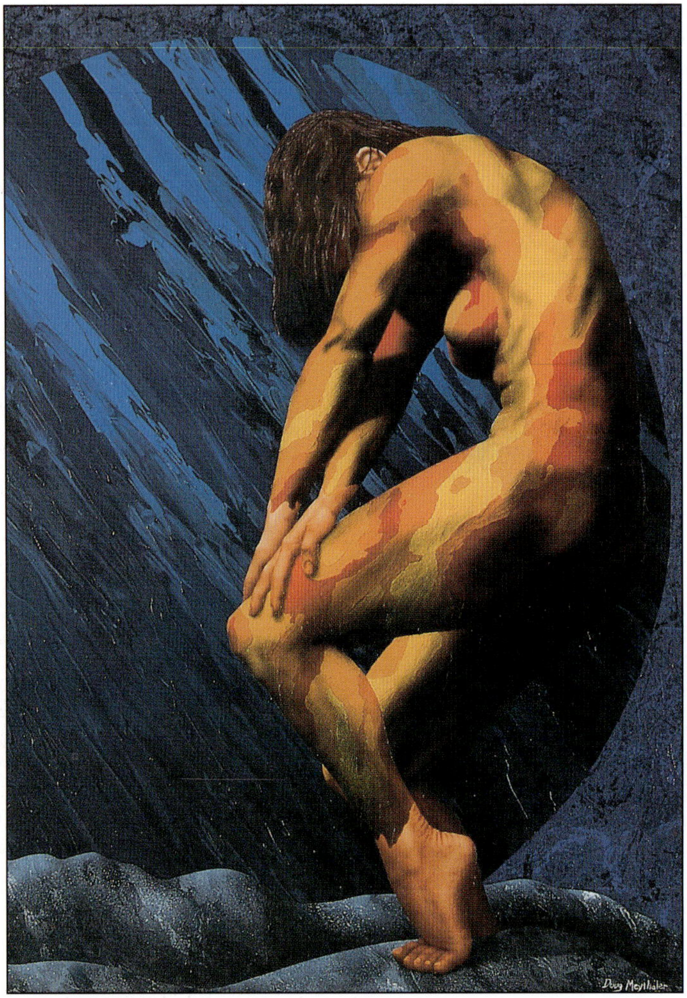

Hearts of space •
Doug Meythaler

CONCEPT
This piece of work was not a commission but an example of the application of the airbrush and other techniques in fine art; the original being specifically meant for hanging in a gallery rather than for reproduction.

TECHNIQUE
Airbrushing in acrylics was used initially to establish the block shapes within FILM MASKING. OVERSPRAYING on top created the application of shape and form, with a strong emphasis on deeply contrasting shadows which almost merge with the depth of color used in the background. FREEHAND SPRAYING gave added depth and shape to the undulations in the female body.

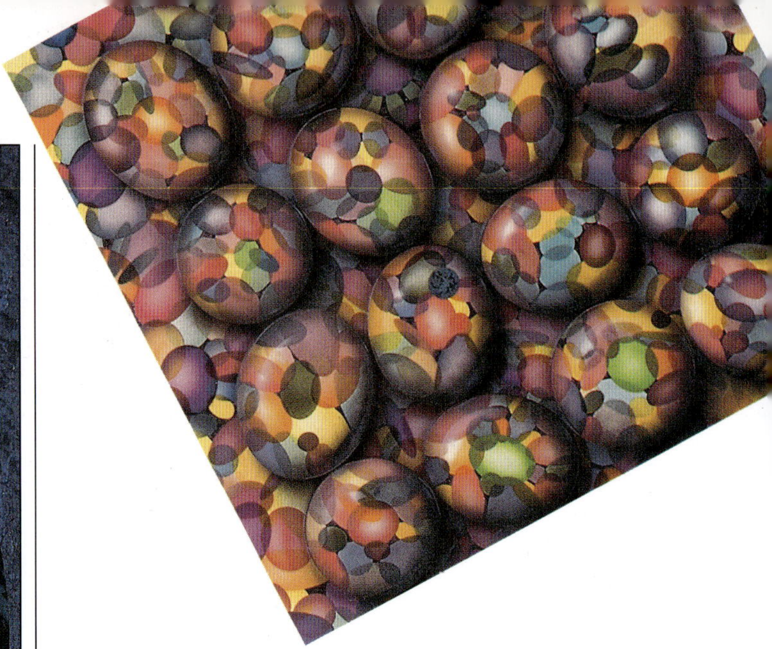

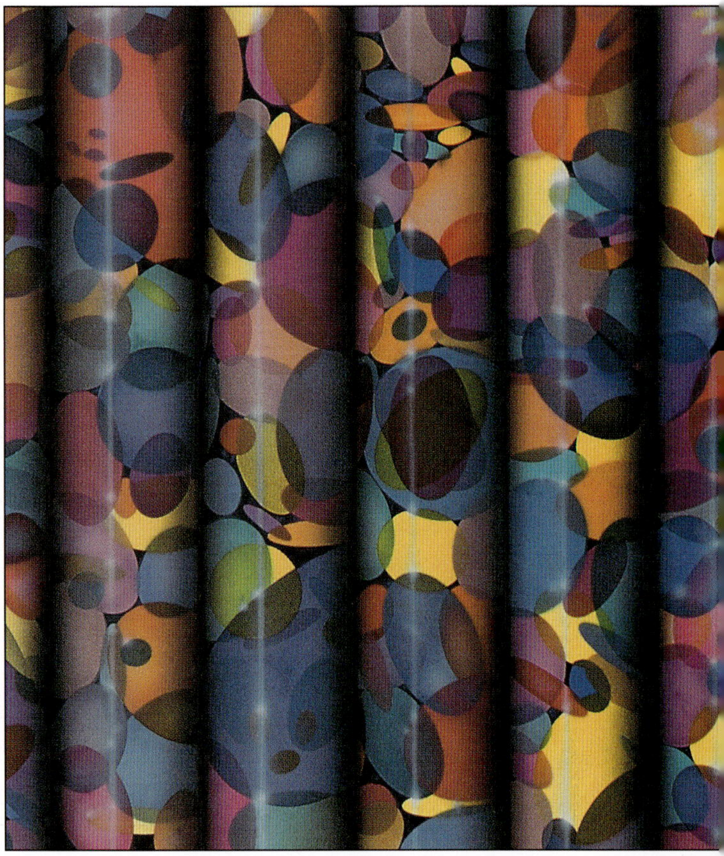

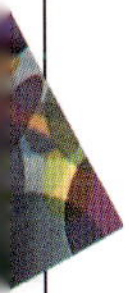

◀ **Jelly bean pool** •
Timothy Stafford
COMPOSITION
Using ellipses of various sizes and angles alongside circles, the artist has produced an abstract image in which there are 16 clearly defined and three-dimensional "beans." These beans are comprised of the same shapes as the flat background ones and all have been sprayed in bold transparent colors. The addition of soft-edged shadows to the 16 beans enhances their three-dimensional quality.

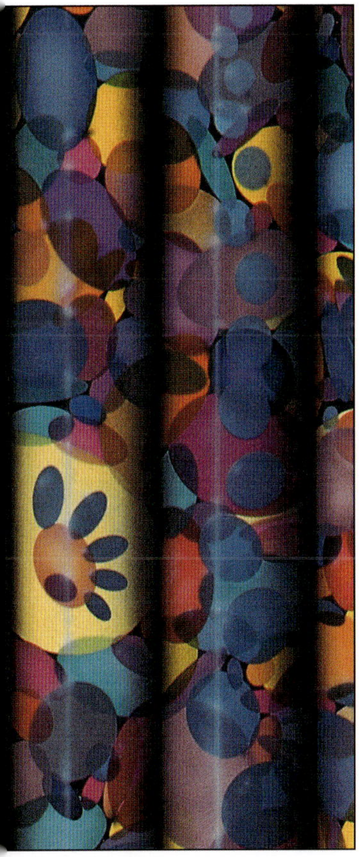

◀ **Happy painting** •
Timothy Stafford
COMPOSITION
Using the same basic shapes as in the previous example, the artist has taken his concept in a different direction. The illusion is of closely packed and vertically stacked tubes, each with a kaleidoscopic range of colored shapes. In producing such paintings as these, an artist may spend more time on the planning and drawing stage than on production of the finished artwork. This is often essential if the final painting is to work as a cohesive whole, whether abstract or realistic.

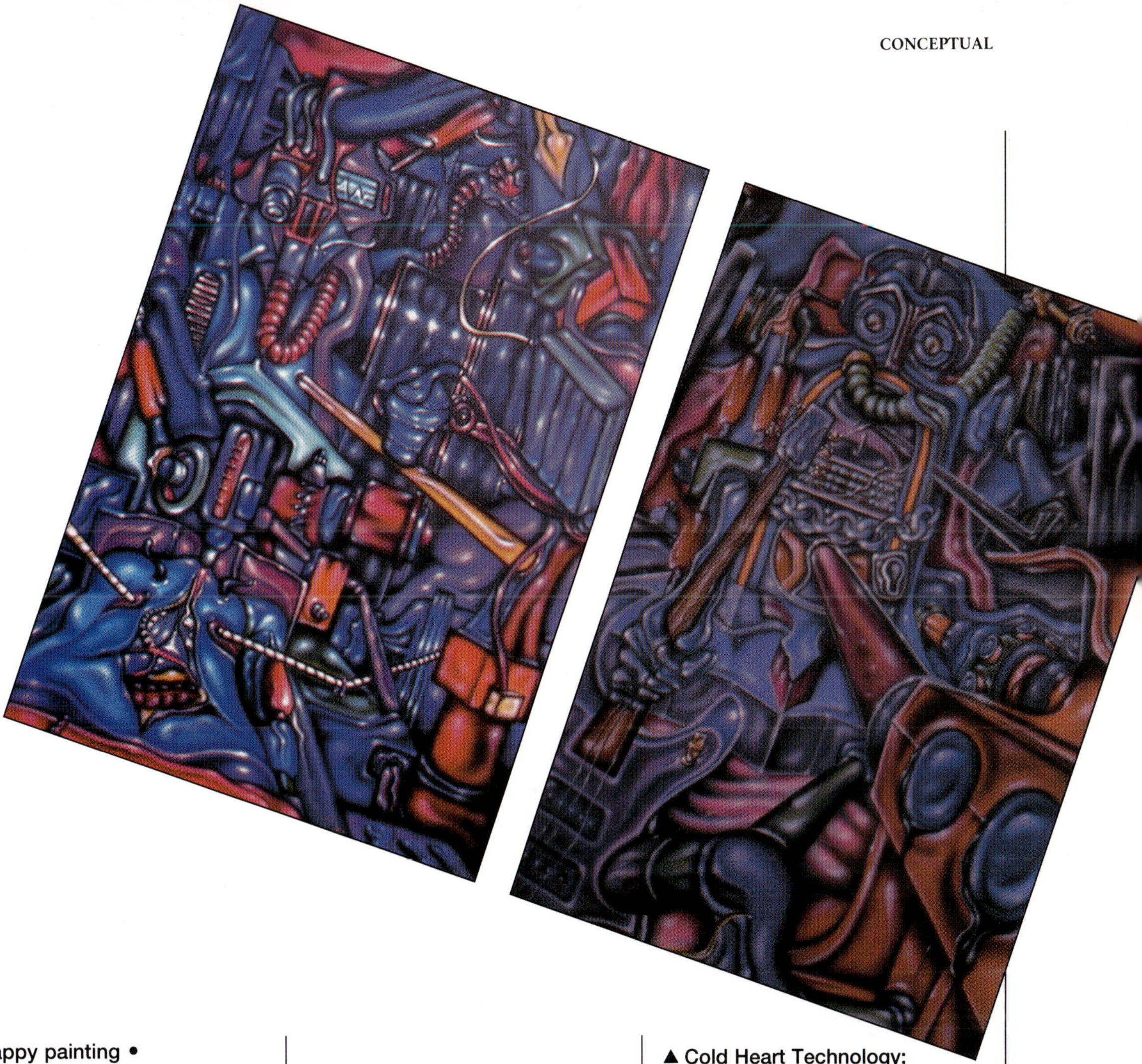

▲ **Cold Heart Technology; The Art of Censorship** •
Joseph Martin
APPROACH AND TECHNIQUE
These very large pieces of work, the first measuring 5 x 7ft and the other 5 x 6ft 8in, are incredibly imaginative and provide good examples of what can be achieved on a large scale, if the artist's patience can be sustained. The narrow band of colors selected demands careful application to maintain the complete tonal and color balance over the duration of a relatively long-term project. Both paintings show excellent FREEHAND SPRAYING, HIGHLIGHTING, and DOT CONTROL, and general mastery of the medium.

CREDITS

Key: *a* above, *l* left, *r* right

Quarto would like to thank all the artists who have kindly allowed their work to appear in this book. We are also grateful to artists' agents Archer Art (Keith Harmer, **pp111, 113, 116**); Arena (Jim Burns, **p152**); and for supplying transparencies, and to the following organisations for permitting us to reproduce copyright material: ABB, Sweden (**p129***l*); Coca-Cola GB (**p138**); David Judd Ltd, London (**p132***r*); London Underground Ltd (**pp120, 127**) and Mars Confectionery (**p133***a*). Coca-Cola and Coke are registered trademarks which identify the same products of the Coca-Cola Company.

All demonstrations in the Techniques section of the book were done by Mark Taylor.

Every effort has been made to obtain copyright clearance and Quarto would like to apologize if any omissions have been made.